Landslide Ecology

Despite their often dangerous and unpredictable nature, landslides provide fascinating templates for studying how soil organisms, plants, and animals respond to such destruction. The emerging field of landslide ecology helps us to understand these responses, aiding slope stabilization and restoration and contributing to progress made in geological approaches to landslide prediction and mitigation.

Summarizing the growing body of literature on the ecological consequences of landslides, this book provides a framework for the promotion of ecological tools in predicting, stabilizing, and restoring biodiversity to landslide scars at both local and landscape scales. It explores nutrient cycling; soil development; and how organisms disperse, colonize, and interact in what is often an inhospitable environment. Recognizing the role that these processes play in providing solutions to the problem of unstable slopes, the authors present ecological approaches as useful, economical, and resilient supplements to landslide management.

LAWRENCE R. WALKER is a Professor of Plant Ecology at the University of Nevada, Las Vegas. His research focuses on the mechanisms that drive plant succession, particularly primary succession on volcanoes, landslides, glacial moraines, floodplains, dunes, mine tailings, and abandoned roads. His landslide research has involved field work in Alaska, Hawaii, Puerto Rico, and New Zealand.

AARON B. SHIELS is a postdoctoral research associate with the USDA National Wildlife Research Center in Hilo, Hawaii. His research is focused on understanding the local and large scale impacts of disturbance and invasive species on plant communities and ecosystems. He has worked on landslides in China, Hawaii, and Puerto Rico.

ECOLOGY, BIODIVERSITY AND CONSERVATION

Series editors
Michael Usher *University of Stirling, and formerly Scottish Natural Heritage*
Denis Saunders *Formerly CSIRO Division of Sustainable Ecosystems, Canberra*
Robert Peet *University of North Carolina, Chapel Hill*
Andrew Dobson *Princeton University*

Editorial Board
Paul Adam *University of New South Wales, Australia*
H. J. B. Birks *University of Bergen, Norway*
Lena Gustafsson *Swedish University of Agricultural Science*
Jeff McNeely *International Union for the Conservation of Nature*
R. T. Paine *University of Washington*
David Richardson *University of Stellenbosch*
Jeremy Wilson *Royal Society for the Protection of Birds*

The world's biological diversity faces unprecedented threats. The urgent challenge facing the concerned biologist is to understand ecological processes well enough to maintain their functioning in the face of the pressures resulting from human population growth. Those concerned with the conservation of biodiversity and with restoration also need to be acquainted with the political, social, historical, economic, and legal frameworks within which ecological and conservation practice must be developed. The new Ecology, Biodiversity and Conservation series will present balanced, comprehensive, up-to-date, and critical reviews of selected topics within the sciences of ecology and conservation biology, both botanical and zoological, and both "pure" and "applied". It is aimed at advanced final-year undergraduates, graduate students, researchers, and university teachers, as well as ecologists and conservationists in industry, government, and the voluntary sectors. The series encompasses a wide range of approaches and scales (spatial, temporal, and taxonomic), including quantitative, theoretical, population, community, ecosystem, landscape, historical, experimental, behavioral, and evolutionary studies. The emphasis is on science related to the real world of plants and animals, rather than on purely theoretical abstractions and mathematical models. Books in this series will, wherever possible, consider issues from a broad perspective. Some books will challenge existing paradigms and present new ecological concepts, empirical or theoretical models, and testable hypotheses. Other books will explore new approaches and present syntheses on topics of ecological importance.

Ecology and Control of Introduced Plants
Judith H. Myers and Dawn Bazely

Invertebrate Conservation and Agricultural Ecosystems
T. R. New

Risks and Decisions for Conservation and Environmental Management
Mark Burgman

Ecology of Populations
Esa Ranta, Per Lundberg, and Veijo Kaitala

Landslide Ecology

LAWRENCE R. WALKER
University of Nevada, Las Vegas, Nevada, U.S.

AARON B. SHIELS
USDA National Wildlife Research Center, Hilo, Hawaii, U.S.

CAMBRIDGE UNIVERSITY PRESS

Cambridge, New York, Melbourne, Madrid, Cape Town,
Singapore, São Paulo, Delhi, Mexico City

Cambridge University Press
The Edinburgh Building, Cambridge CB2 8RU, UK

Published in the United States of America by Cambridge University Press, New York

www.cambridge.org
Information on this title: www.cambridge.org/9780521190527

First published 2013

Printed and bound in the United Kingdom by the MPG Books Group

A catalog record for this publication is available from the British Library

ISBN 978-0-521-19052-7 Hardback
ISBN 978-0-521-17840-2 Paperback

Contents

Color plates are to be found between pp. 178 and 179.

Preface

Landslides are fascinating because they are dangerous and remind us how powerless we are in the face of overwhelming geological forces. Some progress has been made on how to predict their occurrence and how to avoid or reduce the damage that they cause, but humans are still vulnerable to landslides. We find landslides fascinating for another reason. They create a new surface of exposed rock and soil to which plants, animals, and microbes respond. These habitat gaps in the landscape provide great habitats for rock hounds, plant collectors, bird watchers, and other outdoor enthusiasts, in addition to research opportunities for geologists and ecologists. Landslide surfaces are not at all homogeneous, but vary greatly in degree of plant and soil removal, subsequent stability, and soil fertility. Organisms respond to that variability with different patterns of colonization and community development. Understanding these responses can greatly improve landslide stabilization and ecosystem restoration. The new field of landslide ecology examines the biological responses to landslides, including human responses because we avoid, use, cause, and manage landslides. This book synthesizes the growing literature on landslide ecology and provides the first comprehensive examination of landslides as dynamic ecosystems rather than simply as physical phenomena to be predicted, avoided, and mitigated.

We begin this book by emphasizing the relevance of landslides to ecological processes. For instance, landslides act as conduits of soil nutrients and organic matter down slopes and into aquatic habitats including rivers and oceans. Landslides also provide habitats for colonization by early successional species. The spatial complexity of landslides comes both from the contrast with more stable, vegetated surfaces at the undisturbed edge and from variation in fertility and stability along lateral and vertical gradients within a landslide. Such heterogeneity often supports high regional biodiversity. We also discuss the physical causes and consequences of landslides, which is necessary information for any ecological study. These topics have been thoroughly addressed by geomorphologists, so we focus on their potential ecological consequences. For example, post-landslide erosion can reduce rates of ecosystem recovery, which are generally faster in warm, tropical regions than in cooler, temperate ones.

The organisms that colonize landslides are typically adapted to survive on the newly exposed, low-nutrient, and unstable substrates where they may also experience temperature and water stress. These gap specialists are not unique to landslides because they also colonize other disturbed habitats. Microbes, widely dispersed plants, and arthropods such as mites and ants are among the first colonists and they are followed by various plant groups and vertebrates, the latter often just visitors rather than residents on landslides. The colonists interact over time and have both positive and negative influences on each other and on the successional pathways.

Historically, humans could never ignore landslides but as our population grows and we utilize more landslide-prone slopes, landslides become increasingly frequent (we trigger more of them) and lethal (larger human populations are more vulnerable). Humans directly cause landslides through expanding construction, road building, logging, and agriculture, and indirectly (and at broad spatial scales) by altering temperature and precipitation regimes that influence landsliding. Landslide risk assessment continues to improve, with new mapping and modeling tools. In addition, mitigation of landslide damage and restoration of ecosystem processes has become more successful, particularly by the inclusion of ecological principles into restoration plans. We view landslide ecology as a fascinating and emerging discipline, which provides opportunities for understanding temporal and spatial dynamics in heterogeneous habitats; opportunities for management to integrate these insights into improving prediction, prevention, mitigation, and restoration; and opportunities for cultural development through improved approaches to more sustainable use of erosion-prone slopes and education about the dangers posed and damages caused by landslides.

We both have explored the mysteries of landslides through long-term monitoring, experimental manipulations, and modeling. Lawrence is a plant ecologist who studies temporal dynamics of communities in the process of ecological succession. He specializes in primary plant succession, which occurs when a disturbance leaves little or no biological legacy. Landslides are good examples of primary succession because they generally remove all plants and most soil layers. However, the destruction is often patchy, and sometimes islands of original vegetation, soils, and animals result in localized examples of secondary succession. Lawrence has studied landslides in Puerto Rico, Alaska, Hawaii, and New Zealand. Aaron is an ecologist who also studies disturbance and succession, and much of his research is focused on the many factors (e.g., plants, animals, soils) that alter plant communities after a disturbance, including disruptions caused by invasions of non-native species. Most of Aaron's research is in tropical environments, particularly on islands, where he applies his findings to improve restoration and conservation of native ecosystems. He has worked on landslides in Puerto Rico, Hawaii, and China. We have attempted to present a global perspective on both terrestrial and submarine landslides, although inevitably, many local publications were not readily available. We hope that, through our broad approach, this book will advance the search for generalities about landslide ecology, even as we recognize that successional trajectories and specific restoration techniques will always be heavily influenced by both local and stochastic factors.

We thank the many geologists and geomorphologists who have described the physical aspects of landslides. Notable among these is the late David Varnes, whose 1958 drawings of landslide structures are still widely used. Robert Schuster has produced an impressive compilation of landslides around the world, which was helpful in assembling this book. Seminal work by Matthew Larsen on landslides in the Caribbean has influenced us, and a book entitled *Cliff Ecology: Pattern and Process in Cliff Ecosystems* by Larson *et al.* (2000) provided a good model for the organization of this book. A recent contribution that we drew extensively from, particularly for human–landslide interactions and numerous examples of landslides from around the world, is the book *Landslides: Processes, Predictions, and Land Use* by Sidle & Ochiai (2006). We were involved in the first global gathering of landslide ecologists in China in 2006, organized by Carla Restrepo, with a subsequent publication in *BioScience* by Restrepo *et al.* (2009). We are grateful for these resources and collaborations as well as for our interactions among colleagues at conferences on ecological aspects of slope stability, which have provided us with helpful insights about landslide ecology.

We thank our wives, Elizabeth Powell and Laura Shiels, for support and collegial assistance on many landslide projects, our parents for their continual support, and our colleagues Peter Bellingham, Wendy Boneta, Ned Fetcher, Arthur Johnson, Paul Klawinski, Frederick Landau, Roger del Moral, Randall Myster, Liz Neris, Carla Restrepo, Honghua Ruan, Joanne Sharpe, Ashley Sparrow, Sandra and Stephen Talbot, Daniel Thompson, Eduardo Velázquez, Christine West, Xiaodong Yang, and Daniel Zarin with whom we have measured, analyzed, and written about landslides and related phenomena. We also thank Paula Garrett for her fine work on the figures and Richard Bardgett, Peter Bellingham, Marian Chau, Beatrice Cohen, Peter Scott, Eduardo Velázquez, and Xiaodong Yang for kind permission to use their original photographs. We are grateful for the support of our series editor, Michael Usher, and the publishing team at Cambridge University Press, especially Dominic Lewis and Megan Waddington. The staff members at the El Verde Field Station from the University of Puerto Rico deserve special thanks for many years of data collection and plot maintenance under difficult field conditions. We would like particularly to highlight the outstanding and long-term contributions of Rafael De León and Maria Aponte. Eda Melendez-Colom and her data management team at the University of Puerto Rico were also essential to the success of many of our landslide projects. Eduardo Velázquez and Frederick Landau have been wonderful companions and supporters of landslide work in Puerto Rico. Eduardo also has contributed many helpful insights from his work on a landslide in Nicaragua.

We are indebted to the many reviewers of our book who read one or more chapters and contributed their valuable perspectives. These include Peter Bellingham, James Dalling, Claudia Dislich, Rui Elias, Ned Fetcher, Douglas Larson, Jean Lodge, Roger del Moral, Karel Prach, Joanne Sharpe, Alexia Stokes, Frederick Swanson, Eduardo Velázquez, and Margery Walker. Finally, we thank our various sponsors, including the Luquillo Long Term Ecological Research Program (most recently NSF grant DEB-0620910), for supporting us during 20 years of research in Puerto Rico. Lawrence also thanks the US Fish and Wildlife Foundation for work in Alaska; the Wilder Chair Program in the Botany Department at the University of Hawaii at Manoa for support during the 2009–2010 academic year; and Landcare Research in New Zealand. Aaron thanks the Dai Ho Chun fellowship from the University of Hawaii at Manoa; the US Department of Agriculture, National Wildlife Research Center for support during 2011–2012; Xishuangbanna Tropical Botanical Gardens, Chinese Academy of Sciences for work in China; and the Commonwealth Scientific and Industrial Research Organization (CSIRO) for support while working in Alice Springs, Australia.

The publisher has used its best endeavors to ensure that URLs for external websites referred to in this book are correct at the time of going to press. However, the publisher has no responsibility for the websites and can make no guarantee that a site will remain active or that the content is or will remain appropriate.

1 · *Introduction*

Key points

1. The geological characteristics of landslides and their management as physical hazards are well documented. In contrast, the ecological processes that are initiated by landslides, and their relevance to efforts to restore stability to unstable slopes, have never been synthesized.
2. Landslides can cause intense human suffering and human activities can aggravate natural causes of landslides. However, we can ameliorate many of the worst effects of landslides through improved prediction and restoration of landslides and adjoining slopes.
3. Landslides initiate many ecological processes at landscape to local scales, including the process of ecological succession. Although landslides have negative effects on the survival of many terrestrial and aquatic organisms, they also recycle nutrients and provide habitats for colonizing species.
4. Landslides encompass many types of gravity-driven movements of mass. A typical landslide often has material that falls, slides, and flows, thereby creating geologically and ecologically heterogeneous substrates. Landslides cause and are caused by other disturbances, an interaction that creates a disturbance regime.

1.1 Relevance of landslides

A landslide is broadly defined as a sudden mass movement of substrate downhill and occurs on sloping terrain. Landslides can be localized slumps several square meters in size or so large that they are visible from space. Why are landslides important to you? Perhaps your property or farm has been damaged by landslides, or road access to your workplace or vacation site has been blocked. Maybe your telephone, water, or electrical power services were once disrupted. Or perhaps you follow reports of landslides because your home is on a steep slope and you wonder whether or when your property will slide. Regardless of your personal experience with landslides, we demonstrate in this book that landslides are relevant at many levels, both personal and ecological. Landslides are geological events that have obvious immediate impacts on landscapes and humans, but they also provide such ecological services as nutrient enrichment of rivers and creation of new habitats for colonizing organisms unable to survive in the surrounding ecosystem. The geology of landslides and hazard management (e.g., how to minimize property losses through landslide prediction, prevention, and restoration) are well-studied, with several recent summaries of research progress (e.g., Sidle & Ochiai, 2006; Sassa et al., 2007). However, the ecology of landslides (the interaction of organisms with the landslide environment) has received surprisingly little attention, given the dramatic influences that landslides have on the environment. Less than 1% of papers published on landslides between 1970 and 2010 address ecology (Web of Science, 2011). Landslides are a severe type of disturbance because they damage or remove plants, animals, and soil organisms. Landslide habitats are therefore of interest as examples of places where plant and animal communities assemble following disturbances that leave little or no biological legacy (primary succession). These ecological responses, when better understood, can be manipulated to augment restoration efforts that have, until recently, relied largely on modifications of the physical environment such as the construction of debris dams or re-contouring of slopes. Landslide ecology can thus be compared with other disturbances that initiate primary succession (e.g., volcanoes, retreating glaciers, and floods; Matthews, 1992; Reice, 2001; Walker & del Moral, 2003; Elias & Dias, 2009). This book attempts to fill the gap in our ecological understanding of landslides by presenting the first synthesis of the widely scattered literature on landslide ecology. In this opening chapter, we introduce the links among landslides and humans, landscapes, and ecological processes; then, we define the term landslide and describe it from multiple perspectives; finally, we present the central themes of each of the remaining chapters.

1.1.1 Humans

The term "landslide" has negative connotations for most people because of the often highly publicized destructive consequences of landslides. While many small landslides are only temporary inconveniences, some are more catastrophic, resulting in considerable loss of human lives. Perhaps the most lethal ever recorded was the 1920 earthquake-triggered landslide in Gansu, China that killed 200 000 people (Close & McCormick, 1922). Landslides on the coast of Venezuela killed > 20 000 people in 1999. Landslides in the Peruvian Andes (1962, 1970) killed > 6000 people (see Chapter 6). In 1963, a landslide in Europe created a flood that killed 2600 people, while landslides (particularly in Japan, Hong Kong, the Philippines, Indonesia, Colombia, and the Caribbean Islands) have killed scores of people in recent decades (Hansen, 1984a; Petley, 2010). Prehistoric records indicate that large-scale landslides were common (Schuster, 2001), and they remain an important disturbance in today's landscapes, particularly because of human activities such as road building and urbanization.

Landslides can recur at a given site as long as the slope remains unstable. For some residents of unstable, mountainous regions, for example, landslides frequently disrupt their lives by repeatedly eroding pastures, blocking roads, and destroying houses (Haigh et al., 1993; Singh & Pandey, 1996). Several dozen people die each year from landslides in the U.S., but mortality rates can be even higher in some developing countries. In contrast, costs of property damage are higher in developed countries, reaching about $4 billion year^{-1} in the U.S. and Japan (Schuster, 1996b; Gori et al., 2003). In either developing or developed countries, landslides can cause losses that become a significant percentage of a nation's budget (Hansen, 1984a). Costs include the direct losses of property and lives, but also the indirect costs of subsequent disturbances such as floods caused by blocked drainages. Other indirect costs include clean-up, lost productivity from agriculture and fisheries, and reduced revenues from tourists and real estate sales (Schuster, 1996b).

Humans have developed multiple ways to deal with the challenges that landslides present (see Chapter 6). Where population densities are low, landslide-prone areas are often avoided as building sites, unless those sites have desirable features such as views or access to water, fertile soil, or other resources which offset the dangers of building. Where population densities are higher, more people live or work in areas vulnerable to landslides because site selection is driven more by proximity to municipal services than by careful assessments of soil stability. Squatter communities of poor migrants from rural areas rim many large cities in developing countries and these communities are often located on steep, unstable slopes that were previously avoided, but have become the only areas left on which to build. Whether the newcomers build houses in the relatively wealthy suburbs of Los Angeles (U.S.) or grass mat shacks in the poor areas surrounding Lima (Peru), they are equally vulnerable to the geological forces that produce landslides. Wealthier nations may have more to spend on prediction and prevention, but these defensive measures are not always effective. Sometimes, humans accommodate to the presence of landslides in their lives by using the new resources that landslides provide. Examples of such resources include drinking water (E. Velázquez, pers. comm.) and fast-growing trees that are harvested for firewood or fence posts in Nicaragua (Velázquez & Gómez-Sal, 2008); scrambling ferns collected for various medicinal purposes in southeast Asia (Robinson *et al.*, 2010); and tree fern trunks used for growing orchids in Hawaii (Fosberg, 1942) – until tree ferns were protected for conservation purposes (Mehltreter, 2010).

Humans cause landslides in a variety of ways (Sharpe, 1960; Bonuccelli *et al.*, 1996; Singh & Pandey, 1996; Sidle & Ochiai, 2006). Removal of soils or rocks from a slope can destabilize it; this occurs when roads, railroads, and canals are cut across slopes and interrupt surface and subsurface movement of water. Road embankments can slide due to inadequate compaction or heavy rainfall before adequate cover is established (Larsen & Parks, 1997), but also can slide where runoff from roads is not properly channeled. Such construction errors can be particularly dangerous when bridge abutments are destabilized (Alonso *et al.*, 1996). Urban construction involves not only cutting into slopes but adding the water from irrigation and the weight of buildings, vehicles, and fill material (Keller, 1996). Open-pit mines have unstable slopes at their cut edges, but piles of unusable or sorted rocks also can be unstable. Slope failures can occur on other anthropogenic piles such as municipal waste landfills (Towhata, 2007). Sometimes, recreational activities in mountainous regions (e.g., skiing, climbing, off-road driving) result in landslides. Finally, logging and grazing can reduce protective vegetative cover and accelerate erosion.

Rapid deforestation of tropical rainforests (13–16 million ha year^{-1} in the last two decades; Achard *et al.*, 2010) has increased the number of landslides, particularly where soils are shallow. When we alter slope hydrology by adding culverts or retaining walls, we sometimes concentrate previously diffuse drainages and increase erosion. On a larger scale, landslides can be purposefully caused by explosives to create dams for hydropower or protection from future landslides (Schuster, 1996b). Climate change (see Chapter 7) may also lead to more landslides in regions that receive increases in rainstorm intensity, increases in windstorm frequencies (less time for vegetative recovery), or increases in the irregularity of precipitation (and subsequent loss of a protective vegetative cover). However, increased temperatures may also lead to increased evapotranspiration and therefore reduced water content on some slopes while increased vegetation cover in formerly arid regions could improve slope stability (Borgatti & Soldati, 2010).

The prediction of landslide occurrences has become an important aspect of hazard assessment that sometimes saves lives and provides guidance on where to build or live (Sidle & Ochiai, 2006). In some cases, there is an obvious correlation between rainfall duration and intensity and the occurrence of landslides (see Chapter 3; Caine, 1980; Larsen & Simon, 1993), but many other factors (e.g., soil type, slope, vegetative cover, successional stage, land use) usually complicate the prediction of landslides. For example, landslides associated with volcanoes (lahars, debris flows, mud flows) are generally unpredictable. When landslides are predictable, urban planners, architects, farmers, utility companies, and residents on sloped terrain can better adjust land management to reduce the chances of loss of lives and property. With an expanding human population that continues to exploit marginal lands with steep slopes, landslide hazard assessment will continue to be an important component of land management.

Prevention and restoration of landslides are other actions, which, like prediction, have only mixed success. Geological forces can overwhelm the best efforts to stabilize slopes, particularly wide or steep ones within high rainfall regions, but temporary and small-scale prevention can be successful, at least until unusually intense storms occur. In Japan, evacuation procedures have greatly reduced deaths from landslides in the last several decades through a combination of identifying potential hazards and improving preventive techniques (Takahashi, 2007). Many slopes re-slide, so restoring them to prevent further sliding is often attempted. Restoration efforts range in intensity from planting vegetation on the landslide to complete alterations of the local slope or hydrology. Drainage of surface and ground water is frequently successful (Schuster & Kockelman, 1996). Mechanical efforts include building earth buttresses at the base of the slope and various other restraining structures such as walls of wood, concrete, or rock-filled cages (gabions). Surfaces can be stabilized by metallic, plastic, or organic meshes placed over the soil. Metallic meshes are frequently seen covering roadside cliffs (see Chapter 6; Wyllie & Norrish, 1996). Finally, one can sometimes remove all material that could re-slide by reshaping the slope and leaving only exposed bedrock. Using biological tools such as plantings of grasses or trees can be initially straightforward and inexpensive, but learning how to properly restore plant and soil communities that supply lost ecosystem services (e.g., clean water, biodiversity) and undergo natural successional changes takes a long time and it is a poorly understood process (Walker *et al.*, 2009).

1.1.2 Ecological processes within landslide-prone landscapes

Landslides cover about 4% of the earth's terrestrial surface each century (Restrepo & Alvarez, 2006; Hong *et al.*, 2007), but they are most common in earthquake-prone mountain regions and in landscapes heavily modified by human land use (Restrepo *et al.*, 2009). The effects of landslides expand beyond their actual physical limits because they influence downstream sediment loads (Fort *et al.*, 2010) as well as the regional biodiversity and movements of organisms. Landslides are usually discrete events that only last for mere seconds to several minutes. However, some types of mass movement (e.g., creeps) can have persistent consequences, including secondary erosion and alterations of regional hydrology. Gradual changes such as increases in soil water content can lead to the sudden sliding of a slope, while improving conditions for drainage can make a slope less likely to slide again (Keller, 1996).

Landslides help maintain such natural ecosystem processes as nutrient cycling and may promote biodiversity by the promotion of habitat diversity (Geertsema & Pojar, 2007). Landslides can be viewed as fluid systems, much like rivers, except that the medium that moves is soil and its contents, including nutrients and carbon as organic matter (Walker & Shiels, 2008). As part of the erosion of slopes, landslides move critical components down slope, including soil organisms, seeds, wood fragments, and rock-derived nutrients such as phosphorus and calcium, where they enrich down slope habitats. The sediments and nutrients from landslides fertilize aquatic ecosystems either directly (when the base of a landslide enters a river, lake, or ocean) or indirectly (through ground water or surface erosion). Landslides also create habitat gaps in a background matrix of a forest, shrub, or grassland community. These gaps provide refugia for colonizing organisms that, in turn, supply many other organisms with food or habitat (Wunderle *et al.*, 1987). Occasionally, landslides are so common that they become the background matrix for patches of mature vegetation.

Landslide habitats change through ecological succession. The rapidly growing plants that typically colonize landslides (Velázquez & Gómez-Sal, 2007, 2009; Restrepo *et al.*, 2009) serve various functions, including slope stabilization through rain interception and root growth, maintenance of biodiversity, and sinks for carbon dioxide. Sometimes anthropogenic disturbances such as road embankments, clear cuts, and construction zones can provide habitats similar to landslides (e.g., bare soil combined with high light and warm soil conditions favorable to germination and growth). After the early colonists establish on the bare soil that typically characterizes a new landslide surface, they are gradually replaced by later arrivals. As the plant cover on landslides undergoes change, landslides become part of a shifting mosaic of patches in a landscape (Pickett & Cadenasso, 1995). Landslide successional processes often take decades before the landslide becomes indistinguishable from its background matrix (Ferreira *et al.*, 1996). Within landslides, there is also a mosaic of patches of vegetation at different stages of successional development, open areas of recent re-sliding, nutrient-rich and nutrient-poor patches, and patches of varying substrate stability. Animals respond to such habitat diversity by browsing on early successional growth, nesting in cliffs, perching on surviving trees, and using new ponds created in the deposition zone (Geertsema & Pojar, 2007). This spatial and temporal heterogeneity makes a landslide a complex but fascinating ecosystem to study. In this book, we discuss both the abrupt disturbance itself and the longer-term ecological processes that are triggered by the disturbance.

1.2 Terminology and types of landslides

A disturbance is a relatively abrupt event that causes a loss of biomass, ecosystem structure, or function. A disturbance has a cause or trigger (e.g., an earthquake or rainstorm), an event with physical characteristics (e.g., frequency, intensity, extent), and a consequence (e.g., damage caused, new habitat created; Walker, 2012). Landslides, as we use the term here, are both a disturbance event driven primarily by gravity that results from slope destabilization (Fig. 1.1) and the habitat created by the displaced debris. Landslides are a type of erosion but our use of the term erosion will generally imply the presence of landslides. Most studies of the ecological consequences of landslides focus on the post-erosion habitat. There is so much variation in how landslides occur that no standard classification system has emerged (Table 1.1; Hansen, 1984b). Strictly defined, a landslide is a sliding movement of a mass of rock, debris (loose rock or regolith), or earth (finer sediments with or without organic material) down a slope (Cruden, 1991). However, the term landslide is often used to include all types of slope failure or mass wasting (general terms for down slope movement of earth materials) that are

Table 1.1. *Classifications of landslides based on characteristics of hill slope movement*

Sorting variable	Name	Description
Type of movement	Slide	Translational (planar) or rotational (slumps)
	Fall	Outward and downward movement with exposed face (excludes slumps)
	Flow	Merges with creeps and spreads; called mass transport if sediments moved by water, air, or ice
	Complex	Mixture of slides, falls, and flows
Degree of movement	Active	Currently moving; can be advancing, retrogressing, widening, enlarging, or diminishing
	Inactive	Moved within past year
	Dormant	No movement in at least 1 year; cause remains
	Abandoned	No movement and no causes remain (e.g., river changes course)
	Relict	Rediscovered (e.g., due to new road cut); formed under different conditions
	Reactivated	By new or recurring disturbance
Rate of movement	Slow	Creeps (e.g., 0.06 m year^{-1})
	Moderate	Initial and final moments of many slides
	Fast	Initial fall, movement through chute (e.g., 3 m sec^{-1})
Cause of movement	Geological	Weathering, shearing, fissuring; contrasting erosional surfaces
	Morphological	Slope changes due to 1) uplift from volcanoes, earthquakes, glacial rebound; 2) undercutting from waves, river currents, glaciers; 3) internal erosion through seepage; or 4) deposition of mass on the slope or its crest
	Physical	Earthquakes, volcanoes, rapid increase in water content, freeze–thaw weathering, rapid drawdown, vegetation removal by fire, drought, or wind
	Biotic	Plants increase water infiltration, add weight, transfer energy from windblown trees to soil; animals overgraze plants on a slope; humans remove or add rocks, soil, or vegetation and add water or induce vibrations

Sources include Coates, 1977; Varnes, 1978; Hansen, 1984b; Cruden, 1991; Cruden & Varnes, 1996; Cannon, 2001; Wondzell & King, 2003; Sidle & Ochiai, 2006; and Petley, 2010.

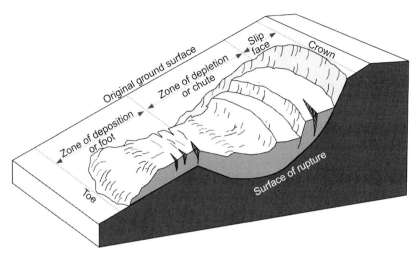

Fig. 1.1. Cross section of a typical landslide. Modified from Varnes (1958), Plate 1-t. Copyright, National Academy of Sciences, Washington, DC. Reproduced with permission of the Transportation Research Board.

Type of material	Type of movement (increasing speed) ⟶				
	Slide		Flow	Fall	
	Rotational	Translational			
Bedrock	Rock slump	Rock slide	Rock avalanche	Rock fall	
Regolith	Debris slump	Debris slide	Debris flow	Debris fall	
Sediments	Sediment slump	Slab slide	Earth flow	Sand flow / Loess flow / Liquefaction flow	Sediment fall	

Debris avalanche (between Debris slide / Debris flow)

Decreasing sediment size

Increasing particle size ↑

Fig. 1.2. Terrestrial landslide classification. Modified from Coates (1977).

broadly defined as slides, flows, and falls (Fig. 1.2). Challenges in defining landslides start with the type of movement. True sliding can occur through rotational movements called slumps (Fig. 1.3) or along a plane (translational slides; Fig. 1.4; Coates, 1977). Flows (Fig. 1.5) consist of mass movement (movement influenced by gravity) and they are similar

Fig. 1.3. Rotational debris slump in Puerto Rico. Photograph by A.B. Shiels.

Fig. 1.4. Translational (planar) debris slide in Puerto Rico (foreground). Photograph by A.B. Shiels.

Fig. 1.5. The deposition zone of a large scale debris flow landslide on Casita Volcano, Nicaragua (top of photo). The debris flow extended 12 km from the volcano, was 1.4 km wide, and reached depths of > 4 m. Photograph by E. Velázquez.

to creeps and spreads (Varnes, 1978) and mass transport (when rock or soil is transported by a moving medium such as water, air, or ice). For example, rock avalanches and debris flows are types of landslides but a snow avalanche composed mostly of snow and ice is generally not classified as a landslide (Hansen, 1984b). Landslides also include falls (Plate 1; Fig. 1.6), which are outward and downward movements of rocks or debris with exposed faces (thereby excluding subsidence (sinking) as a type of landslide). Many landslides are complex mixtures of slides, falls, and flows (Fig. 1.7). The role of air in landslides cannot be discounted, because compressed air in front of a fast-moving landslide can be very destructive (see Chapter 6; Rouse, 1984). Further complications in defining landslides arise because landslides can be caused by a combination of slides, flows, and falls. For example, in a one-time survey of 215 landslides in an 89 km^2 basin in southern Spain, 40 landslides were combinations of slides, flows, and falls; these complex landslides accounted for 42% of the total area affected by landslides (Hamdouni et al., 1996) while the remaining 58% fit into a single landslide category.

Other parameters used in defining landslides include the degree of movement of an erosive slope, the rate of movement, and the causes of movement (Table 1.1). The degree of movement categorizes various levels of landslide activity from active to inactive or dormant. The rate of movement varies both within one event and across types of landslides. Within a single landslide, the initial displacement at the slip face can be rapid, but mass movement (especially falls) down the chute can accelerate, and then, as the material spreads out in the deposition zone, it decelerates considerably. The steepness of the slope, the nature of the material, and the friction from the surface all modify the velocity. Velocity directly affects damage levels, because fast-moving landslides have a greater impact on buildings and leave people less time to escape.

Landslides have both ultimate causes such as weathering or steepness of slope and proximal triggers, such as a particularly intense rainstorm. These causes can be classified as geological, morphological, physical, or biotic (Table 1.1). Abiotic causes are variations of weathering (geological), slope changes (morphological), and changes due to recent disturbances (physical) (Cruden & Varnes, 1996; Petley, 2010) such as fire (Cannon 2001; Wondzell & King, 2003). Water movement in sediments is affected by both abiotic (e.g., fissuring) and biotic (e.g., plant root) factors. Water-soaked surface soils tend to slide when percolation to lower levels is slow or inhibited. Water can also liquify clay-rich soils, causing them to flow. Plants provide cover that generally has a stabilizing influence on

(a)

(b)

Fig. 1.6. (a) Rock fall at the slip face of a landslide on Casita Volcano, Nicaragua. Photograph by E. Velázquez. (b) Debris fall near Crater Lake, Oregon (U.S.). Photograph by A.B. Shiels.

Fig. 1.7. A complex landslide near San Carlos de Bariloche, Argentina with (from top to bottom) debris fall, debris slide, and debris flow. Photograph by L.R. Walker.

slopes because it reduces the impact of rain, facilitates water infiltration, decreases soil moisture through transpiration, and increases soil cohesion through root systems (Keller, 1996). The cohesive properties of roots vary by plant species, increasing with plant age and declining over time as roots decay at species-specific rates when trees are cut (Sidle & Ochiai, 2006). Plants and animals can also destabilize slopes through a variety of mechanisms (Table 1.1). Anthropogenic causes, as noted in Section 1.1.1, include construction and mining activities that remove or add material to slopes, recreation activities, removal of vegetation through logging or agriculture, road construction, and additions of water (e.g., from irrigation or leaky pipes). Artificially induced vibrations from the use of explosives or heavy traffic can also trigger landslides.

Landslides often cause further disturbances, a feature that can also be used to categorize them. For example, landslides can cause small-scale deforestation by removing the above-ground biomass, damage roads and properties, modify slope hydrology, or (when under-water) cause tsunamis (Whelan & Kelletat, 2002; Bardet *et al.*, 2003). Large, submarine landslides can trigger earthquakes, and landslides can alter volcanic or glacial activity (Hewitt, 2009). When landslides partially or totally dam rivers they can divert or block water flow, leading to various secondary disturbances, including additional landslides. Partial landslide dams can trigger landslides on the opposite bank of the river; complete dams can cause landsliding along newly formed upstream lake shores (and create drought conditions downstream); the eventual collapse of a landslide dam can create many more landslides as flood waters rush downstream (see Chapter 2; Fort *et al.*, 2010). The sum of all interacting disturbances at a given site is considered the disturbance regime (Walker & Willig, 1999). Landslides are one of the more severe types of disturbance because of their removal of most organisms and soil.

Submarine landslides also can be categorized as rock falls, slides, or flows, but can occur on much shallower slopes than terrestrial landslides due to the presence of more unconsolidated material. Mass movements that begin as slides can become flows as the debris progressively deteriorates (Prior & Coleman, 1984). Submarine landslides are found throughout the world's oceans, but are particularly common in areas of high relief (e.g., submarine trenches, edges of continental shelves), tectonically active areas, and locations that receive large inputs of sediments (e.g., river deltas). Factors that promote them include volcanoes, earthquakes, water level changes, and sediment deposits from glaciers, deltas, tides, and underwater currents (see Chapter 2; Prior & Coleman, 1982).

In this book, we use a broad definition of landslides that follows Coates (1977) and considers all sudden mass movement from slides, falls, and flows as landslides. There are many related phenomena that we will mention in future chapters as they are relevant, such as solifluction in areas of permafrost (soil creep due to freeze–thaw cycles; Matsuoka, 2001), movements of snow and ice (especially so-called dirty avalanches that transport rock and soil; Bründl et al., 2010), and erosion of road, river, and canal embankments and unstable cliffs (Larson et al., 2000).

1.3 Scope

This book addresses all aspects of landslide ecology and also covers the fundamental geological processes and consequences for human societies that are needed for a full appreciation of the ecological role of landslides. Chapter 2 discusses the spatial distributions of landslides and their ecological consequences. Landslides occur in marine, freshwater, and terrestrial environments. Terrestrial landslides are found mostly in wet, montane habitats and are the primary focus of this book. Groups of landslides in a landscape provide opportunities to examine gap dynamics and gradients across distinct habitat boundaries. Local features of landscapes that shape landslides include soil types, topography, climate, and vegetation. Spatial patterns within landslides are also helpful in examining recruitment, edge effects, and the role of microsites and repeat disturbances.

Chapter 3 considers the causes and physical consequences of landslides, including impacts on soils and post-landslide erosion. The ultimate cause of a landslide is slope instability, but a variety of natural and anthropogenic disturbances represent proximal causes or landslide triggers (see Section 1.2). We examine the various rock and soil types that are most susceptible to landslides. Persistent erosion commonly follows landslides, and it occurs until overall slope stability is achieved. Landslide effects on soil chemistry and soil development have many ecological consequences following a landslide.

Chapter 4 presents the biological consequences of landslides. Landslides can develop floristic and faunal assemblages that are distinct from the surrounding non-landslide areas, due to the altered microclimatic conditions. We examine whether such assemblages are unique to landslides or if generalist colonizer communities are found on other early successional sites. Many abiotic and biotic variables affect these colonists, including soil conditions, soil microbial populations, the presence or absence of seed banks, nitrogen fixing plants, and surviving pockets of residual soil and organisms.

Chapter 5 discusses how landslide ecosystems are dynamic in time as they undergo succession and interact with their immediate and broader surroundings. The process of succession results in species replacements that are driven by species interactions (both positive or facilitative, and negative or competitive), herbivory, other on-going disturbances (e.g., drought, persistent erosion, fire, plant harvesting), and colonization by both later successional native species and non-natives. Non-native species can sometimes alter or arrest successional trajectories because they add a missing ecosystem function (e.g., nitrogen fixation) or rearrange trophic food webs or competitive hierarchies. Finally, successional dynamics alter local and regional biodiversity and landslide patches contribute to biogeographical dynamics including migration, dispersal corridors, and landscape connectivity.

Chapter 6 expands on the human relationship with landslides discussed at the beginning of this chapter. We include more examples of extremely large, damaging, or costly natural landslides, and infamous landslides of anthropogenic origin. We elaborate on the themes of how humans survive and learn to co-exist with landslides and how they cause them. Humans have colonized many landslide-prone habitats, so we also try to predict landslides and prevent them when we can. Finally, we discuss how successful co-existence of humans and landslides is best addressed through efforts to restore ecosystem function and biodiversity on landslide scars.

Chapter 7 places the details of previous chapters into a larger spatial context. We summarize land use changes in mountain societies and note how novel mixtures of native and non-native species will become increasingly common. We discuss how climate change will likely lead to more frequent landslides and how rehabilitation is best addressed at landscape rather than landslide scales. We suggest several lessons that landslide ecology provides and end with nine suggestions for how landslide ecology might develop in the next few decades, using technological, ecological, and cultural approaches.

2 · *Spatial patterns*

Key points

1. Remote sensing tools have greatly improved the mapping of both terrestrial and submarine landslides, particularly at global scales. At regional and local scales, environmental correlates are being found that help interpret spatial patterns and related ecological processes on landslides.
2. Landslides are frequent on only 4% of the terrestrial landscape and coverage varies over time because new landslides do not occur at a constant rate.
3. Multiple landslides triggered by the same event, such as an earthquake or severe rainstorm, can vary in physical characteristics. This variety contributes to a mosaic of landslide conditions across the landscape.
4. A landslide environment contrasts with the more stable conditions found in adjacent habitats. The transitions between landslide and adjacent habitats in light, fertility, stability, and other characteristics can be abrupt to gradual, sometimes making it difficult to define where a landslide begins or ends.

2.1 Introduction

The distribution of landslides is determined by background factors (ultimate causes) such as rock type and soil properties and by immediate triggers (proximate causes) such as rainfall or earthquake occurrence (Dai *et al.*, 2002). While the prediction of the location and timing of a particular landslide remains inexact, mapping of existing landslides at global spatial scales is improving with the use of remote sensing tools such as satellite imagery (Hong *et al.*, 2007). There are also discernible spatial patterns at regional and local scales, driven particularly by the location of landslide triggers (e.g., earthquake epicenters, regions of high rainfall) interacting with topography (Zhou *et al.*, 2002). Within a given landslide, there can also be spatial patterns that influence local ecological processes. The dramatic impacts that landslides have on plants, animals, and soils represent important alterations of the spatial patterns of many ecosystems that can influence future ecosystem processes for decades (Foster *et al.*, 1998).

The consideration of spatial patterns of landslides can be viewed hierarchically, where smaller-scale patterns driven by local erosion events such as microhabitat heterogeneity are nested within patterns driven at regional to global scales by such processes as succession and tectonic activity (regional to global; Fig. 2.1). Time scales are also considered hierarchically (e.g., larger-scale phenomena are measured on longer time scales). Geomorphological (and ecological) events at a given scale are linked to other scales by the exchange of matter, and energy (O'Neill *et al.*, 1986; de Boer, 1992; Restrepo *et al.*, 2009). Brunsden & Jones (1980) consider such links across scales for landslides occurring on coastal cliffs in southern England during a 100-year period. The average rate of erosion during that time by large, occasional landslides was similar to the rate of erosion by smaller, more frequent landslides. Landslides at these two scales were linked through processes occurring at the cliff bases at intermediate temporal and spatial scales that provided a positive feedback loop between large and small scales. Blocks of eroded cliff rocks from large landslides reduced overall erosion rates and the likelihood of further large landslides but promoted local, smaller scale erosion and the break-up of the large blocks. Meanwhile, many small landslides gradually led to the destabilization of larger portions of the cliffs, increasing the likelihood of a larger landslide occurring during the 100-year period. In this chapter, we consider the distribution of landslides at global, regional, and local scales, and then discuss how physical attributes of landslides are spatially heterogeneous. This chapter establishes the visually obvious parameters of physical aspects of landslides, followed in Chapter 3 by the visually less obvious mechanics of how landslides slide and how their soils are altered.

2.2 Where landslides occur

2.2.1 Global scales

Landslides are an occasional feature of over half of all terrestrial landscapes but are only abundant on 4% of the terrestrial surface (Hong *et al.*, 2007). They are most common in the tropics, in earthquake-prone regions, and

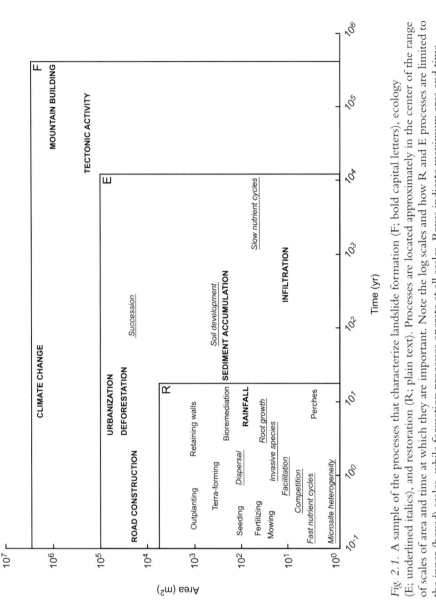

Fig. 2.1. A sample of the processes that characterize landslide formation (F; bold capital letters), ecology (E; underlined italics), and restoration (R; plain text). Processes are located approximately in the center of the range of scales of area and time at which they are important. Note the log scales and how R and E processes are limited to the inner (boxed) scales, while formation processes operate at all scales. Boxes indicate maximum area and time

where rainfall events tend to be short but intense (Plate 2). Lands bordering the Pacific Ocean (e.g., western South and North America, Kam-
chatka, Japan, the Philippines, and New Zealand) are earthquake prone
and therefore susceptible to landslides where the terrain is sloped (see
Chapter 1). Other tectonically active faults include those in Indonesia,
northern India, and Tibet. High levels of rainfall and land degradation by
dense human populations make eastern China, southern India, eastern
Africa, and eastern Brazil particularly susceptible to landslides.

The detection and description of landslides across large spatial scales
can be done using a variety of techniques. Aerial photography (particularly with stereoscopic or digital interpretation) has been a standard way to
map and monitor landslides (Restrepo *et al.*, 2003). Typical data include
estimates of landslide number, local rock type, and regional land use
(Singhroy & Molch, 2004). However, the likelihood of finding landslides
with aerial photographs decreases with landslide age because vegetation
obscures the landform (Turner *et al.*, 2010). More sophisticated tools
(e.g., geographical information systems (GIS), laser altimetry (LIDAR),
and synthetic aperture radar (SAR)) use inputs from both airplanes and
satellites to make remote measurements, even when the landslides are
covered by vegetation (McKean & Roering, 2004). Typical parameters
that can be measured remotely include landslide number, rock type, size
(length, width, depth), distribution of debris types, mass movements
over time, and detailed topographic profiles or digital elevation models
(Metternicht *et al.*, 2005). Creeping (or slow deformation) of landslide
surfaces can also be monitored to help predict when re-sliding will occur
(Chadwick *et al.*, 2005). Advances continue to be made in the accuracy
of prediction of landslides (see Chapter 6) through the analysis of soil
water content using infrared imagery (Carrara *et al.*, 1991), GIS models
(Fabbri *et al.*, 2003), and remote mapping of the volumes of potential
debris flows (Metternicht *et al.*, 2005).

Submarine landslides move sediments from shallow water to deeper
regions of the ocean floor. The source of these sediments is often from
erosion of terrestrial surfaces, especially coastal cliffs (Plate 3). Submarine
landslides resemble terrestrial landslides in general types (slides and flows)
and morphology (slip face, chute, deposition zone) but are often much
larger and frequently slide on less steep slopes (Hampton *et al.*, 1996;
Elverhoi *et al.*, 2010). Flows are more diverse in submarine than terrestrial landslides and include turbidity currents, which are downhill movements of sediment-laden water (Table 2.1). Submarine landslides most

Table 2.1. *Classification of submarine landslide types*

Type of movement	General characteristics	Nature of movement	Classification of landslide
Mass slide	Cohesive material, distinct boundary, fluids have minor role	Indistinct failure surface Distinct failure surface Isolated block collapse	Creep Slide (translational or rotational) Debris avalanche
Gravity flow	No cohesion, indistinct boundary, fluids have major role	Laminar, mass flow Turbulent flow	Debris flow Turbidity current (high or low density)

(Modified from Masson *et al.*, 2006).

commonly occur in regions with rapid accumulations of sedimentary deposits and sloping sea floors (Masson *et al.*, 2006). The collapse of sedimentary deposits often generates tsunamis, and biological forces can both destabilize (e.g., by bioerosion) and stabilize (e.g., by providing fungal hyphae) submarine slopes (see Chapter 4; Diaz *et al.*, 1994; Glynn, 1997; Meadows *et al.*, 1994; Walker, 2012). Six locations that provide conditions that promote submarine landslides are discussed below. These locations include fjords, river deltas, submarine canyons, continental margins, areas experiencing changes in sea level, and volcanic islands.

First, fjords, or glacially eroded valleys inundated by the sea, have sediment-rich inputs from glacial melt water that create unstable debris fans on the steep submarine slopes. The 1964 earthquake in Alaska, for example, resulted in several types of landslides where debris fans had accumulated sediments that were several hundred meters deep in the 7000 years since the glaciers that carved the fjords had receded. These accumulated sediments collapsed as debris falls and debris flows (Lee *et al.*, 2006). Fjord-related landslides are also common throughout the North Atlantic Ocean and are generally limited by the geomorphology of the channel with widths up to 0.5 km, slip faces matching the height of accumulated sediments, and shallower deposition zones because the sediments tend to dissipate through turbidity currents (Hühnerbach & Masson, 2004).

Second, submarine river deltas are created at the mouths of silt-rich rivers. Some are subject to slope failure, particularly where heavy loads of relatively coarse sediments build upon already unstable, finer sediments. River delta landslides have been found at the mouths of the Mississippi (U.S.) and Yellow (China) Rivers (Prior & Coleman, 1980; Prior *et al.*, 1986; Hampton *et al.*, 1996). The absence of landslides in other sediment-rich river deltas (e.g., the Yangtze and Pearl Rivers, China, and the Columbia River, U.S.) suggests that other triggers are needed. Such triggers might include earthquakes, hurricanes (that can affect water currents to 100 m depth; Henkel, 1970), or decaying organic material that destabilizes sediments through the production of methane gas (Nisbet & Piper, 1998).

Third, submarine canyons are conducive to submarine landslides, especially when they have steep, incised walls. Common ways to determine if submarine canyons are locations for landslides are to look for debris fans and displaced blocks at their outlets, or losses of sediments following storms or earthquakes (Malouta *et al.*, 1981).

Fourth, the slopes along continental margins can produce landslides, and there are many examples from around the world (Plate 4; Piper *et al.*, 1985; Hampton *et al.*, 1996). Many of these coastal landslides produce turbidity currents, which can deposit organically rich sediments in deeper ocean water (Fig. 2.2; Heezen *et al.*, 1955a). Earthquakes are presumably the cause of most of these landslides, but this has only occasionally been documented (e.g., for the 220 km^3 Grand Banks landslide near Nova Scotia in 1929; Fine *et al.*, 2005).

Fifth, changes in sea level are presumed to be important in generating submarine landslides, resembling conditions in reservoirs where water level fluctuations within short time intervals can trigger landslides. Changes in temperature and pressure accompanying the lowering of sea level can generate gas bubbles (especially methane) in sediment layers and, as the gases are released, slopes can become destabilized (Kayen & Lee, 1991). Gas hydrates released at the base of a continental shelf are associated with eroding continental slopes (Crutchley *et al.*, 2007). Such zones of instability can experience repeated landslides for thousands of years, as demonstrated off the California coast (Greene *et al.*, 2006).

Sixth, submarine landslides are common on slopes of young, active volcanoes, and other tectonically active parts of the sea floor (Whelan & Kelletat, 2002). On the Island of Hawaii, lava flows have

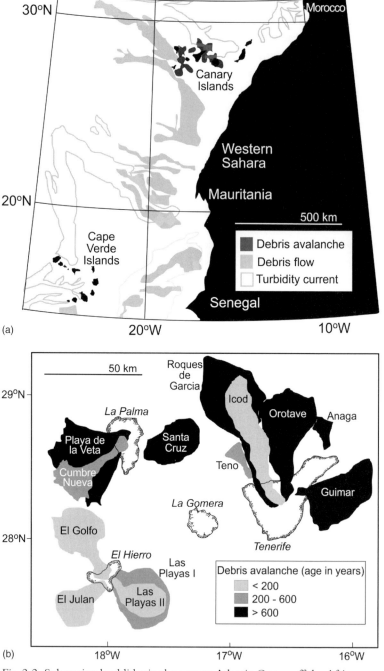

Fig. 2.2. Submarine landslides in the eastern Atlantic Ocean off the African coast. (a) Debris avalanches, debris flows, and turbidity currents; and (b) details of debris avalanches around the Canary Islands with approximate ages of formation. From Masson *et al.* (2006) with permission from The Royal Society (U.K.).

built mountains that are up to 9 km tall (5 km of which is submarine) (Lipman *et al.*, 1988). There appears to be a two-way, causal relationship between magma and landslides, because landslides can modify the location and eruption dynamics of volcanoes and magma displacement can trigger landslides (Moore *et al.*, 1989). Submarine (and terrestrial) landslides are also found on older volcanoes wherever slopes are destabilized (Fig. 2.2). Earthquakes are common causes of landslides but also can be caused by landslides (e.g., on submarine volcanic slopes; Hampton *et al.*, 1996).

The detection of submarine landslides is a relatively new endeavor. Submarine landslides can now be detected remotely using side-scan sonar, acoustic signals, and swath-bathymetry systems (Hampton *et al.*, 1996). Submarine landslides can also be deduced from evidence of deformed sediments in cores of the ocean floor or by terrestrial deposits of marine sediments purported to come from submarine-triggered tsunamis. Examples of the latter come from Hawaii and Scotland. On the south coast of Lanai, Hawaii, gravel deposits reach an elevation of 326 m a.s.l. and contain skeletons of reef organisms presumed to have been brought there by three separate landslide-induced tsunamis (occurring approximately 105 000 years ago; Moore & Moore, 1984). In Scotland, diatom-rich deposits of fine sands 4 m a.s.l. are likely to have originated from a tsunami in the North Atlantic triggered by the second Storegga landslide about 7000 years ago (Fig. 2.3; Box 2.1; Long *et al.*, 1989). Other methods of detection of submarine landslides come from interactions with man-made features. For example, landslides broke submarine telegraph cables off the coast of Newfoundland in 1929 (Heezen *et al.*, 1955a); harbor facilities were lost in Alaska (U.S.), British Columbia (Canada), Norway, and France; and offshore drilling platforms were disrupted in the Gulf of Mexico (Hampton *et al.*, 1996). The 1964 earthquake in Alaska triggered many landslides in Anchorage (Fig. 2.4; Box 2.2) and caused a submarine landslide that removed 75 million m^3 of the harbor at Valdez (Coulter & Migliaccio, 1966). Submarine landslides can also cause earthquakes (Lipman *et al.*, 1985), as well as being caused by earthquakes, so there are multiple avenues to pursue in detecting and studying them. Submarine landslides differ in many intriguing ways from terrestrial ones (e.g., they have much longer run-outs on shallower slopes; Elverhoi *et al.*, 2010), so detection is the first step to increasing our understanding of them.

Landslides also occur in freshwater ecosystems, triggered mostly by river bank erosion but also by abrupt changes in water levels, particularly

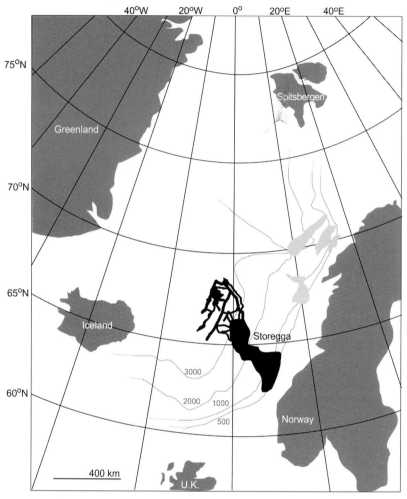

Fig. 2.3. The huge submarine Storegga landslide (black) off the west coast of Norway, which occurred about 7000 years ago. The westernmost, finger-like deposits are from turbidity currents. Other large landslides in the North Atlantic Ocean are shown in light grey. Contour lines of ocean depth in m. From Haflidason *et al.* (2004) with permission from Elsevier.

in lakes and reservoirs. Landslides can affect freshwater ecosystems by the deposition of sediments that alter flow dynamics and the contours of stream and lake beds (Schuster, 2001). Most (e.g., 80%) of the sediment in some rivers comes from landslides, as demonstrated in the Rocky Mountains, Idaho, U.S. (Wilson *et al.*, 1982) and in Puerto Rico

Box 2.1 Storegga: a massive submarine landslide

Recent advances in remote sensing of submarine landslides are showing just how unstable the ocean floor can be, particularly along continental margins. One of the largest submarine landslides ever measured is Storegga ("Great Edge"), located 100 km off the coast of Norway. It is so large that it reaches half the distance from Norway to Greenland (Fig. 2.3), or nearly the length of the U.K. The first of five phases (Elverhoi *et al.*, 2010) was the most massive and occurred about 30 000–50 000 years ago; it created a slide that had enough volume (about 4000 km^3) that it would have covered Alaska 2 m deep and left a scar the size of the state of Maryland (U.S.; Nisbet & Piper, 1998). The second phase mostly occurred on the surface produced by the first event and was composed of a series of landslides in rapid succession (about 6000–8000 years ago) that had a total volume between 2400 and 3200 km^3 and covered about 95 000 km^2 (Haflidason *et al.*, 2004). The remaining three phases were shorter and smaller in volume and continued the erosion toward the coast of Norway. The slip face (headwall) of the second phase was 310 km long and the landslides together had a run-out distance of 410 km of debris and another 400 km of turbidite (from turbidity currents). One of the landslides moved two blocks, each 10 × 30 km in size, 200 km downslope. These landslides were caused by layers of clay-rich sediments deposited from ocean currents (contourites) that become unstable when under great pressure from layers of glacial sediments (Masson *et al.*, 2006). The tsunami created by the second event deposited sediments in Scotland and probably destroyed early human populations on the now submerged land between Denmark and the U.K. called Doggerland.

(Larsen & Torres-Sánchez, 1992). Sediment loads in rivers depend in part on the width of the floodplain, because narrow valleys are more likely to funnel landslide sediments directly into the river (Fig. 2.5) than are wide valleys where (terrestrial) debris fans can accumulate (May & Gresswell, 2004). The input of sediments from landslides can occur quickly through rock avalanches and debris flows or more slowly through slumps and earth flows (Swanston, 1991). Rapid additions of sediments to rivers can increase flood damage downstream, particularly when rivers are already swollen from high levels of precipitation. The damage from

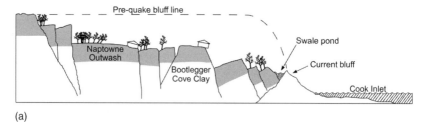

(a)

(b)

Fig. 2.4. The Alaskan earthquake of 1964 and coastal slumping around Anchorage. (a) Artistic rendering of the slump at the edge of the coast of the Cook Inlet (horizontal displacement = several hundred meters; vertical displacement = 11 m, so horizontal scale collapsed relative to vertical scale); (b) current bluff displaced about 11 m downward into the Inlet; (c) swale pond created after the displacement. See Box 2.2 for details. Drawing modified from sign provided by the City of Anchorage. Both photographs by L.R. Walker.

earthquake-triggered landslides on the Reventador Volcano in Ecuador in 1987 was largely from flooding that was aggravated by sediments from the many landslides (Nieto & Schuster, 1991). Landslides also provide a critical conduit of organic matter and nutrients (particularly phosphorus) to freshwater ecosystems (see Chapter 3).

(c)

Fig. 2.4. (cont.)

Fig. 2.5. Landslide entering the Yangtze River in Tiger Leaping Gorge, Yunnan Province, China. Photograph by X. Yang.

Box 2.2 The Alaska earthquake of 1964

On 27 March 1964, southern Alaska experienced a powerful earthquake that registered 9.2 on the Richter Scale, making it the second most intense earthquake ever recorded. With its epicenter on land 125 km east of Anchorage, it caused soil liquifaction, fissures, and many landslides; over 130 people were killed. The port of Valdez, 64 km east of the epicenter, lost its entire port to a large, submarine landslide and subsequent 12 m tall tsunami. Tsunamis caused additional damage as far away as Japan. Marine clays (Bootlegger Cove Clay) deposited by glaciers over many centuries in the Cook Inlet liquified along the coast of Anchorage. A bluff (2500 × 350 m) composed of more recent sediments overlying the clay (Naptowne Outwash) slid with the clay several hundred meters seaward (Fig. 2.4), depositing over 12×10^6 m^3 of sand, gravel, and clay into the ocean. Large areas of forests and wetlands were destroyed, but new habitats were created, including swale ponds. The vertical displacement of about 11 m was not limited to the Cook Inlet, but affected a 250 000 km^2 area of Alaska.

Sometimes landslides dam rivers, especially in steep-walled, narrow canyons where minimal landslide volume is required (Schuster, 1995). Dams rearrange sediment deposits in the floodplain (Mackey *et al.*, 2011), and can trigger further landslides upstream of the dam, particularly if water levels drop quickly when the dam is breached (Kojan & Hutchinson, 1978). Downstream, landslides can also occur during the flash flood following a breach. The amount of sediment transported during a dam failure can be substantial; 3 000 000 m^3 of sediment was deposited 700 m downstream after a 100 m tall landslide dam was breached on the Toro River in Costa Rica (Mora *et al.*, 1993). Most landslide dams are short-lived, with about 90% failing within 1 year (Costa & Schuster, 1991). For example, when the Dadu River in China was dammed by a landslide in 1786, water pooled behind it and it broke 10 days later (Li, 1989). The debris flow that resulted extended 1400 km downstream and killed about 100 000 people (Schuster, 2001). Other landslide dams can last for centuries to millennia. Lake Waikaremoana on the North Island, New Zealand is 250 m deep and was formed by a landslide 2200 years ago (Riley & Read, 1992). The 1911 Usoi landslide in the Pamir Mountains of Tajikistan created the still extant, 500 m deep Lake Sarez (Gasiev, 1984). If the Usoi landslide dam were to fail, the resulting flood could affect 2100 km of floodplain – all the way to the Aral Sea (Schuster, 2002). Long-lived landslide dams can provide clues about past climates. For example, in northwestern Argentina, sediments in lakes that formed from landslide dams between 40 000 and 25 000 years ago have been used to suggest past environmental conditions of increased humidity and more pronounced seasonality, conditions which are generally associated with reduced thresholds for landsliding (Trauth & Strecker, 1999).

2.2.2 Regional scales

At regional levels, several studies have quantified the spatial extent of landslides over time using various tools (Table 2.2). Time intervals for these studies ranged from decades to several centuries over areas from several to hundreds of km^2. The area affected by landslides in these studies (usually expressed as a percentage of the land affected per century) ranged from 0.01% to 15%, although subsets of these examples had over 50% of the land area affected where landslides were most dense. Studies that focused on small areas prone to landsliding had higher percentages of land affected than studies of larger areas; extrapolations using small study areas could therefore be misleading. Although rainfall was the most common trigger in these examples, earthquakes were also important. Return intervals of landslides to a specific site were not always calculated, but in the mountains of Mexico and Central America, return intervals ranged from 75–500 years; more land was affected at low than at high elevations and in wet than in dry forests (Restrepo & Alvarez, 2006). The average size of landslides alters the percentage of land affected. For example, in eastern Puerto Rico, 41 rainstorms between 1960 and 1990 created 1100 landslides, but their total coverage was not large due to their generally small size (Larsen & Torres-Sánchez, 1996). The median size of a landslide was larger (220 m^2) on hill slopes affected by roads than those affected by crops or pasture (70 m^2). Similarly, the mean area of landslides on Oahu, Hawaii, was only 291 m^2 and landslides affected a relatively small percentage of the measured land area (Peterson et al., 1993). The rate of landslide formation varies over time. For example, on the North Island, New Zealand, landslides covered 1.7% of a catchment in 1946 but 2.7% in 1963, likely due to increased rainfall coupled with overgrazing by

Table 2.2. *Land area affected by landslides during time periods > 20 years (in order of decreasing time span). Note the negative correlation between study area and affected land area*

Location	Study period (years)	Study area (km²)	Affected land area (%)[a]	Comments	References
Hawaii	430	4	15	Up to 51% of area affected	Restrepo et al., 2003
Mexico and Central America	110	1.6×10^6	0.30	More landslides with higher elevation and rainfall	Restrepo & Alvarez, 2006
Hawaii	59	222	0.23[b]	Variable frequency by decade; rain-triggered hill slope failures	Peterson et al., 1993
Jamaica	52	218	0.19	Scars persist 500 years	Dalling & Iremonger, 1994
New Zealand	31	40	3.92	More landslides with higher elevation; up to 10% of area affected	Jane & Green, 1983
Puerto Rico	30	930	0.01	Landslides mostly <400 m²	Larsen & Torres-Sánchez, 1996
New Zealand	23	75	2.20	More landslides with higher rainfall	James, 1973

[a] Usually calculated as area affected per century; mean value when several were presented.
[b] Estimated from mean area (291 m²) of 1779 landslides.

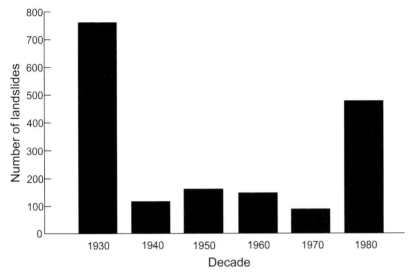

Fig. 2.6. Landslide occurrence on Oahu, Hawaii varied by decade, largely due to rainfall patterns. From Peterson *et al.* (1993).

introduced animals (James, 1973). In Hawaii, large variations in the number of landslide per decade were attributed to rainfall patterns (Fig. 2.6; Peterson *et al.*, 1993).

Many landslides can be generated by a single trigger event (Table 2.3), although the landslides may be quite distinct in size and density, due to underlying environmental correlates. Landslides created in 1989 in Puerto Rico during Hurricane Hugo, for example, ranged in size from 18 to 4500 m^2 (Larsen & Torres-Sánchez, 1992) and density from 0.8 landslides km^{-2} in drainage basins furthest from the path of the hurricane to 15 km^{-2} in drainage basins closest to the hurricane. Landslide densities also vary across a landscape, typically decreasing exponentially with distance from the earthquake epicenter (Fig. 2.7). For example, landslide densities on bluffs along the Mississippi River in Missouri and neighboring states (U.S.) declined with distance from the epicenter of the 1811–1812 New Madrid earthquake (Jibson & Keefer, 1989). Similar concentrations around earthquake epicenters were found in two California earthquakes in 1989 (Keefer, 1994; 2000) and 1994 (Parise & Jibson, 2000). Additional explanations of the spatial distributions of landslides come from lithology, topography, aspect, and vegetation. Landslides created by a 1929 earthquake in New Zealand were most frequent and largest on mudstone and siltstone, particularly along rock folds and steep

Table 2.3. *Characteristics of landslides triggered by the same event*

Year	Location	Trigger	Number of landslides	Study area (km²)	Landslide density (number km⁻²)	Environmental correlates[b]	References
1811–1812	Central U.S.	M 8.4–8.8	146	300 km²[a]	0.5	Tall bluffs	Jibson & Keefer, 1989
1929	New Zealand	M 7.7	1850	120	15.4	Mudstones, rock folds, aspect	Pearce & O'Loughlin, 1985
1987	Ecuador	M 6.1, M6.9	Many[c]	250	ND	River valley walls	Nieto et al., 1991
1989	Puerto Rico	Hurricane Hugo	285	65	4.4	Wind-driven rains, aspect	Larsen & Torres-Sánchez, 1992
1989	California, U.S.	M 6.9	1046	1920	0.5	Steep slopes	Keefer, 2000
1994	California, U.S.	M 6.7	1562	159	9.8	Unconsolidated sediments	Parise & Jibson, 2000
1999	Taiwan	M 7.5	>10 000	11 000	0.9	Sedimentary rocks, steep slopes	Khazai & Sitar, 2003
2007	Northwestern U.S.	Rain & snowmelt	2061	1520	1.3	Younger forests	Turner et al., 2010

[a] 300 km stretch along the Mississippi River.
[b] Landslides were most common in these environments.
[c] About 66% of the area experienced > 25% denudation by landslides.
M = earthquake magnitude (moment magnitude scale); ND = no data.

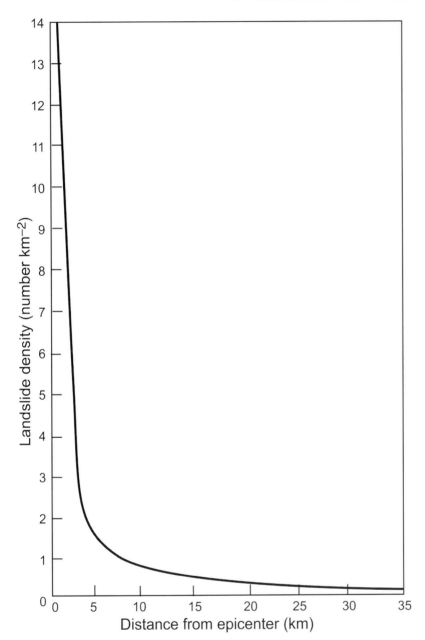

Fig. 2.7. Landslide density decreased with distance from the epicenter of the Loma Prieta earthquake in California in 1989. From Keefer (2000) with permission from Elsevier. Density $= 14.675 \times \text{distance}^{-1.3284}$; $R^2 = 0.97$.

scarps, and least common and smallest on granite and sandstone (Pearce & O'Loughlin, 1985). Unconsolidated sediments and sedimentary rocks were most erosion prone during earthquakes in 1994 (California; Parise & Jibson, 2000) and 1999 (Taiwan; Khazai & Sitar, 2003). Steep slopes are nearly universally more susceptible to sliding than flatter ones, if all other characteristics are similar. Aspect can influence landsliding when slopes exhibit distinct geological formations or when an earthquake features directional differences in seismic shaking (Pearce & O'Loughlin, 1985). In addition, aspect can be a factor when slopes are differentially exposed to relatively horizontal rain, as occurred during Hurricane Hugo in Puerto Rico (Larsen & Torres-Sánchez, 1992). Finally, vegetation cover can provide variable resistance to erosion, as it did in the northwestern U.S. in 2007 when slopes with intermediate-aged forests were most resistant to landsliding during heavy rainstorms combined with snowmelt (Turner *et al.*, 2010). Landslides formed during a single event are therefore quite distinct except for their age.

2.2.3 Local scales

The local distribution of landslides has several environmental correlates, including rock and soil types, topography, climate, and vegetation (Table 2.3). Rocks of sedimentary origin and unconsolidated sediments are most likely to erode (see Chapter 3), while geological faults and areas of folding are also susceptible. Steep slopes, valley headwalls, scarps from former landslides, and undercut cliffs along river channels are some of the topographical features that promote landslides. Rainfall is the principal climatic variable that influences landslide distributions and it is affected by topography, elevation, and vegetation, factors which are all interrelated. Mountain ranges cause air currents to ascend and cool, resulting in increasing precipitation with elevation. Losses of water from vegetation to the air (evapotranspiration) also increase humidity and therefore rainfall. The sudden loss of foliage from Puerto Rican forests following Hurricane Hugo, for example, contributed to a temporary increase in the elevational belt of high rainfall (Scatena & Larsen, 1991). Mountains also provide rain shadows on the leeward side of the prevailing winds because air masses warm up as they descend and thereby moisture is removed from the air. Therefore, leeward slopes may be less prone to landsliding because they are drier than windward slopes. Most landslides in northeastern Puerto Rico, for example, are on north- and north-east-facing slopes (Larsen & Torres-Sánchez, 1996), which are most exposed to the prevailing northeasterly trade winds. In contrast, south-facing slopes had fewest landslides during three large storms (Shiels & Walker, in press). Within a slope prone to landsliding, smaller scale variations in slope and vegetation can be influential in determining whether or not a given portion of the slope erodes. Most landslides do not create homogeneous patches of mineral soil, but instead result in complex surfaces representing a mosaic of erosion rates.

2.3 Spatial heterogeneity

2.3.1 Gaps and patchiness

Landslides create spatial heterogeneity in landscapes and are also internally heterogeneous. The sharpest contrast at both levels is between landslide habitats and adjacent, unaffected habitats. Landslides initially form a gap with more light and bare soil and less vegetation than the undisturbed matrix. Thus, a gradient of resources is created where early successional organisms find refuge. There can also be contrasts among and within landslides. Across a landscape prone to hill slope erosion, there may be several to many landslides differing in size and age. Landslides of similar age may have resulted from a single earthquake or heavy rainstorm (see Section 2.2.2) and form "populations" of landslides (Fig. 2.8). Many of these populations created during different triggering events can be considered "communities" of landslides across wider spatial scales (Restrepo et al., 2009). Landslides within populations may be more similar to each other than to those in other populations, thus forming regional heterogeneity within landslide communities. Alternatively, within-population variability in size, aspect, elevation, or other physical characteristics is also possible. Landslides within a population are also likely to diverge (become more distinct) in their biological characteristics during succession because of their scattered distribution, variation in remnant soil or vegetation, and local dispersal dynamics (Restrepo & Alvarez, 2006; Walker et al., 2010b; see Chapter 5). A mountainous region with landslides is therefore a patchwork of habitats differing in soil, vegetation, and successional stage (Pickett & White, 1985). This patchwork influences regional distributions of nutrients, organic matter, and vegetation, and landslides are important as agents of transfer of these elements from ridges to valleys (see Chapter 3; Restrepo et al., 2003; Walker & Shiels, 2008).

Local heterogeneity is provided both by the distinct change from landslide to undisturbed matrix along landslide edges and by the patchiness of

Fig. 2.8. Multiple earthquake-induced landslides in the Avoca River drainage of the Southern Alps, New Zealand. Photograph by P.J. Bellingham.

Fig. 2.9. Landslide edges are accompanied by often abrupt changes in microsite conditions; Puerto Rico. Photograph by A.B. Shiels.

habitats within most landslides. Increased light levels are the most obvious physical alteration when a landslide occurs in a forested landscape; landslide-forest borders are generally intermediate in light levels (Myster & Fernández, 1995). The increase in light levels within a landslide parallels increases found in forest gaps created by treefalls and hurricanes (Chazdon & Fetcher, 1984; Denslow *et al.*, 1990; Fernández & Fetcher, 1991). Light levels on landslides can be reduced by tall canopies in adjacent forests, an aspect that reduces exposure to the sun (Fernández & Myster, 1995), and by rapid re-growth of vegetation, especially when it produces dense thickets (Walker, 1994; see Chapter 5). Light quality is also altered within landslides, where red:far red ratios are increased compared to adjacent forest edges and forests (Fig. 2.9); these changes have implications for plant colonization, generally favoring germination of early successional species (Vázquez-Yanes & Smith, 1982).

The interior of a landslide derives its heterogeneity from the dynamics of erosion (Hansen, 1984b). Landslide scars often resemble amphitheaters because they have a generally rounded and convex upper boundary (crest) and a rounded, concave lower area (Plate 5). However, those landslides that are elongated do not resemble an amphitheater. The steepness of a landslide is partly determined by the erosion resistance of the underlying bedrock and partly by surface erosion factors such as water flow. Standardized descriptions of landslides help compare variable landslide surfaces. Typical measurements include the width, length, and depth of the rupture and the displaced mass as well as the total length of the landslide (IAEG Commission on Landslides, 1990). Volumes can then be estimated (Fort *et al.*, 2010) based on spoon-shaped models of half an ellipsoid, but such estimates become more problematic when landslide pathways are elongated or irregular in shape.

Terrestrial landslides generally have a recognizable slip face (also called a failure scar or scarp) at the top that is usually a steep, occasionally vertical headwall. The top of the slip face where it meets undisturbed substrate above is called the crown (Plate 6; see Fig. 1.1; Cruden & Varnes, 1996). The entire area that slides is sometimes called the source area (Brunsden, 1984) where most soils are removed and few nutrients remain. The zone of depletion is a related term that indicates where a landslide has lowered the original ground surface. The next discernible feature of most landslides is a chute (or zone of depletion) that is typically the narrowest part of the landslide and it is often clearly delineated from the stable slopes on either side by steep sheer zones (Plate 6). Finally, there is usually a deposition zone where the slope decreases sharply and the transported material stops (see front cover image; Fig. 1.5). The deposition zone can be characterized by lobes of successive flows that often spread out horizontally and where the ground level is raised from its original level. The foot is the area where eroded material has moved beyond the area of rupture and spread onto new ground. The foot can be quite extensive and include portions of both the chute and deposition zones. The mix of vegetation, topsoil, and subsoil that has slid down slope and stopped in the deposition zone provides an area of relatively high fertility when compared to the slip face and chute. Sometimes the end (toe) of the deposition zone is removed by wave action (at the ocean shore), currents (in a river), or bulldozers (on a road).

2.3.2 Sizes and shapes

Terrestrial landslides can vary from slumps of only 10–20 m^2 to massive disruptions of whole valleys or mountainsides reaching as much as $500\,000$ km^2 (Fig. 2.10; Keefer, 1984). The largest landslides are prehistoric and include some with volumes up to 135 km^3; such large

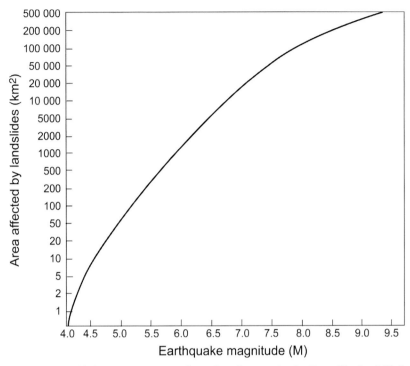

Fig. 2.10. Landslide area increases with earthquake magnitude. From Keefer (1984) with permission from the Geological Society of America.

landslides are usually triggered by earthquakes (Schuster, 2001). In contrast, the largest historical landslide was triggered by the 1980 Mount St. Helens volcanic eruption in Washington, U.S. This landslide was a large debris avalanche that covered about 60 km^2 of a river valley with 2.5 km^3 of material (Fig. 2.11; Box 2.3).

Submarine landslides can be much larger and more massive than terrestrial landslides. The largest known is the prehistoric Agulhas landslide off the coast of South Africa that is 750 km long and has an estimated volume of 20 000 km^3 (about 150 times larger than the largest terrestrial landslides; Schuster, 2001). Other large prehistoric landslides are found off the coasts of Norway and Hawaii. Landslides on the submarine slopes of the Hawaiian Islands (Kay, 1994) and the Canary Islands (Masson *et al.*, 2006) cover more surface area than the current total land mass of all the islands. However, in a survey of the Atlantic coast of the U.S., Chaytor *et al.* (2009) found that most submarine landslides ranged from 1–100 km^2 in size (the entire range of sizes included landslides

Fig. 2.11. Debris flow of the North Fork of the Toutle River, 24 years after the 1980 eruption of Mount St. Helens, Washington (U.S.). This is the largest recorded terrestrial debris flow. See Box 2.3 for details. Photograph by L.R. Walker.

$0.9–2410$ km^2) and $0.1–10$ km^3 in volume (entire range: $0.002–179$ km^3). The elongation of submarine landslides is sometimes due to turbidity currents (dense currents of suspended sediments) down continental slopes, even when the slopes are only slightly inclined (Nisbet & Piper, 1998).

Although large landslides affect more surface area than small landslides, they are usually less frequent (Guariguata, 1990; Dalling & Iremonger, 1994) and therefore may contribute less total sediment erosion than small landslides (Stark & Hovius, 2001). However, large landslides can also contribute more erosion, depending on the group of landslides one compares. For example, in a comparison of the volumes of twelve South American landslides that occurred during the twentieth century, seven were $< 10 \times 10^6$ m^3, five were $10 \times 10^6–99 \times 10^6$ m^3, and only two were $> 1000 \times 10^6$ m^3 (Schuster *et al.*, 2002). The largest (2000×10^6 m^3) was the result of failure of a landslide dam, and it approximated the volume of the Mount St. Helens debris avalanche. Several other recent landslides

Box 2.3 Toutle River landslide: the world's largest recorded debris avalanche

Mount St. Helens is the best known and most studied volcano in the U.S. It erupted in May 1980 and dramatically altered the once heavily forested landscape, in part through the destruction caused by the world's largest historical debris avalanche (area: 60 km^2, volume: 2.5 km^3). One of the lobes of the avalanche entered and passed through a lake, creating a new lake that was larger and shallower. A second lobe overtopped a ridge that reached over 380 m above the lake. A third lobe swept 23 km down the North Fork of the Toutle River in about 10 minutes, erasing existing vegetation and soils and radically altering the region's hydrology. The river valley was transformed into a poorly sorted, hummocky terrain of sand and gravel that was 10–195 m deep (mean: 45 m) (Swanson & Major, 2005). New lakes were formed where tributary streams were blocked. Most of the debris had little organic matter or soil, although some was deposited at the landslide margins and terminus. Over the next few years, the loose debris began to erode and deep new drainage channels were carved out that provided drainage for both entrapped ground water and new inputs from precipitation. Within 10 years, 35% of the surface had been altered into channels and terraces (Meyer & Martinson, 1989). Ponds formed between some of the 30 m tall hummocks and have become centers for plant colonization (Fig. 2.11; Crisafulli et al., 2005). A landslide that caused great landscape changes has become one of the much-studied features of the Mount St. Helens eruption.

have had estimated volumes of 1000–2000 × 10^6 m^3 (e.g., Tajikistan in 1911; New Guinea in 1988), but most are much smaller (Sidle & Ochiai, 2006).

Landslides are typically longer than they are wide (see Fig. 1.7). In a study of over 2000 landslides in Hong Kong, horizontal length varied from 5–785 m (mean = 43 m; Dai & Lee, 2002). Slopes (in conjunction with rainfall patterns and soil structure) largely determine the location of the initial landslide, but the surrounding topography (slopes, ridges, valleys, lakes) continues its influence on the velocity of the sediments and the final shape of the landslide through its effects on re-sliding. Abrupt decreases in slope can slow sediment loss and, where not constrained by valley walls, cause debris fans to spread out over the land surface. Short landslides occur when there is a small volume of soil dislodged from the slope, a sudden decrease in slope, or opposing slopes or structures that restrict sediment flow. On a similar slope, flows normally travel further than falls, while slides are intermediate in length. Short landslides fall, slide, or flow only 5–10 m, while some landslides can travel hundreds to thousands of meters (Schuster *et al.*, 2002).

2.3.3 Gradients

The spatial heterogeneity of landslide surfaces is partly a mosaic of clearly defined patches but it is also a combination of abiotic and biotic gradients. Changes in physical and abiotic conditions on landslides and between landslides and their matrix can be initially abrupt, but more often they are gradual, producing indistinct gradients between landslide and non-landslide surfaces. A fresh landslide scar can be hotter, drier, better lit, more unstable, and less fertile than the surrounding vegetated matrix. However, designating the actual edges of a landslide can be a challenge, especially at smaller scales. Does a landslide begin where there is 0%, <25%, or <75% of the original vegetative cover? Or should landslide edges be defined by soil removal and deposition, thereby disregarding vegetative cover? Are islands of soils and vegetation that survived the landslide or rafted down from the top to be considered as a part of the landslide? Are branches of canopy trees that overhang a part of the landslide a part of the landslide, particularly if tree roots are growing into the landslide soil? How deep do mineral soil deposits over the top of undisturbed soil (e.g., at the base of a landslide) have to be to be included as part of the landslide? A similar problem arises with volcanic ash that can vary in depth from several millimeters to many meters (Zobel & Antos, 1991). The spatial gradients on a landslide are complex and affect not only attempts to draw boundaries or categorize habitats, but also the temporal dynamics of a landslide (Myster & Fernández, 1995; Fetcher *et al.*, 1996). For example, fertile soils and surviving organisms in the deposition zone often accelerate ecological succession on landslides compared to the less fertile patches of a landslide (see Chapter 5; Walker *et al.*, 1996). The boundaries of within-landslide patches and the shapes of entire landslides can also vary with time, because sharp edges erode, nutrients are rearranged, plants grow, and animals return.

2.4 Conclusions

Landslides are distributed around the world wherever there are slopes and at least one trigger such as an earthquake, an intense rainfall, recent volcanic activity, or a construction project. Landslides also can trigger earthquakes, tsunamis, and floods and even modify the eruption patterns of volcanoes. Therefore, landslides are closely linked to many other types of disturbances. Their spatial characteristics at regional and global scales have been much easier to assess since the advent of high-resolution remote-sensing imagery and GIS technology (Keefer & Larsen, 2007). Advances are also being made in the detection and mapping of submarine landslides. Landslides can occur irregularly and often re-slide (Shiels & Walker, in press), so multi-year studies give a better picture of their importance in the landscape. When many landslides are triggered by the same event, they can be considered a population of landslides, but these landslides may vary greatly from each other in size, shape, aspect, and successional recovery trajectories. The local distribution of landslides is affected by topographical and climatic features, including aspect, slope, and rainfall.

Landslides contribute to a heterogeneous patchwork of gaps that influences many subsequent geological and biological processes. Multiple landslide shapes and sizes add variety to this patchwork. The stark differences between a landslide and a stable slope include changes in light and soil conditions. These changes can be abrupt, or gradual, providing many gradients of stability, fertility, and light levels. This spatial complexity provides a rich and fascinating variety of habitats in which to study ecological processes.

3 · Physical causes and consequences

Key points

1. The propensity for a landslide to occur is largely determined by potential slip planes, or weakness planes in the geological substrate, where the driving forces exceed resisting forces.
2. Landslide occurrence across the landscape is often unpredictable; substrates can be resistant to slippage for centuries and then suddenly experience instability that may result from human or non-human changes that disrupt the balance between driving and resisting forces at a slip plane.
3. Post-landslide erosion is common and can contribute as much as 33% of the total sediment loss from the site of landslide initiation. Such post-landslide erosion can continue for years, which reduces rates of ecosystem recovery on landslide scars and alters down slope habitats and watersheds.
4. Landslides greatly alter soils through physical losses, gains, and mixing, as well as through chemical changes. Soil organic matter contains critical nutrients and retains moisture; it facilitates soil and plant recovery in microhabitats present after a landslide. In warm, tropical regions, some landslide soil chemistry may recover to pre-landslide conditions within 55 years, yet such recovery is much slower in cooler, temperate regions.

3.1 Introduction

What causes a landslide? This is an important question, both ecologically and for human safety and hazard management. Landslides occur on sloped terrain, making topography a crucial component for landslide occurrence. However, the underlying factors that control whether or not a landslide is triggered include the conditions of the local soil and rock substrate. Below the ground surface, a complex combination of geological, topographical, hydrological, historical, climatological, and biological factors in addition to random disturbances interact and influence whether a landslide occurs (Table 3.1). Most of the below-ground characteristics that affect landslide occurrence are not fixed, but instead constitute dynamic interactions that can fluctuate in minutes or seconds. Water is absorbed and drained from soils at multiple scales and rates, which disrupts balances between driving and resisting forces. Seemingly static components of a hill slope, such as rock and soil, are also in a state of flux. Rock slabs can be split or pulverized through mechanical weathering, such as when moisture or roots penetrate cracks in bedrock and expand either by freezing or growing, respectively. Moisture, and the organic acids exuded by plants, can degrade rock surfaces and alter soil chemistry. Earthworms may increase infiltration, aeration, and organic matter decomposition (see Section 4.6.1). Changes in above-ground characteristics also influence below-ground properties; dense understory vegetation may restrict precipitation from reaching the soil, and plant abundance and elevated growth rates may dry soils due to evapotranspiration. Clearly, there are numerous interacting variables within the soil and rock medium that are in near-constant flux, and the changes in such variables influence the threshold between a stable slope and one that slides.

The complexities of landslide triggers have made it difficult to predict their exact location, time, and severity (see Chapter 6). Similarly, the consequences of a landslide can be described in general terms. A relatively bare, nutrient-poor substrate generally remains following the loss of multiple soil layers and extends from the zone of rupture or slip face through much of the chute or transport zone, whereas the deposition zone of the landslide is comparatively rich in organic matter and nutrients (see Chapter 2; Fig. 1.1). However, the landslide-affected area is a mosaic of exposed bedrock and soil, transported colluvium (soil, rock, debris), and remnant vegetation. This heterogeneity also makes it difficult to predict how ecosystems will develop following a landslide (see Chapter 5). In this chapter, we describe the mechanisms by which landslides occur, covering the geological and soil conditions that influence landslides, as well as the proximal triggers. The abiotic consequences of a landslide are then discussed (see Chapter 4 for biotic consequences), with our focus on sediment, rock, and organic matter movement, as well as post-landslide erosion. Finally, we cover the effects of landslides on soil properties, including carbon and nutrient cycling and soil development.

Table 3.1. *Eight factors that indicate unstable slopes prone to landsliding*

			Factors indicating slope instability				
Bedrock	Regolith	Topography	Drainage	Historical	Climate	Vegetation	Anthropogenic
High joint density; wide joint openings	Steep slope; deep soil	Deep valley	High drainage density; high pore pressure	Fossil solifluction lobes	High intensity rainstorms	Hydrophytic plants	Large, deep excavations
Hard joint fillings	Low shear strength	Steep slope	Steep river gradient	Fossil gullies	High rainfall variability	Potassium-demanding plants	Excavations at top of slope
Joint wedging by vegetation	Desiccation cracks	Cliffs present	Severe slope undercutting	Previous landslides	Freeze–thaw cycles	High biomass on slopes >45 degrees	Reservoir with fluctuating water levels
Tension cracks	Permeable layer on top of impermeable layer	Concave valley	Seepage; standing water	Deep weathering	Rapid snow-melt	Recent alterations to biomass	Loading from buildings on upper slope

Adapted from Crozier (1984)

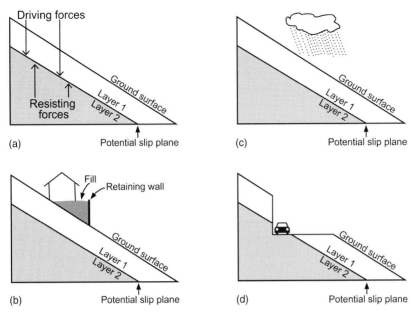

Fig. 3.1. Forces driving and resisting landsliding. (a) A balance of driving and resisting forces keeps a slope stable; destabilization of a slope can come from additional driving forces created by adding mass from (b) buildings and related construction activities or (c) saturation by rain; (d) road cuts and similar disturbances reduce resisting forces. Layer 2 can be the same or a different substrate (soil, saprolite, or bedrock) than layer 1.

3.2 How landslides slide

Slope stability is ultimately determined by the relationship between driving forces, which tend to move material down slope, and resisting forces, which tend to oppose such movement (Keller, 1996). The interface of these two forces occurs at a slip plane, or a geological plane of weakness in the slope material. Slip planes can be abrupt changes in the physical conditions of the below-ground substrate, such as the interface of two geological substrates (e.g., unconsolidated material overlying bedrock or a layer of clay; Fig. 3.1(a)). For example, massive limestone blocks slide down underlying clay slopes when the clay layer becomes wet and compressed in north-central Puerto Rico (Monroe, 1964). Slip planes can also be less abrupt and occur within the same geological substrates, such as when a landslide occurs at a fracture in bedrock or failure within a seemingly heterogeneous soil mass (Wilcke *et al.*, 2003; Sidle & Ochiai, 2006; Fig. 3.1(a)). Slope stability is often evaluated by determining a safety factor (F_s), which is defined as the ratio of resisting forces (S) to the driving forces (T) (i.e., $F_s = S/T$). The slope is stable at this interface if the driving forces are less than or equal to the resisting forces (i.e., when $F_s \geq 1$). However, when the driving forces exceed the resisting forces (i.e., when $F_s < 1$), the slope is unstable and a landslide may occur. An increase in weight of the slope material is perhaps the most common cause of increase to the driving force (e.g., a house; Fig. 3.1(b)); whereas the most common resisting force is the shear strength of the slope material acting along the potential slip planes (Keller, 1996; Sidle & Ochiai, 2006). The shear strength is largely influenced by the substrates adjoining the slip plane, and soils tend to have greater shear strength than rock because of the cohesive strength of the soil, which results from adhesion properties of soil particles (Keller, 1996). Typical examples of increases in driving forces that result from increases in weight of the slope material include vegetation, fill material, and buildings. Additionally, water from rainfall that saturates the soil both adds weight and increases pore pressure, which reduces frictional resistance, or suction, by separating soil particles (Fig. 3.1(c)). The driving forces can increase relative to the resisting forces without any additional mass added to the ground surface simply by reducing the resisting forces, a condition which is common in road cuts resulting from road building (Fig. 3.1(d)). Although vegetation adds weight and therefore increases the driving force of a slope, the roots can also increase the resisting force by growing through potential slip planes (Table 3.2; Schmidt et al., 2001; Stokes et al., 2007b, 2009). Earthquakes cause obvious disruption to local substrates that can weaken the resisting forces and trigger landslides. Earthquakes occur widely in tectonically active locations on other planets such as Mars and Venus where they also trigger landslides (Lucchitta, 1978; Bulmer et al., 2006).

The mechanics of slope failure can be described in greater detail by a series of equations that include numerous variables that ultimately reflect the ratio of the resistance force (S) and the driving force (T). One such equation described by Sidle & Ochiai (2006) includes the weight of soil and vegetation mass (W) along a potential slip plane, as well as the cohesive strength of the soil (c) and roots (ΔC):

$$F_s = S/T = (c + \Delta C)/(W \sin \beta) + (\tan \phi)/(\tan \beta) - (u \tan \phi)/(W \sin \beta)$$

where β is the slope inclination, ϕ is the internal friction angle, and u is the pore pressure, which is an integration of the unit weight of water (γ), vertical depth of the water table above the sliding surface (h), and β, in the following equation: $u = \gamma h \cos^2 \beta$. Due to the model

Table 3.2. *The role of vegetation in promoting slope stability (S) or instability (I)*

Effect	Region	Mechanism	Description
S	Soil	Mechanical	Roots reinforce soil and increase shear strength
S	Soil	Mechanical	Roots anchor into stable substrate
S	Soil	Hydrological	Roots and root channels funnel water into root clusters
S	Plant	Hydrological	Short plants reduce rainfall splash erosion
S	Plant	Hydrological	Plants absorb water and reduce rainfall infiltration into soil
I	Soil	Mechanical	Plant mass increases driving force
I	Soil	Hydrological	Roots and root channels funnel water to soil cracks and impermeable layers
I	Plant	Mechanical	Flammable plants leave soil exposed
I	Plant	Mechanical	Plants shake in wind and transfer vibrations to soil
I or S	Soil	Mechanical	Uphill roots increase pore pressure, downhill roots decrease it
I or S	Soil	Hydrological	Plants increase surface roughness and infiltration
I or S	Plant	Mechanical	Tall plants add stabilizing litter but also increase drip erosion
I or S	Plant	Hydrological	Evapotranspiration decreases soil moisture, increases infiltration, and lowers pore pressure

Sources include Nott (2006), Sidle & Ochiai (2006), Goudelis *et al.* (2007), Morgan (2007), Stokes *et al.* (2009), and Ghestem *et al.* (2011).

assumptions and possible errors in the parameters, the threshold of $F_s < 1$ should be viewed as an index of likely, rather than absolute, slope failure. Landslides generated by earthquakes must have an additional parameter, an earthquake load, integrated with the other variables in the safety factor equation. The earthquake load parameter consists of horizontal and vertical components along the slope (Sidle & Ochiai, 2006). Many of the parameters within slope safety factor equations are challenging to measure prior to slope failure, especially because several variables (e.g., W, c, ϕ, u) constantly change based on the proximal conditions of the environment. However, some generalizations have been reported for certain variables. For example, for shallow soils, the effects of pore water pressure (u) on slope instability are large. On sloped terrain with deep soils, the effects of cohesion and pore pressure are generally smaller, while the more important attributes determining landslide occurrence are typically the inclination of the slope and the potential slip plane (Sidle & Ochiai, 2006). Slope inclination has long been an important component predicting landslides (Walker *et al.*, 1996; Turner *et al.*, 2010). Root strength is often a more important component of slope stability than the weight of vegetation, and this has been demonstrated on a landslide (where $\beta = 42°$) associated with forest clear-cutting in Alaska (Sidle, 1984). Because of the many factors that affect the driving and resisting forces, including slope angle, earth substrate, climate, vegetation, water, and time, the condition and balance between such forces are highly dynamic at the slip plane, which is why a slope may be stable for centuries and then suddenly slide. Sometimes vulnerability to landslides can be calculated with matrices that include some of these variables. For example, in three montane regions in Puerto Rico, Larsen & Torres-Sánchez (1998) determined that slopes most likely to slide were those that were anthropogenically modified, had slopes $> 12°$, were > 300 m in elevation, and faced the predominant northeast trade winds.

3.2.1 Geological context

The geology, or earth substrate, can affect the frequencies and types of landslides that may occur. For rotational slides, which are also known as slumps, the sliding occurs along a curved (concave upward) slip plane (see Fig. 1.3). Rotational slides are most common on soil slopes, but can also occur on weak rock slopes such as shale (Keller, 1996). In contrast to rotational slides, the slip plane of a translational landslide is planar (see Fig. 1.4). Translation slip planes can occur in all rock and soil types and can range from shallow soil slips to deep-seated landslides (Keller, 1996; Sidle & Ochiai, 2006; see Fig. 1.2). Bedrock that is fractured, jointed, faulted, or bedded in the direction parallel to the hill slope constitutes a zone of weakness that can increase the likelihood of a landslide (Pearce & O'Loughlin, 1985; Chen, 2006). Chemical and mechanical weathering, as well as tectonic activity, affects the strength and cohesion of the geological substrate and its propensity for landslides. The interface between two different rock types represents a potential slip plane that can result in devastating landslides, especially when mechanical weathering reduces resistance forces, which is what occurred during the Frank Slide (Box 3.1).

Box 3.1 The Frank Slide disaster of 1903

One of the more famous landslide stories of both survival and devastation is the Frank Slide. On April 29, 1903, at 4:10 a.m., 82 million tons of limestone sheared off Turtle Mountain in the southern Rocky Mountains of Canada. The section of rocky slope that failed was 150 m thick, 650 m tall, and 900 m wide (Dawson, 1995). The landslide lasted less than 90 seconds, and covered 3 km^2 of the valley floor, including some of the town of Frank (population about 600). The landslide dammed the Crowsnest River, covered 2 km of the Canadian Pacific Railroad, destroyed a coalmine entrance and associated infrastructure, and buried seven houses and several rural buildings. Of the approximately 100 people that were in the path of the landslide, at least 70 people died (Bonikowsky, 2012). Miners who were buried in the mine tunnels were later able to dig themselves out, although several miners taking their 4 a.m. lunch break at the entrance of the mine were killed (Bonikowsky, 2012). Many of the survivors of the landslide were children, perhaps the most famous was a 15-month-old girl who was thrown from her house by the slide, and was found afterward in a pile of hay. The mother of a 27-month-old baby found her child face down in the slide's mud and debris, and saved the baby's life by clearing mud from her nose and throat.

The geology of Turtle Mountain was one of the primary causes of the landslide because limestone rock was thrust over weaker rocks and coal (Dawson, 1995). The stratification of these sedimentary rocks was weakened by fracturing and fissures, and such cracks in the rock allowed precipitation to infiltrate and periodically freeze and expand, which further weakened the integrity of the mountain slope. The timing of weather events was also a contributing factor. The winter prior to the landslide had more snow than usual, and April was unusually warm, allowing snowmelt and rain to percolate into the mountain fissures before the weather turned cold again. On the day of the landslide, the resistance forces of the rock layers were weakened past the critical tipping point by the water freezing and expanding in the fissures. Mining activities may have provided an additional trigger (Benko & Stead, 1998).

Although the Frank Slide was a tragic and devastating landslide, reclamation efforts were immediate: the town was moved and life was restored. The coal mine was re-opened within weeks and the buried section of the railroad was rebuilt. In 1906, a road was built through the deposition zone of the landslide. During road improvements in 1922, a construction crew found the skeletal remains of seven people in the rubble. Although the last survivor of the Frank slide died in 1995 in Bellevue, Washington, U.S. (Bonikowsky, 2012), the devastation of Canada's largest landslide will not be forgotten. In fact, geologists currently monitor Turtle Mountain and the changes in the sizes of the fissures because they expect that future displacements are likely.

Landslides can occur on all types of geological substrates or rock types. Although some rock types are more prone to landslides than others, the physical and chemical conditions of the rock types or soil parent material can result in a wide spectrum of substrate conditions (e.g., fine volcanic clays to fresh lava rock), which often affect slope stability more than the type of parent material alone. For example, the characteristics of the sliding surface (potential slip plane) are often more important than the underlying parent bedrock; all three of the main rock types (igneous, sedimentary, metamorphic) are potentially susceptible to landslides (Sidle & Ochiai, 2006). Granite (an igneous rock) is one type of parent material that, when weathered, results in relatively high slope instability, as found on landslides in Korea (Wakatsuki et al., 2005) and Nepal (Ibetsberger, 1996). The instability of granite rocks probably results from relatively slow weathering, which produces shallow soils with low water storage and high permeability (Sidle & Ochiai, 2006). Weak sedimentary rocks, such as mudstone and shale, are also highly susceptible to landslides (Pearce & O'Loughlin, 1985; Chigira & Oyama, 1999). The presence of particular compounds and oxidation in sandstone (another sedimentary rock) determines if it is weakened and therefore more susceptible to landslides, or if it is strengthened by cementation by iron oxide or hydroxide (Chigira & Oyama, 1999). Pyroclastic rocks can also weather quickly by both mechanical and chemical processes, and landslides commonly occur on these substrates (Yokota & Iwamatsu, 1999; Chigira & Yokoyama, 2005). Weathered gneiss (metamorphic rock), in contrast, is often more resistant to sliding than other rock types (Ibetsberger, 1996; Wakatsuki et al., 2005), yet catastrophic landslides can still occur on hill slopes underlain by gneiss (Weidinger et al., 1996; Larsen & Wieczorek, 2006).

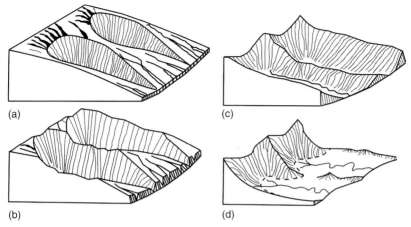

(a)

(b)

(c)

(d)

Fig. 3.2. Stages in the formation of valleys with amphitheater-shaped head walls, (a) to (d), sequentially. From Scott & Street (1976) with permission from Schweizerbart Science Publishers (schweizerbart.de).

Landslides often shape, and re-shape, the topography of many terrestrial and submarine environments. Much of our understanding of topographical changes has come from examining valley formation and the processes of erosion over a chronosequence (i.e., an age sequence of landforms with a common parent material; see Chapter 5). The Hawaiian Islands are a well-studied chronosequence of volcanic landforms because the main Hawaiian Islands range in age from about 5.25 million years on Kauai, to parent material just being formed on the Island of Hawaii (Vitousek *et al.*, 2009; Peltzer *et al.*, 2010). After the volcanic rock is formed from cooling lava, the processes of chemical weathering and landsliding begin to re-shape the topography. Scott & Street (1976) describe the formation of U-shaped "amphitheater" valleys, which are now common landscape features on several of the Hawaiian Islands, particularly on the older islands of Kauai, Oahu (3–4 million years old, and Molokai (2 million years old; Ziegler, 2002). Valley formation in Hawaii can be viewed as a model example for understanding the role of landslides in transforming topography and landscapes. Valley formation begins when major rivers incise the parent substrate and initially create deep, V-shaped valleys (Fig. 3.2). The chemical weathering on the sides of the valley produces soils that deepen to the point where they are unstable. With high rainfall events, the soil is transported down slope by landslides. The valley widens through this process and landslides continue to occur beyond the river profile equilibrium (i.e., when river downcutting ceases). Valley walls undergo parallel retreat to form a broad floor and U-shaped

Fig. 3.3. An amphitheater-shaped valley on Molokai, Hawaii. Amphitheaters form in part because maximum erosion occurs at the top of the valley headwalls. Photograph by A.B. Shiels.

(amphitheater) valleys (Fig. 3.3) with steep sides (Fig. 3.4). This process takes at least 0.8 million years (Scott & Street, 1976). Today, many of the residents of Oahu live in the valley bottoms and on the ridges above such U-shaped valleys that were partially formed by landslides. A related process occurs in U-shaped valleys that are initially carved by glaciers and then further shaped by landslides (Plate 7).

A similar process involving landslides also forms large U-shaped valleys on the ocean floor (Robb, 1984). An important difference between terrestrial and submarine landslides is that submarine landslides occur on slopes that have a mostly constant volume of water (i.e., weight on the slope) and are triggered primarily by seismic activity rather than variation in local precipitation (see Section 3.2.3). One intriguing result of the shifts in soils and/or geological substrate that occur during both terrestrial and submarine landslides is the exposure of rock layers that are millions of years old as well as human artifacts deposited prior to soil or substrate coverage; such prehistoric items can be uncovered by terrestrial landslides occurring on road cuts (Fig. 3.5; Box 3.2).

Fig. 3.4. Landslides on fields (far left, center, and far right of photo) at the base of steep walls (Makua Valley) derived from the inner crater rim of a giant volcano, Oahu, Hawaii. Note that the upper slopes are too steep for soil formation. Photograph by A.B. Shiels.

3.2.2 Soil context

Like all rock types, all soil orders are potentially vulnerable to landslides. Rock weathers through mechanical and chemical processes. Freeze–thaw and wet–dry cycles, direct impacts from dislodged rock, and waterfalls are all examples of mechanical weathering. The primary controls of

Fig. 3.5. A tunnel and an overhead chute used to divert landslide sediments from a road through Arthur's Pass, New Zealand. Photograph by L.R. Walker.

the rates of chemical weathering include rock type, temperature, and moisture (Scott & Street, 1976). Available moisture (affected by local

Box 3.2 Road cuts trigger landslides and expose geological and human history

Road-building is ubiquitous across much of the planet, and where it occurs over sloped terrain it often triggers landslides (Fig. 3.5). Road cuts are often the sites of busy mountainside traffic and may, in unstable regions, cause some anxiety to travelers because of danger or delays resulting from eroding slopes. Road cuts, and the land-slides that occur on them, have two interesting side benefits. The deep cuts provided by roadway excavation and subsequent landslides create steep, vertical, walls, which expose a geological record that intrigues both geologists and anthropologists. Geologists, soil scien-tists, and geomorphologists can use such road cut profiles to differen-tiate among rock layers and interpret a geological story that can date back millions of years. Anthropologists and archaeologists can use the same road cuts and landslides to reveal traces of human cultures that might be centuries old. For example, during road construction in the Asese Peninsula of Lake Nicaragua, a landslide unearthed numerous ceramic vessels (decorated pottery) and artifacts (Wilke *et al.*, 2011) that, when dated using carbon isotope analysis of carbon fragments, were about 1000 years old. Interest in the items unearthed from the small landslides led to the establishment of a formal archeological excavation at the site. The site contained a mass cemetery with not only ceramic vessels, but also human bones and other remains. There were also caches of goods such as knife blades, ear spools, bone tools, ceramic beads, pendants, fishing weights, and a figurine of a shaman (Wilke *et al.*, 2011). Landslides therefore serve multiple purposes, including providing geological insights and improving understanding of our human ancestors.

climate) is the most variable of these controlling factors on the local and watershed scale, which highlights its importance in weathering and landslide occurrence across landscapes (Chen, 2006). Areas with limestone are highly susceptible to chemical weathering and rock decomposition because rainfall is typically acidic (forming carbonic acid) from its reaction with carbon dioxide in the atmosphere and soil (Keller, 1996).

Soil is a mixture of decomposed rock and organic matter that is teeming with living organisms, particularly microbes (e.g., bacteria and fungi) and invertebrates such as arthropods and earthworms (see Chapter 4). Soil formation results from the interactions of climate, biota, topography, parent material, and time (Jenny, 1941, 1980). Climate affects weathering rates via temperature and precipitation. The soil fauna is an important component of all soils because it directly contributes to soil building and its chemical and nutritional status. Soil microbes commonly span all soil layers from the surface to the parent rock, yet they tend to be most active and in highest abundance near the soil surface where organic matter is highest. Vegetation that colonizes landslides creates physical channels in the soil and parent material via rooting; organic acids, both from root exudates and leaf litter, contribute to substrate weathering and soil formation.

The degree to which soils have been weathered can affect landslide occurrence. Coarse-grained, granitic soils are commonly classified as Entisols or Inceptisols, which are the least developed of any soil types. Such soils have abundant air spaces between grains that make them loose (less cohesive) relative to finer grained particles such as silt or clay, which more readily "stick" to one another. Sandier soils are also more permeable and therefore do not have the high water-holding capacity that silts and clays do. Therefore, granitic soils often crumble and erode, resulting in frequent, small landslides (Pearce & O'Loughlin, 1985; Sidle & Ochiai, 2006). A greater frequency of landslides per substrate area occurred on sandy soils derived from granite-like diorite with a lower water-holding capacity than on the clay-rich volcaniclastic soils with higher water-holding capacity in the Luquillo Mountains of Puerto Rico (Shiels *et al.*, 2008; Walker & Shiels, 2008; Shiels & Walker, in press).

The depth to which soils are developed can affect the volume of material eroded and can range from several vertical meters in deep rotational or translational landslides to several centimeters in young, shallow soils (Wentworth, 1943; Pearce & O'Loughlin, 1985; Fort *et al.*, 2010). As with rock layers, the interface of two soil layers in the soil profile is commonly a potential slip plane because the density, permeability, and other soil characteristics change in ways that affect the water dynamics and resistant forces (Fig. 3.1(a)). Such changes can occur at virtually any soil depth. An abrupt type of layering occurs when a developed soil layer abuts bedrock or saprolite (chemically weathered bedrock), either of which is generally more compact and less permeable than the soil above it. The compact substrate that rests below such a soil layer impedes soil water percolation, thereby leading to saturation of the pore spaces in the upper soil layers and changes in the driving and resisting forces. The most common landslides in many areas of sloped terrain are those that are shallow (< 2 m) and small (< 150 m^2; Scott & Street, 1976; Larsen & Torres-Sánchez, 1996; Shiels *et al.*, 2008). These shallow landslides are primarily triggered by intense precipitation on high antecedent soil moisture conditions rather than by earthquakes. Landslides studied in Jamaica by Dalling (1994), and in Hawaii by Scott & Street (1976), were shallow (averaging < 60 cm depth). The variation in depth of Hawaiian landslides reflected differences in plant cover type; landslides that averaged 42 cm depth were initially fern-covered, whereas landslides that averaged 57 cm depth were originally forest-covered (Scott & Street, 1976). Wentworth (1943) studied 200 landslides in a 39 km^2 area on Oahu and found that the depth of landslides averaged 30 cm. Similarly, in a study of nine landslides by Restrepo *et al.* (2003) on the island of Hawaii, the average depth from the surface to bedrock was 34 cm. Such shallow landslides in Hawaii are probably the result of relatively young parent material that has had little time to weather and form soil. When both soil types and substrate ages were considered, the average depths of landslides in the Luquillo Mountains in Puerto Rico were 0.5 m to 7 m (Larsen & Torres-Sánchez, 1990). However, when landslides occur on the 30 million-year-old volcaniclastic substrate they appear to erode more deeply on average than those soils derived from the 10 million-year-old dioritic intrusion (A. Shiels, pers. obs.). Additionally, landslides occurring on dioritic soils in the Luquillo Mountains tend to expose bedrock more frequently than those on volcaniclastic soils, yet saprolite rather than bedrock is typically exposed following landslides occurring on volcaniclastic soils. Therefore, the depth of erosion resulting from landslides is influenced by both physical (e.g., the type and age of parent material) and temporal (e.g., degree of weathering) factors.

Local topography and especially slope not only influence landslide occurrence, but also influence soil development. Although the steepest slopes might be expected to experience the highest landslide frequency, slopes that are too steep to form substantial soil rarely experience landslides involving soil (but can experience rock falls). Many of the slopes on the windward side of Molokai, Oahu, and Kauai (Hawaiian Islands) are too steep (> 75°) for substantial soil formation to occur (Fig. 3.4; Scott & Street, 1976). Therefore, soil-related landslides are most frequent where substantial soil forms, which is commonly on foothills below cliffs or on mountain slopes above cliffs (Scott & Street, 1976). However, slope gradient interacts with geological and biological factors as well. In New Zealand, landslides at high elevation with erosive allophane and poor vegetation cover occurred on slopes as low as 15°, while at lower elevations with more stable soils and vegetative cover, landslides occurred only on slopes > 40° (Jane & Green, 1983). Additional topographic characteristics that affect soil development and landslide activity include proximity to dips, scarps (topographic evidence of faults), rock outcrops, and valley walls; these features can influence the direction and magnitude of seismic shaking, the buildup of pore pressure, and the local microclimate (Pearce & O'Loughlin, 1985). For example, outcrops or walls may provide protection from driving rain along some aspects, and the shade created by topographic features often increases soil moisture, decreases soil and air temperature, and alters plant cover and rooting depth (Larson *et al.*, 2000).

3.2.3 Proximal triggers

Rainfall, earthquakes, volcanic eruptions, and human activities can facilitate landslide occurrence because each of these components alters the balance between driving and resisting forces on the slope. Many of the landslides discussed in the previous section were shallow, terrestrial land-slides that resulted from large rainfall events. While rainfall typically trig-gers smaller landslides than those produced by earthquakes or volcanoes (Schuster, 2001), rainfall-triggered landslides tend to be more frequent worldwide because heavy storms are common, even in areas of little seis-mic activity. For example, Scott & Street (1976) studied 139 landslides that were all triggered by heavy rainfall during a 5-year period in 7 km^2 of the Koolau Mountains, Oahu. A recent landslide survey over 2 years in the Luquillo Mountains (110 km^2) of Puerto Rico found that three significant rainstorms triggered 142 landslides (Shiels & Walker, in press). The average size of the 139 landslides studied by Scott & Street (1976) and the 142 studied by Shiels & Walker (in press) was approximately 100 m^2. However, despite their small sizes, the relatively high frequen-cies of such landslides can affect significant portions of the landscape (see Table 2.2).

Earthquakes can generate tens of thousands of landslides over thousands of square kilometers and dislodge several billion cubic meters of rocks and soils from slopes (Keefer, 1984). In a 154 000 km^2 portion of the South Island, New Zealand, an estimated 40%–67% of all the material that had eroded in that region had originated from earthquake-induced landslides (Adams, 1980). The shaking of the soil profile by either an earthquake or volcanic eruption decreases the resisting forces along potential slip planes. Explosive volcanoes can also create landslides from the blast, which was the case with the largest historic (terrestrial) landslide, which was triggered by the eruption of Mount St. Helens in 1980 (Schuster, 2001; Dale *et al.*, 2005; see Box 2.3). Additionally, landslides can be triggered by the interaction of intense rainfall with seismic activity (Plate 8). For example, Ecuador's 1987 Reventador earthquakes (magnitude 6.1 and 6.9) in Napo Province triggered thousands of landslides (affecting hundreds of km^2) on soils that had been saturated by heavy rainfall during the prior month (Schuster *et al.*, 1996). High pore pressure from the weight of water (1 liter = 1 kg) held in the soil from prolonged rainfall likely increased the driving forces on the potential slip plane; the shaking from the earthquakes then tipped the balance further in favor of driving forces and slope failure. In the absence of high pore pressure, water is not a slippery medium that has a lubricating effect; instead, water holds soil grains through surface tension and therefore provides cohesion in the soil–water interface (Keller, 1996).

Heavy rains typically cause landslides by temporarily raising the water table to a shallower depth. A rising water table results from a greater rate of surface infiltration into the unsaturated (vadose) zone than the rate of deep percolation (Keller, 1996; Dhakal & Sidle, 2004; Chen, 2006). The most extreme case of a rising water table occurs when it reaches the surface, indicating that a potential landslide mass is entirely saturated. Saturation of soil increases the pore pressure. Pore pressure slightly forces the soil grains apart and thus reduces inter-grain friction, cohesion, shear strength, and resisting forces (Sidle & Swanston, 1982). Additionally, the driving forces increase due to the extra weight and pressure of water (Peterson et al., 1993; Chen et al., 1999). Seepage of water from external sources, such as reservoirs, canals, culverts, and septic tanks, can also increase pore pressure and weight on a slope, thereby increasing the likelihood of a landslide.

Water can also reduce soil stability by rapid draw down, or by altering the physical structure of clays. Rapid draw down occurs when the water level of a river or reservoir lowers quickly, usually at a rate of at least 1 m per day (Kojan & Hutchinson, 1978; Keller, 1996). With the drop in surface water, the bank, which the surface water body had previously inundated, is left unsupported and with water-filled pore spaces. The bank therefore reflects an abnormal distribution of pore pressure where the weight of the bank increases the driving forces and reduces the resisting forces, causing bank failures (slumps) to occur. Examples of rapid draw down can occur in most environments after flood waters have receded, including semi-arid ecosystems where ephemeral streams are present. On river valley slopes that contain clay-rich sediment, liquifaction can occur. This process results from disturbance to some clays in the soil profile, which causes them to lose their shear strength and behave like a liquid (flow). Liquifaction of clays is often caused by river erosion at the toe of the slope. Although they start in a small area, these flows (see Table 1.2) can become large events that are very destructive and can result in large losses of human lives (Sidle et al., 1985; Boadu & Owusu-Nimo, 2011).

How much rainfall and what magnitude of an earthquake are needed to trigger landslides? Due to the many factors involved, there is no simple generalization, especially when rainfall interacts with seismic activity. However, there have been several attempts to make both worldwide and regional models to predict landslide occurrence. Using 73 shallow landslides from around the world, Caine (1980) constructed a landslide-triggering equation to predict landslide occurrence based solely on rainfall intensity (I) in millimeters hour^{-1} and duration (D) in hours: $I = 14.82D^{-0.39}$. If at any time the rainfall intensity exceeds the threshold

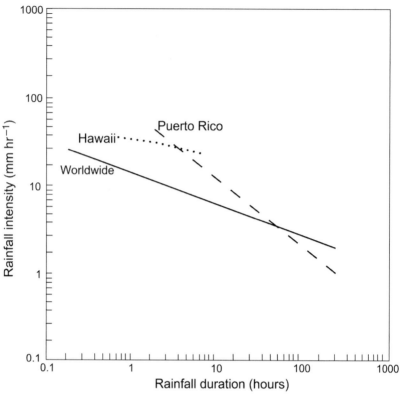

Fig. 3.6. Three rainfall intensity-duration thresholds for triggering landslides. From Larsen & Simon (1993) with permission from John Wiley & Sons.

value I, then shallow landslides may occur (Fig. 3.6). The antecedent moisture content, or the degree of wetness of the soil, is typically positively correlated with D but it will also depend upon local physical characteristics of the environment (e.g., soil properties, vegetation cover). Since Caine (1980) reported this model, it has been tested and altered for improvement; but local and regional models are typically favored over the worldwide model (Sidle & Ochiai, 2006). For example, Larsen & Simon (1993) defined such a model for northeastern Puerto Rico using the same two variables as Caine (1980). Their equation ($I = 91.46D^{-0.82}$), derived from studying 256 storms across 32 years, gives the threshold that, when exceeded, resulted in landslides (Fig. 3.6). Note that in both Hawaii and Puerto Rico more rain is required per unit time than the world average. From their surveys, Larsen & Simon (1993) also estimated that landslide-producing storms in the Luquillo Mountains occur at an average rate of

1.2 year^{-1}. Keefer (1984) developed indicators of earthquake-triggered landslides by applying simple relationships with earthquake magnitude and distance to the epicenter. Keefer (1984) reported that the smallest earthquakes that produce landslides typically have a magnitude of at least 4.0, and an "average" earthquake of magnitude 8.0 would likely trigger landslides over an area of 35 000 km^2 (Keefer, 1984). Using data from 47 earthquakes from various settings around the world, Keefer & Wilson (1989) calculated the following regression relationship to predict the amount of area potentially affected by earthquake-triggered landslides: $\log_{10} A' = M - 3.46$ (± 0.47) where A' is the potential area affected by landslides (km^2) and M is the earthquake magnitude in the range of 5.5–9.2. A similar equation was developed using 22 earthquake-triggered landslides in New Zealand: $\log_{10} A' = 0.96$ (± 0.16) $M - 3.7$ (± 1.1) (Hancox *et al.*, 2002). Such predictive models for landslide occurrence could probably be improved by accounting for particular properties of the local soil and parent material (e.g., soil moisture, rock type). However, predicting exact locations of landslides still remains challenging.

The physical factors responsible for triggering submarine landslides are similar to those for terrestrial landslides because slope failure occurs on weak geological layers (slip planes) when driving forces override resistance forces. Because precipitation is largely irrelevant in triggering submarine landslides, earthquakes are the primary triggering mechanism (Schuster, 2001). Like terrestrial landslides, an earthquake can cause a single landslide or multiple landslides around the earthquake's epicenter. Because submarine landslides often occur at great depths beneath the ocean surface, few have been documented at the time of occurrence (see Section 2.2.1; Hampton *et al.*, 1996).

In addition to earthquakes, submarine landslides may be caused by increased pore pressure due to rapid sediment deposition or by increased wave action due to large storms such as cyclones (Bea *et al.*, 1983; Locat & Lee, 2002). Submarine landslides may also occur through tidal changes in a manner analogous to the way that a rapid draw down causes terrestrial landslides; such landslides occur during low tide when the pore pressure of the intertidal zone does not have sufficient time to reach a steady state with ground water flow (Locat & Lee, 2002). Submarine landslides that occur as a result of tidal change are most common on river deltas, and they are often related to additional co-occurring triggering mechanisms such as road construction and/or increased sediment loading via river outflow (Locat & Lee, 2002). Groundwater discharge and sediment discharge at coastal areas and river mouths can also trigger submarine landslides at high and low tides because these tides increase pore pressure and driving forces on a slope (Robb, 1984; Locat & Lee, 2002). Additionally, some submarine landslides occur from disruption of gas hydrates, which are ice and natural gas mixtures that are stable at constant sea floor temperatures (Sultan *et al.*, 2004). Gas hydrates form by gas (usually natural gas) trapped in sea beds, which are under intermediate pressure and low temperature. These gas hydrates form layers and, at sufficient concentration, cement sediments (Sultan *et al.*, 2004). However, when bottom temperature or pressure changes occur, or drilling disrupts the ocean floor layers, the gas hydrates can melt or otherwise become unstable and can facilitate landslides (Sultan *et al.*, 2004; Crutchley *et al.*, 2007). The reduction in sea level is one way in which natural gas trapped in the seafloor can be released, making the local slope unstable (Locat & Lee, 2002).

Human actions are well known to cause landslides (Locat & Lee, 2002; Sidle & Ochiai, 2006). There are at least three main ways in which humans increase slope instability (see Section 1.1.1): (1) ground-shaking (reducing resisting forces), (2) increasing the slope's load or weight (increasing driving forces), and (3) physically modifying the slope substrate by drilling or removing a portion of the slope and/or vegetation (reducing resisting forces). Construction using large ground-shaking equipment, and blasting or drilling through rock, can cause ground vibrations resulting in slope failure that is similar to that produced by tectonic earthquakes. Even submarine landslides near the coastline have been triggered by nearby (terrestrial) blasting associated with road construction (Kristiansen, 1986). To study liquefaction and other details of landslide processes, explosives have been used to create submarine landslides (By *et al.*, 1990; Couture *et al.*, 1995). For example, the Kenamu River delta in Canada was partially destabilized by a blast using 1200 kg of explosives (Couture *et al.*, 1995).

Humans can directly or indirectly increase the weight of a slope, which consequently increases the driving forces along a potential slip plane (Keller, 1996; Locat & Lee, 2002). Direct increases on a slope include erecting structures, such as buildings, or adding substrate, such as mine tailings or fill material (Fig. 3.1(b)). Although development and building on slopes is common worldwide, slope and substrate surveys combined with site engineering can help alleviate and transfer much of the structure's weight load from the most vulnerable slip planes to deeper soil depths or perhaps bedrock by using ties and pilings. Some indirect weight increases to slopes that result from human activity can increase pore pressure on a slope (e.g., when soil water increases from redirection of drainage patterns). Sediment deposition through increased runoff into water bodies (e.g., for submarine landslides) is another way that humans may indirectly increase the weight load of a slope. Rapid draw down of rivers and reservoirs by humans can also result in pore pressure increases to a slope.

Common practices that physically modify a slope and increase the likelihood of landslides include road building and drilling. Road cuts can decrease resistance forces and lead to landslides (Fig. 3.1(d)), whereas the addition of material placed below a road cut can also increase the weight (driving forces) on the slope below a road. Landslides associated with road building are more common than non-anthropogenic landslides in many regions of the world, such as Puerto Rico (Guariguata & Larsen, 1990). Drilling into the seafloor for petroleum or natural gas can also directly cause landslides either by reducing resistance forces in a similar fashion as road building, or by disrupting or melting gas hydrates (Locat & Lee, 2002; Sultan *et al.*, 2004). Therefore, humans frequently cause landslides through a number of land use practices; Chapter 6 describes in greater detail the various human–landslide interactions.

3.3 Physical consequences

Landslides create gaps or scars in vegetation and surface substrate, and therefore the physical environment is greatly altered following a landslide. The loss of above-ground and below-ground biomass and abiotic material provides opportunity for new colonists (see Chapter 4), and results in widespread microtopographic heterogeneity, exposure of new substrates that have long been covered by soil layers, and microclimatic variation at the surface and near surface. The range of substrates within a land-slide zone can include a patchwork of bedrock, saprolite, deep soils, and even soils that were resistant to the landslide (Miles & Swanson, 1986; Shiels & Walker, in press). Variation in the degree of scouring, depth of soil remaining, and organic matter is often divided into three main zones (slip face, chute, deposition) described in Chapter 2. The physical consequences of landslides also extend out of the landslide area; sediment clouds (turbidity currents) extend for kilometers from submarine landslides (see Fig. 2.3; Locat & Lee, 2002), and mixtures of both sediment and debris are commonly transported through a watershed and deposited into rivers or roads (Chen, 2006; Sidle & Ochiai, 2006). Landslides are more than mass movements of the upper layers of the earth; each landslide leaves a unique signature in the local landscape where its effects extend beyond the immediate landslide scar.

3.3.1 Sediment, rock, and debris movement

The high energy movement of material down slope is often the most impressive, but also most dangerous, portion of a landslide disturbance. Uprooted trees, rocks, branches, leaf litter, and soil fauna travel down slope as part of a sediment-dominated mixture that ultimately comprises the base, or deposition zone, of a landslide. Two landslide events in New Zealand altered stream channels by delivering 4700 m^3 of logs that piled up to 8 m tall and about 60 000 m^3 of sediment reaching depths of 4 m (Pearce & Watson, 1983). The deposition zone can also be removed from the landscape by rivers, and when flooding co-occurs with landslide-producing rainstorms the flood waters can immediately alter the landslide-delivered deposits across the landscape. Based on studies of 19 earth flows, which are slow-moving landslides that creep down slope in a manner analogous to alpine glaciers, an estimated 24 900 tons km^{-2} of sediment was annually deposited during 1941–1975 into the Van Duzen River, northern California (Kelsey, 1978). Landslides and flooding triggered by a large rainstorm deposited as much as 100 000 m^3 km^{-2} sediment from a 200 km drainage area in Venezuela (Larsen & Wieczorek, 2006). Sediment loads may not have immediate effects on waterways if they are far from stream networks, composed of large particle sizes (Pearce & Watson, 1986), or landslide dams retain them. It took 2 years for river erosion to remove half of the total landslide debris generated by an earthquake in New Guinea (Pain & Bowler, 1973). Keefer (1994) proposed an equation to describe the total volume of terrestrial landslide material dislodged by earthquakes. The equation is: $V = M_0 / 10^{10.9(\pm 0.13)}$, where V is the volume and is measured in m^3, and M_0 is the seismic moment of the earthquake measured in dyn cm (where 1 dyn is the force required to accelerate a 1 g mass at a rate of 1 cm second^{-2}). The M_0 is related to the magnitude (M) of an earthquake but also takes into account rigidity, average slip fault, and rupture area (Keefer, 1994). Through such modeling of sediment production in 12 earthquake-prone regions, Keefer (1994) found that four regions, including Hawaii, New Zealand, Irian Jaya (West Papua), and San Francisco Bay (U.S.) had very high sediment production (> 200 m^3 km^{-2} year^{-1}) generated by earthquake-triggered landslides. Additional regions in California, Japan, and Turkey had moderately high sediment production (20–200 m^3 km^{-2} year^{-1};

Keefer, 1994). Advances in seafloor mapping technology have enabled the sizes and depths of past submarine landslides to be better estimated (see Chapter 2; Locat & Lee, 2002); and the largest known submarine landslide transported approximately 20 000 km^3 of material down slope (Schuster, 2001).

Land use plays a critical role in altering sediment loads. For example, the Cayaguás watershed in Puerto Rico was intensely farmed from 1820 to 1970. Despite recent revegetation efforts, a total of 666 000 m^3 km^{-2} of sediments (3805 m^3 km^{-2} year^{-1} during the last 175 years) have been eroded by landslides (Larsen & Santiago Román, 2001). An additional 113 000 m^3 km^{-2} of colluvium has accumulated in the Caguas watershed from landslides during this time period. If mobilized, this colluvium would be sufficient stored material to supply the annual fluvial sediment yield for up to 129 years (Larsen & Santiago Román, 2001). Logging and associated road building in Malaysian rainforest resulted in annual sediment yields from landslides that were double the pre-logging levels even 6 years after logging had ceased (Clarke & Walsh, 2006). Although there are a wide variety of scar sizes, scouring depths, and debris and sediment deposition volumes, all landslides create immediate and long-term effects that alter biotic and abiotic environments.

3.3.2 Post-landslide erosion

Erosion that occurs after a landslide event is often neglected because of its apparent subtlety relative to the landslide itself. However, landslides often initiate a complex and lengthy process of changes in both geological (Swanson & Major, 2005) and biological aspects of a landscape (see Chapter 5). The exposure of vegetation-free substrate, for example, promotes subsequent erosion through a number of mechanisms, including reduced interception of precipitation, increased overland flow, and creation of channel incisions along landslide surfaces and edges (Stokes et al., 2007b; Walker & Shiels, 2008). Such post-landslide erosion can last for years and affect the biotic recovery on the landslide scar and the habitats below the landslide (Scott & Street, 1976; Larsen et al., 1999; Clarke & Walsh, 2006). Vegetation diverts and intercepts rainfall, physically impedes surface sediment runoff, and anchors soils (Table 3.2; see Section 6.5.3; Sidle et al., 2006; Stokes et al., 2007a,b, 2009; Dung et al., 2011). Similarly, the multi-layered broad leaf forests of the Himalayan Mountains experience fewer landslides than those dominated by the more sparsely layered pine trees (Tiwari et al., 1986). Organic matter (e.g., litter layer) generated by vegetation helps in water absorption and infiltration, and it helps reduce the incidence of sediment dislodging from rainfall splash (Sidle *et al.*, 2006; Ghahramani *et al.*, 2011). Roots (both dead and alive) provide channels for water to infiltrate and help provide lateral drainage of hill slopes, which ultimately reduces surface flow and sediment runoff (Noguchi *et al.*, 1997; Sidle *et al.*, 2001). Similarly, the depth of the soil relative to the rooting depth and root density can also influence slope stability; deep roots and high root density enable greater water diversion through the soil profile (Sidle *et al.*, 1985; Pla Sentís, 1997; Schmidt *et al.*, 2001). Vegetation also removes soil water from the rooting zone via transpiration (Stokes *et al.*, 2009). Species composition and disturbance history also influence root cohesion on landslides, with the contributions of plant roots in undisturbed coniferous forests in Oregon, for example, far exceeding that of clear cuts and plantations (Schmidt *et al.*, 2001). Severe fires that reduce vegetation cover on slopes can promote new landslides or re-sliding by reducing root cohesion (Swanson, 1981; Cannon, 2001; Wondzell & King, 2003). The spatial distribution of vegetation on recent landslides is also important because clumpy vegetation cover can lead to concentrated flow between clumps, thereby increasing water flow velocity, sediment movement, and gully formation (Morgan, 2007; Dung *et al.*, 2011).

Bare (vegetation-free) soil is often the immediate consequence of a landslide, and therefore the amount of post-landslide erosion that occurs on landslide slopes can be significant (Scott & Street, 1976; Douglas *et al.*, 1999; Larsen *et al.*, 1999; Walker & Shiels, 2008). For example, in Malaysian rainforest, the ground-lowering rates due to post-landslide erosion were 10–15 cm year^{-1} for the first 2 years following landslide disturbance (Clarke & Walsh, 2006). Post-landslide erosion occurring during the first year on ten Oahu landslides resulted in approximately half of the amount of sediment lost by the initial landslide disturbances (Scott & Street, 1976). On 30 8–13 month old landslides in Puerto Rico, the rates of sediment runoff from post-landslide erosion on volcaniclastic and quartz–diorite substrates were 20 and 67 g m^{-2} day^{-1} (7.3 and 24.4 kg m^{-2} year^{-1}), respectively (Fig. 3.7; Walker & Shiels, 2008). This amount of annual sediment runoff was much greater than on two other landslides studied with similar methods in the same forest (0.03–0.12 kg m^{-2} year^{-1} for a 4-year average; Larsen *et al.*, 1999). There was no reduction in post-landslide erosion throughout the 13 months in the Walker & Shiels (2008) study, but some decline was reported in post-landslide erosion during the 4-year study (Larsen *et al.*, 1999). The

Fig. 3.7. A gurlach trough (white object in foreground) used on a Puerto Rican landslide to measure sediment from post-landslide erosion. Photograph by A.B. Shiels.

propensity for post-landslide erosion is also affected by the particle sizes of surface sediments. For example, water flows over clay soils faster than over coarser-grained soils, such as sands, which impart greater roughness and therefore erode more readily (Morgan, 2007). Soil type and fertility can also indirectly influence post-landslide sediment loss through their effects on plant recovery (Shiels *et al.*, 2008).

Landslide edges provide another site of post-landslide instability (see Fig. 2.9). Distinct edges, or those which have clear boundaries, are typically steep and unsupported. Through the same forces that cause landslides (i.e., the imbalance between driving and resisting forces), material at the landslide edge topples or sloughs off into the landslide (Adams & Sidle, 1987; Zarin & Johnson, 1995a). In contrast to most post-landslide erosion originating from within the landslide, sloughing at the landslide edge adds soil into the landslide matrix that often contains elevated organic matter, nutrients, microbes, and seeds, which potentially accelerate plant and soil recovery (Adams & Sidle, 1987; Shiels *et al.*, 2006). Post-landslide erosion that originates both from the landslide edge and within the landslide can be a significant factor that may persist for many months after the landslide and comprise up to one-third of the total sediment lost from a landslide (Scott & Street, 1976).

In addition to the instability of landslide surfaces and edges after a land-slide, it is not uncommon for all, or a substantial portion of, the landslide to experience additional landslides on top of the first. This process, called re-sliding, often occurs in the steep regions of the landslide such as the slip face. However, any of the unsupported slopes, including edges and interior mounds, can erode and further scour or cover portions of the original landslide. Re-sliding differs from sediment loss and sloughing because it is spatially more extensive and represents a mass movement event. In Tanzania, six out of 14 landslides experienced re-sliding within 7 years of each initial landslide (Lundgren, 1978). During 2003–2004, nearly half (40%–48%) of the ≤ 2-year-old landslides generated near roads and trails in the Luquillo Mountains of Puerto Rico re-slid (Shiels & Walker, in press).

Sediment deposited in rivers, either via post-landslide erosion, or the initial landslide disturbance, can significantly alter water flow, tem-perature, light, and biota (see Section 2.2.1; Schuster, 2001; Mackey *et al.*, 2011). Within a landslide scar, the post-landslide aggregate stabil-ity, woody debris, slope gradient, topographic complexity, and exposed rock affect the velocity of the water and sediment movement down slope (Ziegler *et al.*, 2004; Morgan, 2007; Ghahramani *et al.*, 2011). Below the landslide, the distance to a river, tributary junction angles, channel and hill slope gradients, vegetation type and cover, extent of boulders and woody debris, and land uses influence the amount of landslide material deposited into streams (Pearce & Watson, 1983; Douglas *et al.*, 1999; Chen, 2006; Sidle *et al.*, 2006; Dung *et al.*, 2011). Many microtopo-graphic changes to landslide scars continue long after the landslide dis-turbance, and the sediment losses affiliated with such changes alter down slope habitats including waterways (Clarke & Walsh, 2006).

Large rain events are the most common cause of post-landslide erosion (Douglas *et al.*, 1999), but the lack of tight correlations between rainfall quantity and sediment loss is a reminder that there are likely to be mul-tiple interacting factors influencing soil, sediment, and debris transport both within and down slope of landslides (Walker & Shiels, 2008). Such material exports from landslides scars can begin immediately after the landslide disturbance, and may continue for years (Larsen *et al.*, 1999; Clarke & Walsh, 2006; Shiels & Walker, in press). On a chronosequence of landslides in the Himalayan Mountains, sediment losses did not return to pre-disturbance forest conditions within 40 years of landslide development (Pandey & Singh, 1985)

3.4 Geochemical consequences

One of the most obvious changes resulting from a landslide is the loss and redistribution of surface soils. Massive soil loss across the landslide, and a mixture of soils, rocks, and organic matter in the deposition zone, are key characteristics that make landslides unique disturbances. The majority of the landslide scar is typically infertile and is represented by undeveloped soils, saprolite, and possibly bedrock. The mosaic of various substrate types also has different microtopographic characteristics such as slopes, gullies, mounds, and remnant plant parts. The removal of the topsoil layers during a landslide alters the physical conditions of remaining soils, and can result in increased soil bulk density when compared to adjacent undisturbed soils (e.g., 0.78 g cm^{-3} in landslides vs. 0.37 g cm^{-3} in undisturbed soils in Jamaica; Dalling & Tanner, 1995). Remnant soil patches that survived the landslide, or small "islands" of developed soil that are rich in plant-available nutrients and organic matter, may also be common and contribute to soil and surface heterogeneity (Adams & Sidle, 1987; Shiels *et al.*, 2006). Depending upon the depth of soil removed and the amount of scouring, the landslide edge may initially be as infertile as interior soils. However, with time, plants bordering the landslide edge provide shade and litterfall that can enhance soil conditions (e.g., soil moisture and nutrients) at the landslide edge more than at the interior (Fetcher *et al.*, 1996). Therefore, soils within a landslide are highly heterogeneous and gradients of soil physical and chemical conditions are present from the top (slip face) to bottom (deposition zone) of the landslide, from edge to center, and from the bare soil or rock matrix to remnant patches of soil that were resistant to landsliding (see Section 2.3.3; Guariguata, 1990; Myster & Fernández, 1995; Shiels & Walker, in press).

3.4.1 Soil chemistry

Following landslides, soils and other substrate layers that had previously been covered become exposed to chemical weathering. Soil pH is one of the most important measurements needed to understand soil chemistry because most nutrients are only available to biota under particular pH ranges. Outside of these ranges, nutrients are tightly bound to other soil elements so that, when water is present, the elements are not displaced into solution and therefore are not available for plant uptake. Landslides typically have elevated soil pH relative to adjacent, undisturbed soils (Adams & Sidle, 1987; Guariguata, 1990; Dalling & Tanner, 1995). There are a number of reasons for the substrate pH to be higher after a landslide, all of which have to do with the loss of the surface soil layers. First, the surface soil layers contain the most organic matter, which is almost always acidic (Shiels, 2006; Shiels *et al.*, 2006). Second, the surface soil layers also contain the greatest density of plant roots (Schmidt *et al.*, 2001; Stokes *et al.*, 2009), which commonly exude organic acids into the soil (Schlesinger, 1991). And finally, the pH commonly decreases with soil depth because of the slightly acidic nature of rainfall and the less frequent percolation to the deeper soil depths relative to surface soils (Keller, 1996). Water is the primary medium by which chemical reactions occur in the soil. Elements and compounds are transported through soil by water, and the hydrogen and oxygen atoms can be exchanged, through oxidation and reduction reactions, within the soil column (Schlesinger, 1991). With the absence of topsoil in the upper landslide zone (slip face and upper chute), soil pH tends to be slightly higher than in the more organically rich lower zone (deposition zone), and this pattern is supported by evidence from landslides in Puerto Rico (pH in upper is 4.8 vs. lower is 4.7; Guariguata, 1990) and Alaska (pH in upper is 5.3 vs. lower is 5.1; Adams & Sidle, 1987). However, as a reminder of the great surface heterogeneity possible both within and among landslides, the soil pH on one landslide studied by Adams & Sidle (1987) did not differ between the upper and lower zones.

Potassium and phosphorus are rock-derived nutrients that are critical for plant growth and survival. Exposure of lower depths of soil coincidental with landslides (e.g., up to 60 cm depth) can result in elevated concentrations of potassium (Zarin & Johnson, 1995b) and phosphorus (Guariguata, 1990) following landslides. Despite the overall increase in these rock-derived nutrients, their availability for biotic uptake is dependent upon further breakdown from chemical weathering or by biota (Walker & Syers, 1976). Therefore, plant-available forms of potassium and phosphorus are often higher in habitats with intact surface soils (e.g., adjacent forests) relative to landslides (Guariguata, 1990; Dalling & Tanner, 1995) or in deposition zones relative to the upper portion of the landslide (Adams & Sidle, 1987; Guariguata, 1990). Calcium and magnesium are also important cations that derive from rock or organic matter. Landslides typically have a reduced cation exchange capacity, reflecting pronounced infertility, and many of the nutrient cations that are released by subsequent weathering or by external deposition into a landslide are often lost if biota are not present to absorb them (Pandey & Singh, 1985; Zarin & Johnson, 1995a).

Soil nitrogen and phosphorus are often the most limiting nutrients for plant growth, and both soil nitrogen and phosphorus limited seedling growth on young landslides in Jamaica (Dalling & Tanner, 1995) and Puerto Rico (Fetcher *et al.*, 1996; Shiels *et al.*, 2006). Because plant-available soil nitrogen (i.e., nitrate and ammonium) is either derived from atmospheric nitrogen, if nitrogen fixing bacteria are present in the soil, or from decomposition of organic matter, it should not be surprising that landslide soils are largely low in available nitrogen. For example, landslide soils in Jamaica had over four times less ammonium than soils in the adjacent forest understory (Dalling & Tanner, 1995). In relatively recent landslides in Puerto Rico, including those < 2 years old and < 5 years old, soil nitrate concentrations were below detection levels (i.e., < 1 µg nitrogen g dry soil^{-1}; Shiels & Yang, unpublished data). Total soil nitrogen, also expressed as organic nitrogen, is also greatly reduced by landslides. In Himalayan India, the total nitrogen concentration of 6- and 13-year-old landslides was approximately half that of the undisturbed forest (Pandey & Singh, 1985). In Puerto Rico, Guariguata (1990) found that total soil nitrogen was two times higher in the forest understory adjacent to landslides than in the landslide deposition zone, and five times higher in the forest than the upper landslide slip face. In Alaska, Adams & Sidle (1987) also found that the deposition zone had approximately twice as much total soil nitrogen as the chute for one landslide; the other two landslides studied did not differ in total soil nitrogen content between landslide zones despite very low concentrations (< 0.5% by dry weight). Although nitrogen fixation has not been well studied in landslides, nitrogen fixing bacteria are found on many temperate and tropical landslides (see Chapter 4), and Dalling (1994) found that nitrogen fixing lichen (*Stereocaulon virgatum*) were common on the upper portions of four 15-year-old landslides in Jamaica (see Fig. 4.3). Such examples of nitrogen fixation are important for nitrogen deprived landslide substrates.

3.4.2 Nutrient cycles and carbon flow

Organic matter is perhaps the most critical substrate that influences landslide soil conditions because it affects soil nutrient availability and cycling, moisture content, pH, the presence and activity of microbes and other soil fauna, and successional development (Guariguata, 1990; Zarin & Johnson, 1995a; Walker *et al.*, 1996; Wilcke *et al.*, 2003; Shiels, 2006). Organic matter derives from dead organisms, and because dead tissue includes proteins, organic matter is a common and crucial source of nitrogen that benefits landslide colonists (Dalling & Tanner, 1995; Shiels *et al.*, 2006). The carbohydrates and proteins in organic matter are readily sought by soil fauna where they are used for energy. Through decomposition, as well as additional chemical reactions in the soil (e.g., organic acid exudates from plants), complex compounds are broken down into more biologically usable states (Schlesinger, 1991).

Landslides are generally depauperate in organic matter (Walker *et al.*, 1996; Wilcke *et al.*, 2003). For example, on 14 landslides in Tanzania that were < 1 year old, organic carbon in surface soils (0–10 cm deep) was < 0.5%, which was less than half the concentration of soil carbon sampled in adjacent undisturbed habitats (Lundgren, 1978). Similarly, in India, the soil carbon in landslides aged 6 and 13 years was approximately half that of the undisturbed forest (Pandey & Singh, 1985). Within a given landslide, the deposition zone commonly has elevated organic matter concentrations relative to the chute and slip face (Adams & Sidle, 1987; Guariguata, 1990). The landslide deposition zone typically has a wide variety of organic matter substrates present, including soil organic matter (i.e., < 2 mm organic particles), partially decomposed material originating from the organic-horizon of previously up slope soils, coarse woody debris (e.g., partially decomposed logs), and whole plants or trees that may contain some living tissue even after being detached and transported into the deposition zone (Guariguata, 1990; Wilcke *et al.*, 2003; Sidle & Ochiai, 2006). The level of decomposition of such wide-ranging types of organic substrates directly influences the amount of available soil nutrients and subsequent biotic growth and activity (Shiels *et al.*, 2006). For example, because logs and other woody material have a higher carbon:nitrogen ratio relative to leaf blades or dead animals, the woody material decomposes more slowly and therefore has less immediate effect on increasing soil nutrient availability (Schlesinger, 1991). Most decomposition studies conducted on landslides have examined leaf degradation. When pioneer plant species' decomposition rates were examined on fresh landslide scars in Puerto Rico, Shiels (2006) found that tree fern leaves of *Cyathea arborea* decomposed more quickly than those of the tree *Cecropia schreberiana*, and therefore had different effects on soil nutrients (Shiels *et al.*, 2006). The importance of soil fauna to decomposition rates on two recent landslides in Taiwan was demonstrated by Hou *et al.* (2005)

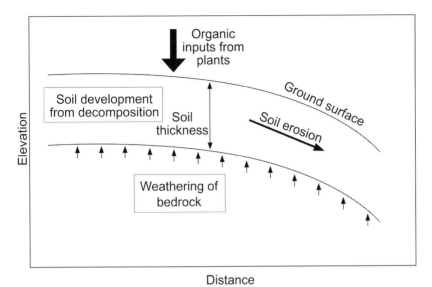

Fig. 3.8. A schematic diagram of processes affecting hill slope thickness and soil development. Down slope soil erosion is driven by physical weathering of bedrock and mixing of organic inputs; as a result, soil is transported down slope. From Yoo *et al.* (2006) with permission from Elsevier.

by using mixed species of leaf litter; decomposition rates were reduced when soil fauna was removed.

Because organic matter and carbon are well integrated with nutrient cycling, several studies have described various aspects of carbon dynamics on landslides. In addition to the large gradient of carbon from the top (slip face) to the bottom (deposition zone) of a landslide, the movement of carbon in and out of landslides is also important. Post-landslide carbon inputs to landslides originate from adjacent habitats beyond the landslide edge (e.g., via litterfall or sloughing), as well as from litterfall from new plant colonists or remnant patches of vegetation that were resistant to landsliding. Soil thickness is considered a critical control over soil carbon storage; slope thickness is influenced by the balance between soil production and erosion. Soil production occurs through a combination of physical (e.g., decomposition of bedrock) and biological (e.g., gross primary production minus respiration and decomposition) processes while erosion is controlled largely by slope, including topographical context and whether the slopes are convex or concave (Fig. 3.8; Yoo *et al.*, 2006). On very young landslides, carbon losses can be substantial. For example, on 8–13-month-old landslides in Puerto

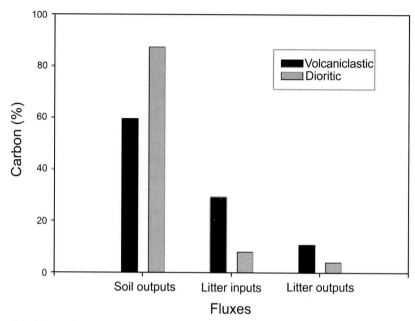

Fig. 3.9. Carbon fluxes of surface soils (0–10 cm depth) and litter from 30 landslides in Puerto Rico with two contrasting soil types (8 volcaniclastic and 12 dioritic). Landslides were ≤ 13 months old. The proportions of total carbon within each soil type are based on means (g C m^{-2}) of biweekly measurements over a 6-month period. From Walker & Shiels (2008) with permission from Springer.

Rico, Walker & Shiels (2008) quantified carbon standing stocks, inputs, and outputs. While post-landslide litter inputs were substantial, and were two to three times higher than litter outputs, much more carbon was found in landslide soils than in plant biomass. The losses of soil carbon down slope represented the largest carbon fluxes (60%–80% in flux) in the landslide ecosystem at 6%–24% (depending on soil type) of the standing stock carbon within the first year of a landslide (Walker & Shiels, 2008; Fig. 3.9). The rapid turnover of carbon is indicative of highly unstable substrates; such post-landslide erosion (see Section 3.3.2) will directly affect soil development and nutrient cycling. The short-term carbon dynamics were combined with longer-term carbon movements from chronosequence studies, which suggested that Puerto Rican landslides represent net down slope movements of carbon despite the various carbon inputs from outside landslides (Walker & Shiels, 2008; Fig. 3.10). Over longer periods, carbon pools generally increase on landslides in parallel with increasing soil thickness. One model suggested that rates of increase

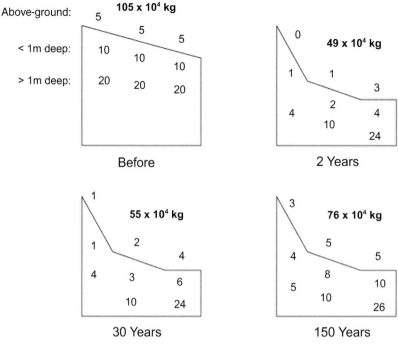

Fig. 3.10. A model of how erosion from a landslide involving 1 ha of land moves carbon down slope in northeastern Puerto Rico. Note that during 150 years of post-landslide succession, the total amount of carbon in a typical 30–1000 m long landslide (bold values in kg ha^{-1} C) drops following a landslide then slowly recovers, first in the lower above-ground (plant) carbon and then gradually in soils < 1 m deep. Little change occurs in soils > 1 m deep (the bottom numbers in each column; all values in kg ha^{-1} C). The three columns represent the slip face, chute, and deposition zone from left to right. From Walker & Shiels (2008) with permission from Springer.

can be rapid for the first 500–1000 years, then decline but continue to increase for many centuries (Yoo *et al.*, 2006). These findings support others that have demonstrated that landslides can affect regional carbon cycles (Restrepo *et al.*, 2003). Landslide-derived, fossilized carbon can be sequestered in ocean sediments when coastal mountains erode quickly and oxidation is minimal (Hilton *et al.*, 2011).

The quantities of nutrients (e.g., nitrogen, phosphorus, potassium, calcium) in runoff from landslides are greater than the losses from undisturbed habitats adjacent to the landslide (Larsen *et al.*, 1999). Nutrient losses tend to be highest on young landslides and decrease with landslide age such as found across a Himalayan chronosequence of 6, 13, 21, and 40 year old landslides (Pandey & Singh, 1985). Such losses in landslide nutrients from post-landslide erosion decreased with an increase in herbaceous and shrub biomass (Pandey & Singh, 1985). The reduction in nutrient loss with increased vegetation cover is likely due to the physical presence of vegetation that limits runoff, as well as to nutrient uptake by plants.

Precipitation, solar radiation, and atmospheric chemistry are additional abiotic factors that can affect soil nutrient cycles on landslides. Landslides experience more intense precipitation and solar radiation at the ground surface than do adjacent undisturbed habitats (Walker, 1994; Myster & Schaefer, 2003; Shiels *et al.*, 2006), and these two factors magnify the soil wetting and drying cycle and enhance substrate breakdown. With the majority of organic matter removed and transported down slope by the landslide, precipitation becomes an important mechanism of nutrient input and soil chemistry changes following landslides. Pandey & Singh (1985) determined that nutrient inputs in rainfall near landslide scars in the Himalayas were 6.0, 1.0, 8.4, 12.0, and 7.5 kg ha^{-1} year^{-1} for nitrogen, phosphorus, potassium, calcium, and organic carbon, respectively. Atmospheric inputs can also be significant sources of nutrients into landslides characterized by infertile soils. For example, atmospheric inputs of nitrogen, phosphorus, calcium, and magnesium that are derived primarily from sea salt can range from 0.3 to 15 kg ha^{-1} year^{-1} in the Luquillo Mountains (McDowell *et al.*, 1990; McDowell & Asbury, 1994), which adds yet another source of potential soil nutrient variability within local landslides.

3.4.3 Soil development

One of the long-standing mysteries in landslide ecology is a decisive answer to the time it takes for landslide soil and plant properties to resemble conditions of a pre-landslide state. The exact conditions of the pre-landslide state will not likely be realized because of the complex physical changes to the soil which concomitantly alter biotic patterns and processes following a landslide (Fig. 3.8). Because long-term sampling (at least decades, and probably centuries) is needed, detailed estimates of the recovery times of the many attributes embedded within landslides remain elusive. Chronosequence studies have been used in attempts to establish the time required for soil carbon and nutrients to return to pre-landslide conditions. On Puerto Rican landslides, total soil nitrogen, phosphorus, potassium, and magnesium can return to levels of the moist tropical forest within 55 years (Zarin & Johnson, 1995b). In temperate moist oak forests in India, total soil phosphorus recovered to pre-landslide conditions within 40–60 years, and carbon recovered within 35–40 years (Pandey & Singh, 1985; Reddy & Singh, 1993). However, total soil nitrogen varied widely between sites and studies for the temperate moist oak forest, with estimates of 40 (Pandey & Singh, 1985) to 120 years (Reddy & Singh, 1993) to recover to pre-landslide levels. In contrast, landslides in temperate pine forest in central India took the least amount of time (about 25 years) for soil carbon and phosphorus to recover to nearby forest levels; however, estimates for soil nitrogen recovery were > 25 years (Reddy & Singh, 1993). Many factors can influence soil development and plant recovery on landslides, making estimates largely site specific.

3.5 Conclusions

Landslides have an important role in shaping Earth's landscapes. These mass movements on sloped terrain have been a dominant force in creating terrestrial and submarine valleys. Landslides occur as a result of driving forces exceeding resisting forces on a given slope's slip plane. All rock and soil types are potentially vulnerable to landslides. Many factors affect the balance between the driving forces and resisting forces on a slip plane, including soil properties that affect water movement and storage on a slope. These factors also affect the depth to which a landslide scours a slope; on young substrates such as those in the Hawaiian islands, terrestrial landslides rarely exceed 50 cm depth, yet others like submarine landslides can scour tens of meters deep and extend tens of kilometers in length. Slopes that are > 75° can be too steep for substantial soil formation and landslide occurrence. Landslides can be triggered by heavy rains, earthquakes, volcanic eruptions, and human alterations to sloped terrain. Earthquakes usually result in the largest landslides, while rain-triggered landslides tend to be smaller and more frequent. Road-building is a common cause of landslides, either from ground vibrations or, more commonly, through the reduction of resisting forces by the contouring of slopes. Driving forces on a slope are often increased by humans due to construction or by increasing seepage and concentrating runoff onto slopes. The weight of water on a slope can be formidable, mainly due to the great capacity of soils to hold water. With a rising water table, the potential for landslides greatly increases.

Landslides are gaps or scars on the landscape that are represented by a substrate that has not previously been exposed because of its past protection by upper soil layers. There is pronounced heterogeneity in soil physical and chemical conditions following a landslide. Patches of organic matter are often absent in most areas of a new landslide except in the deposition zone. With time, inputs of organic matter from litterfall and sloughing of soils from beyond the landslide edge are important sources of nutrients for the largely infertile landslide substrate. Additional nutrient inputs from atmospheric deposition and rainfall are also important for alterations to soil chemistry and soil development. The impacts of landslides are not restricted to the landslide scar; rock, sediment, and woody material pass through watersheds and block streams, and an abundance of post-landslide erosion affects soil development and new colonists to landslides as well as ecosystems down slope from the landslide. Much still remains to be learned about the interactive mechanisms that trigger landslides. There is also too little known about how post-landslide soil conditions regulate soil development and re-colonization of landslide surfaces by plants and animals. The next two chapters address these biological consequences of landslides.

4 · *Biological consequences*

Key points

1. Landslide colonists have adaptations to survive low-nutrient, unstable substrates, where they may also experience temperature and water stress. Many of the species that colonize landslides are found exclusively in disturbed habitats and are known as gap specialists. Other colonists are common species in the adjacent undisturbed environment where their proximity to the landslide may have enabled rapid dispersal.
2. Microbes (including bacteria and fungi) are probably the first organisms to disperse to and colonize landslides. Symbiotic relationships, such as lichens, and plants with mycorrhizal fungi or nitrogen fixing bacteria, represent adaptations for survival in newly exposed, low-nutrient landslide substrates.
3. All plant life forms are found on landslides, but tend to segregate by slope. Small plants including bryophytes and forbs tend to dominate steep slopes, while tree ferns and trees tend to dominate less steep slopes. Grasses, vines, vine-like scrambling ferns, and shrubs, as well as most wind-dispersed plants, are common colonists on many landslides.
4. Arthropods are typically the first animals to colonize landslides, and include mites, Collembola, and ants, which are well adapted to temperature extremes and drought conditions.
5. Vertebrates associated with landslides are generally visitors rather than residents of the landslides. Birds and small mammals are the most common visitors, yet most vertebrates do not visit landslides until sufficient ground cover or foraging material has become established.

4.1 Introduction

Landslides have much in common with many other types of disturbances because they result in gaps in the landscape vegetation that attract organisms with life histories adapted to survival in such openings. However, landslides create unusual gaps because most of the physical structure is removed, and only bare, nutrient-poor substrates commonly remain. Treefalls also occur in many of the same forest environments as landslides, but treefalls generally disturb much smaller areas than landslides and result in gaps of mostly intact soils, often retaining the structural complexity of the understory (Reagan & Waide, 1996). Because of the physical consequences of the disturbance, landslides initially have a negative effect on biota. However, the loss of biomass and species creates opportunities for species that are not typically present or abundant in undisturbed habitats. Like any patch that has experienced a disturbance, a range of organisms with different morphological and ecological attributes can colonize a landslide as it undergoes successional change (see Chapter 5). The diversity of organisms that occupy a landslide is therefore partly influenced by the mode of arrival (e.g., wind vs. animal dispersal) and timing (e.g., early vs. late in succession). Following its arrival, an organism's length of stay on a landslide can also vary; species well adapted to minimizing water loss and temperature stress can become established and dominate for decades (e.g., ants and scrambling ferns in tropical landslides), whereas others such as forest birds might visit landslides for mere seconds to forage.

This chapter begins by describing how organisms are dispersed into landslides and outlines some of the general adaptations that allow such organisms to colonize successfully. We then focus on behaviors and adaptations of specific groups of organisms that colonize tropical and temperate landslides, including bacteria, fungi, lichens, bryophytes, ferns, gymnosperms, grasses, forbs, woody angiosperms, invertebrates, and vertebrates.

4.2 Dispersal

The conditions in gaps created by landslides can present strong barriers to potential colonists. Remnant patches of vegetation and soil, if present at all, represent a minor portion of the landslide. Therefore, landslide-colonizing organisms must generally have been dispersed from outside the landslide gap (exogenous propagules). In contrast, dispersal into a treefall gap can occur from sources within the gap because the soil seed bank and understory vegetation remain largely intact. Exogenous propagules (e.g., spores, seeds, plant parts, larvae, eggs) are transported to landslides passively by gravity, wind, water, or animals, or actively by their own motility (e.g., worms, insects).

Many propagules, including a suite of microorganisms (e.g., bacteria, fungi, nematodes, protozoa, rotifers, and mites), are dispersed into landslides from the edges while attached to or incorporated within roots, rocks, soil, and organic matter. Despite the presence of appendages used for walking and crawling, most microfauna (< 0.1 mm in size) and mesofauna (0.1–2.0 mm) typically spend their entire lives within a square meter of soil (Coleman *et al.*, 2004). Macrofauna (> 2 mm; earthworms, spiders, pill bugs, beetles, slugs, snails, and ants) are generally more mobile than smaller organisms and are therefore more likely to disperse into landslides on their own accord. All of these invertebrates can potentially faciliate establishment of plants and other organisms through their effects on soil development and nutrient cycling during early primary succession (Hodkinson *et al.*, 2002).

The distribution of plant propagules from parent sources is directly influenced by distance, and most species have limited dispersal distances (Malanson & Cairns, 1997; Fenner & Thompson, 2005). Therefore, landslide size affects the dispersal of propagules into a landslide because of the positive relationship between area and edge-to-center distance (Miles *et al.*, 1984). Many conditions in landslide environments, including the abundance of propagules, vary spatially along an edge-to-center gradient (see Chapter 2). On two tropical landslides, Walker & Neris (1993) found that seed rain (numbers of seeds m^{-2}) tended to increase from landslide interior to edge, and was highest in the surrounding forest. However, the number of seeds deposited into a landslide can reach annual levels from tens to thousands of individuals m^{-2} for small-seeded species such as graminoids (Shiels & Walker, 2003) and Asteraceae (Dale, 1986; Myster & Sarmiento, 1998). These initial landslide colonists greatly influence subsequent seed dispersal and the spread of vegetation within the landslide. Small-seeded, wind-dispersed seeds were the dominant types dispersed to landslides in Japan (Nakashizuka *et al.*, 1993), Ecuador (Myster & Sarmiento, 1998), and Puerto Rico (Shiels & Walker, 2003), a pattern typical of early successional plants (Fenner & Thompson, 2005). However, the likelihood of wind dispersal into a gap is strongly influenced by the environment, including the distance to parent plants, the height of the seeds on the parent plants, the height and density of surrounding vegetation, and proximal weather conditions (Fenner & Thompson, 2005). Larger seeds therefore face a greater barrier to dispersal to landslides than

86 · **Biological consequences**

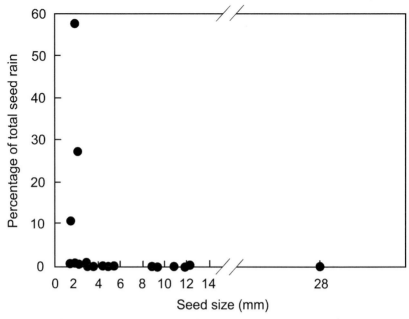

Fig. 4.1. The percentage of seed rain of various seed sizes collected over 14 months
in six young (< 6 year old) landslides in the Luquillo Mountains, Puerto Rico.
Three graminoids (two grass species, *Andropogon bicornis* and *Paspalum conjugatum*,
and one sedge species, *Rhyncospora holoschoenoides*) comprised > 95% of the seed
rain when all six landslides were combined. Seeds > 2.2 mm in longest axial length
were rarely trapped in these recent landslides unless artificial perches were present.
Seed traps excluded all spores and seeds < 1 mm in longest axial length. Seed rain
data were taken from Shiels & Walker (2003) and excluded seed traps beneath
artificial perches. The largest seed shown (28 mm; tabonuco tree, *Dacryodes excelsa*)
represents one of the dominant tree species in the forest and it, like most mid- and
late-successional species (many not shown), was largely absent from the landslide
seed rain.

do smaller seeds, and larger seeds are often adapted to dispersal by animals
(Parendes & Jones, 2000; Shiels & Walker, 2003; Matt *et al.*, 2008). The
vast majority of seeds dispersed into six relatively young landslides in
Puerto Rico were wind-dispersed grasses and sedges, each of which had
small seeds that were ≤ 2.2 mm in longest axial length (Fig. 4.1). Seeds
that blow into landslides can also be trapped by foliage of already established plants, which may provide amenable conditions (e.g., increased
shade and soil moisture) for germination (Dale, 1986). In addition to
seed rain, seed plant dispersal into landslides may be concentrated at the
edges due to secondary erosion from the edge, which can frequently

deposit both seeds and other plant propagules (e.g., roots, rhizomes, seedlings) into the landslide (Dale, 1986).

Non-seed plants such as bryophytes and ferns are also common on landslides, and the small, bouyant, and abundant nature of their spores promotes dispersal (Walker & Sharpe, 2010). Although spore-bearing structures (e.g., sporocarps, sporophylls) are commonly elevated on spore-bearing plants, most of the non-seed plants remain low to the ground relative to shrubs and trees. Spore-bearing tree ferns are an exception, sometimes reaching heights of 20 m (Large & Braggins, 2004). Tree ferns colonize landslides across their range in some temperate forests (mainly in the Southern Hemisphere) and many subtropical and tropical forests (Mark *et al.*, 1964; Walker & Sharpe, 2010). Spore-rain produced by landslide-colonizing tree ferns from the genus *Cyathea* in Puerto Rico can reach 3–5 billion spores annually from a single leaf (Conant, 1976), whereas a single leaf of a different *Cyathea* species was reported to produce 600 million spores in 1 year (Tryon & Tryon, 1982). Myster & Fernández (1995) estimated that *Cyathea* (likely *C. arborea*) spore rain over a period of 2 months on 6 to 20 year old landslides in Puerto Rico was approximately 700 spores m^{-2}. Spores readily travel by wind and can survive transport over thousands of kilometers in large air masses including jet streams (Punetha, 1991; Kessler, 2010). Fern dispersal patterns are similar to those of seed plants because most fern spores are deposited in close proximity to the parent plant. For example, an 8 m tall Puerto Rican *Cyathea arborea* deposited most spores within 7.5 m of the parent plant, yet some spores were recovered 30 m away (Conant, 1976). Roads, powerline tracts, and other gaps provide corridors that likely enhance dispersal distances of spore- and seed-bearing plants that rely upon wind dispersal (Parendes & Jones, 2000). Even in forests where spore disperal may be limited by physical interference from tall trees, spore-bearing plants such as ferns apparently disperse well, as shown by their dominance on many tropical landslides in early stages of succession (Walker, 1994; Walker & Sharpe, 2010). Differences in air temperature between landslides and adjacent vegetated surroundings may also affect spore dispersal. Spore dispersal into landslides may increase when lower nighttime temperatues lead to sinking air masses over landslides. Enhanced spore dispersal may also result from warm daytime temperatures in landslides creating ascending air that lofts spores released from landslide colonists high into the atmosphere (Ricklefs *et al.*, 1995). In addition to dispersal via wind, water can also transport spores and assist down slope colonization along sloped terrain. A combination of wind and water dispersal of spores may explain the lichens, mosses, ferns, and fern allies (e.g., *Selaginella*) that grew from incubated landslide soils in Ecuador (Myster & Sarmiento, 1998).

Animals can play an important role in dispersing spores (McIlveen & Cole, 1976; Cázares & Trappe, 1994) and seeds (McDonnell & Stiles, 1983; Levey, 1988; Wunderle, 1997; Holl, 1998) into gaps, yet this process has received little study in the context of landslides. Soil-consuming fauna (e.g., earthworms, wasps, and birds that use mud for nest construction) may disperse fungal spores (McIlveen & Cole, 1976). Fecal pellets of many types of mammals are also likely sources of mycorrhizal spores and perhaps seeds of early successional plants (Cázares & Trappe, 1994; Janos *et al.*, 1995; Mangan & Adler, 1999). Ants are common dispersers of seeds in both arid (Fenner & Thompson, 2005) and mesic (Bryne & Levey, 1993) habitats, but whether ants disperse seeds to landslides is unknown. Birds are probably the most common vectors of animal-assisted seed dispersal (zoochory) into landslides. In Puerto Rico, addition of artificial perches increased the dispersal of several species of forest seeds (Fig. 4.2). Dispersal mechanisms included both gut-passage for small seeds, as well as regurgitation for larger seeds (Shiels & Walker, 2003). Mammals can also be important vectors of seed dispersal into landslides. Like birds, frugivorous bats may fly through landslides but will not likely stop within the landslide unless perches (usually > 5 m tall) are present (M. Gannon, pers. commun.). Bats are particularly important dispersers of seeds into tropical landslides (Matt *et al.*, 2008). Bat droppings that contained hundreds of *Cecropia schreberiana* seeds were found in seed traps on an old (> 50 year) landslide with trees > 10 m tall in Puerto Rico (A. Shiels, pers. obs.). In addition to *C. schreberiana*, several species of gap-colonizing *Piper* are bat-dispersed in Puerto Rico (Devoe, 1989). In Mexico, two opposums (*Philander opossum* and *Didelphis marsupialis*) dispersed landslide-colonizing *Cecropia obtusifolia* as far as 70 m from a source plant (Medellín, 1994). Rats also disperse seeds into landslides. In seed traps on several relatively recent (< 6 year) Puerto Rican landslides, Shiels (2002) frequently found droppings of introduced black rats (*Rattus rattus*) that each contained tens to hundreds of seeds of native *Miconia* spp. The prevalence of non-native *Miconia calvescens* on some Pacific Island landslides may also be partly due to black rats dispersing the small seeds (Meyer & Florence, 1996; Shiels, 2011). Larger mammals such as monkeys may disperse seeds and spores into landslides. For example, 42% of the diets of Afro-montane monkeys (*Circopithecus l'hoesti*) in a forest in Rwanda included fruits and seeds, at least two species of fern fronds were consumed, and the monkeys commonly visited landslides to forage,

Fig. 4.2. Bird perches (5 m tall saplings) erected on Puerto Rican landslides to encourage bird visitation and seed dispersal of forest species. Photograph by A.B. Shiels.

socialize, rest, and scan (Kaplan & Moermond, 2000). Ungulates can also disperse seeds and spores into landslides following direct consumption and gut passage or by attachment of seeds and spores to the outside of the animal (epizoochory). Members of the genus *Desmodium* are epizoo-chorous forbs that colonize landslides in Hawaii (Restrepo & Vitousek, 2001), Nicaragua (Velázquez & Gómez-Sal, 2007), and Puerto Rico (Shiels & Walker, 2003), where birds or mammals are probably responsi-ble for their dispersal. Similarly, there are two species of sedges (*Uncinia* spp.) found on landslides in Fiordland, New Zealand that are likely dis-persed by epizoochory (Mark *et al.*, 1964). Seed dispersal to landslides by mammals is probably underestimated due to the fleeting nature of mammalian passage through such habitats, as well as the nocturnal habits and unobtrusive feces of many mammals. A variety of invertebrates and vertebrates may disperse spores and seeds into landslides. For any given species of plant or microbe, there are typically multiple mechanisms enabling propagules to reach and colonize disturbed sites (Pakeman *et al.*, 1998).

4.3 Colonization and species adaptations

Colonization reflects the ability of an organism to tolerate and survive the conditions of a landslide. For plants, colonization is defined as survival through germination and establishment; thus, the seeds of seed plants must germinate and establish true leaves (i.e., survive the cotyledon stage), the spores of bryophytes must germinate and produce a gameto-phyte, while ferns must survive the gametophyte phase and produce a leafy sporophyte. For animals and microorganisms, colonization simply reflects survival while in the landslide, and we therefore do not distin-guish dispersal from colonization for animals and microbes. An animal visitation to a landslide, for example, can be considered a colonization event. In terms of the number of individuals and species, the successful colonists are a subset of those organisms dispersed into a landslide. Stud-ies of plants on landslides highlight the survival barrier between dispersal and colonization (Dale, 1986; Walker & Neris, 1993; Shiels & Walker, 2003). Clearly, there are many species that lack the necessary adaptations to survive within the landslide environment.

Landslide colonists are largely species that are well adapted to toler-ate water and temperature stress (Lundgren, 1978; García-Fayos *et al.*, 2000). Species that are only found in landslides, known as landslide specialists, apparently do not exist (Box 4.1); yet many of the species that colonize landslides are found exclusively in disturbed habitats

Box 4.1 Landslide specialists

Successful landslide colonists have dispersal and colonization characteristics that favor survival on relatively bare, sloped terrain, as well as conditions of high light, extreme temperatures, and water and nutrient stress. A landslide specialist is a species unique to landslides and otherwise absent in all other types of environments. We know of no such species that are only found on landslides. This may not be surprising because landslides are relatively random events and specialization requires long-term adaptations to specific conditions. If a landslide specialist did exist, it would require a landscape that experienced frequent landslides that essentially supported the characteristics of the specialist. Specialists are fragile because they can lead to evolutionary dead-ends if, for example, available landslide habitat becomes rare or unavailable. One example of specialization to landslide habitats that occurs within a species is evident for the pioneer tropical tree *Trema micrantha*. Recent work has shown some morphological distinctions (e.g., seed and leaf size), as well as functional differences in growth responses to nutrients, mycorrhizae, and herbivory, between landslide morphotypes relative to treefall gap morphotypes (Silvera *et al.*, 2003; Pizano *et al.*, 2011). Genetic comparisons between the morphotypes would help explain the extent to which such traits may be genetically fixed, yet this example with *T. micrantha* highlights the extent to which landslide colonizing species adjust to landslide conditions. Although landslide specialists (species level) may not exist, gap specialists are common colonizers of landslides. Gap specialists are organisms that are only found in disturbed habitats such as forest gaps (Denslow, 1980). Some of the gap specialists that are found in landslides include lichens with members in the genus *Stereocaulon* (see Section 4.4), scrambling ferns in the Gleicheniaceae (see Section 4.5.2), many representatives in the grass family Poaceae (see Section 4.5.4), the pioneer tree species in the genera *Alnus* and *Cecropia* (see Section 4.5.6), and *Wasmannia auropunctata* fire ants (see Section 4.6.1). Pikas (*Ochotona princeps*) live in talus environments formed by rock falls or landslides (Hafner, 1993). Several characteristics of the landslide environment (e.g., size, age, exposed rock, cracks in substrate, remnant soils or biota) influence the composition of the colonizing community and its similarity to or difference from that of other types of non-landslide disturbances, including the presence of gap specialists.

(gap specialists), and some species have morphological and/or functional adaptations that distinguish landslide morphotypes from other morphotypes found in disturbed habitats such as treefall gaps (e.g., *Trema micrantha* in Panama; Silvera *et al.*, 2003; Pizano *et al.*, 2011; Box 4.1). Species that colonize unstable or newly disturbed environments such as landslides tend to be categorized as pioneer or r-selected species, and they possess a suite of life-history characteristics that reflect adaptation to such unstable environments. Traits of r-selected species include high fecundity, small body (or seed) size, reduced time to reproduction, and the ability to disperse offspring widely. In contrast, K-selected species are those that are commonly found in stable environments, have low fecundity, large body size, a longer time to reproduction, and relatively poor dispersal (Townsend *et al.*, 2008). The r-selected life-history strategy is favored in environments such as landslides that allow for rapid population growth and expansion due to the initial presence of few individuals and few competitors.

4.3.1 Plant adaptations

There are several plant adaptations that favor colonization in the nutrient-poor landslide environment. To survive in low-nutrient substrates, some plants form symbiotic relationships with fungi (forming lichens, or mycorrhizal associations) and/or with nitrogen fixing bacteria in roots (see Section 4.4). Typical plant characteristics that aid survival in hot and dry environments include leaves that are reduced, dissected, thickened, waxy, hairy, or deciduous (Raven *et al.*, 2005). Each of these leaf adaptations helps to prevent water loss. Photosynthesis is a highly water-dependent process, and water stress on landslides may favor colonization by plants with water-efficient C_4 and CAM (crassulacean acid metabolism) pathways over less water-efficient C_3 plants, at least on tropical landslides (see Section 4.5.4).

4.3.2 Animal adaptations

Animals that successfully colonize landslides typically have small body sizes and structures and behaviors for increasing water retention. Some animals acquired traits long ago that improved their survival in dry and disturbed habitats; for example, during the Jurassic, insects evolved a waxy epicuticle, which enabled them to become day-active (Kronfeld-Schor & Dayan, 2003). This diurnal strategy may be altered in response to temperature and water stress. For example, in the Chihuahuan Desert, ants (typical landslide colonists) foraged during the daytime in winter, whereas their summer foraging was restricted to nighttime and cloudy days (Whitford et al., 1981). Other animals have behaviors that allow them to avoid environmental stresses on landslides by conducting short diurnal visits, visits around sunrise and sunset to avoid midday heat, and nocturnal visits. In Puerto Rico, the majority of observed bird visits to landslides were during the morning (A. Shiels, unpublished data); these visits were short (often just several seconds in duration, but averaging 1.1 minutes on artificial perches), and the birds typically returned to the cooler and more shaded confines of the nearby forest at the end of their landslide visit (Shiels & Walker, 2003). Many of the mammals that have been documented in landslides through sightings, tracks, or scat are nocturnal (see Section 4.2). Nocturnal activity in animals can often be linked to behavioral adaptations, such as avoidance of elevated daytime temperature and water loss in warm environments (Whitford et al., 1981; Lourens & Nel, 1990; Kronfeld-Schor & Dayan, 2003). Nighttime temperatures in gaps are typically a few degrees cooler than adjacent non-gap environments, where the insulating properties associated with high vegetation cover create slightly warmer air temperatures. Cooler nighttime temperatures in gaps can potentially provide an accessible water source for animals in the form of dew (Richards, 2006), yet we know of no studies that have associated animal behaviors with nighttime water availability on landslides.

4.4 Bacteria, fungi, and lichens

Bacteria and fungi are important landslide colonists that often improve the nutrient conditions of the landslide through their metabolism, symbioses with other organisms, and role in decomposition and nutrient cycling. Although bacteria are prokaryotes and fungi are eukaryotes, they are discussed here in a single section because both are microscopic for all or part of their existence. Cyanobacteria, and several other types of bacteria, contain the enzyme nitrogenase, which allows them to convert atmospheric nitrogen to forms of nitrogen that are available for biotic uptake and use. Without bacteria providing such forms of nitrogen, plants (and other organisms which rely upon them) could not exist with their present physiology and biochemistry because they lack nitrogenase (Schlesinger, 1991).

Cyanobacteria (blue – green algae) are particularly well adapted to survival in harsh environments because they couple nitrogen fixation to their photosynthetic reaction. Organisms living closely with cyanobacteria would therefore benefit from nitrogen availability, and for this reason, many types of cyanobacteria form symbioses with other organisms. One such interaction that occurs on several landslides is the symbiosis between a cyanobacteria (*Nostoc*) and plant species in the genus *Gunnera*. This unique interaction occurs when *Nostoc* enters the plant stem through specialized pores and initiates an intracellular symbiosis where the bacterium is thought to provide the plant with fixed nitrogen in return for fixed carbon from the plant (Bergman *et al.*, 1992). This symbiosis is particularly beneficial to plants that occupy nitrogen limited soils such as found on landslides (see Chapter 3). *Gunnera* is a gap-specialist (Palkovic, 1978), and it is found on landslides in several parts of the world, including New Zealand (Mark *et al.*, 1964), Chile (Veblen & Ashton, 1978), and Costa Rica, where it was the dominant plant species on two landslides (Myster, 1997).

The nitrogen fixing bacteria *Rhizobium* and *Frankia* are involved in symbioses with roots of several plant species, forming macroscopic nodules on the roots. This symbiosis represents yet another adaptation to nitrogen-deficient soils. Nodular nitrogen fixing symbionts colonize landslides frequently; their abundance on landslides (63%) resembles their abundance on mine tailings (64%) and floodplains (48%) but they are less frequent on other types of primary succession (Walker, 1993). Like the *Nostoc* – *Gunnera* symbiosis, *Rhizobium* or *Frankia* provide the plant with fixed nitrogen in return for fixed carbon. Many nodular nitrogen fixing symbioses involving *Rhizobium* and *Frankia* occur with plant colonists in temperate and tropical landslides (Table 4.1). *Rhizobium* has established nodular nitrogen fixing symbioses with most species in the Fabaceae, and with one genus in the Ulmaceae (Soltis *et al.*, 1995). *Rhizobium* is particularly well represented on landslides worldwide because of the relatively high incidence of Fabaceae in the landslide plant community. All other plants known to have nodular nitrogen fixing symbionts are associated with *Frankia*, including some genera from each of the following eight plant families: Betulaceae, Casuarinaceae, Coriariaceae, Elaeagnaceae, Datiscaceae, Myricaceae, Rhamnaceae, and Rosaceae (Soltis *et al.*, 1995). A variety of forbs, shrubs, and trees form nodular nitrogen fixing symbioses with *Rhizobium* or *Frankia* in landslides (Table 4.1).

Lichens are another symbiotic association between a fungus and a photosynthetic partner (green algae or cyanobacteria). Nitrogen fixation occurs in lichens when cyanobacteria (e.g., *Nostoc*) are involved as a symbiont. Lichens commonly colonize landslides and in some cases can be the dominant life form on portions of the landslide, such as the slip face

Table 4.1. *Plant species occurring on landslides that are from genera with nodular nitrogen fixing symbionts (cf. Schubert, 1986; Soltis et al., 1995)*

Location	Species	Life form	Family	References
Temperate				
Queen Charlotte Islands, Canada	*Alnus rubra*	T	Betulaceae	Geertsema & Pojar, 2007
Montana Rocky Mountains, U.S.	*Alnus sinuata*	T	Betulaceae	Malanson & Butler, 1984
Mount St. Helens, U.S.	*Alnus rubra*	T	Betulaceae	Dale, 1986
	Lupinus latifolius	F	Fabaceae	
Alps, Switzerland	*Alnus viridis*	T	Betulaceae	Van der Burght et al., 2012
Lake Thompson, New Zealand	*Coriaria arborea*	S	Coriariaceae	Mark et al., 1964
Oregon Cascade Mountains, U.S.	*Alnus rubra*	T	Betulaceae	Miles & Swanson, 1986
	Ceanothus integerrimus	S	Rhamnaceae	
	Ceanothus velutinus	S	Rhamnaceae	
	Lotus purshiana	F	Fabaceae	
	Lotus micranthus	F	Fabaceae	
New Hampshire White Mountains, U.S.	*Alnus crispa*	T	Betulaceae	Flaccus, 1959
Andes Mountains, Argentina	*Coriaria ruscifolia*	S	Coriariaceae	Veblen & Ashton, 1978
	Lotus uliginosus	F	Fabaceae	
	Trifolium dubium	F	Fabaceae	
	Trifolium repens	F	Fabaceae	
Colorado Rocky Mountains, U.S.	*Lupinus sericeus*	S	Fabaceae	Langenheim, 1956
	Vicia americana	F	Fabaceae	
Virginia Appalachian Mountains, U.S.	*Robinia pseudoacacia*	T	Fabaceae	Hull & Scott, 1982
Mount Kiyosumi, Japan	*Albizia julibrissin*	T	Fabaceae	Sakai & Ohsawa, 1993
Flores Island, the Azores	*Lotus pedunculatus*	F	Fabaceae	Elias & Dias, 2009
Himalayan Mountains, Nepal	*Alnus nepalensis*	T	Betulaceae	Devkota et al., 2006

(cont.)

Table 4.1. (cont.)

Location	Species	Life form	Family	References
Tropical				
Hawaii Koolau Mountains, U.S.	Casuarina equisetifolia	T	Casuarinaceae	Russo, 2005; A. Shiels, pers. obs.
Hawaii Mauna Loa Volcano, U.S.	Desmodium sp.	F	Fabaceae	Restrepo & Vitousek, 2001
Luquillo Mountains, Puerto Rico	Desmodium incanum	F	Fabaceae	Myster & Walker, 1997; Shiels &
	Inga laurina	T	Fabaceae	Walker, 2003
	Inga vera	T	Fabaceae	
Blue Mountains, Jamaica	Myrica cerifera	T	Myricaceae	Dalling, 1994
Andes Mountains, Bolivia	Alnus acuminata	T	Betulaceae	Kessler, 1999
Casita Volcano, Nicaragua	Clitoria ternatea	F	Fabaceae	Velázquez & Gómez-Sal, 2007,
	Calopogonium mucunoides	F	Fabaceae	2008, 2009b
	Desmodium incanum	S	Fabaceae	
	Desmodium nicaraguense	S	Fabaceae	
	Galactia striata	F	Fabaceae	
	Mimosa pudica	F	Fabaceae	
	Stizolobium puriens	F	Fabaceae	
	Zornia thymifolia	F	Fabaceae	
Monteverde Cloud Forest, Costa Rica	Pithecellobium costarricense	T	Fabaceae	Myster, 1993
Uluguru Mountains, Tanzania	Acacia mearnsii	T	Fabaceae	Lundgren, 1978
	Crotalaria natalitia	F, S	Fabaceae	
	Eriosema psoraleoides	F	Fabaceae	
	Indigofera paniculata	F	Fabaceae	
	Myrica salicifolia	S, T	Myricaceae	
	Phaseolus vulgaris	F	Fabaceae	

Rhizobium is the prokaryote forming the symbiosis with representative taxa in Fabaceae, whereas *Frankia* is the prokaryote forming the symbiosis with all other taxa listed. Life forms are trees (T), shrubs (S), and forbs (F). References are indicative of the plant's presence on landslides and do not necessarily reflect confirmation of the presence or activity of nodular symbionts. Entries are listed in descending order by latitude for both temperate and tropical environments.

Fig. 4.3. A common lichen (*Stereocaulon virgatum*) on a Puerto Rican landslide. Photograph by A.B. Shiels. See also background of Plate 9.

or on rocks (Plate 9; Flaccus, 1959; Dalling, 1994). Unlike most plants, lichens do not require soil to establish and therefore lichens commonly colonize bare rock surfaces such as lava flows where they fix nitrogen (Vitousek, 1994); however, lichens were also found growing on incubated landslide soils in Ecuador (Myster & Sarmiento, 1998) and can occur on bark (Mark *et al.*, 1964). In Chile, lichens were found on approximately half of the earthquake-generated landslides sampled, and the microsites where lichens were most abundant were bedrock and rock debris (Veblen & Ashton, 1978). Lichens tend to be most common in early succession on steep slip faces and chutes and least common in deposition zones and on older landslides. For example, young landslides in Puerto Rico (< 1 year old; A. Shiels, pers. obs.), New Zealand (15 years; Mark *et al.*, 1964), Jamaica (15 years; Dalling, 1994), and Tanzania (3–7 years; Lundgren, 1978) had abundant lichen cover. *Stereocaulon virgatum*, for example, represented more than half of the landslide biomass in Jamaica (Dalling, 1994) and primarily inhabits exposed bedrock on landslides in Puerto Rico (Fig. 4.3; Plate 9). In some cases, lichens are present only on older landslides (19 and 35 years old but not 2 and 9 years old;

Flaccus, 1959), or present throughout a chronosequence of landslides (Mark *et al.*, 1964) or lava flows (Vitousek, 1994). Bacteria, fungi, and lichens can have disproportionally large and important effects on other organisms (e.g., plants) and processes such as decomposition and nitrogen cycling (see Chapter 3; Schlesinger, 1991; Coleman *et al.*, 2004). Their early colonization and symbiotic relationships with plants make them critical components of landslide recovery.

Free-living bacteria and fungi are also found in landslide soils, yet few surveys have been conducted that establish their relative abundances. Instead, total soil microbial biomass is more commonly sampled. Soil microbial biomass is greatly reduced by landslides. Arunachalam & Upadhyaya (2005) sampled soils over a short (4 year) landslide chronosequence in moist tropical deciduous forest in India, and found that there was 2–20 times more microbial biomass in the nearby forest than in any of the landslides sampled. Li *et al.* (2005) found that microbial biomass, and its constituent bacteria and fungi, were generally lower in two Puerto Rican landslides than in adjacent forest soils, and were lower on slip faces than deposition zones within the landslides. Soil fungi accounted for at least three times as much biomass as bacteria. There were no seasonal (wet vs. dry) differences in the soil bacteria biomass on landslides or in forest plots (Li *et al.*, 2005) but spatial variability was pronounced (see Chapter 2). Soil microbial biomass can be patchy in landslides, and it often correlates with soil carbon. Soil microbial heterogeneity was particularly pronounced in young landslides in India; some microsites in 6 month old landslides had ten times more microbial biomass than 4 year old landslides (Arunachalam & Upadhyaya, 2005). Experimental studies have shown that both bacteria and fungi have soil-binding properties that increase slope stability, and this effect is accentuated with fungi more than with bacteria because of the strand-like characteristics of the hyphae (Meadows *et al.*, 1994). Although the abundance of microbes may take many years to reach pre-landslide levels, the often immediate colonization of bacteria and fungi clearly plays an important role in plant species survival and succession.

Fungal infection can occur in both plants and animals that colonize landslides. Seeds of landslide colonists in Puerto Rico and Costa Rica were colonized by fungi and such infection (presumed to be pathogenic) correlated with greater seed loss than animal seed predation (Myster, 1997). The fungi inhabiting seeds on Puerto Rican landslides included species in the genera *Colletotrichum*, *Pythium*, *Arthrosporium*, and *Fusarium*, whereas the fungal taxa inhabiting seeds in Costa Rican landslides were not identified (Myster, 1997). Fungi (species in the genera *Col-letotrichum*, *Fusicladium*, *Phoma*, *Phyllachora*, *Phyllosticta*, and *Rhizoctonia*) also colonized leaves of early successional trees (*Cecropia schreberiana* and *Inga vera*) on two Puerto Rican landslides (Myster, 1997, 2002). The effects of the fungal infection on leaf area losses were minimal, and ranged from < 1% to 3% for both tree species (Myster, 2002). While the dispersal pathways of the fungal colonists were not apparent, dispersal via insects visiting the plants (de la Cruz & Dirzo, 1987) and wind dispersal were proposed as potential vectors of the plant-inhabiting fungi (Myster, 2002).

Mycorrhizal fungi may reside in landslides as symbionts with plants (Myster & Fernández, 1995; Fetcher *et al.*, 1996), or they may be present as dormant spores (Li *et al.*, 2005). Vesicular–arbuscular mycorrhizal fungi (VAM) were sampled on two Puerto Rican landslides, aged 6 years and 20 years, by examining fine-root infection frequency (Myster & Fernández, 1995). The majority (67%) of the landslide plots sampled, including all those in the upper slip face (top 40 m of the landslide), did not have any roots with VAM. The amount of VAM fungal colonization in root samples taken from within the landslide was never greater than 10%, whereas in the forest bordering the landslide there was typically 25% of the fine root length converted to VAM (Myster & Fernández, 1995). Therefore, even on relatively old landslides (one was 20 years old), VAM fungal colonization did not appear to recover to infection levels in the forest. The VAM genera that have colonized Puerto Rican landslides in the past include *Sclerocystis*, *Glomus*, and *Acaulospora* (D.J. Lodge, pers. comm.). Some landslide colonists studied in Puerto Rico do not appear to depend on mycorrhizal affiliations. *Cecropia schreberiana* did not show any positive growth when inoculated with VAM in landslide soils (Lodge & Calderon, unpublished data). However, both the facultatively mycor-rhizal *C. schreberiana* and the non-mycorrhizal *Phytolacca rivinoides* showed positive spatial correlations with areas of high soil phosphorus availability on Puerto Rican landslides (Lodge & Calderon, unpublished data).

4.5 Plants

4.5.1 Bryophytes

Bryophytes, which include mosses, hornworts, and liverworts, are com-mon at different stages of plant recovery on landslides (Plate 10). While bryophytes most commonly grow in moist environments, there are many species that thrive in dry environments such as deserts and landslides (Tuba et al., 2011). Bryophytes therefore occupy many of the same micro-habitats as lichens. Their adaptations to landslides include spore dispersal and vegetative reproduction, the ability to withstand great fluctuations in temperature and moisture, and tolerance of a wide variety of abiotic and biotic substrates. Because bryophytes often harbor cyanobacteria and fungi (that aid in the acquisition of nutrients; Raven et al., 2005), they are also potentially adapted to low-nutrient landslide soils.

Bryophyte frequency, cover, and biomass can all be substantial on temperate landslides. On landslides triggered by earthquakes in Chile in 1960, bryophytes were recorded on 50%–100% of all plots (Veblen & Ashton, 1978). In New Zealand, Mark et al. (1964) documented bryophytes on both the ground and as epiphytes along a 78 year old landslide chrono-sequence. On the ground, bryophyte cover decreased through succes-sion and was most prevalent on the slip face of the 15 year old landslides where its biomass was nearly double that of the bryophytes inhabiting the ground in the nearby forest (Mark et al., 1964). In contrast, epiphytic bryophytes were more common as succession proceeded. Typical genera included *Macromitrium* and *Weymouthia* (mosses), and *Metzgeria*, *Porella*, and *Radula* (liverworts) (Mark et al., 1964). Other genera found on temperate landslides include *Sphagnum* and *Polytrichum* mosses. *Sphagnum* covers more than 1% of the Earth's surface (Raven et al., 2005), and in the Azores, *Sphagnum* spp. was the dominant or co-dominant plant in the upper (slip face) portion of young, intermediate, and old landslides (Elias & Dias, 2009). Blue–green algae are also found associated with *Sphagnum*, which can be an important source of fixed nitrogen in pri-mary succession (Sheridan, 1991). *Polytrichum* spp. occurred on the upper parts of all ages of landslides sampled in the Azores, but its prevalence was greatest in the intermediate-aged landslides (representing 10%–15% cover; Elias & Dias, 2009). In New Hampshire, U.S., *Polytrichum* spp. occurred on 61% of all 9 year old landslides, making it the most fre-quently observed non-woody plant on these relatively young temperate landslides (Flaccus, 1959). The frequency of *Polytrichum* declined through succession, and it was only observed in 3% of the forest plots sampled. As a likely consequence of woody plant dominance later in succession, mosses were generally restricted to bare rocks and rock ledges in the 19 year old and 35 year old landslides (Flaccus, 1959).

Bryophyte studies on landslides are apparently less frequent in the tropics. However, mosses ranked second in total biomass on landslides in montane wet forest, Jamaica (Dalling, 1994). On 15 year old landslides, bryophyte biomass was exceeded only by lichens, while on landslides > 50 years old, only woody plants had more biomass (Dalling, 1994). In Tanzania, bryophytes were only found near the perimeters of landslides where secondary erosion (e.g., sloughing) was common (Lundgren, 1978). Bryophytes are a substantial part of landslide vegetation, found mostly on slip faces and chutes, or anywhere that there are exposed rocks.

4.5.2 Ferns

Ferns are one of the most prominent plant life forms that colonize landslides in both temperate and tropical locations (Walker & Sharpe, 2010). Their success in disturbed environments is most likely due to the same adaptations listed for bryophytes above, plus the following: extensive rhizome growth, effective nutrient uptake or immobilization, a vertical, scrambling, or climbing life form, and rapid growth rates. We discuss the colonization of landslides by ferns and lycophytes (hereafter: ferns, as per ferns *sensu lato;* Mehltreter *et al.*, 2010), focusing on club mosses, horsetails, bracken, scrambling ferns, and tree ferns.

Club mosses (Lycopodiaceae) and horsetails (*Equisetum*; the only surviving genus in the Equisetaceae) dominated the vegetation of the Carboniferous Period and often grew to be tree-sized (Raven *et al.*, 2005). Their present-day relatives rarely exceed 50 cm in height. Both have adaptations to landslides that include small leaves, spore dispersal, and vegetative reproduction. Although club mosses can be outcompeted by scrambling ferns (e.g., Gleicheniaceae) and woody vegetation, Walker *et al.* (2010a) found that, when scrambling ferns were removed, club mosses (predominantly *Lycopodiella cernua*) dominated the vegetation on Puerto Rican landslides. Club mosses were also described on landslides in Jamaica where they comprised 3% of plant biomass (Dalling, 1994), and in New Zealand where they accounted for 25% of the vegetation cover on slip faces (Mark *et al.*, 1964). Horsetails can account for up to 20% of the cover of young landslides in Oregon (Miles & Swanson, 1986), Tanzania (Lundgren, 1978), Chile (Veblen & Ashton, 1978), and India (Arunachalam & Upadhyaya, 2005). Dominance by horsetails is likely to be only temporary, and it lasted only 4–7 years on landslides in Tanzania (Lundgren, 1978).

Pteridium aquilinum (bracken) is perhaps the most widespread fern on Earth, and it is a well-known colonist of disturbed sites (Walker & Sharpe, 2010). Kessler (1999) found that bracken was an important colonist of landslides in Bolivia, but also noted that it did not reach densities in landslides as great as it did in most anthropogenic gaps. Bracken was also an important colonist of landslides in Tanzania where it appeared within 1 year of disturbance and persisted through 4 years (Lundgren, 1978). Part of bracken's post-establishment success in spreading may be due to vigorous vegetative reproduction via rhizomes. *Odontosoria aculeata* is in the same family as bracken (Dennstaedtiaceae) and it increased in cover after a fire swept through a landslide in Puerto Rico (Walker & Boneta, 1995). Aside from some grasses, *O. aculeata* represented the only plant surviving the fire, perhaps due to the abundance of partially buried rhizomes (Walker & Boneta, 1995). *Dennstaedtia punctilobula* is a temperate member of Dennstaedtiaceae that is known for rampant vegetative reproduction, and it was found on 68% of the plots among 22 landslides examined in the White Mountains, New Hampshire, U.S. (Flaccus, 1959).

A number of other fern genera comprise between 2% and 80% of vegetation cover on a particular landslide. Two of the most dominant genera reported were *Pityrogramma* and *Blechnum*. *Pityrogramma calomelanos* was a dominant colonist on tropical landslides on volcanoes in Nicaragua (Velázquez & Gómez-Sal, 2009b) and Mexico (Spicer *et al.*, 1985), and *P. ebenea* was found on landslides in Jamaica (Dalling, 1994). In the Azores, *Blechnum spicant* covered 3%–5% on young landslides but increased to 35%–75% on intermediate-aged landslides (Elias & Dias, 2009). In New Zealand, *Blechnum* spp. dominated the herbaceous layer of vegetation on slip faces (Mark *et al.*, 1964), yet the only *Blechnum* representative on Jamaican landslides (*B. lineatum*) was relatively uncommon (Dalling, 1994). Other fern genera commonly found on temperate landslides include *Dryopteris* in the Azores (Elias & Dias, 2009) and in New Hampshire (Flaccus, 1959), *Polystichum* in Oregon, U.S. (Miles & Swanson, 1986), and *Nephrolepis* in Hawaii, U.S. (Restrepo & Vitousek, 2001).

Scrambling ferns are tropical ferns with leaf tips that have indeterminate growth, branching rhizomes at the soil surface, and recumbent leaves that spread across the surface and over other vegetation (Walker & Sharpe, 2010). The most widespread scrambling ferns are in the Gleicheniaceae, and they often colonize disturbed habitats resulting from landslides, fires, and roads (Dalling, 1994; Walker & Boneta, 1995; Negishi *et al.*, 2006; see Fig. 5.5). In particular, species in this family are prominent on tropical landslides where they often form thickets that stabilize soils and competitively exclude other species (Walker, 1994; Russell *et al.*, 1998; Slocum *et al.*, 2004; Walker *et al.*, 2010a). *Dicranopteris curranii* colonized roadside slopes in Malaysia, where it reduced water and sediment runoff and potentially ameliorated the ground layer microclimate by forming thickets (Negishi *et al.*, 2006). *Gleichenella pectinata* and *Sticherus bifidus* were also colonists of roadside landslides in Puerto Rico where they dominated the plant community for many years (Guariguata, 1990; Walker, 1994; Shiels & Walker, 2003). Similarly, on Oahu, Hawaii, *Dicranopteris linearis* was the dominant species for more than a decade after colonizing landslides with bare soils (Scott & Street, 1976). However, species in the Gleicheniaceae do not always form dominant thickets on landslides even when they are part of the local flora. For example, on the Island of Hawaii, Restrepo & Vitousek (2001) did not find *D. linearis* on their youngest landslides (4–42 years), but it was present on old landslides (approximately 130 years) and in forests (325–525 years). On intermediate-aged landslides in Bolivia where flowering plants dominated, *Sticherus* spp. and *Diplopterygium bancroftii* constituted 6%–12% of the vegetation cover, which was the highest among all ferns on all landslides sampled (Kessler, 1999). Interestingly, in the Blue Mountains of Jamaica, *Gleichenia jamaicensis* was absent from landslides > 50 years old, but present in relatively low abundances on three of the four 15 year old landslides that were sampled (Dalling, 1994).

Tree ferns are the largest ferns to colonize temperate and tropical landslides and they range in height from < 1 m to over 20 m (Plate 11; Large & Braggins, 2004; Walker & Sharpe, 2010). This height helps disperse their spores many meters from the parent (Conant, 1976; Tryon & Tryon, 1982; Myster & Fernández, 1995), thereby facilitating dispersal to and within landslides. Tree ferns have an erect rhizome (trunk or caudex) and occur in a number of families. Their taller stature and longevity can give them a competitive advantage over other ferns and seedlings, and sometimes they form monospecific stands on landslides (Walker *et al.*, 2010a; see Fig. 5.5). Although many tree ferns are good colonizers of landslides and grow rapidly (up to 40 or more cm year^{-1}; Walker & Aplet, 1994), they may also survive for decades to several centuries, becoming a part of the forest matrix (Tanner, 1983; Large & Braggins, 2004). Therefore, tree ferns can be present during some or all of the stages of landslide succession. For example, in Hawaii, *Sadleria pallida* was found on landslides of all ages sampled, yet *Cibotium glaucum* was only found on intermediate-aged (18–42 years) landslides (Restrepo & Vitousek, 2001). In the Azores, *Culcita macrocarpa*, which is apparently the only tree fern native to Europe, was found only on one old landslide (Elias & Dias, 2009). In Jamaica, two species of *Cyathea* colonized several > 50 year old landslides, yet they had not colonized 15 year old landslides (Dalling, 1994). In Puerto Rico, *Cyathea arborea* is an important colonist of new landslides, but can also invade scrambling fern thickets, eventually displacing them, while inhibiting subsequent forest development (Walker *et al.*, 1996, 2010a). Tree fern trunks have additional ecological relevance as a substrate on which forest seedlings often germinate (Newton & Healey, 1989), thereby potentially increasing species diversity on landslides.

4.5.3 Gymnosperms

Seed plants are the dominant vegetation on many landslides in temperate and tropical ecosystems. Because of the initial paucity of animal colonists on landslides that are capable of dispersing seeds, most early landslide colonists have adaptations for wind-dispersal as well as many other traits of r-selected species that assist in colonizing landslide gaps (see Sections 4.2 and 4.3). Gymnosperms are seed plants that are more common on temperate than tropical landslides (Table 4.2). In some tropical areas prone to landslides, native gymnosperms are rare (e.g., Puerto Rico) or absent (e.g., Hawaii), but are sometimes planted to stabilize slopes (Acevedo-Rodríguez & Strong, 2005; A. Shiels, pers. obs.). Conifers are the most common form of gymnosperm found on temperate landslides and many are adapted for dispersal and colonization into disturbed areas including landslides, as shown by wind pollination, wind dispersal, and additional features of drought tolerance such as waxy, thickened leaves (Arno & Hammerly, 1984).

Douglas fir (*Pseudotsuga menziesii*) is the dominant conifer tree in forests on many western slopes of the Cascade Mountains in Oregon and Washington, U.S., and was the most common of 140 species of landslide colonists in that region (Miles *et al.*, 1984; Miles & Swanson, 1986), including a large landslide resulting from Mount St. Helen's eruption (Dale, 1986). *Larix decidua* colonized a large rockslide in Switzerland within 2 years and established dominance within 20 years (Van der Burght *et al.*, 2012). Despite these two examples, many conifers establish in landslides after angiosperms and non-seed plants provide shade or other habitat amelioration. For example, conifers dominated landslides that were at least 40 years old in both British Columbia (*Picea sitchensis* and *Tsuga heterophylla*; Geertsema & Pojar, 2007) and New Hampshire (*Picea rubens* and *Abies balsamea*; Flaccus, 1959). However, many conifers need exposure of mineral soil to germinate (Zasada *et al.*, 1992), so early

Table 4.2. *Dominant trees (both gymnosperms and angiosperms) documented in landslide studies*

Location	Species	Family	References
Temperate			
Queen Charlotte Islands, Canada	*Alnus rubra*	Betulaceae	Geertsema & Pojar, 2007
Montana Rocky Mountains, U.S.	*Populus tremuloides*	Salicaceae	Malanson & Butler, 1984
	Alnus sinuata	Betulaceae	
Mount St. Helens, U.S.	*Pseudotsuga menziesii*	Pinaceae	Dale, 1986
	Salix spp.	Salicaceae	
The Alps, Switzerland	*Larix decidua*	Pinaceae	Van der Burght *et al.*, 2012
	Betula pendula	Betulaceae	
Lake Thompson, New Zealand	*Leptospermum scoparium*	Myrtaceae	Mark *et al.*, 1964, 1989
	Aristotelia serrata	Elaeocarpaceae	
Oregon Cascade Mountains, U.S.	*Pseudotsuga menziesii*	Pinaceae	Miles *et al.*, 1984; Miles & Swanson, 1986
	Alnus rubra	Betulaceae	
New Hampshire White Mountains, U.S.	*Betula papyrifera*	Betulaceae	Flaccus, 1959
	Betula lutea	Betulaceae	
Matiri Valley, New Zealand	*Nothofagus fusca*	Nothofagaceae	Vittoz *et al.*, 2001
Andes Mountains, Argentina	*Nothofagus dombeyi*	Nothofagaceae	Veblen & Ashton, 1978
	Eucryphia cordifolia	Cunoniaceae	
Virginia Massanutten Mountain, U.S.	*Tsuga canadensis*	Pinaceae	Hupp, 1983
	Betula lenta	Betulaceae	
Virginia Appalachian Mountains, U.S.	*Liriodendron tulipifera*	Magnoliaceae	Hull & Scott, 1982
Waitakere Ranges, New Zealand	*Agathis australis*	Araucariaceae	Claessens *et al.*, 2006
Akaishi Mountains, Japan	*Salix bakko*	Salicaceae	Nakamura, 1984
	Carpinus japonica	Betulaceae	

(*cont.*)

Table 4.2. (cont.)

Location	Species	Family	References
Mt. Kiyosumi, Japan	*Euptelea polyandra*	Eupteleaceae	Sakai & Ohsawa, 1993
Flores Island, the Azores	*Juniperus brevifolia*	Cupressaceae	Elias & Dias, 2009
Himalayan Mountains, Nepal	*Alnus nepalensis*	Betulaceae	Devkota *et al.*, 2006
Himalayan Mountains, India	*Quercus* spp.	Betulaceae	Reddy & Singh, 1993
	Pinus roxburghii	Pinaceae	
Tropical			
Mauna Loa Volcano, Hawaii	*Metrosideros polymorpha*	Myrtaceae	Restrepo & Vitousek, 2001
Luquillo Mountains, Puerto Rico	*Cecropia schreberiana*	Cecropiaceae	Myster & Walker, 1997
	Psychotria berteriana	Rubiaceae	
Blue Mountains, Jamaica	*Clethra occidentalis*	Clethraceae	Dalling, 1994
Casita Volcano, Nicaragua	*Trema micrantha*	Cannabaceae	Velázquez & Gómez-Sal, 2008
	Muntingia calabura	Muntingiaceae	
Monteverde Cloud Forest, Costa Rica	*Palicourea standleyana*	Rubiaceae	Myster, 1997
	Cecropia polyphlebia	Cecropiaceae	
Darien Province, Panama	*Trema micrantha*	Cannabaceae	Garwood *et al.*, 1979

Dominance was based on stem abundance, frequency, biomass, or cover, and included one to many landslides. Entries are listed in descending order by latitude within both temperate and tropical categories. When more than one species is listed for a location, the most common species is listed first. All studies were conducted in forests or forest–farmland habitats.

succession on landslides can be optimal for their establishment (e.g., *Pinus roxburghii* in the Himalayas; Reddy & Singh, 1993). In a study in the Azores, different morphological forms of the same species were found at different stages of landslide development. While some *Juniperus brevifolia* seedlings colonized the most recent landslides (those without any soil), the shrub form of *J. brevifolia* expanded to 25%–50% of total vegetation cover on intermediate-aged landslides, and *J. brevifolia* trees dominated the oldest landslides (Elias & Dias, 2009).

In the southern hemisphere, conifers in the family Araucariaceae occupy landslides in both temperate Argentina and New Zealand (Table 4.2; Plate 12; Veblen & Ashton, 1978; Claessens *et al.*, 2006). Additionally, Denslow (1980) classified several species of Araucariaceae as gap specialists in New Zealand, Solomon Islands, and New Guinea. In New Zealand, regeneration of kauri trees (*Agathis australis*) appears to depend on landslides or treefall gaps (Claessens *et al.*, 2006). Using landscape modeling techniques, Claessens *et al.* (2006) determined that mature kauri trees tend to occur on sites with moderate to high landslide hazard in northern New Zealand. Furthermore, mature kauri trees have a positive feedback on retaining kauri dominance in a patch; upon death of a mature kauri through wind damage or a landslide, increased light from the newly formed gap promotes kauri seedling regeneration (Claessens *et al.*, 2006). The presence of conifers such as *A. australis* can help identify past landslides as well as help predict future landslides. However, other types of conifer-dominated vegetation on landslides, featuring such species as *Pseudotsuga menziesii* in the Pacific Northwest (U.S.) and *Juniperus brevifolia* in the Azores, resemble the adjacent, less-disturbed forest and therefore the landslide may only be discernible from the forest by reduced plant size and a uniform age class structure (Elias & Dias, 2009). Conifers may therefore be a dominant feature of landslides at all stages of succession, although some are gap specialists.

4.5.4 Grasses

Grasses represent one of the most successful groups of plants on the planet, and they can rapidly colonize and dominate landslides for several years following disturbance (Velázquez & Gómez-Sal, 2009b). Key features of grasses that colonize landslides include: pollination and dispersal adaptations to dry habitats, extensive fine-root systems, frequent vegetative reproduction, leaf adaptations to discourage herbivory and limit water loss, relatively high incidence of C_4 photosynthesis, rapid growth, and short periods to reproduction (Raven *et al.*, 2005). Like gymnosperms, grass pollination generally occurs by wind and therefore the open and often dry landslide environment likely aids in reproduction of early grass colonizers. Grasses often produce hundreds of seeds on a single plant and some have accessories to aid in wind dispersal. For example, species in the genus *Andropogon* have hairy spikelets that help dispersal by wind and they are common landslide colonists in Puerto Rico (Walker & Boneta, 1995; Shiels & Walker, 2003), Hawaii (Restrepo & Vitousek, 2001), and Ecuador (Myster & Sarmiento, 1998). However, many other grasses do not have hairs or other accessories to help with movement via wind but instead (like spore-bearing plants) rely on their small size. The fruit of a grass is a caryopsis, which is dry and fused to the seed coat, and it generally allows the seeds to be moved easily by the wind. Most landslide colonists that are grasses do have small (< 3 mm in length) seeds in both temperate (Flaccus, 1959; Veblen & Ashton, 1978; Miles & Swanson, 1986) and tropical (Lundgren, 1978; Restrepo & Vitousek, 2001; Shiels & Walker, 2003) environments.

The extensive, fine-root systems of grasses help stabilize soils and improve water and nutrient uptake, which is an advantage on unstable, dry, nutrient-poor landslides. Nutrient-poor landslides support increased root growth compared to roots on more fertile landslides (Walker & Shiels, 2008). Landslide soils are also not readily colonized by mycorrhizal fungi (Shaw & Sidle, 1983; Guariguata, 1990; Myster & Fernández, 1995), but the frequent absence of mycorrhizae in landslides can provide a competitive advantage to plants that have fine root systems for nutrient uptake, such as grasses (Lambers *et al.*, 1998). Microsites where rooting is possible on landslides can also be limited, especially in the slip face and chute where exposed bedrock or shallow soils predominate (see Chapter 3; Adams & Sidle, 1987; Sakai & Ohsawa, 1993). Nevertheless, the shallow rooting depth of grasses and their ability to grow in cracks in rocks aid in the colonization of these microsites (Mark *et al.*, 1964; Ziemer, 1981). Additional graminoids such as sedges (e.g., *Carex*) and rushes (e.g., *Luzula* and *Juncus*) also colonize cracks and thin soils on a wide range of landslides (Flaccus, 1959; Mark *et al.*, 1964; Elias & Dias, 2009). Graminoids can be important to help stabilize landslides in restoration efforts (Walker *et al.*, 2009; see Chapter 6).

Grasses have both morphological and physiological adaptations to limit water loss. Narrow, strap-shaped leaves enable prolonged exposure to sunlight in relatively dry habitats, and a protective sheath at the base of each leaf helps retain moisture. C_4 grasses are frequently found on

Fig. 4.4. The C$_4$ grass *Schizachyrium condensatum* on a landslide along the Na Pali Coast, Kauai, Hawaii. Photograph by A.B. Shiels.

tropical landslides (Fig. 4.4), while C$_3$ grasses dominate temperate land-slides (Table 4.3), perhaps because most temperate landslides occur in moist, cooler conditions where C$_3$ grasses are competitively successful. In the tropics, C$_4$ grasses tend to dominate in the driest regions. For example, in a large landslide occurring in dry forest in Nicaragua, all of the landslide-colonizing grasses were C$_4$ (Velázquez & Gómez-Sal, 2007). In the Uluguru Mountains, Tanzania, 10 of the 13 grass species that colonized landslides were C$_4$ grasses (Lundgren, 1978). In wet-ter tropical landslides, such as those studied by Restrepo & Vitousek (2001) on the Island of Hawaii, both C$_4$ and C$_3$ grass species colonized. Therefore, although C$_4$ photosynthesis is a more efficient carbon fixing process than C$_3$ in sunny and dry conditions, it is not a feature of all landslide-colonizing grasses. Clearly, there is a range of adaptations that helps account for successful landslide colonists.

Tropical landslides with bare soils can be quickly covered by grasses. Velázquez & Gómez-Sal (2009b) found that grasses, particularly *Sporobo-lus indicus* and *Hyparrhenia rufa*, were the dominant initial colonists and persisted as dominants through the first 4 years of succession on a large

Table 4.3. *Grasses (Poaceae) that have been documented in landslides and their photosynthetic pathway*

Location	Annual precipitation (mm)	Species	Carbon fixation process	References
Temperate				
Lake Thompson, New Zealand	2500	*Agrostis parviflora*	C₃	Mark *et al.*, 1964, 1989
		Chionochloa flavescens	C₃	
		Chionochloa conspicua	C₃	
Oregon Cascade Mountains, U.S.	2400	*Agrostis* spp.	C₃	Miles & Swanson, 1986
		Deschampsia elongata	C₃	
		Festuca arundinacea	C₃	
		Festuca occidentalis	C₃	
		Holcus lanatus	C₃	
New Hampshire White Mountains, U.S.	1000–1600	*Agrostis scabra*	C₃	Flaccus, 1959
Andes Mountains, Argentina	3000–4000	*Agropyron* sp.	C₃	Veblen & Ashton, 1978
		Agrostis sp.	C₃	
		Holcus lanatus	C₃	
		Poa pratensis	C₃	
Colorado Rocky Mountains, U.S.	71	*Bromus inermis*	C₃	Langenheim, 1956
		Koeleria cristata	C₃	
		Poa pratensis	C₃	
		Sitanion hystrix	C₃	
		Stipa columbiana	C₃	

Location		Species		Reference
Flores Island, the Azores	5632	Agrostis sp.	C_3	Elias & Dias, 2009
		Deschampsia foliosa	C_3	
		Festuca francoi	C_3	
		Holcus rigidus	C_3	
		Holcus lanatus	C_3	
Tropical				
Hawaii Na Pali Coast, U.S.	1700–2100	Chloris virgata	C_4	A. Shiels, pers. obs.
		Schizachyrium condensatum	C_4	
Hawaii Mauna Loa Volcano, U.S.	2900–4100	Andropogon virginicus	C_3	Restrepo & Vitousek, 2001
		Isachne distichophylla	C_3	
		Paspalum conjugatum	C_4	
		Schizachyrium condensatum	C_4	
Luquillo Mountains, Puerto Rico	3000–4000	Andropogon bicornis	C_3	Myster & Fernández, 1995; Shiels & Walker, 2003; Shiels et al., 2006
		Ichnanthus pallens	C_3	
		Lasiacis divaricata	C_3	
		Paspalum conjugatum	C_4	
		Paspalum millegrana	C_4	
Blue Mountains, Jamaica	2500–3000	Chusquea abietifolia	C_3	Dalling, 1994
		Melinis minutiflora	C_4	
		Zeugites americana	C_3	
Casita Volcano, Nicaragua	1250	Hyparrhenia rufa	C_4	Velázquez & Gómez-Sal, 2007
		Panicum maximum	C_4	
		Sporobolus indicus	C_4	

(cont.)

Table 4.3. (cont.)

Location	Annual precipitation (mm)	Species	Carbon fixation process	References
Monteverde Cloud Forest, Costa Rica	3300	Chusquea pohlii	C_3	Myster, 1993
Uluguru Mountains, Tanzania	950–1920	Agrostis lachnantha	C_3	Lundgren, 1978
		Andropogon dummeri	C_3	
		Arthraxon quartinianus	C_3	
		Beckeropsis uniseta	C_4	
		Brachiaria umbratilis	C_4	
		Digitaria velutina	C_4	
		Eragrostis racemosa	C_4	
		Eragrostis schweinfurthii	C_4	
		Hyparrhenia rufa	C_4	
		Panicum trichocladum	C_4	
		Pennisetum purpureum	C_4	
		Rhynchelytrum repens	C_4	
		Sorghum vulgare	C_4	
Andes, Ecuador	800–2000	Chusquea scandens	C_3	Stern, 1995a,b

C_3 and C_4 grasses were distinguished based on Edwards & Still (2008). Sage et al. (1999), Dengler et al. (1994), and Klink & Joly (1989). Poaceae taxonomic classifications have not been updated and reflect the nomenclature specific to each study (e.g., Rhynchelytrum is synonymous with Melinis; Panicum maximum is synonymous with Urochloa maxima). All studies were conducted in forest or forest-farmland habitats. Entries are listed in descending order by latitude for both temperate and tropical environments.

landslide in a Nicaraguan dry forest. The prevalence of grasses was particularly high in the slip face and chute of the landslide, and there was little grass colonization in the deposition zone (Velázquez & Gómez-Sal, 2009b). In the upper regions of several Puerto Rican landslides where there was bare soil, Shiels *et al.* (2006) found that the grass *Paspalum millegrana* had 60%–90% germination success within 45 days of sowing seeds. Further experiments revealed that seedling growth, biomass, and survival of *P. millegrana* greatly exceeded a common pioneer forb species, *Phytolacca rivinoides* (Shiels *et al.*, 2006). Bamboo (*Chusquea* spp.) can be a frequent colonist of landslides in tropical America and the Caribbean, yet its relative abundance can vary greatly in the landslide plant community, perhaps because of its rare reproduction via seed (Dalling, 1994; Stern, 1995a,b; Myster, 1997; Kessler, 1999). In Monteverde Cloud Forest Reserve, Costa Rica, for example, *Chusquea pohlii* was the dominant colonist of two landslides (Myster, 1997), and it was also a common early colonist of landslides in Ecuador (Stern, 1995a,b). In Bolivia, *Chusquea* spp. was found in mid- and late-succession on landslides (Kessler, 1999), whereas in Jamaica *C. abietifolia* was only present on one of three > 50 year old landslides (Dalling, 1994), and *Chusquea* spp. was on one of two landslides in Ecuador (Myster & Sarmiento, 1998). Sedges (Cyperaceae) are also common landslide colonists in the tropics; sedges in the genus *Rhynchospora* are found on landslides in both Puerto Rico (Shiels & Walker, 2003; Fig. 4.1) and Jamaica (Dalling, 1994).

Grasses are also common colonists of temperate landslides (Table 4.3). Veblen & Ashton (1978) in Chile found several native and non-native grasses (e.g., *Holcus lanatus*, *Poa pratensis*, *Agrostis* sp.) that frequently colonized landslides. In 9-year-old landslides in New Hampshire, grasses occurred in 45%, and sedges in 65%, of all plots sampled (Flaccus, 1959). However, graminoids were infrequent ($\leq$ 5%) in 30 and 72 year old landslides. Grasses, especially *Deschampsia foliosa* and *Festuca francoi*, dominated vascular plant cover on the upper and middle portions of young landslides in the Azores (Elias & Dias, 2009). *Festuca francoi* was one of the co-dominants in one of two intermediate-aged landslides where rushes (Juncaceae) were also found, and all graminoids comprised little (mean < 5%) of the vegetative cover in the oldest landslides studied in the Azores (Elias & Dias, 2009). Although a variety of graminoids were found on 15–78 year old landslides in Fiordlands, New Zealand, none comprised > 5% of the herbaceous cover (Mark *et al.*, 1964). Therefore, graminoids of both temperate and tropical regions appear readily to colonize landslides but their dominance decreases through time.

However, some grasses may rely on landslide habitats even when their abundance is relatively low, as with the case of the rare New Zealand tussock grass (*Deschampsia cespitosa*) that persists on a prehistoric landslide scar (Mark & Dickinson, 2001).

Largely owing to life history traits such as rapid colonization, vigorous vegetative expansion, and potential dominance, introduced (non-native) grasses have been problematic species in some landslide environments. The non-native African grass (*Hyparrhenia rufa*) was an abundant colonist on a Nicaraguan landslide where Velázquez & Gómez-Sal (2007) suggested that it increases the grass-fire cycle. In two young (4–17 year old) landslides in Hawaii, Restrepo & Vitousek (2001) found two non-native grass species (*Schizachyrium condensatum* and *Paspalum conjugatum*) were abundant colonists. Even after grass removal, many non-native species (including other grasses) returned (Restrepo & Vitousek, 2001). These two examples highlight how substantial shifts in community recovery on landslides can occur from colonization by one or a few non-native species (see Section 5.2.6).

4.5.5 Forbs

Forbs, which are herbaceous seed plants other than graminoids, colonize both temperate and tropical landslides. Where spatial and temporal distributions of forbs on landslides have been examined, they predominate on the slip face and in the chute in early succession, rather than in the deposition zone or later in succession. Typical forbs that colonize landslides include representatives forming nitrogen fixing symbioses (e.g., Fabaceae, *Gunnera*), vines, tall forbs (up to 2 m or more), orchids, and species in the Asteraceae.

The spatial and temporal distributions of forbs on landslides are more likely to be limited by competition than by dispersal. Forbs are well represented in landslide floras because many of them have high rates of seed production and wind-dispersed seeds, as exemplified by species in the family Asteraceae (see below). Often forbs dominate immediately following a disturbance but then are quickly confined to the more erosive surfaces such as the slip face and the chute, where larger, woody plants are less successful. For example, on a single landslide in Glacier National Park, U.S., the forb cover was dense but restricted to the inner (central) portion of the chute (Malanson & Butler, 1984). In Nicaragua, Velázquez & Gómez-Sal (2009b) found that forb cover, including species in the Fabaceae (Table 4.1), initially dominated the chute and deposition zones of the landslide, but after 2 years the forb cover declined in both of those zones. Grasses, rather than forbs, dominated the slip face on this landslide. Similarly, in New Hampshire, colonizing forbs were found in bedrock cracks in the steepest zones of 9 year old landslides, but forb abundance successively declined in 19, 30, and 72 year old landslides (Flaccus, 1959). *Astelia nervosa*, *Helichrysum bellidioides*, and *Gunnera monoica* (a forb that can have cyanobacteria symbionts in the stems; see Section 4.4), were the most abundant species on the slip faces of the youngest (15 year old) landslides sampled in New Zealand, but were less abundant on 49 and 78 year old landslides (Mark *et al.*, 1964).

Sometimes forbs can be competitively dominant and even increase in cover during succession. In Japan, *Cirsium purpuratum* was one of the dominant pioneers to colonize fresh landslides (Nakamura, 1984), while *Nepsera aquatica* and *Sauvagesia erecta* initially dominated a Puerto Rican landslide immediately following a fire (Walker & Boneta, 1995), and forbs comprised 63% of the vegetation cover on 22 recent (14 month old) landslides in Puerto Rico (Shiels *et al.*, 2008). When forbs form dense thickets, they can inhibit the establishment and growth of other species. In Nicaragua, the annual forb *Tithonia rotundifolia* developed high cover in the landslide chute where it probably inhibited germination of other species (Velázquez & Gómez-Sal, 2009b). In Puerto Rico, dense thickets of forbs inhibited forest development (Walker *et al.*, 2010a). Forb cover may also increase with time since disturbance. Pandey & Singh (1985) did not distinguish between grasses and forbs but found that the herbaceous layer increased approximately tenfold during a 90 year chronosequence study in temperate oak forests in the Himalayas. Consequently, forbs vary from < 5% of vegetation cover in the Azores (Elias & Dias, 2009); to intermediate levels of 10%–35% in New Zealand (Mark *et al.*, 1964) and volcaniclastic soils in Puerto Rico (Shiels *et al.*, 2008); to at least 50% on a different set of Puerto Rican landslides (Myster & Fernández, 1995).

Vines can represent a substantial portion of forb cover on landslides. For example, vines accounted for approximately 75% of the forb cover on eight recent Puerto Rican landslides with volcaniclastic parent material (Fig. 4.5), yet just 10% of forb cover on 22 landslides with dioritic parent material (Shiels *et al.*, 2008). Also in Puerto Rico, the vines *Ipomea* spp. and *Cissus sicyoides* colonized landslides after fire (Walker & Boneta, 1995). In Japan, *Clematis stans* was a common landslide colonist, especially in convex microhabitats where little post-landslide plant damage occurred from burial by rock and falling gravel (Nakamura, 1984). Some vines, such as *Rubus* spp. and *Lonicera japonica*, can form dense thickets on

116 · Biological consequences

Fig 4.5. Vines comprise the dominant cover on some recent (<1 year old) landslides in Puerto Rico. Photograph by A.B. Shiels.

landslides that are nearly impenetrable (Hull & Scott, 1982). If the vine is woody (i.e., producing secondary growth) it is called a liana, such as *Smilax melastomifolia* growing on old (130 year) landslides in Hawaii (Restrepo & Vitousek, 2001). Because landslide vegetation generally lacks substantial vertical structure early in succession, most vines that colonize landslides are prostrate or restricted to growing on remnant stems that survived the landslide or on new landslide colonists. The rapid growth rates of vines on landslides can extend over rock surfaces and reduce post-landslide erosion by entrapping litter and soil and reducing their down slope movement (Hull & Scott, 1982; Fig. 4.5).

Large forbs that reach 2 m tall can colonize landslides in both temperate and tropical locations (Lundgren, 1978; Malanson & Butler, 1984; Walker *et al.*, 2010a). For example, species in the genus *Phytolacca* become established early on landslides in Puerto Rico (Fetcher *et al.*, 1996; Shiels *et al.*, 2006) and in Tanzania (Lundgren, 1978). Additionally, in temperate landslides in the Rocky Mountains, U.S., *Heracleum lanatum* and *Veratrum viride* are 2 m tall forbs that dominate the herbaceous plant community (Malanson & Butler, 1984). Without protective bark and woody stems and branches, such large forbs would seem vulnerable to herbivore attack. However, *H. lanatum*, *V. viride*, and *Phytolacca* spp. have toxins that help defend against herbivores (Malanson & Butler, 1984; Ravikiran *et al.*, 2011). In addition to chemical defenses, physical defenses occur among forbs on landslides. Stinging nettle (*Urtica dioica*) is a common landslide colonist in Glacier National Park, and it has leaf hairs (trichomes), which contain stinging toxins and deter herbivores (Malanson & Butler, 1984). *Urera baccifera*, which is a shrub that is also in the nettle family (Urticaceae), has similar defensive properties and it colonizes landslides in Puerto Rico (Myster & Walker, 1997). Additional physical defenses and anti-herbivory traits found in herbaceous species include silica deposits in the leaves and stems, pubescence, and sticky or glandular excretions in some landslide-colonizing grasses such as *Melinis minutiflora* (Dalling, 1994).

Trapping and digestion of animals can be another adaptation of forbs to obtain limiting mineral nutrients in landslides, particularly in acidic and nitrogen limited microsites. The insect-trapping plant *Drosera rotundifolia* (honeydew) was found in rock cracks and crevices that contained saturated sediments on landslides in New Hampshire (Flaccus, 1959). In the nutrient-poor landslide environments, physical adaptations for both nutrient acquisition and retention appear important to survival of forbs that colonize landslides.

Orchids are occasional colonists of tropical landslides. Orchid cover constituted < 5% of the vegetation cover in 10 year old landslides in both Ecuador (Myster & Sarmiento, 1998) and Puerto Rico (Walker *et al.*, 2010a). Similarly, the non-native orchid *Arundina graminifolia* invaded 4–17 year old landslides in Hawaii where it commonly resprouted after above-ground biomass was removed (Restrepo & Vitousek, 2001). In a study of seven Jamaican landslides, orchids were only present on one 50 year old landslide (*Phaius tancarvilleae* and *Stelis micrantha*; Dalling, 1994). In montane forests in Central America, the orchid *Epidendrum radicans* can dominant roadside landslides (Wolfe, 1987; J. Dalling, pers. comm.). Orchids do not appear to be early colonizers of landslides initially as indicated by their absence from 1 year old landslides in Puerto Rico (Shiels *et al.*, 2008) and Hawaii (A. Shiels, pers. obs.). The scarcity of orchids on landslides may be due to a lack of mycorrhizal symbionts needed for most orchids to establish (Lambers *et al.*, 1998). In addition, most landslide habitats may be too dry for successful orchid establishment. Although many orchids utilize the water efficient CAM photosynthetic pathway, the two orchids commonly found on 4–17 year old landslides in Hawaii and Puerto Rico (*Spathoglottis plicata* and *A. graminifolia*; Restrepo & Vitousek, 2001; Walker *et al.*, 2010a) both have the C_3 pathway (Goh *et al.*, 1977). Bromeliads (Bromeliaceae) do, however, have CAM photosynthesis, and have been reported on tropical landslides in Bolivia (Kessler, 1999) and Jamaica (Dalling, 1994).

One of the most well-represented plant families among landslides is the Asteraceae. Adaptations for wind dispersal, such as small achenes that are assisted by a hairy pappus, are common among many species in the Asteraceae and these features have likely facilitated seed arrival into landslide gaps (Myster & Sarmiento, 1998; Shiels & Walker, 2003). Other Asteraceae are adapted for epizoochory, as evident with the awns in *Bidens* spp., which are found in 15 year old landslides in Jamaica (Dalling, 1994). In two 10 year old Ecuadorian landslides, the dominant seed rain and the seedlings that emerged from the landslide seed bank were Asteraceae, including *Vernonia patens*, *Hieracium* spp., *Baccharis latifolia*, and *Elephantopus mollis* (Myster & Sarmiento, 1998). *Elephantopus mollis* was also found in the seed rain and established on three of six landslides surveyed in Puerto Rico (Shiels & Walker, 2003). In Jamaica, nearly half of the 23 forb species documented across seven landslides were Asteraceae, including *Baccharis scoparia*, *Bidens shrevei*, *Erigeron karvinskianus*, *Eupatorium* spp., *Gnaphalium americanum*, *Lapsana communis*, and *Vernonia pluvialis* (Dalling, 1994). Similarly, in New Hampshire, *Aster acuminatus* had the highest presence of all herbs (86% of all landslides), whereas several other Asteraceae were also common, including *Anaphalis margaritacea* (77%) and *Solidago graminifolia* (59%) (Flaccus, 1959). Therefore, forb colonists in the Asteraceae are common in a variety of different types and ages of landslides, and, like most other forbs, are particularly successful colonists of the slip face and chute of landslides.

4.5.6 Woody angiosperms

Woody angiosperms dominate the vegetation of many temperate and most tropical landslides (Table 4.2). Some species colonize immediately after landslide formation, while others do not appear on landslides until much later in succession and replace early colonists such as grasses or forbs. Woody angiosperms rarely colonize the slip faces, but are often found in chutes, and are most abundant in deposition zones and landslide edges (Malanson & Butler, 1984; Guariguata, 1990). Woody angiosperms on landslides may or may not resemble adjacent vegetation on undisturbed slopes. Their success on landslides can be attributed to a variety

of traits, depending on the species, including their superior competitive abilities (particularly to shade out competitors of smaller stature);
their drought tolerance (from extensive root systems, deciduousness,
and reduced water loss from thick or small leaves); their resistance to
herbivory; widespread dispersal through light seeds, animal vectors, or
vegetative expansion; and the ability of some to establish nitrogen fixing symbioses. We discuss how these traits and others permit successful
colonization of landslides by woody angiosperms. We begin with shrubs
(< 4 m tall; Arno & Hammerly, 1984), then cover tropical trees, and
finally temperate trees.

Shrubs can become relatively abundant on landslides after several years
of herbaceous dominance (Sakai & Ohsawa, 1993; Kessler, 1999), and
they can occupy all landslide zones and establish dominance near the
edges (Malanson & Butler, 1984), the slip face, or the chute (Mark *et al.*,
1964). In moist oak forests in the Himalayan Mountains, India, shrubs
appeared 6 years after a landslide had occurred (Pandey & Singh, 1985).
On a 2 year old Rocky Mountain landslide, *Amelanchier alnifolia* and *Cor-
nus stolonifera* were the most abundant shrubs (Malanson & Butler, 1984).
Veblen & Ashton (1978) determined that the most common shrubs
to colonize landslides in Chile immediately after the 1960 earthquake
were *Baccharis* spp., which belongs to a genus of (mostly herbaceous)
landslide-colonizing species in the Asteraceae (Dalling, 1994; Myster &
Sarmiento, 1998). On tropical landslides, shrubs in the Melastomataceae,
particularly those in the genus *Miconia*, are among the first woody plants
to colonize and can spread and persist for several years (Myster, 1993;
Meyer & Florence, 1996; Walker *et al.*, 2010a; see Section 5.2.6). Some
genera of landslide-colonizing shrubs are found in both temperate New
Zealand and tropical Hawaii, such as *Leptecophylla* and *Coprosma* (Mark
et al., 1964; Restrepo & Vitousek, 2001). *Leptospermum scoparium* was the
most common shrub colonizing landslides on slip faces of landslides in
Fiordland, New Zealand (Mark *et al.*, 1964). *Leptospermum scoparium* is
very drought tolerant, surviving in some areas with < 620 mm of annual
rainfall. Similarly, *Dodonaea viscosa* survives well in dry areas and grows
as a shrub on landslides in Hawaii (Restrepo & Vitousek, 2001), yet it
grows as a tree in some less disturbed sites in Hawaii (Wagner *et al.*, 1999)
and on 15 and 50 year old Jamaican landslides (Dalling, 1994).

Perhaps the most ubiquitous genus of landslide-colonizing shrubs is
Rubus; it colonizes temperate landslides in the U.S. (Flaccus, 1959; Hull
& Scott, 1982; Malanson & Butler, 1984; Miles & Swanson, 1986),
the Azores (Elias & Dias, 2009), New Zealand (Mark *et al.*, 1964), and

Chile (Veblen & Ashton, 1978), as well as tropical landslides in Hawaii (Restrepo & Vitousek, 2001), Jamaica (Dalling, 1994), Puerto Rico (A. Shiels, unpublished data), and Tanzania (Lundgren, 1978). Species in this genus can colonize within 6 months of landslide formation (Lundgren, 1978) and persist for over 50 years (Mark *et al.*, 1964; Dalling, 1994). Some species of *Rubus* form thickets, while most spread through vegetative reproduction in addition to sexual reproduction (Hull & Scott, 1982; Miles & Swanson, 1986; Wagner *et al.*, 1999). Their persistence on landslides may also be due to an abundance of prickly physical defenses.

Ericaceae is another common family that colonizes landslides, with representatives as both shrub and tree growth forms. *Vaccinium meridionale* was a tree found on all seven 15 and 50 year old landslides in Jamaica, and *Lyonia octandra* and *Rhododendron arboreum* were additional tree species in the Ericaceae found on some of the landslides (Dalling, 1994). *Vaccinium cylindraceum* was also found in old landslides in the Azores (Elias & Dias 2009); and in Hawaii, *V. calycinum* was present in initial landslide sampling but the species was absent during the following year of sampling (Restrepo & Vitousek, 2001). In a temperate landslide in the Rocky Mountains, *V. scoparium* appeared in 13 of 20 plots and *V. globulare* appeared in 5 of the 20 plots; *Arctostaphylos uva-ursi* was a less common member of the Ericaceae that appeared in just 2 of the 20 plots (Malanson & Butler, 1984). *Gaultheria shallon* is a dense shrub that appeared in 22% of the plots surveyed on landslides in the Oregon Cascades, yet comprised just 7% cover (Miles & Swanson, 1986). Landslide colonists in the Ericaceae may greatly benefit by forming symbioses with ericoid mycorrhizae, which flourish in nutrient impoverished soils. Ericoid mycorrhizae are able to degrade organic matter to access nitrogen, including absorbing whole amino acids, which can ultimately improve plant nutrition (Read, 1996; Hodge *et al.*, 2000).

The Rubiaceae is generally considered a tropical/subtropical plant family and is well represented on tropical landslides, including those in Jamaica (Dalling, 1994), Puerto Rico (Myster & Walker, 1997; Walker *et al.*, 2010a), Costa Rica (Myster, 1993), Hawaii (Restrepo & Vitousek, 2001), and Tanzania (Lundgren, 1978). The dominant tree genera in the Rubiaceae on these tropical landslides include *Psychotria* and *Palicourea* (Myster, 1993; Dalling, 1994; Myster & Walker, 1997; Walker *et al.*, 2010a). Interestingly, native members of the Rubiaceae are also represented on landslides in both New Zealand and Oregon (Mark *et al.*, 1964; Miles & Swanson, 1986). In New Zealand, there were seven species of *Coprosma* found on a range of surface ages (15, 49, and 78 years old) and in both slip face and deposition zone microsites (Mark *et al*, 1964). In Oregon, 41% of the sampling plots among 25 landslides had *Galium* spp. (Miles & Swanson, 1986). Although most landslide colonists in the Rubiaceae are trees and shrubs, *Galium* spp. in Oregon and *Anthospermum herbaceum* and *Rubia cordifolia* in Africa are herbaceous.

A great diversity of tree species colonize landslides (Table 4.2), including both gymnosperms (see Section 4.5.3) and angiosperms. Trees are the tallest of all woody life forms, and they can be successful landslide colonists for years when they overtop all other vegetation. Like shrubs, trees can colonize landslides at all stages of succession. Tree seedlings may arrive in the first years following landslides and dominate after 5–10 years in both tropical and temperate environments (Garwood *et al.*, 1979; Miles & Swanson, 1986; Myster & Walker, 1997; Velázquez & Gómez-Sal, 2008). Adaptations by some landslide-colonizing trees to dry habitats such as the Casita landslide in Nicaragua (Velázquez & Gómez-Sal, 2008), may include C_4 or CAM photosynthesis. Two genera with both shrubs and trees that have C_4 photosynthesis include *Chamaesyce* and *Euphorbia* (Batanouny *et al.*, 1991). Trees that utilize CAM photosynthesis, such as members in the genus *Clusia* (Ting *et al.*, 1987), also colonize landslides (Myster, 1993; A. Shiels, pers. obs.). Species of *Clusia* are similar to most bromeliads because their early life stages are epiphytic, typically requiring a host tree for initial colonization, and therefore are unlikely to colonize landslides early in succession.

One of the well-studied tree genera found in tropical disturbances is the angiosperm *Cecropia* (Brokaw, 1998; Shiels, 2006; see Fig. 5.4). In addition to landslides, *Cecropia* rapidly colonizes soil pits created by treefalls (Walker, 2000) and the forest understory following hurricanes (Guzmán-Grajales & Walker, 1991; Shiels *et al.*, 2010). *Cecropia* has many r-selected traits, such as fast growth rates and time to reproduction, small seeds, low resistance to wind disturbance, and shade intolerance (Brokaw, 1998; Walker, 2000). Unlike most r-selected species, *Cecropia* has large leaves; however, the leaves can be slightly to greatly dissected, which is an adaptation for reducing water loss. On tropical landslides in both Puerto Rico and Costa Rica, *Cecropia* is co-dominant with trees and shrubs in the Rubiaceae (Myster, 1997; Myster & Walker, 1997; Table 4.2). A viable seed bank allows for rapid colonization following hurricane disturbance for both *Cecropia schreberiana* and *Psychotria berteriana* in Puerto Rico (Shiels *et al.*, 2010), and the presence of a seed bank in the deposition zone of Puerto Rican landslides may also aid in the establishment of both *C. schreberiana* and *Psychotria* spp. on landslides (Guariguata, 1990).

Trema is a New World and Old World tropical tree genus that readily colonizes landslides in Central America (Garwood *et al.*, 1979; Velázquez & Gómez-Sal, 2008; Pizano *et al.*, 2011) and Pacific islands (Taiwan, J. Dalling, pers. comm.; Hawaii, A. Shiels, pers. obs.). In Panama, Garwood *et al.* (1979) determined that *T. micrantha* became the dominant species within 8 months on a 2 ha earthquake-triggered landslide because it accounted for 66% of all species present. Similarly, Velázquez & Gómez-Sal (2008) found that *T. micrantha* established dominance within 3 years on a rainfall-triggered landslide that was 3 km long and passed through dry forest and farmland in Nicaragua. *Trema*'s successful colonization of recently disturbed habitats is likely due in part to relatively small and slightly thickened leaves, which deter herbivores because they are rough or pubescent, and small fleshy-fruited seeds that facilitate dispersal by birds (Wagner *et al.*, 1999).

The genus *Alnus* (Betulaceae) is an important colonist of tropical and temperate landslides, and it can become a dominant or co-dominant tree on many landslides (Malanson & Butler, 1984; Miles & Swanson, 1986; Kessler, 1999; Geertsema & Pojar, 2007; Table 4.2). Wind-dispersed seeds, enhanced seedling establishment on mineral soils, and rapid growth rates in temperate (Miles & Swanson, 1986; Haeussler *et al.*, 1995; Geertsema & Pojar, 2007) and tropical (Kessler, 1999; Russo, 2005) ecosystems contribute to its successful establishment in disturbed habitats. The genus is well known for its important symbiotic relationship with the nitrogen fixing bacteria *Frankia*, which reside in the root nodules (see Section 4.4; Table 4.1), as well as its important association with mycorrhizal fungi (Russo, 2005). In addition to improving landslide soils by nitrogen fixing symbiosis, *Alnus* may also improve soil fertility by seasonally shedding its nitrogen-rich leaves into the disturbed site (Fig. 4.6). Deciduousness is an adaptation for avoiding low water availability and leaf damage due to freezing. Recovery of *Alnus rubra* on both landslides and logged areas in British Columbia, Canada, was rapid relative to the dominant conifers (*Tsuga heterophylla* and *Picea sitchensis*) of the adjacent forest (Schuster, 2001). Owing to its rapid colonization of disturbed habitats such as landslides, as well as its deciduous and nitrogen fixing symbiotic properties, *Alnus* spp. may also provide favorable habitat for soil-, litter-, and leaf-colonizing animals.

Betula is in the same family as *Alnus*, yet lacks nitrogen fixing symbionts (Soltis *et al.*, 1995). However, the functional role of *Betula* is similar to *Alnus* because both are relatively shade intolerant and wind dispersed (Carlton & Bazzaz, 1998), they both form ectomycorrhizae with

Fig. 4.6. A grove of leafless *Alnus rubra* trees (winter scene) growing on a rotational sediment slump in coastal Oregon, U.S. Photograph by A.B. Shiels.

wind-dispersed basidiomycete fungi (Russo, 2005), and they can establish on landslides quickly and persist as a dominant or co-dominant (Flaccus, 1959; Van der Burght *et al.*, 2012; Table 4.2). On a large rockslide in Switzerland, *Betula pendula* was a dominant tree species that grew larger in exposed microhabitats characterized by boulders than on finer-grained substrates (Van der Burght *et al.*, 2012). In New Hampshire, two species of *Betula* (*B. papyrifera* and *B. lutea*) were the dominant pioneer species 9 years after landslide formation, and both persisted as co-dominants through at least 30 years of succession (Flaccus, 1959). These same two species of *Betula* also dominated early succession on treefall mounds, pits, and forest gaps in the same region in northeastern U.S. (Carlton & Bazzaz, 1998).

Populus tremuloides (Salicaceae) can be a dominant colonist of landslides in montane temperate zones (Mitton & Grant, 1980; Malanson & Butler, 1984; Table 4.2) and is the most widespread deciduous tree in North America. Its vigorous vegetative reproduction enables a single clone to cover many hectares (Mitton & Grant, 1980). Malanson & Butler (1984) found that the dominant tree on a Rocky Mountain landslide was *P. tremuloides*, and that, while it initially colonized the relatively bare portions of the landslide, it also spread to the forest–landslide edge. The ability of *Populus* spp. to form ectomycorrhizae with air-dispersed fungi facilitates its colonization of bare portions of landslides, and such ectomy-corrhizae affiliations allowed *Populus* spp. to colonize buildings wrecked by war in Poland (Dominik, 1956; Vittoz & Hacskaylo, 1974). Additional colonists of Rocky Mountain landslides included members of the genera *Acer* and *Alnus* (Malanson & Butler, 1984), and these genera were also represented on most landslides sampled in the Cascade Mountains (Miles & Swanson, 1986) and on a large rockslide in the Swiss Alps (Van der Burght *et al.*, 2012). *Populus tremuloides* and *Salix bebbiana* were frequent landslide colonists in the White Mountains (Flaccus, 1959), and *S. bacco* was the dominant tree colonist in central Japan (Nakamura, 1984). Like *Populus* spp., *Salix* spp. have wind-dispersed seeds and successfully reproduce vegetatively.

Nothofagus is a genus of landslide-colonizing trees that naturally occurs in the southern hemisphere, and it often dominates forests in less disturbed habitats in New Zealand, Chile, and Argentina. *Nothofagus dombeyi* was the most common tree that colonized Chilean landslides in 1960, and it established in both bare and rocky debris sites (Veblen & Ashton 1978; Table 4.2). In New Zealand, Mark *et al.* (1964) found that *N. menziesii* forests are the climax forest species, yet where such forests surrounded a series of 15–78 year old landslides, *N. menziesii* was a minor component of the vegetation, particularly on the 15 year old landslide. Instead, *Leptospermum scoparium*, in both shrub and tree forms, dominated the New Zealand landslides (Mark *et al.*, 1964). After *N. dombeyi*, the next most common tree on Chilean landslides was *Weinmannia trichosperma*, which is also an evergreen tree that is native to Chile and Argentina. In addition to *N. menziesii*, a southern hemisphere species of *Metrosideros* (*M. umbellata*; Myrtaceae) was found in low abundance on the same landslides in New Zealand (Mark *et al.*, 1964). However, *M. polymorpha* is the dominant native tree in much of Hawaii, and Restrepo & Vitousek (2001) found that it was the most abundant tree that colonized landslides > 4 years old (Table 4.2). Therefore, landslide colonists may be the dominant tree species in the forest that surrounds a landslide (e.g., Veblen & Ashton, 1978; Miles & Swanson, 1986; Restrepo & Vitousek, 2001), or they may be uncommon in the surrounding forest (e.g., Mark *et al.*, 1964; Malanson & Butler, 1984; Nakamura, 1984). In the latter case, landslides promote regional biodiversity (Moss & Rosenfeld, 1978).

In summary, most plant life forms may be represented within the landslide community shortly after disturbance. In the most extreme

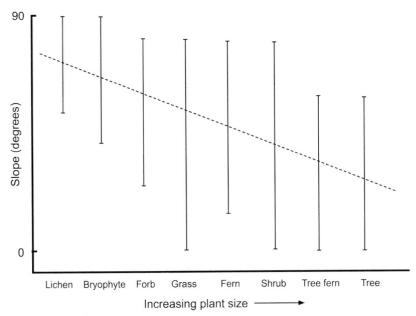

Fig. 4.7. Plant groups on landslides separated by the degree of slope they commonly colonize. The dashed line represents an overall estimate in the relationship between slope and plant size. The presence at some slopes may represent preferred habitat or reflect remaining habitat left by other dominant plant groups. Lichens are included because they are symbiotic with green algae or cyanobacteria (blue–green algae). Free-living cyanobacteria are present on all types of slopes within landslides.

microhabitats of landslides, which include near-vertical substrates and bare rocks in the slip face portion, lichens and bryophytes are able to colonize and in many cases flourish (Fig. 4.7). Free-living or symbiotic relations that include nitrogen fixing bacteria such as cyanobacteria, *Rhizobium*, and *Frankia*, aid in colonization of landslides by *Gunnera* and woody and herbaceous plants, as well as lichen and bryophyte establishment and survival. Mycorrhizal fungi also aid in plant colonization in nutrient depauperate landslide soils. Grasses and ferns colonize all but the steepest, near-vertical, slopes of a landslide and are among the most ubiquitous of all plant life forms that colonize temperate and tropical landslides. The C_4 grasses that colonize tropical landslides are more efficient at carbon fixation in dry habitats; once established, both grasses and ferns successfully spread on landslides through both sexual and asexual reproduction. Forbs are a frequent colonist of all landslides, yet they often play the most important role during early succession in the chute and slip face of the landslide. The spatial separation of plant groups within landslides may result from both habitat preference and competitive exclusion by other, more dominant species. Woody plants are typically rare on the steep slip face, and many shrubs and trees colonize landslides either early or late in succession and often establish long-term dominance. Herbaceous plants often inhibit other herbaceous plants early in succession, whereas shrubs and trees play a more facilitative role (Gómez-Aparicio, 2009; Walker et al., 2010a). Further discussion of species interactions on landslides occurs in Chapter 5.

4.6 Animals

4.6.1 Invertebrates

Crawling and flying arthropods are probably the first animals to establish on landslides (Hou et al., 2005; Shiels & Yang, unpublished data). Characteristics that likely enhance arthropod establishment on landslides include high tolerance to water and temperature stress (Lavelle & Spain, 2001), as well as the ability to disperse from landslide edges, either by using their appendages or by transport associated with soil and organic matter. Studies of arthropods and other invertebrates are relatively sparse for temperate landslides. However, Růžička and Zacharda (1994) studied arthropod communities on talus slopes in the Krkonoše Mountains of the Czech Republic and found that the most abundant species was a rhagidiid mite (*Evadorhagidia oblikensis*). Additionally, 33 species of spiders (Araneae), 31 species of beetles (Coleoptera), as well as flies (Diptera) and aphids (Aphidinea) were among the most abundant arthropods discovered from year-long pitfall trapping. Stony debris in the talus provided a wide range of temperatures that supported the co-existence of such diverse arthropod communities (Růžička & Zacharda, 1994). Spiders were among the most frequently observed arthropods in the talus slopes of the Niagara Escarpment in Canada (Larson et al., 2000). Based on tropical studies, landslide colonization by arthropods can be rapid; arthropod abundance and richness can reach 6–7 orders and 18–30 families within a few years after a landslide (Myster, 1994), where overall abundances may be comparable to undisturbed forests (Hou et al., 2005; Chien, 2007). Among the most abundant soil arthropods found on landslides as well as in undisturbed forests are mites and springtails (Collembola), and they may comprise 86%–90% of the total individuals in the soil–litter community (Hou et al., 2005) and become landslide dominants within 2 years in

Fig. 4.8. A nest of the ant *Wasmannia auropunctata* on a young (< 5 year old) Puerto Rican landslide. Caliper length is about 20 cm. Photograph by A.B. Shiels.

both Puerto Rico (Shiels & Yang, unpublished data) and Taiwan (Hou *et al.*, 2005). Part of the success of such landslide-colonizing arthropods, particularly mites, is reproduction via parthenogenesis, when unfertilized eggs develop into new individuals (Chien, 2007).

Ants (Hymenoptera) also recruit to disturbed areas, and they can be one of the most abundant colonists in landslides (Myster, 1994) as well as in other newly formed gaps such as those created by clear cuts (Schowalter *et al.*, 1981). In landslides < 2 years old in Puerto Rico, ants extracted from litterbags were the most abundant arthropod observed and were over twice as abundant as on 4–15 year old landslides and in the adjacent forest (Shiels & Yang, unpublished data). The fire ant *Wasmannia auropunctata* appears to be common in young landslides, as indicated by the high abundance in leaf litter and colony nesting on recent Puerto Rican landslides, and because this ant species was not found in any of the nearby forest understory plots (Shiels & Yang, unpublished data; Fig. 4.8). *Wasmannia auropunctata* prefers Collembola, rather than leaf litter, as a food source (B. Edwards, pers. comm.), making it one of the earliest colonizing predators on Puerto Rican landslides. Like most other ground nesting ants, *W. auropunctata* nest building results in substantial soil mixing within landslides (A. Shiels, pers. obs.). *Wasmannia auropunctata* has invaded disturbed sites in many tropical and subtropical regions outside of its native range of Central and South America, and the human and ecological threats that it poses have resulted in its being listed as one of the world's 100 worst invasive species (Lowe *et al.*, 2000). Additional landslide-colonizing ants may play important roles as seed predators. Ants fed on *Cecropia schreberiana* seeds when offered multiple seed species in landslide feeding trials (Myster, 1997), and ants were observed taking seeds of *Clusia rosea* from beneath perches placed on landslides (Shiels, 2002).

Through insect censuses on 5–20 year old landslides in Puerto Rico and Costa Rica, Myster (1994) found that insect abundances within landslides from two tropical sites were similar, and that flying insects (nectivorous midges and gnats) were the most abundant insects. Additional nonnectivorous insects that are common to landslides in both Costa Rica and Puerto Rico include ants, beetles, flies, and thrips (Thysanoptera) (Myster, 1994), yet each of these insect groups accounted for just 1%–3% of the total animals on landslides in Taiwan (Hou *et al.*, 2005). With insects establishing on landslides relatively early after disturbance, it would seem reasonable that spiders, a common insect predator, would also establish. Spiders did not appear in ground samples from recent (1–2 year old) landslides in Puerto Rico, but did appear in some 4–5 year old and 14–15 year old landslides (Shiels & Yang, unpublished data). Perhaps the absence of spiders on young landslides in Puerto Rico is a reflection of a lack of vegetation complexity for web-building spiders, or simply a result of a sampling bias where only ground-dwelling arthropods were captured. The relatively rapid recovery of litter arthropods in the study by Hou *et al.* (2005) may have also resulted from partial sampling bias because findings were based on small landslides (approximately 50 m^2) that had patches of residual forest soil.

Aerial and arboreal insects, although poorly studied on landslides, can play an important role in nutrient cycling on landslides when they consume plants. For example, Myster (2002) found that 25%–34% of the leaf area of the nitrogen fixing *Inga vera* tree experienced herbivory on Puerto Rican landslides. Aerial insects can also be important pollinators of landslide-colonizing plants. On a large (25 km long) landslide created by Mount St. Helens' eruption in Washington, Dale (1986) measured bumblebee (*Bombus* spp.) visitation to *Lupinus latifolius*, which was an early plant colonist with a *Rhizobium* symbiont (Table 4.1). *Lupinus latifolius* requires bumblebees to transfer pollen between plants for seed set (Dale, 1986), and 11 bumblebees from at least two *Bombus* species (*B. occidentalis* and *B. californicus*) were observed flying between and foraging on *L. latifolius* on the landslide. Dale (1986) reasoned that, due to the sporadic plant spacing, the bumblebees might travel at least 1 km to transfer *L. latifolius* pollen and that the below-ground bumblebee nests would have been destroyed in the landslide. However, the blow down area (< 1 km from some parts of the landslide) would have provided important sources of surviving bumblebees (Dale, 1986).

Earthworms are a globally important component of the soil fauna in both disturbed and undisturbed sites; over 4000 species of earthworms have been named (Sims & Gerard, 1985). Earthworms can be less abundant in landslides than adjacent forest understories (Hou *et al.*, 2005), or they can differ in species composition when landslides and adjacent forests are compared (Li *et al.*, 2005). In Puerto Rico, Li *et al.* (2005) found two species of earthworms present, but only one species (*Pontoscolex corethrurus*) was found occupying landslides whereas both *P. corethrurus* and *Amynthas rodericensis* occupied the soil in the forest understory. A possible explanation for this species segregation is that *A. rodericensis* is an anecic earthworm, which means it lives only in the leaf litter and organic-rich soil layer and only eats organic matter. *Pontoscolex corethrurus* is an endogenic earthworm that builds complex lateral burrow systems through all of the soil layers and eats both organic matter and mineral soil (Fig. 4.9). With the paucity of organic matter on landslides, the findings from Li *et al.* (2005) fit the expectation that earthworm colonists in recent landslides were the types that survive by eating soil (endogenic) rather than solely organic matter (anecic). Li *et al.* (2005) also found that earthworm abundances in the landslide soils were positively correlated with soil bacteria, leaf litter, and soil carbon.

There have been few studies of invertebrates larger than earthworms on landslides. Slugs and snails are common in disturbed environments and they frequently colonize rock piles at the bases of rock slides, where they survive largely by feeding upon lichens (Lawrey, 1980; Baur & Baur, 1990). The snail *Chondrina clienta* was the only gastropod that occupied exposed vertical surfaces within talus slopes in Sweden because it survives sudden changes in temperature and feeds exclusively upon lichen that grows in such microhabitats (Baur & Baur, 1990). In tropical environments, some snails exist in higher abundances in gaps (e.g., *Caracolus caracolla* in Puerto Rican rainforests) relative to the undisturbed forest, whereas other snail species are equally abundant in gaps and non-gaps

Fig. 4.9. Earthworm castings at the base of a Puerto Rican landslide. Photograph by A.B. Shiels.

(Alvarez & Willig, 1993). Land crabs such as *Epilobocera sinuatifrons* have been observed after heavy rains on landslides in Puerto Rico (A. Shiels, pers. obs.). This particular crab is relatively common in the Puerto Rican rainforest and forages widely from streams and burrows, especially on wet nights (Stewart & Woolbright, 1996). Submarine landslides can be readily colonized by clams in the family Vesicomyidae (e.g., *Calyptogena kilmeri*), which can help date landslides by using growth rates of the clams (Barry & Whaling, 2003). Long-distance displacement of organic matter by turbidity currents likely has an important role in burial of invertebrates living on the sea floor, improvement in nutrient content, and promotion of marine organism diversity and growth (Heezen *et al.*, 1955b; Diaz *et al.*, 1994).

Landslides can also affect down slope ecosystems and the invertebrates that occupy them. In alpine areas in Austria, streams and springs draining from landslides create habitats that can host a variety of aquatic invertebrates (Staudacher & Füreder, 2007). Despite such positive effects of landslides on aquatic invertebrates, landslides are more typically damaging to organisms via sediment deposition (also see Chapter 5; Schuster,

2001; Mackey *et al.*, 2011). While simulating the sediment deposition conditions of a landslide, Norkko *et al.* (2002) found that macrobenthic organisms suffered greatly in estuaries; the numbers of macrobenthic individuals were reduced by 50% after 3 days and 90% after 10 days. Mud crabs (*Helice crassa*), which commonly dig in the benthic zone, were the only animals to emerge from the sediment deposit. Organisms such as bivalves that commonly bed deeply in the sediment suffered the greatest losses (Norkko *et al.*, 2002). Therefore, landslides can greatly affect the invertebrates that occupy the soil, ground surface, and submarine environment, as well as the aquatic organisms that occupy habitats downslope from landslides.

4.6.2 Vertebrates

Birds and small mammals are the dominant vertebrates that generally occupy landslides; however, the initial paucity of vegetation cover and available structure after landslide occurrence generally restricts their use to short visits, especially during early succession. Foraging, perching, courtship, and territoriality are common behaviors of vertebrates on landslides of all ages (Shiels & Walker, 2003; Geertsema & Pojar, 2007).

Gaps with some vegetation can be particularly important for bird visitation (Wunderle *et al.*, 1987). In New Zealand, landslides were apparently important nesting and foraging habitats for the now extinct flightless moa (Wood *et al.*, 2011; Box 4.2). After Hurricane Hugo passed through a Puerto Rican rainforest, the available food sources for birds were largely lost or reduced to gaps containing pioneer vegetation. Such gaps became hotspots for novel bird assemblages, including those bird species that typically occupy the understory or canopy of undisturbed forest (Wunderle, 1995). This behavior was most likely a result of the gaps acting primarily as refuge sites containing some of the only available fruit in the hurricane-affected forest and secondarily as protective sites from predators (Wunderle, 1995). In addition to serving as important forage locations, gaps with emergent vegetation can also be important perches for birds (McDonnell & Stiles, 1983; McClanahan & Wolfe, 1993; Holl, 1998; Shiels & Walker, 2003). The frequency of such perching and feeding behavior on landslides was observed during a 14-month study in which seven species of birds were recorded on artificial perches (4–5 m tall saplings) that were placed on relatively recent landslides (Shiels & Walker, 2003; Fig. 4.2). Another 15 species were recorded either foraging or perching at the landslide–forest edges, or less frequently flying over

---

Box 4.2 Landslides were refuge sites for moa (prehistoric birds)

The moa were giant flightless birds (some up to 3.5 m tall and 200 kg) that were endemic to New Zealand. Their natural predators were birds of prey, including the impressive Haarst Eagle (*Harpagornis moorei*), which had a 2–3 m wingspan and large (> 10 cm) talons that could crush bone up to 6 mm thick under 50 mm of skin and flesh (Bunce *et al.*, 2005). However, moa were driven to extinction by human hunters shortly following human colonization of New Zealand. Because of their large size, flightless nature, and prehistoric presence, moa have long intrigued archeologists, ornithologists, ecologists, and natural historians. Moa bones recovered during an archeological survey on a large rock fall have recently been used to date the landslide and the rupture of the Alpine fault in New Zealand (Wood *et al.*, 2011). Further surveys by paleoecologists have determined that the remnant rocks in the rock fall provided both shelter and nesting sites, as evidenced by egg shells, bones, and nests, for at least three species of moa from the time of the rock fall until the sites were revegetated with forest when human arrival caused their extinction (J. Wilmshurst, pers. comm). The remains were from three species, the South Island giant moa (*Dinornis robustus*), the upland moa (*Megalapteryx didinus*), and the heavy-footed moa (*Pachyornis elephantopus*). The abundance of moa bones on a single rock fall deposition zone indicates that landslides would have been attractive sites for these large birds, likely because of the abundant vegetation for both forage and cover and the large rock overhangs for shelter. Further excavation uncovering moa coprolites (preserved droppings) from beneath rock overhangs within the rock fall have allowed for reconstruction of the moa diets via pollen analysis, seed identification, and ancient plant DNA (J. Wilmshurst, pers. comm.).

---

the landslides (Shiels & Walker, 2003). The most common birds observed were gap specialists such as grassquits (*Tiaris bicolor* and *T. olivacea*) and gray kingbirds (*Tyrannus dominicensis*), and forest birds such as tanagers (*Nesospingus speculiferus* and *Spindalis zena*) (Wunderle, 1995; Shiels, 2002; Shiels & Walker, 2003). The only nesting observed in the vicinity of the landslides was by the gray kingbird, which nested on a 10 m tall utility pole (Shiels, 2002). Many island birds that live in areas of high disturbance, including the gray kingbird, are facultatively omnivorous (Waide, 1996; Shiels & Walker, 2003), and therefore may forage within landslides for fruits, seeds, and arthropods. Rock falls and rotational landslides often form cliffs, which may be colonized by swallows and kingfishers; cliffs may also serve as burrow habitats for seabirds on coastal landslides (Schuster, 2001; Geertsema & Pojar, 2007).

New landslides that contain freshly exposed soil with little vegetation can provide birds with mineral soil used to aid digestion of plant material (i.e., geophagy). On a recent landslide in a montane rainforest in New Guinea, at least four species of parrots, two species of pigeons, one hornbill, one crow, and possibly one cassowary were documented feeding on the bare soil (Diamond *et al.*, 1999). Parrots typically fed on the landslide soil in the morning, while pigeons would frequent the exposed soil in the afternoon. Because of the paucity of landslides in the area, and the relatively long distances that birds would have to travel to get to a landslide, recent landslides with some bare soil appear to be important destinations for many birds in this region. Laboratory tests of the clay-rich soils consumed by the birds revealed a particularly high cation exchange capacity and binding capacity for tannins and quinine. Therefore, Diamond *et al.* (1999) suggested that the consumption of landslide soil by birds in New Guinea served to bind bitter tasting secondary compounds in previously ingested fruit and seed.

Heterogeneous microhabitats within landslides attract many mammals, amphibians, and reptiles. Talus slopes resulting from temperate landslides are used by a variety of amphibians (e.g., tree frogs, toads) and reptiles (e.g., lizards, skinks, snakes) for feeding and reproduction (Maser *et al.*, 1979). More than 60% of the amphibians and reptiles that occur in Oregon and Washington, U.S., utilized talus habitats (Herrington, 1988). Cracks, crevices, and trees on talus slopes were attractive habitats for rodents, voles, and bats (Maser *et al.*, 1979). Insectivorous bats may frequent relatively young landslides because of the open space and presence of aerial insects (Willig & Gannon, 1996), and potentially roost in cliff faces formed by rock falls or rotational landslides (Schuster, 2001; Geertsema & Pojar, 2007). Frugivorous bats commonly visit tropical landslides (Matt *et al.*, 2008). Rodents, which comprise over 40% of the world's mammal species, can be found in a wide variety of habitats and ecosystems that includes landslides (Long, 2008). Rodents have been observed visiting both tropical and temperate landslides (Larson *et al.*, 2000; Shiels, 2002; Geertsema & Pojar, 2007). For example, pikas (*Ochotona princeps*) commonly occur on talus (Hafner, 1993). Additional rodents that occupy temperate landslides include mice and rats (Muridae; Maser *et al.*, 1979), chipmunks, and squirrels (Sciuridae; Matheson, 1995). When ponding results from landslides, beavers (*Castor canadensis*) may colonize

Fig. 4.10. An invasive black rat (*Rattus rattus*) in Hawaii. Note the shiny ear tags. Black rats have been introduced to most islands and continents worldwide. They are known to forage in landslides where they have been recorded as both seed dispersers and predators. Photograph by A.B. Shiels.

(Geertsema & Pojar, 2007). One study in a montane cloud forest in the Chiapas region of southern Mexico sampled rodents on landslides and adjacent undisturbed forest following an El Niño year where 10%–12% of the landscape was affected by landslides (Samaniego-Herrera, 2003). Three species of native rodents (*Peromyscus guatemalensis, P. aztecus*, and *Heteromys goldmani*) were collected from landslides and an additional five rodent species were collected from adjacent forest understories, suggesting that the majority of the rodent species in the Chiapas forest did not frequent landslide gaps (Samaniego-Herrera, 2003). Despite differences in species composition, rodent abundances did not differ along the gradient from landslide to adjacent forest understory, which may benefit rodent predators such as raptors that commonly forage in disturbed areas rather than in the forest understory (Samaniego-Herrera, 2003). Black rats (*Rattus rattus*) have been observed in landslides and adjacent forest in both Puerto Rico and Hawaii (Fig. 4.10; A. Shiels, pers. obs.); this non-native species has invaded most continents and islands and may alter plant communities through both seed predation and dispersal (Shiels, 2011; Shiels & Drake, 2011).

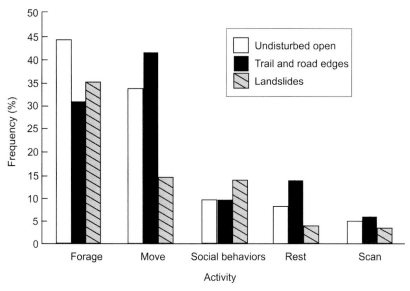

Fig. 4.11. Observed activities of the mountain monkey, *Circopithecus lhoesti*, when it is on the ground in a forest in Rwanda. Social behaviors included play, aggression, and grooming. From Kaplan & Moermond (2000) with permission from Wiley & Sons.

Mammals larger than bats and rodents have been documented on landslides in temperate and tropical ecosystems (Maser *et al.*, 1979; Kaplan & Moermond, 2000). Thirty-six mammal species, including raccoons, porcupines, coyotes, foxes, weasels, badgers, skunks, lynx, bobcat, and bear, were listed as using talus slopes in Wyoming, U.S. (Maser *et al.*, 1979). Bears (*Ursus* spp.) eat emerging graminoids and forbs in landslides, and moose (*Alces alces*) have also left evidence of heavy browsing on landslides (Geertsema & Pojar, 2007). Several non-native mammalian herbivores visit landslides and consume vegetation in New Zealand and elsewhere (Plate 13), including deer (*Cervus elaphus*), goats (*Capra hircus*), and possums (*Trichosurus vulpecula*) (James, 1973). Mountain goats (*Oreamnos americanus*) feed and rest on landslides and mountain slopes during the afternoon and then return to nearby cliffs before dark where fewer predators are present (Geist, 1971). Forest-dwelling monkeys (*Circopithecus l'hoesti*) in Rwanda preferentially visit landslides and other disturbed habitats to forage on the ground for herbaceous plants (Kaplan & Moermond, 2000; Fig. 4.11). Vertebrates visit landslides primarily for forage, yet some also reside on landslides for extended periods of time, such as when they use landslide microhabitats for nesting and predator escape.

4.7 Conclusions

Biota that disperse onto landslides are generally those that are small (e.g., Fig. 4.1); yet adaptations for wind-dispersal (plants) or appendages for locomotion (animals) enable a greater range of organisms to disperse onto landslides, including those from areas well beyond the adjacent habitats. The majority of landslide colonists are gap-specialists with adaptations to survive in mostly bare, low-nutrient environments where temperature and water stress are commonly experienced. There do not appear to be landslide specialists, or organisms that only colonize landslides. Instead, most landslide-colonizing species occur in other types of recently disturbed habitats; however, in some cases, landslides are also important habitats for late-successional species regeneration. Landslide colonists tend to have life-history characteristics that include high fecundity, small body (or seed) size, reduced time to reproduction, and the ability to disperse widely. Water conservation strategies appear important among landslide-colonizing plants, including small and thickened leaves, deciduousness, and C_4 photosynthesis for many tropical grasses. Plant adaptations to nutrient-poor conditions on landslides include symbioses with microbes, particularly nodular nitrogen fixing bacteria. Lichens represent an additional symbiosis common on the steepest portions of landslides, including rocks and bare soil. The first animals to colonize landslides are soil and litter arthropods, particularly mites, Collembola, and ants. Parthenogenesis facilitates rapid expansion and survival of some arthropods on landslides. Most of the remaining animals that colonize landslides are visitors, rather than residents, at least until sufficient habitat structure has developed. A suite of birds, bats, rodents, ungulates, and monkeys has been observed on landslides. Observed behaviors of such animal colonists have included foraging, nesting, perching or resting, reproduction, geophagy, and playing (monkeys).

Our limited understanding of animal colonists on landslides, and their roles in landslide ecology, represents an area deserving future attention and investigation. In addition to more widely documenting animals that occupy landslides, an understanding of the types and frequencies of biotic interactions will also improve our understanding of landslide ecology. For example, how are the roles of animals as pollinators, herbivores, seed predators, and seed dispersers on landslides different than those in non-landslide environments? To what extent do such interactions, and additional interactions within the landslide food web, change through succession? Does the success of early plant colonists on landslides reflect their natural independence from mutualisms with animals? For example, many plants are able to self-fertilize, which may, along with frequent asexual reproduction, facilitate dominance on landslides. Lastly, symbiotic relationships are common within landslide biota. The quantity of nitrogen fixed by various symbionts (lichens, root nodules, *Gunnera*, and free-living organisms) needs future investigation, as do the relative effects of such nitrogen fixers on biotic development within landslides. In summary, much more documentation of landslide-colonizing biota is needed, in addition to investigations of how these colonists interact with each other and alter ecosystem functions. Comparisons of the role of microbes, plants, and animals on landslides and non-landslide environments will help explain the importance of landslide habitats across the landscape.

5 · *Biotic interactions and temporal patterns*

Key points

1. Landslide succession is the sequential replacement of plant communities following landslide creation. It is affected by biotic interactions and abiotic conditions and occurs in the intervals between recurrent erosion events.
2. Plant species can facilitate or inhibit landslide succession by direct species interactions or indirectly by the alteration of resources including light levels, soil stability, soil moisture, or soil nutrients. Species replacements may also occur due to differences in the life histories of landslide colonizers.
3. Herbivores, pathogens, and non-native species influence landslide succession and contribute to the variety of successional trajectories found on landslides, potentially with long-term consequences.
4. Landslides contribute to temporal heterogeneity of landscapes through their destruction and creation of habitats and sharp physical gradients. This heterogeneity generally has a net positive effect on biodiversity at landscape scales, but landslides generally decrease biodiversity at local scales.

5.1 Introduction

As soon as organisms colonize new landslide surfaces, they begin to alter the environment, often in ways that are not favorable for continued establishment of additional individuals of the same species. When changes in the landslide environment favor a new set of species better adapted to the changing conditions, species replacements occur. This process is considered succession (i.e., the change of ecological communities in structure and composition through time) (Glenn-Lewin *et al.*, 1992). Primary succession occurs on surfaces where a disturbance has

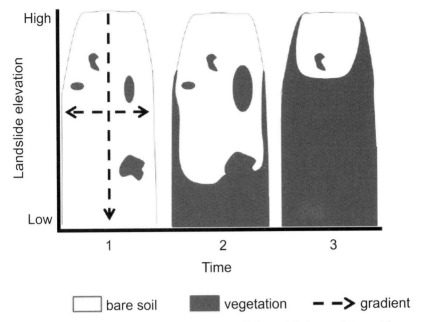

Fig. 5.1. Prominent spatial gradients within landslides and their association with patterns of vegetation recovery. Top to bottom and side to side gradients (arrows point toward increasing nutrients and propagule density) are modified by surviving patches of vegetation at time 1. At time 2, vegetation has expanded from the lower edges and enlarging patches. At time 3, all but the slip face and erosion zone just below it have recolonized. From Shiels & Walker (in press) with permission from the Oikos Editorial Board.

left little or no biological legacy (e.g., new volcanic surfaces); secondary succession occurs where soils remain relatively intact (e.g., following logging). Landslides are generally categorized as examples of primary succession because the initial disturbance removes most of the soil and vegetation (Walker & del Moral, 2003). However, because landslides frequently contain remnants of pre-disturbance soils and plants, change on those remnants often occurs along a continuum of disturbance severity between primary and secondary succession (Vitousek & Walker, 1987).

Several cycles of species replacements typically occur during a sere (successional sequence) while the landslide environment is gradually colonized (Fig. 5.1). Within decades, the landslide scar may no longer be visible to the casual observer. Succession can result in the recovery of an ecosystem that resembles the original, pre-landslide ecosystem, but sometimes new species assemblages are formed. Two or more landslides created at the same time, as well as different locations within the same landslide, may follow similar or different rates and trajectories of succession. These variable pathways enrich the spatial and temporal heterogeneity of landslides and provide a complexity to landslides not always found in other examples of primary succession (Shiels *et al.*, 2008).

Drivers of landslide succession include both regional and local variables where abiotic and biotic factors may drive landslide succession in a hierarchical fashion (Myster *et al.*, 1997). Landslide colonists respond to regional abiotic gradients (e.g., topography, elevation, precipitation) and the regional species pool that determines which species are available and their relative abundance. Landslides contribute to regional biodiversity, particularly when species survive on landslides that cannot survive on less disturbed habitats (see Chapter 4). For example, several species of trees in Patagonia (*Nothofagus* spp., *Fitzroya cupressoides*, *Austrocedrus chilensis*) rely on landslides (and other disturbances including fires and floods) for regeneration (Veblen *et al.*, 1992, 2003) and *Juniperus brevifolia* trees in the Azores rely on landslides, volcanic eruptions, and treefall gaps for regeneration (Elias & Dias, 2004, 2009). The ephemeral nature of many landslides means that they sometimes offer a limited refuge to specialists of disturbed environments.

Local landslide dynamics include abiotic variables such as nutrient availability or surface stability, which affect biotic variables including patterns of species colonization and establishment. Residual soil or surviving organisms can also alter landslide succession. Initially, dispersal and colonization dynamics are important, but as available niches get filled, landslide succession becomes increasingly driven by species interactions; those interactions most carefully examined include facilitation, competition, herbivory, and invasions by non-native organisms. Other potential biotic drivers that are less well studied include mycorrhizae, predation, and disease (Pickett *et al.*, 1987), in addition to the timing of key events in the life cycles of colonizing organisms (e.g., their reproduction, dispersal, and senescence).

Landslides are ecosystems with many spatially and temporally variable habitats which interact with the characteristics of their colonists to shape the still poorly understood process of landslide succession. In this chapter, we summarize what is known about landslide succession, first from a mechanistic perspective of the role of species interactions as drivers of change and then from a landscape perspective of how landslides are a part of larger-scale spatial and temporal dynamics (see Fig. 2.1).

5.2 Succession

5.2.1 Overview

Succession of plant and animal communities has intrigued ecologists for over a century and become the most studied aspect of temporal dynamics, perhaps because of its immediacy and relevance to humans. Many early studies of succession emphasized the role of physical factors. Erosion was recognized as part of a geological cycle of uplift and subsequent erosion (Davis, 1909), but was considered more a background dynamic of all habitats rather than a specific type of disturbance. Cowles (1901) noted that similar results (bare surfaces) such as talus slopes are produced from different processes, including both erosion and deposition. Clements (1928) noted that erosion that creates extensive bare surfaces on slopes and initiates primary succession can be caused by water, wind, gravity, or ice. Clements (1928) also described how low-growing vegetation can help stabilize bare slopes at the surface and how roots can contribute to stabilization at varying depths. Practical efforts such as tree planting began to address slope erosion aggravated by deforestation in the early twentieth century. Efforts in northeastern New Zealand, for example, reduced sediment yield from deforested slopes by 50% within a 10-year period from 1949 to 1958 (Derose *et al.*, 1998). Similar soil conservation efforts were widespread at that time, including in Europe (Coelho, 2006) and North American (Vincent *et al.*, 2009).

Vegetation dynamics on landslides (sometimes explicitly addressing successional changes) were not examined extensively until the mid to late twentieth century, mostly in studies from temperate climates found in North America (Langenheim, 1956; Flaccus, 1959; Miles & Swanson, 1986; Adams & Sidle, 1987), South America (Veblen & Ashton, 1978; Veblen *et al.*, 1980), New Zealand (Mark *et al.*, 1964; Johnson, 1976), Australia (Melick & Ashton, 1991), Africa (Lundgren, 1978), and Asia (Pandey & Singh, 1985). Studies of vegetation dynamics on tropical landslides followed, particularly in the Caribbean (e.g., Garwood, 1985; Guariguata, 1990), and within a decade numerous aspects of landslide succession could be summarized (Walker *et al.*, 1996). Landslides have also been studied as parts of regional disturbance regimes. Garwood *et al.* (1979) found that landslides covered up to 10% of certain regions in Panama and 49% in New Guinea, while Restrepo & Alvarez (2006) determine that at least 0.3% of Central American montane ecosystems were affected by landslides each century. Matthews (1992) recognized landslides as a disturbance associated with glacial moraines and Oliver

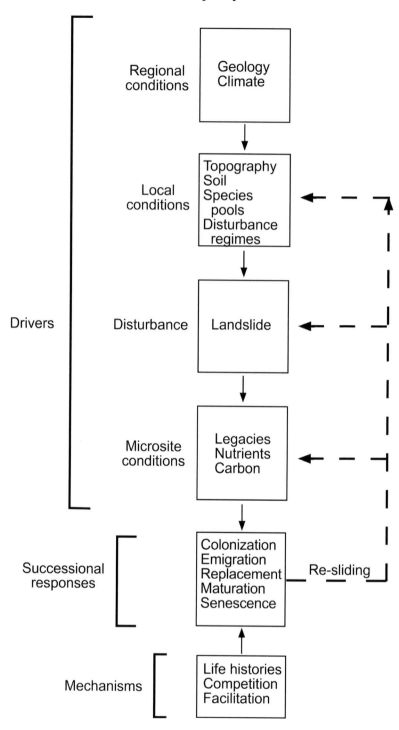

et al. (1985) estimated that nearly 25% of a deglaciated area in Washington, U.S. was subject to rock slides. Landslides can also be triggered by dunes, earthquakes, floods, mines, roads, and volcanoes. Succession has been monitored closely on the resulting surfaces (Crisafulli *et al.*, 2005; Dale *et al.*, 2005). Landslides can, in turn, trigger floods, treefalls, and herbivore outbreaks, among other disturbances (Walker, 1999). For example, landslides frequently dam rivers and cause flooding when the dams erode (see Chapter 2; Schuster, 1995). Interest in landslide succession has developed in part from concerns about landslides as hazards to human lives and properties (Cruden & Fell, 1997; Petley, 2010) and in part from the need to conserve (Usher & Jefferson, 1991; Usher, 1993) and restore (Pandey & Singh, 1985; Chaudhry *et al.*, 1996) their unique ecosystems (see Chapter 6). As noted in Chapter 1, geological studies of landslides have a longer history than ecological studies and provide an excellent source of information on temporal changes in the physical aspects of landslides (Sharpe, 1960) and practical tools for predicting and mitigating landslide hazards (see Chapter 6).

Factors that affect landslide succession are complex, incorporating both abiotic and biotic features of an ecosystem. Geology and climate provide the regional conditions, which over time determine the local conditions of topography, soils, species pools, and disturbance regime (Fig. 5.2). The abiotic features of the disturbance (intensity and severity) determine the

---

Fig. 5.2. Major drivers of landslide succession. Drivers of landslide succession are presented as a hierarchy of long and large regional drivers (geology and climate) that direct local conditions of topography (slope, aspect), soil status (chemistry, texture, stability, and organic content), and the pool of available species (regional fauna and surrounding vegetation and its phenological status). The current disturbance regime is also influential in determining the course of landslide succession. Once a landslide is triggered, microsite conditions drive the successional response. These conditions include legacies of undisturbed patches of soils or seed banks, nutrient inputs (mineral weathering, atmospheric deposition, bird inputs, nitrogen fixation, plant uptake) and outputs (leaching, denitrification, volatilization), and carbon inputs (plant litter, dead animals, rafts of surrounding soils) and outputs (erosion). Microsite conditions constrain the process of landslide succession through their influence on colonization (wind, water, and animal dispersal), emigration (of colonists as high-light niches fill), species replacements (driven by the mechanisms of competitive, facilitative, and neutral, life history-related interactions), maturation (increases in nutrients, biomass, mycorrhizae, seed banks but decreases in light and erosion rates), and senescence of canopy vegetation (more light and erosion but less biomass and available nutrients). Re-sliding (dotted lines) effectively resets landslide succession through its influences on microsite and local conditions.

conditions upon which the successional response proceeds. Many other variables provide site conditions that influence successional responses, particularly the changing availability of resources such as nutrients and carbon that can move in or out of a landslide during succession. Walker *et al.* (1996) proposed that soil stability and fertility determined successional pathways on Puerto Rican landslides (Fig. 5.3). Further evaluation of this model suggests that soil nitrogen and slope stability are both important (Shiels *et al.*, 2008) and that organic carbon is more likely to come from sloughing of forest soil into the landslide than from growth by new colonizing plants (Shiels *et al.*, 2006). In general, a young landslide is characterized by high light, low soil nutrients, and low biomass; an older landslide is usually more shaded and more nutrient- and biomass-rich (see Chapters 3 and 4).

The biotic response to site conditions is the sequential replacement of plant and animal communities, which is a function of their life history characteristics and interactions (positive, negative, or neutral). Interactions that promote successional change are considered facilitation while interactions that delay successional change are considered competitive inhibition (Table 5.1). These processes are not exclusive, can be "turned on" or "turned off" (Odum 1959; Walker, 2012), and can even co-occur or vary in sequence, so it is the relative balance of all species interactions that drives successional change (Walker & Chapin, 1987; Callaway & Walker, 1997). Herbivory (see Section 5.2.5) and non-native species (see Section 5.2.6) can also affect successional dynamics on landslides, sometimes in unexpected ways. Successional trajectories are therefore determined by the mutual influences of abiotic factors such as post-landslide erosion, cyclones, soil texture and moisture, and microclimates (Fig. 5.4; see Section 3.3.2) and biotic factors such as species composition and relative abundances, above-ground structure and growth rates, and root densities. When erosion re-occurs, landslide succession is reset, but it can take either a similar or a different trajectory (see Section 5.2.7). The numerous variables that influence landslide succession make predictability low, although similar responses to limiting variables can occur among groups of landslides (Shiels *et al.*, 2006).

The importance of facilitative interactions is likely to be higher in early than late succession because of the difficulties of establishing in a harsh environment (see Section 4.3; Walker, 1999). Competitive interactions often dominate later, as competition among plant species for nutrients, water, and light becomes more intense (Walker & Chapin, 1987). Landslides are a good place to examine interactions among species because

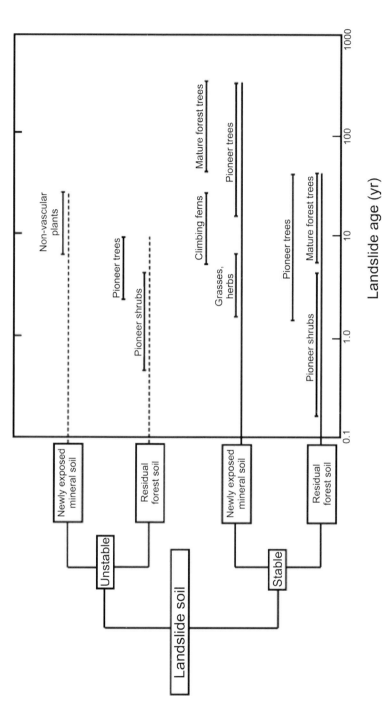

Fig. 5.3. Four proposed successional trajectories for Puerto Rican landslides, depending on soil stability and organic content (highest in residual forest soils). Succession proceeds most rapidly on stable, organic soils. From Walker *et al.* (1996), with permission from John Wiley & Sons.

Table 5.1. *Types of species interactions in primary succession on landslides*

Interaction type	Description	Successional implications and mechanisms	Selected references (see text for more)
One-way			
+	Obligatory facilitation	Succession only if facilitator present	Clarkson & Clarkson, 1995
+	Facultative facilitation	Accelerates succession	Shiels & Walker, 2003
	Direct	Dispersal	
	Indirect		
	Immediate	Site amelioration	Dalling & Tanner, 1994; Walker, 1994
	Delayed		Chaudhry et al., 1996; Shiels et al., 2008
−	Competitive inhibition	Delays succession	
	Direct	Removes light, water, nutrients; prevents germination	Veblen et al., 1980; Reddy & Singh, 1993; Velázquez & Gómez-Sal, 2009a,b
	Indirect	Changes disturbance regime	Singh et al., 1984; Velázquez & Gómez-Sal, 2007
+/−	Commensalism	Nurse plants	Guariguata, 1990; Francescato et al., 2001
Two-way			
0/0	Tolerance	No direct interactions among species	Pandey & Singh, 1985
+/+	Double facilitation	Mutualisms, nurse plants that benefit	Chaudhry et al., 1996
+/−	Contramensalism	Facilitator later out-competed	Francescato et al., 2001
−/+	Competitive inhibition (or competitive displacement)	Inhibition benefits inhibitor	Claessens et al., 2006[1]
−/−	Non-hierarchical	Effects depend on life histories	Walker et al., 2010a
	Hierarchical	Increasing competitiveness during succession	Pandey & Singh, 1985; Velázquez & Gómez, 2009a[2]
Three-way			
	Indirect facilitation or competition	Promotes species diversity	Walker et al., 2010a
	Differential response	Promotes species diversity	Bellingham et al., 2001
	Cyclical	Promotes species diversity	Kessler, 1999; Elias & Dias, 2009

[1] Competitively superior on new landslide scars.
[2] Asymmetric, intraspecific competition for light.

Modified from Walker & del Moral (2003).

(a)

Fig. 5.4. Successional sequence on landslide ES-1 near the El Verde Field Station, Luquillo Mountains, Puerto Rico. (a) 6 mo; (b) 18 mo; (c) 22 mo (note Hurricane Hugo damage to young *Cecropia schreberiana* stems seen in (b); and (d) 80 mo (note full canopy of *Cyathea arborea* tree ferns). Photographs by L.R. Walker.

(b)

Fig. 5.4. (cont.)

(c)

Fig. 5.4. (cont.)

(d)

Fig. 5.4. (cont.)

they provide sharp physical gradients where the relative importance of different types of interactions can be contrasted (Shiels & Walker, in press; Walker, 2011).

5.2.2 Facilitation

The harsh physical environment typical of early primary succession can be quite difficult for potential colonists to tolerate. New landslide surfaces can be exposed to winds and rains and vulnerable to secondary erosion; a lack of shade can result in extreme temperature ranges and soil nutrient levels are generally low (see Section 3.4.2). For some species, however, landslides provide a favorable habitat to establish, particularly if the species are not adapted to the shade and root competition of adjacent forest understories (Dalling & Tanner, 1995) or because they are small-seeded (Metcalfe *et al.*, 1998) and require exposed soil surfaces free of obstructing leaf litter (e.g., *Clethra occidentalis* in Jamaica). A plant species that establishes a resident population in such environments can ameliorate the harshness for other species, thereby facilitating their dispersal, colonization, growth, reproduction, or survival (Bellingham *et al.*, 2001; Walker & del Moral, 2003). For example, on landslides in southern New Zealand, *Leptospermum scoparium* is a shrub that apparently facilitates succession by ameliorating new landslide scars and promoting establishment of later successional trees (Mark *et al.*, 1989). Facilitation can be direct when another species is the direct benefactor of the facilitator (e.g., when the facilitator protects another species from herbivory). Facilitation can be indirect through general (not species-specific) habitat amelioration (e.g., improved soil fertility), or when species that inhibit successional turnover are themselves inhibited (a three-way interaction). Facilitation can alter the rate of turnover among successional stages, frequently by accelerating community change. In some successional models, facilitation was thought to be obligatory, whereby the environmental changes that the first colonists made were required for the second wave of colonists (obligatory facilitation or relay floristics model; Clements, 1916; Egler, 1954; Connell & Slatyer, 1977). A corollary to this facilitative effect was the idea that the changes made by the first colonists did not improve their own chances of reproduction so they were eventually replaced. However, there is much more evidence for facultative succession (optionally facilitative) than obligatory succession (where facilitation is required; Walker & del Moral, 2003). Facilitation is now recognized as just one of many contributing factors driving landslide succession.

Evidence for facilitation of landslide succession comes from several sources and includes direct facilitation, indirect facilitation through habitat amelioration, or indirect facilitation through three-way interactions. Direct facilitation occurred on Puerto Rican landslides when trees facilitated bird dispersal of seeds of forest species (see Fig. 4.2; Shiels & Walker, 2003). Indirect facilitation occurred on several tropical landslides where fast-growing pioneer trees such as *Trema micrantha* (Vázquez-Yanes, 1998; Velázquez & Gómez-Sal, 2009a) and *Cecropia schreberiana* (Brokaw, 1998) produced shade and abundant leaf litter that moderated temperature and moisture extremes and improved soil stability and nutrient availability. Similarly, *Alnus nepalensis* was effective in ameliorating landslide soils in the Himalayan Mountains of India because its nitrogen fixing abilities, fast growth, and copious leaf litter improved soil nutrients and organic matter (Chaudhry *et al.*, 1996). Miles *et al.* (1984) also noted the importance of *Alnus rubra* on landslides in Oregon where it was a dominant pioneer. The facilitative role of nitrogen fixing plants is well recognized in primary succession, including on landslides (Walker & del Moral, 2003). In one survey, nitrogen fixing plants were of intermediate abundance on landslides (mostly as herbaceous legumes or actinorhizal plants) compared to glacial moraines where they were more abundant, and volcanic surfaces where they were less abundant (Walker, 1993). The facilitative role of nitrogen fixers can be overstated because the nitrogen fixing plant may dominate available resources and recycle its own nutrients, which in turn delays succession (Walker, 1999; Pabst & Spies, 2001; Halvorson *et al.*, 2005). Alternatively, both the nitrogen fixer and adjacent plants can benefit, in a two-way mutualism or double facilitation (Chaudhry *et al.*, 1996). Another mode of facilitation from habitat amelioration comes from dense thickets of Gleicheniaceae ferns that stabilize landslide soils (Fig. 5.5(a); Shiels *et al.*, 2008), permit the buildup of soil organic matter, soil nitrogen, and soil moisture (Walker, 1994; Walker & Shiels, 2008), and provide shade that can promote germination of woody colonizers (Ohl & Bussmann, 2004), such as *Tabebuia heterophylla* on Puerto Rican landslides (Walker, 1994). Finally, three-way facilitation occurred when Puerto Rican landslides were colonized by woody pioneers that indirectly facilitated succession to late successional forests by inhibiting the growth of vines, forbs, grasses, and thicket-forming ferns (Gleicheniaceae); these herbaceous plants, in turn, inhibited late successional tree growth, so the inhibition of an inhibitory interaction results in net facilitation (Walker *et al.*, 2010a). Another type of three-way interaction occurred on New Zealand landslides where several tree

(a)

Fig. 5.5. Thickets of colonizing plants on Puerto Rican landslides.
(a) Gleicheniaceae ferns (*Sticherus bifidus* & *Gleichenella pectinata*); (b) forbs and
graminoids; and (c) tree ferns (*Cyathea arborea*). Photographs by A.B. Shiels
(a) and L.R. Walker (b), (c).

species responded differently to facilitation by a nitrogen fixing shrub
(Bellingham *et al.*, 2001).

5.2.3 Competition

Interspecific competition, or the negative effect of one species on
another, has an important role in directing successional trajectories. Certain species slow or arrest succession by preventing establishment of
species representing the next successional stage, either by resource pre-
emption or antagonistic effects (allelopathy). This process is called competitive inhibition and can last as long as the inhibitor lives. Competitive
displacement, on the other hand, involves one species replacing an established species (Walker & Chapin, 1987) and can accelerate succession.
Competition for resources often focuses on light (particularly in mid to
late stages of succession) and nutrients (often in early and late stages).

(b)

Fig. 5.5. (cont.)

Late successional declines in productivity and nutrient availability (and concomitant increases in light) can result from long-term resource consumption and leaching. These declines are termed retrogression and may occur over millions of years (Peltzer *et al.*, 2010). Species replacement

(c)

Fig. 5.5. (cont.)

may, in some cases, be largely determined by the initially decreasing and eventually increasing light:nutrient ratios (Tilman, 1985) as suggested for succession to oak forests on several Himalayan landslides (Reddy & Singh, 1993).

Thicket-forming species are often inhibitors of succession on landslides (Langenheim, 1956; Velázquez, 2007) for several reasons. They typically take advantage of the high light, low nutrient conditions; spread vegetatively; and, through their dominance of early successional resources, reduce or eliminate establishment of later successional plants. The inhibitory effects of thicket-forming species are related to their longevity, size, canopy cover, and density relative to similar characteristics of species of later successional plants (Walker *et al.*, 1996; Callaway, 2007). Thicket-formers on landslides can be trees (Reddy & Singh, 1993; Pabst & Spies, 2001), shrubs (Langenheim, 1956), ferns (Guariguata, 1990; Walker, 1994; Walker *et al.*, 2010a), or forbs and graminoids (Fig. 5.5; Velázquez & Gómez-Sal, 2009b; Walker *et al.*, 2010a). For example, where pine trees (*Pinus roxburghii*) were the initial colonizers of landslides in the central Himalayas, they maintained their dominance throughout a 25 year chronosequence (Reddy & Singh, 1993). The low nutrient content of pine litter likely inhibited the invasion of oak trees (*Quercus leucotrichophora*; Singh *et al.*, 1984). Similarly, the dense shade of *Alnus rubra*, the dominant tree in early succession on landslides in coastal Oregon (U.S.), led to the decline or elimination of forbs and tree seedlings of other species, even those of the shade-tolerant *Tsuga heterophylla* (Pabst & Spies, 2001).

Scrambling ferns in the Gleicheniaceae are the first colonizers on many tropical landslides (see Section 4.5.2) and typically form thickets that can delay forest succession for several decades by monopolizing resources (Walker & Sharpe, 2010). Their dispersal by spores, subsequent vegetative expansion with indeterminate growth, dense layers of senesced leaves and rhizomes up to several meters thick, live rhizome mats, slow decomposition, rapid recovery after fire, and potential allelopathic traits make them effective inhibitors of landslide succession (Fig. 5.6; Slocum *et al.*, 2004, 2006; Walker *et al.*, 2010a). While there can be some promotion of germination of tree seeds under scrambling fern thickets, perhaps due to higher soil water, early seedling growth is inhibited by the 12- to 100-fold reduction of light levels under the thickets (Walker, 1994; Shiels & Walker, 2003). Dead rachises and leaflets remain for several years on the live portion of the leaves, contributing to the reduction of light transmission to the landslide surface. Rhizome mats can also develop that are > 30 cm deep (Slocum *et al.*, 2004), further deterring the establishment of other plants. For example, more seeds of forest species were found on landslides in Puerto Rico that were bare or covered with grass than on landslides covered with scrambling fern thickets (Shiels & Walker, 2003). Even if seeds of forest species were able to germinate, their lack of contact with mineral soil would limit growth. In addition, the slow decomposition of scrambling ferns immobilizes nitrogen and phosphorus (Maheswaran & Gunatilleke, 1988), but may allow the gradual accumulation of soil carbon (Russell *et al.*, 1998; Walker & Shiels, 2008) and long-term erosion control on landslides.

Tree fern thickets can also inhibit landslide succession (Fig. 5.5(c); Walker *et al.*, 2010a). Tree ferns are common landslide colonists (see Section 4.5.2; Walker & Sharpe, 2010) and tend to outcompete scrambling ferns in fertile patches on landslides in the Dominican Republic (Slocum *et al.*, 2006), Tanzania (Lundgren, 1978), Bolivia (Kessler, 1999), and New Zealand (Stewart, 1986). In addition to reducing light levels, they tend to sequester a high proportion of available nutrients (Vitousek *et al.*, 1995). On several Puerto Rican landslides, decomposition rates

Fig. 5.6. Dense mats of dead rachises and live rhizomes of two ferns in the Gleicheniaceae (*Sticherus bifidus* and *Gleichenella pectinata*). Photograph by L.R. Walker.

of the dominant tree fern (*Cyathea arborea*) were higher than those of the dominant woody species (*Cecropia schreberiana*; Shiels, 2006), suggesting that dominance in that case was due to characteristics other than nutrient immobilization. Tree ferns can facilitate the growth of epiphyte communities on their trunks or serve as nurse logs for both herbaceous and woody plant species (Walker & Sharpe, 2010).

Many thicket-formers are weedy plants promoted by human activities such as fire (Velázquez & Gómez-Sal, 2009b). For example, in areas adjacent to a large landslide in Nicaragua, farmers commonly burned crop residues during the dry season. These fires expanded into the landslide where the fire-prone grass *Hyparrhenia rufa* was dominant, creating a positive feedback loop because the grass returns quickly after being burned (Velázquez & Gómez-Sal, 2007). In contrast, in Taiwan, the aggressive native grass *Arundo formosana* helped stabilize landslides, reducing erosion by 80% in 6 years without human intervention (Lin *et al.*, 2006). Alternatively, grass cover can be replaced within several years by vegetative expansion of nearby scrambling ferns, particularly when soil nutrients remain at levels that limit the establishment of forest species (Walker & Boneta, 1995). Scrambling ferns may (Aragon, 1975) or may not (Walker, 1994) be allelopathic, but their other traits make them effective inhibitors in landslide succession (Slocum *et al.*, 2004). Ultimately, despite their initial inhibitory effects, scrambling ferns may have a delayed and indirect facilitative effect on landslides, where they increase soil stability and increase soil organic matter, thereby improving the conditions for later successional species (Shiels *et al.*, 2008; Walker & Shiels, 2008). Thicket-forming species, therefore, can have both negative and positive influences on landslide succession (Fig. 5.7).

Intraspecific competition for resources occurs among the same species. This type of interaction can have successional implications on the wide range of habitats that landslides present, particularly when the species of concern is dominant across that range. On a large Nicaraguan landslide, Velázquez & Gómez-Sal (2009a) found evidence supporting intraspecific competition among populations of *Trema micrantha*, a common woody pioneer of disturbed tropical environments (Garwood, 1985; Campanello *et al.*, 2007). In fertile and stable depositional zones, *T. micrantha* individuals competed with each other through asymmetric competition for limiting light (the tallest trees won). The short-stemmed individuals that survived during the 2 year study period were ones that grew rapidly in height. In less stable erosional zones of the landslide, which were also relatively low in soil nutrient availability, *T. micrantha* individuals did not develop canopy hierarchies. Instead, all individuals remained small, although those with greate diameter growth were more likely to survive. *Trema micrantha* is clearly a versatile type of pioneer species that is able to allocate resources to height or diameter

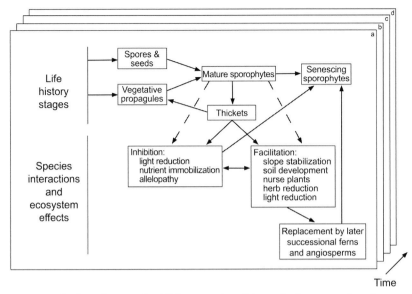

Time

Fig. 5.7. Thicket effects on landslide succession. Dispersal of spores and seeds or vegetative propagules to a site results in development of mature sporophytes that eventually senesce. Sporophytes can either inhibit or facilitate transitions to sequential successional stages (planes b, c, d, etc.) as individuals (dotted arrows) or through a variety of changes that thickets create in the local environment. Modified from Walker & Sharpe (2010) with permission from Cambridge University Press.

growth depending on the landslide environment that it inhabits. Such versatility suggests that its use as a stabilizer of disturbed habitats for restoration activities is warranted (Velázquez & Gómez-Sal, 2009a). Intraspecific competition is likely a common feature among thicket-forming species on landslides.

5.2.4 Life history characteristics

When species growing together do not appear to facilitate or compete with each other, the tolerance model of succession can be applied (Connell & Slatyer, 1977). This model is sometimes associated with the initial floristics model (Egler, 1954), which suggests that many species arrive early in succession but that sequential dominance occurs due to variability in lifespans and serial conspicuousness (visual dominance). However, in Connell & Slatyer's original model, although species initially do not interact immediately following a disturbance, later success is achieved by the species that can best tolerate reduced resource levels. This process is essentially a form of competitive displacement (Walker & Chapin, 1987). On some Himalayan landslides, pioneer annual forbs persisted throughout 40 years of succession, even while perennials gradually gained dominance (Pandey & Singh, 1985). Thus, there was a gradual shift of dominance without any clearly defined successional stages. On landslides in northern New Zealand, kauri trees (*Agathis australis*) are early colonists that are also long-lived. This combination of traits plus return intervals of landslides that are frequently within the lifespan of a given tree allow the kauri trees to out-compete angiosperm tree species (Claessens *et al.*, 2006) in a type of relationship where the inhibition benefits the inhibitor (contramensalism) (Table 5.1). Similarly, *Fraxinus platypoda* trees are frequent and abundant colonists of landslides in Japan, forming dominant, single-cohort forests (Sakio, 1997).

Life forms are often a factor in determining the nature of an interaction between two species. For example, on Bolivian landslides scrambling ferns and club mosses were early colonists and may facilitate succession by stabilizing the surface (Kessler, 1999). They were outcompeted by tree ferns, which were, in turn, outcompeted by forest tree species. Some tree ferns remained but eventually died from senescence, and forest canopies tended to open up with age from intraspecific competition (self-thinning, *sensu* Westoby, 1984) and senescence. A second period of inhibition of tree establishment by scrambling ferns then occurred, as the ferns more readily colonized forest gaps than did tree seedlings. Intriguingly, fern species richness did not necessarily decline, but rather shifted to yet another life form – the emergence of epiphytic ferns on remaining tree ferns and tree trunks (Kessler, 1999). Thus, even within a single taxonomic group such as ferns, life forms have a role in determining patterns of landslide succession. Similar shifts in fern life forms occurred on Hawaiian landslides (Restrepo & Vitousek, 2001), with the erect but short *Nephrolepis multiflora* and the creeping but open-canopied *Odontosoria chinensis* dominating for the first several decades, followed by the denser canopies of the scrambling ferns and tree ferns. Tree ferns were present in mature forests in Hawaii (Restrepo & Vitousek, 2001), unlike Caribbean forests where tree ferns are largely restricted to landslides and other gaps (Slocum *et al.*, 2006; Walker & Sharpe, 2010). On Japanese landslides, herbaceous life forms colonized first, followed by shrubs and then trees; one of these colonists (a grass, *Miscanthus sinensis*) may facilitate the establishment of woody species by stabilizing landslide soils (Nakamura, 1984). Similarly, large moss cover on Ecuadorian landslides enhanced germination of woody pioneers both by compensating for the loss of water after a landslide and by facilitating scarification of seed coats (Myster & Sarmiento, 1998). Mosses also facilitated woody species establishment on landslides in the Azores on the most stable sites. However, on unstable portions of the landslides, the moss carpets, which can reach 1 m in depth, increased the risk of re-sliding when they absorbed large amounts of water (Elias & Dias, 2009). The influence of life form on landslide dynamics is therefore not always predictable.

Life stage is another determinant of the balance between facilitative and competitive interactions (Walker & del Moral, 2003; Walker *et al.*, 2003) in landslide succession, as seen from some of the examples already discussed. Each stage in the life of an organism, including dispersal, germination, establishment, growth, survival, and reproduction, can potentially be facilitated or inhibited by other species (Walker, 1994; Shiels & Walker, 2003; Walker & del Moral, 2003; Slocum *et al.*, 2004; Cammeraat *et al.*, 2005; Velázquez, 2007). Dispersal can be facilitated by trees that provide birds a place to perch and defecate seeds onto landslides, but those trees or other ground cover that attracted the birds can also inhibit establishment through their shading and leaf litter (Shiels & Walker, 2003). Woody plant germination can be facilitated by ferns from the Gleicheniaceae on Puerto Rican landslides, but when trees overtop the ferns, they can eventually outcompete and replace them (Walker, 1994). Establishment, growth, and survival are facilitated by species that stabilize the slope, ameliorate the microsite, or decrease the frequency or intensity of other types of disturbances such as secondary erosion. For example, on abandoned agricultural terraces dominated by fruit trees in a landslide-prone area of Spain, grasses and forbs were the initial colonists and they contributed to the development of soil strata, aeration, and carbon accumulation as well as to a reduction in surface erosion (flow; Fig. 5.8; Cammeraat *et al.*, 2005). These changes likely facilitated the establishment and growth of later successional shrubs (*Ulex parviflorus* and *Crataegus monogyna*) and trees (*Pinus halepensis*). Finally, reproduction can be facilitated by species that provide food for pollinators, or otherwise promote reproduction (Walker & del Moral, 2003), although we know of no evidence for this hypothetical interaction on landslides.

5.2.5 Herbivory and pathogens

Herbivory has been recognized as an important plant–animal interaction in secondary (Brown & Gange, 1992) and primary (Walker & del

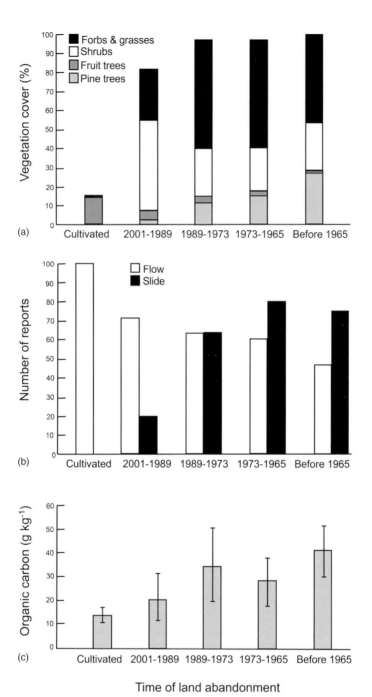

Fig. 5.8. Changes in (a) vegetation cover, (b) erosion type, and (c) soil organic carbon (mean ± S.D.) following abandonment of agricultural terraces in Spain. From Cammeraat *et al.* (2005) with permission from Springer.

Moral, 2003) succession. Granivores can influence colonization of landslides. Black rats (*Rattus rattus*) are a formidable seed predator in most ecosystems where they have been introduced (Towns *et al.*, 2006; Shiels & Drake, 2011), and droppings of these rats were found on Puerto Rican landslides (Shiels, 2002). Seed predation by insects has been reported for *Cecropia schreberiana* in Puerto Rico and for *Urera caracasana* and *Witheringia coccoloboides* in Costa Rica, but fungal pathogens may have caused more seed loss than predation (Myster, 1997).

Herbivory can slow successional change when a plant facilitator is negatively affected by herbivory. For example, stem borers and leaf miners periodically damage thick stands of the nitrogen fixing herb *Lupinus lepidus* that have colonized the erosive volcanic slopes of Mount St. Helens since its 1980 eruption (Fagan & Bishop, 2000). Herbivory can accelerate succession when early successional species are preferred. For example, seedlings of *Salix* spp. and *Populus balsamifera* trees are preferred by hares (*Lepus arcticus*) and moose (*Alces alces*) over seedlings of *Picea glauca* trees on central Alaskan floodplains (Bryant & Chapin, 1986). Sometimes disturbances can temporarily reduce herbivore pressure in succession. In the Aleutian Islands of Alaska, for example, *Lupinus nootkatensis* is one of just a few species to establish successfully (from surviving, buried propagules) on the newly ash-covered and highly erosive slopes of Kasatochi Volcano (Fig. 5.9; Box 5.1; Talbot *et al.*, 2010). However, the 2008 eruption apparently destroyed populations of its most abundant insect herbivores (Sikes & Slowik, 2010), giving *L. nootkatensis* a temporary reprieve from herbivory (except by some hungry gulls; Plate 14). *Lupinus nootkatensis* appeared most robust in the deposition zone of landslides below cliff bases where erosion of new ash deposition has been rapid (Talbot *et al.*, 2010). Herbivory is often stage-specific, especially when its host population is not an early colonizer. For example, the largely coniferous forests in the Rocky Mountains of Colorado (U.S.) do not sustain large insect outbreaks until trees reach at least 70 years of age. In regions where snow avalanches regularly kill the dominant *Picea engelmannii* trees, insect herbivores have a minor role in the early decades of plant succession (Veblen *et al.*, 1994). Alternatively, early successional vegetation and distinct microclimates found on landslide scars can attract both insect and mammalian herbivores. Effects of herbivory on plant succession can be difficult to distinguish from other factors governing changes in species composition. In the landslide-strewn Kokatahi Valley in New Zealand, non-native possums (*Trichosurus vulpecula*) have been suggested as causes of the decline in late successional, native forests dominated by

Fig. 5.9. An earth flow on the rapidly eroding ash deposits from a 2008 eruption of Kasatochi Volcano, Alaska. See Box 5.1. Photograph by L.R. Walker.

Metrosideros umbellata and *Nothofagus* spp. (Rose *et al.*, 1992). However, cohort senescence of the trees, inhibition of germination by litter of other species, increased landslide or earthquake frequency, or climatic shifts may also influence succession (Veblen & Stewart, 1982; Allen *et al.*,

Box 5.1 Plant succession despite high rates of erosion

When Kasatochi Volcano erupted in 2008, it provided an excellent laboratory to study primary succession. Lawrence and other scientists have been visiting the island each year since it erupted to document the rapid changes. The eruption deposited tens of meters of ash on Kasatochi Island in the Aleutian Islands, Alaska. Rapid erosion of that ash in debris slides and debris flows has led to the formation of one 40 m deep canyon and many smaller gullies and rills across the southern slopes of the island (Fig. 5.9). Following the eruption, volcanic ash eroded at rates of 10^4 m^3 km^{-2} year^{-1}, causing the shoreline of this 3 km diameter island to recede about 100 m (Waythomas et al., 2010). Colonists of this largely barren, landslide-covered landscape appear to be almost entirely from survivors of the eruption. Plants that survived as roots, underground stems, or seeds, including *Lupinus nootkatensis* (Plate 14), are now slowly expanding in areas where the ash layer was eroded (e.g., cliffs and cliff bases, landslides, and bluffs) (Talbot et al., 2010). About 500 000 seabirds, half of which were least auklets (*Aethia pusilla*), nested on the island prior to the eruption and are now attempting to nest again. However, the rock crevices and vegetation that they and other seabirds prefer for nest sites are still unavailable. Once seabird colonies re-establish, they will have a strong positive effect on soil nutrients and therefore on plant succession. Gulls are introducing some dead plant matter from other islands (the nearest are 25 km away) to make their temporary nests, but no germination has been observed at these scattered gull nests. Gull colonies have altered primary plant succession on other volcanoes in Iceland (Magnússon et al., 2009), New Zealand (Clarkson & Clarkson, 1995), and elsewhere (Walker, 2012) by introducing plants and fertilizing the nutrient-poor volcanic substrates. For now, we have the unusual situation that plant growth is limited to survivors of the eruption with no significant inputs from elsewhere. Areas of active erosion are removing many of the few survivors (Plate 8), but are also uncovering others, so expansion of the vegetation is beginning.

2003), confounding any simple interpretation of the role of herbivory (Bellingham & Lee, 2006).

Biotic interactions such as herbivory and plant pathogens are potentially weaker on tropical islands than on continents due to shorter periods of co-evolution (Janzen, 1973; Augspurger, 1984). In contrast, island flora and fauna are highly vulnerable to recently introduced herbivores and pathogens for which they have not evolved any defenses (Atkinson, 1989; Courchamp & Caut, 2005). Weaker interactions might have less influence on succession than strong ones. However, Myster (1997) did not find differences in levels of herbivory between Puerto Rican and Costa Rican landslides. Myster (2002) also examined insect herbivory and foliar pathogens on two landslides in Puerto Rico and found < 7% leaf loss in *Cecropia schreberiana*, a common woody landslide colonist, and 25%–34% leaf loss for *Inga vera*, a nitrogen fixing tree, which is a later colonizer of landslides and forest gaps. Continental studies had generally equivalent or lower levels of herbivory and disease than found in Puerto Rico (Myster, 2002), and one possible explanation is that *Cecropia* spp. trees are defended from herbivores by ants on the continent, but not on islands such as Puerto Rico (Putz & Holbrook, 1988). Additional protective factors, such as leaf phenolics and tannins, vary among studies (usually on sites other than landslides) so conclusions about the role of herbivory in succession across regional gradients seem premature, even if there are some similarities in the herbivores found on landslides on islands and continents (Myster, 1994).

5.2.6 Non-native species

Typical non-native invaders of landslides have small seeds, are wind-dispersed, and reproduce rapidly. Such r-selected species include grasses, ferns, plants in the Asteraceae, and other small-seeded species; they also tolerate temperature and moisture stress (see Chapter 4) and sometimes spread via rhizomes or stolons (Lundgren, 1978; Francescato & Scotton, 1999). Succession can be altered by the colonization of non-native species in a variety of ways (Prach & Walker, 2011). A few of the potential effects of non-native species include the creation of novel communities, alteration of ecosystem structure and function, inhibition or facilitation of native species, and the arresting or diverting of successional trajectories. A successional framework provides a useful template within which to study the effects of non-native species (Meiners *et al.*, 2007), including the consequences of their eradication or control. Novel communities (Hobbs *et al.*, 2009) make it more difficult to predict the outcome of succession because they are poorly understood but potentially critical in determining successional trajectories. Disturbance is not always a good predictor of non-native invasions (Moles *et al.*, 2012). Non-native species can alter ecosystem properties directly, such as when they introduce a new function like flammability (Hughes *et al.*, 1991; D'Antonio & Vitousek, 1992; Smith *et al.*, 2000) or nitrogen fixation (Vitousek & Walker, 1989). Non-native species often alter the relative success of native species, leading to changes in species turnover and diversity (Yurkonis *et al.*, 2005) and these changes, in turn, can alter trajectories and increase divergence. Landslide succession in Jamaica, for example, is altered by the tree *Pittosporum undulatum* (Dalling, 1994) and arrested by the herb *Polygonum chinense* (P. Bellingham, pers. comm.). Alternatively, early successional dominance by non-native species can decline with succession, as reported for landslides in New Zealand (Smale *et al.*, 1997). Despite the rapid increase in studies of non-native species, the effects of landslide disturbances on invasions have not been well studied.

The mixtures of native and non-native species that disperse to and colonize new landslide surfaces generally reflect the surrounding biota. For example, landslides that are in the center of large reserves where native species prevail (e.g., in the Azores; Elias & Dias, 2009) are much less likely to be colonized by non-native species because of the great distances to non-native propagule sources. In contrast, dispersal of non-natives is facilitated by human-altered landscapes such as farms, villages, and roads. Non-native plants, such as the forb *Desmodium nicaraguensis* and the grass *Hyparrhenia rufa*, were abundant on the large landslide on Casita Volcano, Nicaragua, where farms and villages were intermixed with forest (Velázquez & Gómez-Sal, 2007). Where farmland had fragmented remaining forest in Tanzania, Africa, non-native shrubs (e.g., *Lantana trifolia*), trees (e.g., *Acacia mearnsii* and *Eucalyptus maidenii*), and crop plants (*Sorghum vulgare* and *Phaseolus vulgaris*) colonized 1–7 year old landslides (Lundgren, 1978). Similarly, roads increased the spread of non-native plant species to landslides in the Cascade Mountains of Oregon (Parendes & Jones, 2000) and facilitated landslide colonization by *Miconia calvescens*, which is one of the most problematic non-native plants on Tahiti and other Pacific islands (Meyer & Florence, 1996). Additional disturbances, such as cyclones, can also facilitate the spread of non-native species in tropical forests (Bellingham *et al.*, 2005; Murphy *et al.*, 2008). For example, in the Blue Mountains of Jamaica, Hurricane Gilbert triggered the spread of *Pittosporum undulatum* throughout the forest (Bellingham *et al.*, 2005) and landslides (Dalling, 1994).

Landslides alter ecosystem conditions by damaging or destroying native communities and their seed banks; by exposing low-nutrient, often unstable soils; and by altering competitive balances among native and non-native communities (Willmott, 1984). These altered conditions can favor invasion by non-native species (Restrepo *et al.*, 2003) and sometimes lead to shallow-rooted plant communities, which could possibly increase the frequency of landslides and abundance of non-natives (Miles *et al.*, 1984; Meyer, 1996). However, more evidence of the effects of variable root structure on slope stability is needed (Stokes *et al.*, 2009). Fire-promoting, non-native invaders of landslides are also likely to promote an increase in fire frequency and reduce long-term slope stability (see Section 5.2.3; Chapter 6).

The Hawaiian Islands are a hotspot for non-native species invasions and they contain among the largest numbers of non-native species of all Pacific Islands (Denslow *et al.*, 2009). The Hawaiian flora now has more non-native plant species that have naturalized than native species, which is in part a result of the relatively recent geological and biological development on very isolated islands (Wagner *et al.*, 1999). The number of non-native seedlings that invaded landslides in Hawaii outnumbered native species invasions both in numbers of species (14 vs. 6) and individuals (895 vs. 322) (Restrepo & Vitousek, 2001). Furthermore, removal of non-native grasses and orchids from landslides resulted in the recruitment of additional non-native plants, which included some species previously unrecorded on the landslides (Restrepo & Vitousek, 2001).

On Hawaiian landslides, a non-native tree fern (*Sphaeropteris cooperi*) from Australia out-competes native tree ferns (*Cibotium glaucum*; Fig. 5.10). *Sphaeropteris cooperi* grows faster, produces more leaves, and retains its leaves longer than does *C. glaucum*; leaves of *S. cooperi* are also faster to decompose than *C. glaucum*, more shade tolerant, and have higher nitrogen and phosphorus content than *C. glaucum* leaves (Durand & Goldstein, 2001a; Allison & Vitousek, 2004; Amatangelo & Vitousek, 2009). These traits allow *S. cooperi* to colonize not only landslides but intact rainforests as well, and the higher nitrogen content of *S. cooperi* potentially increases rates of nitrogen cycling (Durand & Goldstein, 2001b). Experiments suggest that *S. cooperi* leaf litter differentially facilitates growth and nutrient status of some native species under controlled conditions, but its net effect under field conditions is likely to be inhibitory for most native species (Chau *et al.*, in press). Tree ferns are not the only non-natives altering landslide succession in Hawaii. Experimental removal of non-native species of grasses and orchids on landslides on the island of Hawaii led to improved recruitment and growth of the dominant native tree (*Metrosideros polymorpha*), and, in some cases, to invasion by other non-natives (e.g., *Rubus argutus*,

Fig. 5.10. The invasive tree fern *Sphaeropteris cooperi* in Hawaii (canopy) and native tree fern *Cibotium glaucum* (understory). Photograph by M. Chau.

Epilobium ciliatum; Restrepo & Vitousek, 2001). Clearly, non-native plants can be an important component of landslides in both temperate and tropical locations. Knowledge of the level of disturbance and the types of species that comprise the matrix surrounding a landslide can help predict non-native species invasions on landslides. Due to the high frequency of human visitation to erosion-prone mountain environments, future landslide plant communities will likely be novel mixtures of native and non-native species, perhaps with novel successional trajectories.

5.2.7 Trajectories

Multiple successional trajectories on landslides result from the sum of the complex factors that drive landslide succession. Landslides are among the most heterogeneous of surfaces on which primary succession occurs (Walker *et al.*, 2009). The initial conditions can include a range of substrate conditions, from exposed bedrock to patches of intact remnant soil. Soil remnants often contain their original complement of plants and animals (biological legacy; Dalling, 1994; Senneset, 1996). The role of these legacies can be pivotal in determining initial colonists and subsequent species transitions (Shiels *et al.*, 2008), or have little influence if the survivors of the pre-landslide biota fail to colonize the more eroded patches of the landslide (Walker *et al.*, 1996). Legacy effects are most strongly noted in the lower deposition zone, where original pools of seeds and vegetative propagules are supplemented by additions from the upper landslide erosion. Velázquez & Gómez-Sal (2008) noted that succession in the deposition zone of a Nicaraguan landslide was dominated by fast-growing tropical trees, while slower colonization occurred in the upper landslide where soil fertility and instability limited colonization. Trees also typically dominate the deposition zone of temperate landslides (see Fig. 4.7; Flaccus, 1959; Miles & Swanson, 1986). Initial substrate heterogeneity is further complicated by secondary erosion, which can introduce patches of fertile soil into a relatively infertile habitat (see Section 3.3.2). Additional heterogeneity is introduced by litter addition from surrounding vegetation, variable shading, and uneven dispersal of propagules. Propagule dispersal and successful colonization of favorable microsites is still a very poorly understood process (Walker *et al.*, 2009). Thus, the trajectories of succession among several landslides often diverge (Fig. 5.11). Myster & Walker (1997) examined successional trajectories on 16 landslides in Puerto Rico over a period of 5 years and found little convergence of pathways among landslides or between landslides and surrounding forest vegetation (Fig. 5.12). Part of that variation was likely due to differences in soil type, elevation, aspect, and other physical features (Shiels *et al.*, 2008; Shiels & Walker, in press). There were tendencies toward increased shade tolerance following initial soil stabilization;

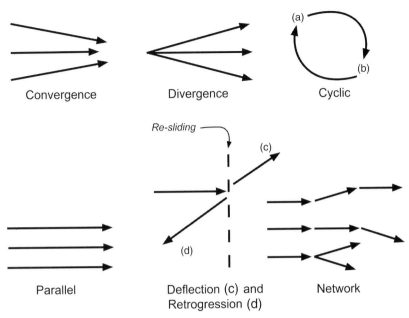

Convergence   Divergence   Cyclic

Parallel   Deflection (c) and   Network
Retrogression (d)

Fig. 5.11. Successional trajectories. Cyclic succession can involve two or more communities (e.g., (a), (b)). Re-sliding can lead to divergence (c) or retrogression (d). Networks can have multiple stable states. Modified from Walker & del Moral (2003) with permission from Cambridge University Press.

soil nutrient availability and local seed availability were also important determinants of landslide successional trajectories. In contrast, Zarin & Johnson (1995b) did find some convergence of soil nitrogen, phosphorus, potassium, and magnesium values in adjacent mature forests within 55 years on Puerto Rican landslides (but much slower recovery of carbon and calcium); Dalling (1994) found slower responses on Jamaican landslides, with estimates of 500 years for convergence to pre-disturbance levels of above-ground biomass.

In addition to convergence and divergence, successional trajectories can be cyclic, parallel, diverted, networked, or retrogressive (Fig. 5.11; Walker & del Moral, 2003). First, landslides can undergo cyclic succession when there are several stages that are replaced in a regular pattern (Elias & Dias, 2009). Landslides in Bolivia that are dominated initially and later in succession by scrambling ferns represent cyclic aspects of vegetative cover (see Section 5.2.3; Kessler, 1999), although total species composition varied substantially. Second, parallel development was shown by Myster & Walker (1997), where total species composition developed

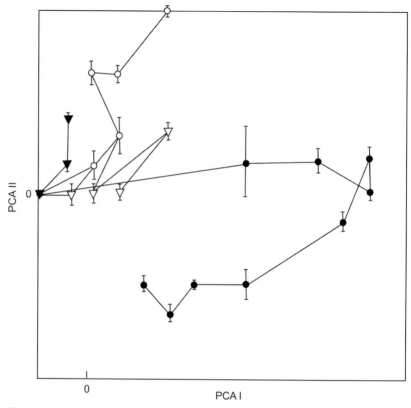

Fig. 5.12. Successional pathways for four Puerto Rican landslides (denoted by four different types of symbols) starting at the same left-most point on the graph. Each point is the average PCA score (coordinate) for all plots sampled for a given landslide at a given sampling date. Modified from Myster & Walker (1997) with permission from Cambridge University Press.

in a similar pattern on some of their 16 Puerto Rican landslides and most plots were dominated by the same common species. In northern Canada, landslides in three areas followed parallel trajectories of vegetation development, although warmer inland locations were more favorable to growth (Cannone *et al.*, 2010). Third, diverted successional trajectories are most common on landslides where secondary disturbances such as erosion (Shimokawa, 1984) and fire (Velázquez & Gómez-Sal, 2007, 2009b) occur and the stochastic nature of early succession results in a new community. This trajectory is particularly likely where non-native species are newly established in the perimeter of the landslide and are able to compete with the traditional colonists (e.g., *Sphaeropteris* on Hawaiian landslides). Fourth, networks are complex trajectories with multiple pathways. For example, landslides can be dominated for decades by forbs, scrambling ferns, or tree ferns in Puerto Rico (Walker *et al.*, 2010a) and elsewhere (Slocum *et al.*, 2004), giving rise to multiple stable states (Suding & Hobbs, 2009b). Finally, retrogression occurs when carbon and nutrient accumulations cease and begin to decline. This pattern occurs in late stages of succession, often after thousands of years (Wardle *et al.*, 2004; Peltzer *et al.*, 2010), but can occur at much shorter scales and even cycle with periods of progressive succession (increase in carbon or nutrients) at decadal scales (Walker & del Moral, 2009). On landslides, re-sliding (see Chapter 3; Walker & Shiels, 2008; Elias & Dias, 2009), particularly after a period of carbon and nutrient accumulation, can be considered a form of retrogression. On Japanese landslides, re-sliding occurred with sufficient frequency to deter the growth of mature forests (Nakamura, 1984; Shimokawa, 1984).

The study of successional trajectories can be direct or indirect. Direct measures of change involve repeated measurements over many years and are feasible only where there is a long-term research program or very dedicated individuals. Therefore, most measurements of landslide succession are done using chronosequences that involve a space-for-time substitution (Pickett, 1989). Sites of different age are assumed to represent a sequence of development, where the older sites went through the successional stages currently represented by the younger stages. Given the lack of predictability and frequent divergence of landslide seres, the chronosequence approach can be problematic (Johnson & Miyanishi, 2008). The best use of the chronosequence approach is when there is good evidence of temporal links among the stages (Fastie, 1995). These links can be established through aerial photos, presence of transition vegetation, tree rings, lichen growth, fossils, pollen cores, changes in soil depth, carbon isotope ratios, and other techniques (Nott, 2006; Walker *et al.*, 2010b). Bull and colleagues (Bull & Brandon, 1998; Bull, 2010) dated the ages of New Zealand landslides (rock falls) to within about 5 years by using lichen dating. Spatial patterns of rocks of a certain age were then used to create seismic maps. Some parameters (species richness, cover, vegetation structure, and soil organic matter accumulation) are more likely than others (e.g., species abundance and composition) to show convergence and therefore are appropriate to measure in chronosequence studies (Walker *et al.*, 2010b). For the study of millennial-scale changes in vegetation and soil development on landslides, chronosequences are the best available tool. Multiple short-term processes (e.g., nutrient pools, microbial biomass) are often predictable within the longer chrono-sequence framework (Chapin *et al.*, 2003; Bardgett *et al.*, 2005).

5.3 Temporal dynamics at landscape scales

The spatial heterogeneity that landslides contribute to landscapes (see Section 2.3) is not a static phenomenon, but one that changes over time as landslides and the matrix of vegetation that they are embedded in undergo succession and are impacted by the regional disturbance regime (Pickett & White, 1985) and longer-term geological forces (Swanson *et al.*, 1988). For example, post-landslide erosion and more extensive re-sliding (see Section 3.3.2) can reset succession, initiating new spatial and temporal patterns. When landslide return intervals are long (e.g., > 200 years), succession can reduce the contrast between the landslide scar and its matrix (Shimokawa, 1984). Moreover, landslides interact with other types of disturbances (e.g., deforestation, Restrepo & Alvarez, 2006; or fire, Walker & Boneta, 1995; Cannon, 2001) that affect a given land-scape to create a disturbance regime. These interactions can alter patterns of landslide occurrence and landslide succession, providing a shifting backdrop that can contribute to the variety of successional trajecto-ries. The sometimes sharp physical gradients both within landslides and across landscapes that contain landslides help generate a variety of biotic responses but these physical drivers are also in flux, albeit at relatively slower turnover rates than biological drivers. For example, successional changes in flora and fauna usually occur more frequently than geological changes such as re-sliding or uplift (see Fig. 2.1). Biotic responses to both geological (e.g., fertile soil patches) and biotic (e.g., competition among colonizers) drivers contribute to an overlay of temporally dynamic patches on a relatively stable geological template (Swanson *et al.*, 1988).

Dispersal is an important determinant of temporal heterogeneity within a landslide (see Chapter 4) because neither its timing nor its end result is easily modeled (Hupp, 1983; Dalling, 1994; Shiels & Walker, 2003). For example, seeds of the pioneer tree *Cecropia schreberiana* can be dispersed to landslides by bats (Wunderle *et al.*, 1987) or survive landslides in situ, germinating when exposed to increased red:far red light ratios (Vázquez-Yanes & Smith, 1982). Similarly, birds may disperse seeds to landslides, but the rate of dispersal is dependent on the presence of perches and on the type of ground cover that may already exist on the landslide (Shiels & Walker, 2003). On two Puerto Rican landslides located only

Fig. 5.13. Talus slopes are prominent landscape features in the Swiss Alps. Photograph by B. Cohen.

a few kilometers apart, Walker & Neris (1993) found many different species of wind-dispersed seeds. Such differences have led to different successional outcomes on the two landslides (Myster & Walker, 1997).

Landslides contribute to the physical diversity of landscapes through their influences on topography, soils, and habitats (Table 5.2; Geertsema & Pojar, 2007). For example, topographical changes created by landslides include the formation of cliffs, gullies, ridges, talus, and the damming of rivers and formation of lakes (Fig. 5.13; Schwab, 1983; Cruden *et al.*, 1993; DeLong *et al.*, 1997; Geertsema & Pojar, 2007). Some of these changes can have long-term consequences, as when succession is very slow on exposed talus slopes in New Zealand (Whitehouse, 1982) and new landslides are created before the vegetation recovers (Allen *et al.*, 1999). Landslides also alter soils by exposing new parent material, changing existing soil chemistry, mixing organic and inorganic soils, and creating islands of infertility (e.g., slip faces) and fertility (e.g., rafted vegetation from above the landslide) (Huggett, 1998; Zarin & Johnson, 1995a,b; Butler, 2001). These topographical and soil changes create novel and altered habitats to which the local flora and fauna respond.

Table 5.2. *Physical diversity created by landslides and its ecological consequences, with an emphasis on ecosystems in British Columbia, Canada*

Type of diversity	Type of landslide	Landslide influence	Ecological consequences	References
Site	Many	Scarps and cliffs formed	Increased slope	Geertsema & Pojar, 2007
	Debris flows	Gullies formed	New microhabitats, climates	Schwab, 1983
	Spreads, flows	Hummocks and ridges formed	Drier, warmer than surroundings	DeLong et al., 1997
	Rock slides	Rubble	Increased drainage	Geertsema & Pojar, 2007
	Many	Rivers dammed	Wetter, cooler, new aquatic habitat	Cruden et al., 1993
	Rotational; flows	Lake creation	Wetter, cooler, new aquatic habitat	Geertsema, unpublished observations
Soil	Many	Parent material exposed	Resets soil development	Huggett, 1998
	Many	Change in chemistry	Changes in organic matter and nutrient availability	Lambert, 1972; Geertsema & Schwab, 1995; Zarin & Johnson, 1995a
	Flows	Mix of organic and inorganic	Changes in hydrology, texture, density, porosity; layering of soil types	Butler, 2001
	Translational	Rafted soil and vegetation	Increased heterogeneity	Smith et al., 1986

Habitat			
Rock cliffs	New, steep surfaces formed	Snags, debris for raptors, fish; resets forest succession	Swanson & Franklin, 1992; Geertsema, 1998
Debris flows	Longitudinal variation in sediments	Betula spp. on outer, sandy edges; transition to Picea on inner cobble	Yajima et al., 1998
Debris flows	Variable habitats	Alnus to Picea and Tsuga except on upper zone (no Alnus)	Smith et al., 1986
Debris flows	Gullies formed	Populus trees	Lewis, 1998
Rock slides	Talus	Lichens	Bull & Brandon, 1998; Geertsema & Pojar, 2007
Rotational; cliff collapses	Talus	Nest holes for birds	Geertsema & Pojar, 2007
Many	New mineral soil surfaces	Pioneer vegetation supports herbivores including bears	Geertsema & Pojar, 2007
Rock slides	Exposed mineral soil; entrapment of water by rough surfaces	Populus outcompetes tundra-grassland vegetation on new surfaces	Lewis, 1998
Rock falls	Covered Picea muskeg	Salix and Betula shrubs invade	Geertsema & Pojar, 2007
Mud flows	Silt exposed; rafted vegetation	Herbs and horsetails; surviving shrubs, sedges, mosses, lichens	Lambert, 1972
Earth flows	Lakes formed	Beavers use dams, lakes, and colonizing vegetation	Geertsema & Pojar, 2007

Modified from Geertsema & Pojar (2007) and references therein.

Regional biodiversity can be maintained by landslides because of the habitat heterogeneity that they contribute to; but locally, landslides often reduce habitat for organisms (Schuster & Highland, 2007). Landslides can denude 1%–2% of forested areas every 100 years in mountainous terrain such as found in Chile (Veblen & Ashton, 1978) or British Columbia, Canada (Smith *et al.*, 1986). However, much larger percentages of the landscape can be affected by disruptions of faults, such as the Alpine Fault in New Zealand (Wells *et al.*, 2001), or when human activities increase landslide frequencies (see Chapter 6). In Chile, old-growth forests were reduced in area by landslides and the fast-growing landslide colonists *Nothofagus* spp. predominated (Veblen *et al.*, 1980). Freshwater organisms can also be affected by landslides through sediment inputs to rivers and lakes. Fish are particularly vulnerable because the sediments can reduce light and therefore algae production, reduce populations of insects and other invertebrates, damage fish gills, and damage spawning grounds (Sidle *et al.*, 1985; Swanston, 1991; Schuster, 2001; Staudacher & Füreder, 2007). Coastal aquatic organisms face similar problems from sediment inputs by landslides; sedentary organisms such as barnacles, clams, and corals do not have the ability to escape high levels of turbidity resulting from up slope landslides (Schuster & Highland, 2007).

Despite their destructive aspects, landslides do provide habitats suitable for colonization by many plants and animals (see Chapter 4). Cliffs provide habitats for birds and rodents (Swanson *et al.*, 1988; Williams *et al.*, 2010) and escape terrain for goats and sheep (Sappington *et al.*, 2007). Debris flows create habitats with variable topography and soil texture. Gullies and ridges provide wetter or drier microhabitats favored by different species. On a debris flow in Japan, tree colonization depended on soil texture, with *Betula* spp. on sand and *Picea glehnii* on cobble (Yajima *et al.*, 1998). The exposed rocks of talus slopes are often colonized by lichens (Kubešová & Chytrý, 2005; Nott, 2006), favor burrowing rodents such as pikas (Millar & Westfall, 2010), and provide some birds with nesting habitat (Sheffield *et al.*, 2006). Exposure or deposition of mineral soil can remove or bury existing vegetation and provide new surfaces that favor colonization of pioneer herbs in tundra (Lambert, 1972) or *Populus tremuloides*, *Betula* spp., or *Salix* spp. trees in taiga (Lewis, 1998; Yajima *et al.*, 1998; Geertsema & Pojar, 2007). Such pioneer vegetation can attract herbivores from rodents to bears, while wolverines and other predators sometimes feed on animals killed in annual snow avalanche chutes in British Columbia (Rozell, 1998). Later successional stages on landslides can provide habitats for organisms that utilize more complex forest

Plate 1. Rock fall (upper part) and rock avalanche (lower part), Grand Canyon, U.S. Photograph by L.R. Walker.

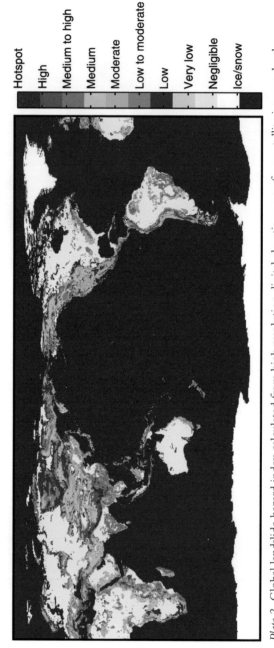

Hotspot
High
Medium to high
Medium
Moderate
Low to moderate
Low
Very low
Negligible
Ice/snow

Plate 2. Global landslide hazard index calculated from high resolution digital elevation maps from satellite imagery by the National Aeronautics and Space Administration. Over half of the land surface is susceptible to landslides and 4% (mostly in subtropical and tropical regions) is highly susceptible. From Hong *et al.* (2007) with permission from the American Geophysical Union.

Plate 3. Coastal erosion is both a persistent cause of terrestrial landslides and a source of sediment for submarine landslides, as seen on this peninsula on the coast of Cornwall, England, where the remains of Tintagel Castle (upper center portion of photo) are found. Photograph by L.R. Walker.

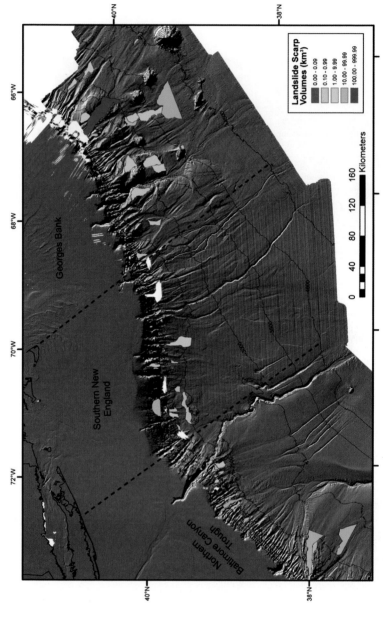

Plate 4. Submarine landslide distribution along the continental slope in the western Atlantic Ocean. From Chaytor *et al.* (2009) with permission from Elsevier.

Plate 5. An amphitheater-shaped landslide near Yanji, Jilin Province, China. Photograph by L.R. Walker.

Plate 6. The slip face and chute zones of a Puerto Rican landslide. Photograph by L.R. Walker.

Plate 7. A valley carved by glaciers and subsequent landslides in the Odelwinkelkees region of the Austrian Alps. Photograph by R.D. Bardgett.

Plate 8. Rapid erosion of volcanic ash from Kasatochi Volcano, Aleutian Islands, Alaska that erupted in 2008. The gully where the people are working was < 1 m deep one year before the photograph was taken (2010) but was > 3 m deep in 2011. Photograph by I. R. Walker.

Plate 9. Cyanobacteria (foreground), lichens, forbs, and ferns are early colonists on a planar (translational) landslide in Puerto Rico. Photograph by A.B. Shiels.

Plate 10. A moss (*Philonotis fontana*) growing on a recent landslide on Kasatochi Volcano, Aleutian Islands, Alaska. Water droplets remain on the vegetation from a recent rainstorm. Photograph by L.R. Walker.

Plate 11. A tree fern (*Cyathea arborea*) on a Puerto Rican landslide with an understory of scrambling ferns in the Gleicheniaceae. Tree ferns are common in all stages of primary succession on landslides throughout the tropics. Photograph by A.B. Shiels.

Plate 12. The monkey puzzle tree (*Araucaria araucana*) is a common tree on landslides in the southern Andes in western Argentina. Photograph by L.R. Walker.

Plate 13. The Spanish ibex (*Capra pyrenaica*) uses steep, eroded slopes in the mountains of the Sistema Central, Spain as escape terrain from predators. Photograph by E. Velázquez.

Plate 14. The nitrogen fixing shrub, *Lupinus nootkatensis*, growing on Kasatochi Volcano, Aleutian Islands, Alaska. This plant and a few others survived the eruption as seeds or vegetative parts in soil that was subsequently exposed by erosion. Note the herbivory by seabirds on some of the seed pods. Photograph by L.R. Walker.

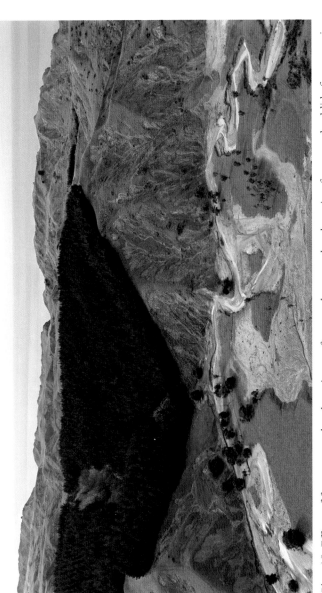

Plate 15. Effects of forest removal and grazing vs. forest replacement by plantation forests on landslide frequency in hilly parts of New Zealand. Note that numerous landslides end in the floodplain where they contribute sediments and alter water quality. See also back cover image. Photograph by P. Scott.

Plate 16. Grazing effects in Iceland. Over 1000 years of heavy grazing have removed most of Iceland's original forest cover, leaving soils exposed and subject to severe erosion. Photograph by A.B. Shiels.

structures, including epiphytes (Kessler, 1999) and monkeys (Kaplan & Moermond, 2000).

Long-term effects of landslide inputs to rivers can be beneficial, particularly when landslides increase habitat complexity by providing large rocks or woody debris to aquatic ecosystems (Sedell *et al.*, 1990). When landslides dam rivers (see Section 2.2.1) and create lakes, forests become flooded, new floodplains are formed, and new erosion and deposition patterns are established. In and adjacent to the newly flooded habitats, floodplain succession is initiated or accelerated, dead snags from drowned trees provide perches for birds, fish obtain new habitats, terrestrial wildlife benefits from new watering holes, and animals like beavers may experience food and habitat improvements (Naiman *et al.*, 1986; Swanson & Franklin, 1992; Geertsema, 1998; del Moral & Walker, 2007). Migratory birds may also benefit from new aquatic habitats resulting from landslides (Amezaga *et al.*, 2002) and fish diversity can increase where gene flow of migratory fish is blocked (e.g., ocean-run trout in the Eel River in California; Mackey *et al.*, 2011). The net effect of landslides on biodiversity is therefore probably beneficial, although not predictably so, especially given the dynamic fluctuations in species composition through colonization and succession. Landslides that increase habitat diversity will most likely increase biodiversity, while large or persistent landslides may decrease both local and regional biodiversity, particularly when they promote dominance by a few aggressive colonists.

5.4 Conclusions

Landslide succession is a dynamic process that is characterized by high spatial heterogeneity, sharp and diffuse abiotic gradients, on-going disturbances, and interactions between abiotic and biotic drivers within landslides, between landslides and their surrounding matrix, and among landslides across a landscape. Spatial heterogeneity contributes to temporal heterogeneity. For example, incomplete or irregular removal of vegetation and topsoil creates differential starting conditions for succession in the slip face, chute, and deposition zones. On-going disturbances within landslide scars include rafting of forest remnants from above, which introduces further temporal heterogeneity in the form of propagules, organic matter, and nutrients. Post-disturbance erosion of landslide edges or unstable soils can disrupt succession in local patches, while more extensive and severe re-sliding can entirely reset succession.

Biotic drivers of plant succession on landslides include stochastic variables such as dispersal, and positive (facilitative), negative (inhibitory), or neutral interactions among colonists. These interactions can accelerate or inhibit rates of succession. Because a given species can be facilitated and inhibited at different stages of its life cycle, the net effect of all interactions is what ultimately drives succession. Colonizing plant species also affect abiotic conditions including light, soil nutrients, and soil stability. Animals interact with the plant colonists by eating them and dispersing them, or by using the altered habitats; herbivores, pathogens, and non-native species readily alter successional trajectories. Successional trajectories on landslides reflect seres initiated by other types of disturbances, with elements of both convergence and divergence of community properties such as biodiversity. Biodiversity is generally enhanced by landslides because of the increase in habitats in both space and time, which allows colonization by species not found in abundance in undisturbed local habitats.

This chapter has reviewed a number of descriptive and a few experimental studies of terrestrial landslide succession, but there are still many questions that remain. At the scale of individual landslides, humans still do not understand the highly stochastic processes of dispersal and establishment and the interaction of propagules with favorable microsites. We have also not yet explained the role of soil biota in the colonization process, or the influence of early colonists on later ones (priority effects). In addition, surviving organisms and patches of fertile soil (legacies) clearly play an important, but poorly understood role in landslide colonization. Despite much effort, there is still more to determine about how species on landslides interact with each other and how these positive and negative interactions influence successional trajectories. At landscape scales, we need more evaluation of the role of landslide communities in maintaining biodiversity, functional diversity, and carbon and nutrient cycles, particularly in light of increasing influences of humans on landslides (e.g., implications of non-native species; see Chapter 6). For example, are natural landslides more important for biodiversity than anthropogenic ones? Regular, systematic, and standardized observations and experiments will help to address these issues, which are of both theoretical and practical interest (del Moral, 2011). Finally, this chapter has focused on temporal patterns and species interactions on terrestrial landslides, but very little is known about similar processes on submarine landslides (Paull *et al.*, 2005).

6 · *Living with landslides*

Key points

1. Human interactions with landslides have become more frequent and lethal as our populations expand into less stable terrain. This trend suggests that we must better understand what causes landslides and how to mitigate future damage.
2. Disturbances created by road construction, urban expansion, forestry, and agriculture are major contributors to anthropogenic landslides, and each has increased in frequency during the last several decades.
3. The field of landslide risk assessment is growing rapidly, and many new mapping and modeling tools are addressing how to predict landslide frequency and severity. Mitigation of landslide damage is also improving, particularly when new landslides follow patterns similar to previous ones. Despite a broad understanding of landslide triggers and consequences, detailed predictions of specific events remain elusive, due to the stochastic nature of each landslide's timing, pathway, and severity.
4. Biological tools are valuable additions to efforts to mitigate landslide damage. Biological protection of soil on slopes and restoration of species composition, food webs, and ecosystem processes ultimately must supplement technological approaches to achieve long-term slope stability because biological systems are generally more resilient than man-made structures.

6.1 Introduction

Human lives have long been shaped by natural disturbances. Early human societies avoided predictable disturbances by moving to less disturbed lands. Such responses influenced early human migrations, as humans sought refuge from droughts, active volcanoes, glacial advances, and highly erosive slopes (Oliver-Smith & Hoffman, 1999; Keys, 2000).

As human population densities increased and agrarian societies replaced hunter–gatherers, humans adjusted their behaviors to tolerate rather than avoid disturbances. Farmers sought fertile soils that were often in disturbed habitats such as floodplains and on the sometimes unstable slopes of volcanoes covered with mineral-rich ash (e.g., Ilopango Volcano in El Salvador or Mt. Etna in Sicily; Sheets, 1999; Pareschi *et al.*, 2006; Chester *et al.*, 2010; Box 6.1). Temporary evacuations during floods, eruptions, or landslides were followed by former residents returning to the original locations that had become fertilized with nutrient-rich sediments, ash, or topsoil. Humans developed numerous other strategies to be able to live with natural disturbances, including modifying their dwellings (e.g., building on stilts), changing their diets (e.g., eating early successional plants and animals that colonized disturbances), and altering other behaviors (e.g., seasonal migrations to avoid droughts or winter storms). With the advent of industrial societies, anthropogenic disturbances have increased (see Section 6.4); at the same time, humans developed even more sophisticated ways to tolerate or defend against disturbances that included architectural advances (e.g., better foundations to build on unstable, landslide-prone surfaces, levees to endure floods, and stronger infrastructures to resist earthquake damage). However, our phenomenal successes have led to more, rather than fewer, encounters with disturbances (del Moral & Walker, 2007). Global deaths due to landslides show an increasing trend: in the 1970s about 600 people were killed each year by landslides (about one out of every million) whereas by 1990, several thousand were killed each year (about 35 out of every million; Brabb, 1991). Rather than limit road building in mountains vulnerable to landslides, for example, we have continued to expand road networks into previously remote terrain to connect villages with markets, exploit mineral resources, extract forest products, or promote tourism, thereby triggering more landslides and placing more people in harm's way. Temporary evacuations still occur, as during recent landslides in Cameroon (Zogning *et al.*, 2007). Similarly, urban expansion has not been adequately restricted in gullies, on hillsides, or on mountain slopes. This synergism of successful adjustments to disturbance, coupled with our population explosion, has ironically resulted in an increase in the role of landslide disturbances in our lives rather than a decrease (Fig. 6.1; del Moral & Walker, 2007). In addition, we are now creating disturbances, which potentially increase landslide risks and range from local spatial scales (e.g., slope destabilization), to regional (e.g., deforestation, urbanization) and global scales (e.g., climate change). For example,

Box 6.1 Double trouble beneath Peru's tallest mountain

The highest peak in the Peruvian Andes (Mt. Huascarán) is infamous for having spawned two destructive debris flows, one in 1962 and one in 1970. The 1962 debris flow originated at 6300 m a.s.l. from the failure of a hanging glacier due to a sudden warming of air temperatures. As it descended 4000 m in elevation in 5 minutes (maximum estimated speed of 170 km hour^{-1}), it picked up rocks and debris, and then destroyed nine towns and killed 4500 people (Table 6.1; Schuster et al., 2002). Huge boulders were deposited at the base of the debris flow; the largest was 3600 m^3 and weighed over 6000 tons. Lawrence visited the area in 1964 with his family to enjoy the mountain scenery, visit the open-air markets, and soak in some hot springs. The scar from the landslide was still a raw mark on the landscape, with rubble and buried houses as well as bitter memories among the residents of their recent losses. Despite warnings of further instability, the same mountain eroded again in 1970 when a 7.75 M earthquake struck off the coast of Peru. The city of Huaraz was leveled by the earthquake and thousands of landslides were triggered in a 30 000 km^2 area (Schuster et al., 2002); about 70 000 people died in that region from the earthquake and landslides. Disrupted glaciers on Mt. Huascarán again triggered a major debris flow, which killed 18 000 people and wiped out the city of Yungay. The debris flow in 1970 also descended 4000 m in a few minutes and had such high speeds (up to 480 km hour^{-1}) that it overtopped a 150 m high spur as it descended and created a destructive air-blast that preceded it and demolished buildings (Rouse, 1984). Only about 300 people survived, including those who climbed a hilltop cemetery and children visiting a circus that was on relatively high ground. The 1970 debris flow also formed a temporary dam in the Rio Santa which soon burst, sending a destructive flood all the way to the ocean. Today, a new city of Yungay has been erected nearby but the old city remains buried as a memorial to those who died. The remains are marked by remnants of the original cathedral and four palm trees that survived in the original town square (Peruvian Times, 2009).

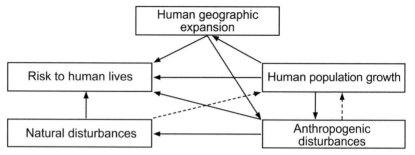

Fig. 6.1. Human population growth leads to geographic expansion, and both of these changes increase anthropogenic disturbances, which in turn intensify natural disturbances and increase risks to human lives. Solid lines indicate a positive influence, dashed lines a negative influence. Modified from del Moral & Walker (2007), with permission from Cambridge University Press.

higher air temperatures are increasing atmospheric moisture and potentially increasing the frequency and magnitude of landslides in some parts of the world (Lateltin *et al.*, 1997). New technical approaches are continually being developed to address our on-going encounters with both natural and anthropogenic disturbances. Local areas prone to earthquakes, hurricanes, volcanic eruptions, and landslides are monitored closely to improve forecasts and give people as much time to evacuate as possible. Landslide risk assessment is a well-developed field of study and addresses how to best live with landslides (Cruden & Fell, 1997; Alcántara-Ayala & Goudie, 2010). Unfortunately, localized erosion is harder to predict than weather patterns. Proactive approaches to minimize the negative effects of landslides on humans include mostly unpopular but ultimately necessary tools such as removing ourselves from regions prone to landslides (e.g., tectonically active zones), relying less on infrastructures to deliver goods and services (e.g., roads that are vulnerable to sliding), and generally mimicking the avoidance patterns of our ancestors. Such a total rearrangement of human lives will not be easy, however, with a much larger human population.

Landslides have affected humans for as long as they have lived in mountainous terrain. Some of the earliest records of landslides are from Asia. In Matsushima Bay, Honshu, Japan, a mega-landslide 6000 years ago led to the collapse of a coastline covering 1×10^6 km^2. The many picturesque islands in the 150 km^2 bay were created by the large deposits from that landslide. We have no direct evidence of the effects of such a landslide on the local human population but can imagine it was catastrophic, particularly because people of the dominant culture at that time

(Jomon) relied heavily on coastal resources (Habu, 2004). In 1556, about 800 000 people were killed by an earthquake and subsequent landslides in Shaanxi Province, China (Hou *et al.*, 1998). During the last century, there have been many recorded deaths from landslides, with five that have killed > 10 000 people (Table 6.1). The human tendency to live in fertile valleys and along waterways results in many of the deaths attributed to landslides. Death tolls appear to be highest in regions with less developed hazard warnings and more fragile dwellings. In this chapter, we discuss how humans interact with landslides. We review how humans have survived, used, and caused landslides; then we cover the modern tools of management of landslide hazards, including prediction, mitigation, and restoration. In Chapter 7, we continue to explore landslide–human synergies at global scales.

6.2 Humans are vulnerable to landslides

Humans inhabit slopes for a variety of reasons, even when those slopes are unstable and prone to landslides. In addition to soil fertility, humans sometimes choose to live on unstable slopes because any future dangers are offset by the immediacy of scenic views, such as along coastal cliffs of California (U.S.). Economic hardship, high population densities, a need to expand farming to marginal lands, and ignorance about potential dangers can also compel humans to reside on unstable slopes. Many residents of Caracas, Venezuela, and Rio de Janeiro, Brazil live on hill slopes because that is the most affordable location to live and still be close to the city and employment opportunities. Residents of suburban areas northeast of Los Angeles, California live at the base of the landslide-prone slopes of the San Gabriel Mountains (DeBiase *et al.*, 2010). Although their wealth is much greater than that of the residents of Caracas and Rio de Janeiro, costs, and concerns about the quality of life in the city (e.g., crime, air pollution, lack of open space) have driven them to the mountains. Ignorance of potential landslide dangers is common, particularly where landslides are not recent and evidence of old landslide scars may not be apparent to most people. House buyers may not be informed about floods, drainage patterns, or the earthquake history of the area. Hills may be considered a scenic plus rather than a potential danger. Even when a house buyer is informed of potential (geological) risks, other factors (e.g., price, scenic views, overall quality of neighborhood, proximity to good schools and work) may override what is seen as acceptable risk of a possible landslide. Whether poor or rich, obligated to living in a

Table 6.1. *A sample of large and lethal landslides in the past 100 years, in decreasing order by volume of displaced material (when known). Larger death tolls are estimates. Where landslides were complex, type represents the most common process*

Volume (10^6 m³)	Location and cause	Type	Date	Deaths
2800	Mount St. Helens, U.S. (volcanic eruption)	Debris flow	1980	5
2000	Usoy, Tajikistan (earthquake)	Rock avalanche	1911	54
2000	Rio Barrancas, Argentina (reservoir failure)	Debris flow and flood	1914	None
1800	Papua, New Guinea (earthquake)	Debris flow	1988	74
1600	Huancavelica, Peru (rainfall, erosion)	Debris avalanche	1974	450
450	Yunnan, China (unknown)	Rock slide	1965	444
300	Longarone, Italy (reservoir failure)	Rock slide	1963	1899
200	Papua, New Guinea (earthquake)	Debris avalanche (dam failure)	1986	None
>150	Sichuan, China (earthquake)	Debris slide	1933	9300
75–110	Napo, Ecuador (earthquake)	Rock and debris slide	1987	1000
60	Nevado del Ruiz, Colombia (volcanic eruption)	Debris flow	1987	23 000
30–50	Yungay, Peru (earthquake)	Debris avalanche	1970	18 000
35	Gansu Province, China (rainfall)	Rotational slump	1983	227
30	Rocky Mountains, Canada (snowmelt and mining)	Rock slide	1903	70
27	Cauca, Colombia (earthquake)	Debris flow	1994	271
25	Rio Paute, Ecuador (rainfall, mining)	Rock slide	1993	None
21	Utah, U.S. (snowmelt and rainfall)	Debris slide	1983	None
15–20	Vargas, Venezuela (rainfall)	Debris flow	1999	15 000
15	Leyte Island, Philippines (earthquake)	Rock slide and debris avalanche	2006	1100
13	Mt. Huascarán, Peru (ice and rock avalanche)	Rock and debris avalanche	1962	4500
Unknown	Gansu Province, China (earthquake)	Sediment flow	1920	180 000
Unknown	Caracas, Venezuela (rainfall)	Debris flow	1999	30 000

Sources (where further examples can be found) include: Hansen (1984b), Schuster (1996a, 1996b), Schuster *et al.* (2002), Sidle & Ochiai (2006), Evans *et al.* (2007), Fort *et al.* (2010), and http://www.landslides.usgs.gov.

landslide-prone area or choosing to, many humans still suffer the consequences of landslides. Sometimes it is just bad luck when one lives near a historically stable slope that erodes due to a particularly intense earthquake or rainstorm or new land use practice up slope. In 1985, Tropical Storm Isabel caused 2 days of intense rain in Puerto Rico, resulting in a landslide in Ponce killing more than 120 people – the highest loss of life from a landslide in the U.S. (Jibson, 1989; Larsen & Torres-Sánchez, 1998).

Submarine landslides that can cause devastating tsunamis are a potential risk for coastline inhabitants. Drilling platforms can also be at risk when their foundations are disrupted by submarine landslides (Bea, 1971; Bea *et al.*, 1983). Harbor facilities are vulnerable for several reasons. Typically, they are built on deltas where sedimentary deposits are inherently unstable and prone to collapse (Hampton *et al.*, 1996). Fjords and other steep-walled shorelines are also popular for harbors because they provide deep-water anchorage for large boats. Harbor facilities are typically constructed on unconsolidated fill, which is particularly vulnerable to earthquakes and the landslides and tsunamis that earthquakes generate (Prior *et al.*, 1982). The damage can be through shaking, flooding, or the loss of hydrostatic support during a tsunami drawdown (Hampton *et al.*, 1996). Finally, extensive harbor development, including support structures and even urban development, destabilizes already unstable deltas or steep shorelines with added mass. Similar concerns occur around newly filled (or emptied) reservoirs where shifting hydrostatic pressures can cause slope instability (Günther *et al.*, 2004).

A final category of people exposed to landslides includes professionals and outdoor enthusiasts who willingly expose themselves to the risk of a landslide. The former include miners, geologists, volcanologists, ecologists, and construction crews, while the latter include rock climbers, skiers, and hikers. For them, the risks are offset by the reward of their jobs or recreational activities.

6.3 Humans use landslides

For those living in landslide-prone regions, there are many ways to co-exist with and even benefit from landslides. Landslides increase habitat heterogeneity and biodiversity (see Chapters 4 and 5), both of which potentially provide benefits to humans. For example, hunters often pursue wild game attracted to the productive, early successional plants that grow on landslides. This same suite of plants also attracts berry pickers, those needing firewood or fodder for livestock, and seekers of decorative ferns or horsetails (*Equisetum*, L. Walker, pers. obs.) and medicinal plants such as scrambling ferns (Robinson *et al.*, 2010). Residents of small farms adjacent to a large (3 km long) landslide in Nicaragua remove *Trema micrantha* trees for firewood from the landslide (Velázquez & Gómez-Sal, 2008), harvest medicinal plants, and access drinking water from springs in the upper portion of the landslide (E. Velázquez, pers. comm.). Firewood is also harvested from landslides in Costa Rican cloud forests (*Alnus acuminata* trees; Kappelle *et al.*, 2000) and medicinal plants from landslides in the Himalayan Mountains of Pakistan (Khan *et al.*, 2011) and India (Uniyal *et al.*, 2000). In India, where medicinal plants such as *Nardostachys grandiflora* and *Rheum moorcroftianum* are abundant on landslides, they are harvested whole for personal use by indigenous people and for sale in local markets (Uniyal *et al.*, 2000). However, high demand for these plants, in addition to grazing by domesticated sheep and goats, has reduced their abundance. These ongoing anthropogenic uses can alter rates and trajectories of landslide succession (Lundgren, 1978) and must be considered in any regional restoration efforts.

Humans also use landslides for intellectual, recreational, and aesthetic activities. Geologists use landslides to study faults and rock strata (see Box 3.2), while ecologists examine successional responses to landslides and explore how they function as gaps in a larger matrix (see Chapters 2 and 5). Sometimes, scientists use landslide deposition zones as helicopter landings in dense forests in New Guinea (Diamond *et al.*, 1999) and Hawaii (A. Shiels, pers. obs.). Cliffs and associated talus slopes are also used recreationally by bird watchers, rock climbers, and hikers (Krajick, 1999), sometimes to the detriment of plant and animal communities (Camp & Knight, 1998; Farris, 1998; McMillian & Larson, 2002). Landslides also provide an aesthetic variety to mountain landscapes, especially when the foliage of plants such as aspen (e.g., *Populus tremuloides*) stands out as light green in spring and summer or yellow, orange, and red in the autumn.

6.4 Humans cause landslides

Humans cause landslides both deliberately and unintentionally. Landslides are deliberately created when engineers want to stabilize slopes (e.g., road cuts, edges of urban lots), create dams, or study the process of landsliding. Several attempts have been made to cause liquefaction of coastal sediments to understand how coastal construction might be affected. In one such effort in Lake Melville, Canada, 1200 kg of explosives were

Fig. 6.2. Landslides often close mountain roads in high rainfall areas such as in the Luquillo Mountains of Puerto Rico. Photograph by A.B. Shiels.

used but caused little displacement of sediments (Couture *et al.*, 1995; Locat & Lee, 2002). In another example, the edge of an old quarry was destabilized by deliberately increasing pore pressure at the base of the slope to follow the movement of the subsequent landslide through inclinometers that had been inserted into the slope (Cooper *et al.*, 1998). Managers of ski areas often trigger snow avalanches to make slopes safer for skiers (Tremper, 2008). However, most anthropogenic causes of landslides are unintentional and are the consequences of various types of land use. In this section, we discuss how various forms of land use trigger landslides, including construction (e.g., roads, railroads, mines, and urbanization), species removals and additions (e.g., forestry, agriculture, non-native species, and failed erosion control efforts), fire, and tourism.

6.4.1 Construction: roads, railroads, mines, urbanization

Construction of roads and railroads is perhaps the most common way that humans cause landslides (Fig. 6.2). Road construction creates landslides by undercutting slopes, reducing root stabilization, adding unstable

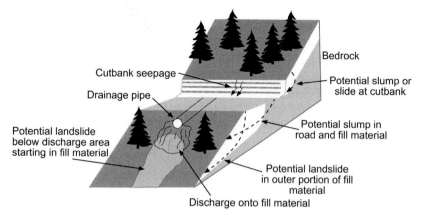

Fig. 6.3. Road effects on slope stability and drainage. Modified from Sidle & Ochiai (2006) with permission from The American Geophysical Union.

fill to a slope, and altering slope morphology and hydrology (Fig. 6.3). These actions alter the balance at a slip plane between the driving and resisting forces (see Chapter 3). The depth beneath the surface of any impermeable layer of soil or bedrock relative to the depth of the road cut will influence how much subsurface flow is intercepted by the road cut, with exposed bedrock intercepting the most flow (Sidle & Ochiai, 2006). Roads on ridges can increase overland flow down slope by reducing absorption by soil and roots; roads in the middle of slopes and in valleys intercept both over land and subsurface flow. Concave slopes and roads in valleys with inadequate or poorly maintained drains also tend to intercept and divert overland flow and subsurface flow from wetlands (Forman *et al.*, 2003). Concentrated overland flow from drains, however, can trigger landslides below the road and alter stream volumes, so drainage management becomes a concern for the entire slope that a road cut crosses (Montgomery, 1994; Wemple *et al.*, 1996, 2001).

Regionally, roads increase soil erosion (Sidle *et al.*, 2006), restructure biotic communities, and alter such ecosystem processes as the flow of nutrients and water (Shiels *et al.*, 2008). Landslides are frequent and problematic along roads in humid and mountainous terrain (e.g., Nepal; Petley *et al.*, 2007), but can also be present in other types of terrain, particularly when roads cut through clays, shales, and other unconsolidated rocks (Forman *et al.*, 2003). Well-studied examples of road effects on erosion come from India, Puerto Rico, and the north-western U.S. In northern India, landslides caused by intense monsoonal rains are frequent hazards along roadsides (Bansal & Mathur, 1976); an estimated 550 m^3 km^{-1} year^{-1} of debris is removed from roadsides (and added to down hill slopes; Haigh *et al.*, 1988), and landslides affect about 60% of the road edges. Similarly, in one study in the Luquillo Mountains in Puerto Rico, landslides from the last 50 years were analyzed with GIS to determine their relationship with roads. Along 268 km of roads in this 276 km^2 tropical forest region, Larsen & Parks (1997) found 1859 landslides within 350 m distance from a road, or about seven landslides km^{-1} of road. The proximity to a road directly influenced landslide abundance; landslides were 2.5 times more frequent and six times more severe within 100 m of a road than between 100 and 350 m from a road. About 25%–50% of all fluvial sediments that erode from the Luquillo Mountains come from landslides (about 110 of a total of 200–400 metric tons km^{-2} year^{-1}). Most landslide sediments (94 tons) come from landslides within 100 m of a road (Larsen & Parks, 1997). In the northwestern U.S., about half of several thousand landslides examined were associated with roads (Montgomery, 1994). For many decades, sediment production from landslides associated with unpaved roads in this region exceeded sediment from forests without roads (Reid & Dunne, 1984; Forman *et al.*, 2003). In addition, one survey noted that landslide damage occurred along 20% of the entire road system in the U.S. between 1985 and 1990 (Walkinshaw, 1992), costing the government $142 million in repairs. Other regions that have reported high costs of road maintenance due to landslide damage include California, the Caribbean, Japan, China, Ecuador, Switzerland, and Turkey. Even the best-constructed and maintained roads can fail, and can sometimes lead to fatalities where they were least expected (Sidle & Ochiai, 2006).

Landslides along railroads are caused by the cut or fill associated with railroad construction and can affect both passengers and maintenance crews. Sometimes, however, roads and railroads are damaged by landslides unrelated to the transportation corridor. For example, the 1903 Frank Slide in the Canadian Rockies was due to freeze – thaw cracks in limestone, but destroyed a section of a railroad and a mine situated further down slope, killing 70 people (see Box 3.1). Similarly, in 1953 in Tangiwai, New Zealand, a rapid debris flow from Ruapehu Volcano weakened a bridge just before a train crossed it, resulting in the death of 151 people (Box 6.2; Stewart, 2004). Occasionally, trains have been able to outrun landslides, as was the case on Mt. Stephen, British Columbia in 1937, when a train narrowly escaped a debris flow (Evans *et al.*, 2002). Transportation corridors through forests generally increase

Box 6.2 The Christmas Eve disaster in Tangiwai, New Zealand

On Christmas Eve, 1953, a night train full of holiday passengers was heading north from Wellington to Auckland on the North Island of New Zealand. As the train approached the hamlet of Tangiwai and a bridge over the flooded Whangaehu River, a lone motorist, realizing the danger, desperately signaled to the train to stop. Apparently, the driver did try to stop the train, saving many in the back, but five railroad cars and the engine raced onto the bridge, which then collapsed, sending 151 people to their deaths. Minutes before the train arrived, a volcanic debris flow (lahar) containing water, ice, rocks, mud, and uprooted trees had raced down the Whangaehu River Valley and weakened the bridge. A volcanic ash dam had broken from pressure due to an increase in water levels inside the crater lake on nearby Ruapehu Volcano. This tragic confluence of train and debris flow remains one of the worst train disasters in history. The poignant tale of rescue efforts and disrupted lives is the subject of several books and documentaries (e.g., Stewart, 2004; Grant, 2012) and lots of speculation. Did a bridge trestle weakened in a 1925 debris flow cause the bridge to fail? What if the debris flow had occurred minutes earlier or the train had been running just a few minutes faster that night? Ruapehu Volcano has been triggering debris flows for thousands of years, with 50 recorded since 1861 and several since 1953 (Lecointre *et al.*, 2004; Graettinger *et al.*, 2010). Warning systems have been installed up slope from railroad and road crossings, and functioned effectively to save vehicles and trains from any damage during a 2007 debris flow.

landslide erosion by two orders of magnitude compared to undisturbed forests (e.g., from 30 to 300 times more in the Cascade Range in Oregon, U.S.; Swanson & Dyrness, 1975) and about one order of magnitude more than clear cuts (O'Loughlin & Pearce, 1976; Sidle & Ochiai, 2006). Clearly, roads and railroads are major causes of anthropogenic landslides.

Mining involves the creation of roads for access and transport, but can also destabilize slopes through the excavation of tunnels and pits, piling of wastes, and impeding drainage. Open-pit mines, including rock and sand quarries, are susceptible to rain-induced erosion (Johnson & Rodine, 1984; Wang *et al.*, 2011), while underground mines are eroded by ground water and subsidence (Oh *et al.*, 2011); both types are vulnerable to earthquake-induced landslides (Moreiras, 2004; Koner & Chakravarty, 2011). Mining activities can destabilize existing slopes through blasting, undercutting, or overloading them. Mines can also alter surface chemistry and texture in ways that do not promote the growth of stabilizing vegetation (Courtney & Mullen, 2009). Dams created intentionally to provide water for mine activities or unintentionally by piling of mine wastes can fail and cause debris flows, sometimes rather spectacularly as has occurred in Spain (López-Pamo *et al.*, 1999), Romania (Bird *et al.*, 2008) and Greece (Steiakakis *et al.*, 2009). When landslide-caused dams fail, there can be similar results (see Section 2.2.1). Mining activities frequently lead to deaths from landslides (Sidle & Ochiai, 2006), but regulations for stabilizing mined slopes in many countries have reduced recent fatalities. Mines are important triggers of landslides across large regions, although the exact extent of mine-related landslides is not clear. Approximately 8% of landslides in one region of West Virginia (U.S.) were associated with mine waste piles, and landslides affected 6% of a mined outcrop in Kentucky (Sidle & Ochiai, 2006). Sometimes active mines are affected by past mining activities, as was the case of the rockslide-debris flow in Wulong, Chongqing (China) in 2009 (Xu *et al.*, 2009). Failure of a karst slope along a layer of shale, influenced by past mining in the region, led to a massive (about 5×10^6 m^3) debris flow and the trapping of miners in an active mine.

Construction of buildings in urban areas may also lead to local destabilization, particularly when it occurs on sloped terrain in high rainfall climates and where population densities are high (Slaymaker, 2010). Additions of buildings or other structures (e.g., walls, dams, bodies of water) to a slope can be destabilizing due to the added weight, particularly when combined with new road construction. Many urban slopes are overloaded by concrete block walls, houses, lawn watering, leaky water pipes, septic systems, construction of building pads, and unstable fill of excavated material, and are therefore at increased risk of sliding (Fig. 6.4). Increased surface runoff from impermeable streets can concentrate in vulnerable areas and trigger landslides. Fill material is particularly vulnerable to sliding when it is poorly compacted and contains organic matter because water readily infiltrates and increases the weight or pressure on the potential slip plane. Because poorly compacted fill material is relatively porous, it is also susceptible to earthquakes, with the height and width of the fill influencing the extent of erosion (Kamai *et al.*, 2004). Urban slopes often lack stabilizing vegetation (Fernandes *et al.*, 2004). Finally, as with road cuts, any excavation into a slope, particularly one

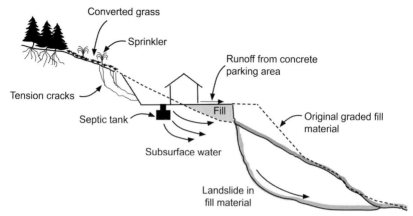

Fig. 6.4. Urban and residential influences on slope stability. From Sidle & Ochiai (2006) with permission from The American Geophysical Union.

composed of inherently unstable clays, will increase instability (Sidle & Ochiai, 2006).

Along the coast near Los Angeles, an infamous but slow-moving landslide called the Portuguese Bend Landslide illustrates the effects of urban land use on slope stability. Part of a much older landslide system, the instability of this region was exacerbated in the 1950s by road building and deposition of construction material, as well as by alteration of ground water conditions from urban development. Drainage wells were installed to remove ground water, but the land still moved about 200 m toward the coast at rates of 0.3 to 2.5 cm day^{-1} (Ehley, 1986; Keller, 1996). Adjustments to this type of steady erosion include frequent attention to broken above-ground utilities, repositioning of houses with hydraulic jacks, and a ban on further development (Keller, 1996).

The expansion of urban areas into sloped terrain is a questionable proposition because it risks both property and human lives. Conditions are particularly conducive to landslides in low-income areas that tend to have poorly built structures and often lack proper water supplies, drainage, and waste disposal (Smyth & Royle, 2000). In Rio de Janeiro, the famous rock spires and steep hills were originally forested but now are mostly denuded due to logging, agriculture, and urban sprawl. Frequent landslides plague this city and occur regularly during periodically intense rains (Jones, 1973). In February 1988, 12 cm of rain in 4 hours caused numerous landslides that killed about 90 people, mostly in towns on the steep slopes (Keller, 1996). Similarly, just one large, earthquake-triggered landslide killed almost 600 people when it swept through a low-income residential area in Santa Tecla, El Salvador in 2001 (Evans & Bent, 2004). Low-income communities are vulnerable in many other cities as well (e.g., Hong Kong, Kingston (Jamaica), and Dunedin (New Zealand); Sidle & Ochiai, 2006). Wealthier residents also reside on steep slopes for aesthetic or cultural reasons (see Section 6.2). Coastal cliffs are also popular but expensive places to live. About 60% of sea cliffs in southern California are affected by landslides (Keller, 1996) and many of these cliff habitats are within the zone of urban expansion. Construction of waterfront structures destabilizes coastlines through damage to stabilizing reefs, dunes, and the excavations needed to build docks, dikes, canals, bridges, and dams (Bush *et al.*, 2009; Walker, 2012). River floodplain construction can also divert the course of a river and lead to new cut banks and erosion.

6.4.2 Species removals and additions: forestry and agriculture

Land use involves manipulations of natural ecosystems through species removals or additions. Both forestry and agriculture usually involve changes in species composition and density that can have both positive and negative effects on slope stability, depending on the relative change in root and canopy characteristics or flammability (see Section 6.4.3). Removal of trees and other vegetation can destabilize slopes by the loss of a protective cover to intercept rain, by increased soil water from reduced evapotranspiration, and by damage to stabilizing root systems (Plate 15; Sidle & Ochiai, 2006). Landslide sediment inputs generally increase several fold in clear cut forests compared to background rates in unlogged forests (Sidle *et al.*, 1985; Clarke & Walsh, 2006) and peak about 5–6 years after deforestation when decomposing tree roots no longer bind the soil and their root channels maximize infiltration (Alexander, 1993). Logging activities (both roads and clear cuts) on unstable slopes can cause more landslides than when done on more stable slopes (Swanson & Dyrness, 1975); and logging slopes at short intervals (e.g., < 25 years) can lead to more landslides than logging at longer intervals (> 25 years; Imaizumi *et al.*, 2008). Increased susceptibility to landsliding following logging typically lasts several decades but declines during that time interval (Sidle & Wu, 1999), perhaps due in part to greater root growth during the longer intervals between logging events (Sidle *et al.*, 2006). Landslide frequency can be reduced by low-impact helicopter-based logging compared to conventional, cable-based, clear-cut logging, but the effect can be less pronounced in gullies than on open slopes (Roberts *et al.*, 2005). Partial clearing does not generally increase landslide rates, probably because of the stabilizing influence of remaining trees and relatively undisturbed ground cover vegetation (Sidle & Ochiai, 2006). Deforestation also can have long-term effects in drainages because landslides alter the rate and content of woody debris that enters streams. Clear cutting provides a short-term increase in smaller debris that enters streams, but tends to decrease overall large woody debris inputs for decades (Potts & Anderson, 1990; Millard, 2000). Woody debris has a central role in providing habitats and nutrients for stream organisms (Gomi *et al.*, 2002), and there is usually a succession of stream invertebrates that respond to decreasing levels of woody inputs from forest clear cutting and debris flows (Kobayashi *et al.*, 2010). Scouring of stream beds by landslide sediments tends to have more deleterious than positive effects on aquatic organisms because it removes benthic organic matter and aquatic vegetation and results in decreased biodiversity (Crozier, 1986; Cover *et al.*, 2010). However, rapid growth of disturbance-adapted trees along riparian corridors can reverse some of these processes (D'Souza *et al.*, 2011).

Conversion of natural forests to timber crops (Fig. 6.5) may or may not destabilize slopes, depending on the resultant root and canopy structure and forest age (Pain & Bowler, 1973; Crozier *et al.*, 1981; Sidle *et al.*, 2006), as well as harvest rotation schedules (Imaizumi *et al.*, 2008) and root decay rates (Schmidt *et al.*, 2001). Sometimes the change in erosion rates from forest transitions can be extreme, as when replacement of native *Nothofagus* spp. forests in New Zealand by *Pinus radiata* plantations led to a 40-fold increase in erosion volume and a 20-fold increase in landslide density. *Pinus radiata* has weaker roots than *Nothofagus* and its roots fail to penetrate the sandstone substrate where it is grown (O'Loughlin & Pearce, 1976). Abandonment of plantation forests or other tree crops can also lead to erosion, particularly when there is a period of low vegetation cover or the new cover is less effective at preventing erosion (Ghestem *et al.*, 2011). Fruit crop abandonment on slopes in Spain led initially to higher erosion rates despite increased vegetative cover because the colonizing grasses had shallower roots than the fruit trees (Cammeraat *et al.*, 2005; see Section 5.2.4; Fig. 5.8).

Conversion of forests to herbaceous crops is likely to decrease overall root strength (Fig. 6.5). However, effects on soil erosion depend on the magnitude, rate, and timing of the conversion. Traditional shifting agriculture, where forests are removed and burned to provide light and nutrients for temporary agriculture, generally is more destabilizing than

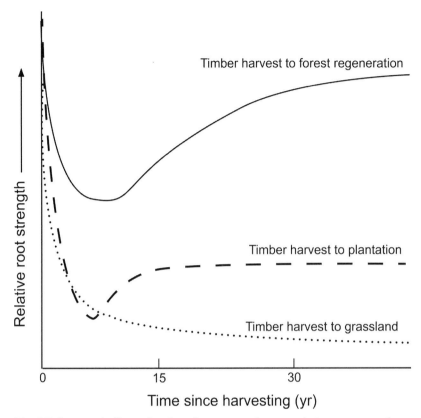

Fig. 6.5. Suggested effects of various forest conversions on relative root strength: timber harvest followed by forest regeneration; timber harvest followed by conversion to agroforestry with plantations; and timber harvest followed by conversion to grassland. Modified from Sidle & Ochiai (2006) with permission from the American Geophysical Union.

logging – in part because it removes both protective ground cover and soil nutrients and thereby delays forest recovery (Perotto-Baldiezo *et al.*, 2004), although generalizations must account for the magnitude of the disturbance. Shifting agriculture can be less disruptive when it is practiced at smaller scales than logging. Forest conversion to crops such as potatoes (India), tea (India and Japan), and corn (Honduras) has been associated with increased sediment loss (Sidle & Ochiai, 2006). Sometimes deforestation is linked to the growing of illicit crops such as coca leaves in Colombia, which can result in increased landslide occurrence (López-Rodríguez & Blanco-Libreros, 2008). Harvesting peat for fuel or sod for landscaping also destabilizes slopes. Agricultural conversion does not always result in more landslides, particularly when there is little burning, and weeds are mulched on site (Lundgren, 1980). Similarly, rates of sediment loss will depend on the type of cover a crop provides. Sidle *et al.* (2006) observed higher rates of erosion from secondary bamboo forests than from coffee plantations in Sumatra. Terracing, used for centuries to maximize agricultural productivity on slopes, can reduce erosion compared to slopes without terraces. However, terraces are also often associated with landslides when they concentrate water (e.g., on flooded rice fields) or are not properly made or maintained. Sediments dislodged from terraces often remain on the slope, but are just redistributed to lower terraces (Shresta *et al.*, 2004).

When forests are converted to pasture, sediment loss from landslides often increases (Plate 16; Heshmati *et al.*, 2011), presumably due largely to the shallower roots of grasses but also potentially due to other factors, including increased fire frequency or decreased interception and uptake of precipitation by vegetation. Grazing, like logging and intensive agriculture, usually involves indirect loss of the topsoil and lower soil layers from reduced plant cover, as well as direct loss or destruction from trampling, plowing, and the use of heavy machinery. Soil compaction reduces water infiltration and sustained grazing can have cumulative and destabilizing effects on slope stability. New Zealand and Iceland are examples where historically recent conversions from forests to grasslands have resulted in extensive erosion (Walker & Bellingham, 2011). In New Zealand, European settlers converted many forested hillsides and native grasslands to pastures of grasses of European origin. This conversion, which happened very rapidly, led to deforestation of 50% of the country between 1840 and 1940, supported in part with rock phosphate from the nearby island Republic of Nauru in Micronesia to offset phosphorus-deficient soils (Walker & Bellingham, 2011). Overgrazing by sheep and cattle further exacerbates erosion and can increase landslide frequency and severity (Glade, 2003). Another pasture grass addition that has altered landslide dynamics is *Hyparrhenia rufa*, which was introduced to Central America from its native Africa for cattle fodder; it now dominates many landslides in the region (Velázquez & Gómez-Sal, 2007, 2009b). Its adaptation to frequent fires has led to arrested landslide succession, fewer trees, and presumably increased erosion on landslides due to less root stabilization by trees (see Chapter 5). Seasonal sediment loss can increase if annuals replace perennials, or if scattered trees replace dense understory species (Versfeld & van Wilgen, 1986; Walker & Smith, 1997). When grasslands are reconverted to forests, sediment and carbon losses can decrease, but there can also be potentially undesirable reductions in biodiversity and stream flow (Whitehead, 2011).

How land use affects slope stability depends on the intensity of a disturbance as well as on climatic factors. The landscape conversion from forest to agriculture took millennia in Europe and Japan (Kerr, 2000; Stringer, 2006), but as agricultural societies expanded and became more efficient at forest destruction, conversion rates accelerated. For example, the forests of Iceland and many forested regions in the Hawaiian Islands were converted to agricultural uses within only a few centuries after the arrival of humans (Walker & Bellingham, 2011). Current rates of conversion to agriculture across wide swaths of humid tropical forests are in the order of years (Larsen & Santiago Román, 2001). Deforested slopes are particularly susceptible to landsliding in the humid tropics with shallow soil development and frequent rains. In one 26.4 km^2 watershed in eastern Puerto Rico, an estimated 2000 landslides have occurred since forest clearing and farming began in 1820 – the equivalent of 80 landslides km^{-2} every 100 years (Larsen & Santiago Román, 2001). Many of the farms were small and intensively cultivated, often on steep slopes. The sediments from all these landslides not only depleted soil fertility and delayed recovery, but also degraded freshwater and marine environments. At the peak of deforestation in the 1940s, nearly the entire original forest cover was lost in Puerto Rico, but subsequent urbanization, industrialization, and emigration resulted in large-scale abandonment of farms and recovery of almost half of the original forest cover (Grau *et al.*, 2003). This reforestation, from 9% to 37% of the island's area between 1950 and 1990, was the fastest reforestation in the world during that period (Rudel *et al.*, 2000). Unfortunately, landslides still continue on Puerto Rican slopes and soil and forest recovery on landslide scars will likely take many more decades (Larsen & Santiago Román, 2001).

6.4.3 Fire

Human-induced fires cause landslides and fire frequency and intensity have been increased by human activities, including fires set for clearing vegetation or burning refuse following logging or agriculture. In Nicaragua, fires that were used to clear agricultural fields often escaped and burned the vegetation on a nearby landslide, thereby altering successional trajectories (see Section 5.2.3; Velázquez & Gómez-Sal, 2008, 2009b) as noted above. Humans also purposefully ignite fires to change vegetation composition and promote grasslands for animal fodder. The most obvious effect of fire on slope stability is the destruction of stabilizing vegetation by the removal or reduction of canopies, ground cover, and roots. Over longer periods, roots decay and increase infiltration rates. Fires also increase water-repellent properties in some soils (DeBano, 2000), which may either increase landslide frequency by promoting overland flow or decrease frequency by reducing infiltration (Sidle & Ochiai, 2006). Burning intervals influence the severity of erosion; maximum erosion is likely to occur when fires burn often enough that large or extensive roots cannot get re-established (Rice *et al.*, 1982). Fires can also promote down slope movement of individual soil and rock particles (dry ravel) because of the loss of cohesion with organic matter (Sidle *et al.*, 2004). Dry ravel is particularly common on granite substrates and sometimes affects debris flows in drainage channels (Cannon *et al.*, 2001). When fires on hillsides increase sediment and debris inputs into drainage channels, they increase surface roughness (decreasing overland flow) and debris mass (potentially destabilizing channel basins). Large storms following fires can result in debris flows that widen drainage channels by triggering landslides along the channel edges. Fires can also remove built-up debris in channels and thereby destabilize stored sediments. Debris flows and drainage channel morphology are therefore potentially affected by fires; the extent to which they are altered depends on the timing and intensity of the rainfall relative to each fire (Sidle & Ochiai, 2006).

6.4.4 Tourism

Tourism is another human activity associated with landslides. Localized erosion is promoted by construction of vacation homes, hotels, and ski areas and the roads needed to access them. Recreational impacts that contribute to erosion include deforestation for ski trails and golf courses, heavy use of trails (sometimes by pack animals), rock climbing, and off-road vehicle use (Webb *et al.*, 1978). Fires triggered by outdoor enthusiasts or arsonists all contribute to localized erosion (Sidle & Ochiai, 2006; Sidle, 2010). Hiking trails over steep terrain afford access to remote beaches and coastlines, but sometimes require hikers to traverse landslides (Fig. 6.6). Interactions of multiple factors accelerate erosion more than single factors. For example, ski trails in Poland eroded two to three times faster when they were also the site of summer hiking trails (Lajczak, 2002). Regions such as the Pakistani Himalayas are experiencing growing resident and tourist populations, which both contribute to an already high frequency of landslides (Rahman *et al.*, 2011). Residents and visitors

Fig. 6.6. A popular trail crosses landslides on the north shore of Kauai, Hawaii. Photograph by A.B. Shiels.

both impact slopes in Malaysian cloud forests, particularly through road construction and house building on steep slopes (Peh *et al.*, 2011). Similarly, increasing tourism in mountainous Turkey is a potential threat to slope stability (Kurtaslan & Demirel, 2011). Sometimes recreational plans are altered to accommodate landslides. In the ski town of Vail, Colorado, buildings from the 1960s, when avalanche predictions were not well developed, have been removed from predicted avalanche chutes. Those chutes are now used as parks in the summer, and barriers have been built to deflect any future avalanches from the remaining buildings (Oaks & Dexter, 1987). Expanding human populations ensure that landslides triggered by recreation in mountainous areas will continue to increase.

6.5 Humans manage landslide hazards

6.5.1 Prediction

The causes of landslides are well known (e.g., earthquakes, rainfall, construction, land use) but predicting when, where, and how a given slope will fail is difficult (Sidle & Ochiai, 2006). Many factors that indicate slope instability have been identified. These include topographical and drainage features, properties of bedrock and regolith, and influences of gravity and pore pressure as well as vegetation-related factors (see Section 3.1). Yet soil properties and slope conditions are highly variable within even short distances and the timing, nature, and location of trigger events are difficult to predict (Keefer & Larsen, 2007). The spatial distribution, type, and severity of past landslides are important components of predicting future landslides because of the assumption that future landslides are most likely to occur under conditions that led to past ones (Zêzere et al., 2004). Predictions of landslide hazards typically focus on either site-specific analyses of individual slopes or on larger, regional risks (Haigh et al., 1988; Gryta & Bartolomew, 1989; Kull & Magilligan, 1994; Cruden & Fell, 1997). Local predictions use a combination of various types of field instruments and modeling. Detailed field examinations of vulnerable sites can help detect the timing and extent of historical landslides in the area (Larsen & Wieczorek, 2006). Field measurements include predisposing factors such as slope angle, aspect, pore pressure, root cohesion, subsurface slippage, and surface deformation, in addition to analyses of current and past land use (see Table 3.1). Laboratory analyses examine shear strength, mineralogy, and density of the substrate. These data are entered into various models to predict landslides, including recent ones that incorporate heat and ground water flow (Keefer & Larsen, 2007).

Regional assessments of landslide hazards can involve integration of data about geological conditions, topography, ground water flow, infiltration rates, seismic records (including distance from an earthquake epicenter), rainfall patterns, and land use (see Table 3.1). Relevant predisposing factors (e.g., slope angle, aspect) for past slope instability can be identified using GIS technology. This way, landslide susceptibility maps are obtained that indicate a spatial probability of future landslides (Brenning, 2005). Landslide hazard maps additionally involve a temporal aspect by taking into account recurrence patterns of landslide triggers (e.g, rainfall; Guzzetti et al., 1999; Zêzere et al., 2004). The integration of data through GIS technology (Gupta & Joshi, 1990; Wu & Sidle, 1995) increases the objectivity of the data compared to earlier methods that relied more on professional judgment (Carrara et al., 1991). A combination of satellite images and aerial photographs can supply information on topography, including slope and aspect, and the water content of vegetation or soils (Menéndez-Duarte et al., 2003). Slope and aspect both influence radiation and therefore potential evapotranspiration and rainfall (Moore

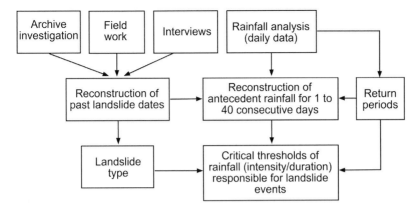

Fig. 6.7. Historical data used to calculate rain thresholds for landslides. Modified from Zêzere *et al.* (2004) with permission from the author.

et al., 1993). Rainfall intensity and duration preceding a past landslide can be used to define critical thresholds for future landslide occurrence (Fig. 6.7; Zêzere *et al.*, 2004). The prediction of ongoing erosion after a landslide is complicated by additional factors including soil type (Walker & Shiels, 2008). Also visible from aerial photographs of large landslides are scarps, debris fans, and lakes in dammed valleys where future landslides might occur (Nott, 2006). Where forests cloak landscapes, a standardized vegetation index can be computed during droughts and wet periods; landslides are typically found where the vegetation is wettest (Kondratyev *et al.*, 2002). Vegetation cover also can indicate where plant communities that have colonized previous landslides differ from the surrounding matrix (see Table 3.1; see Section 6.5.2; Lerol *et al.*, 1992; Smith, 2001), and suggest disturbance frequencies. For example, in Switzerland, bare soil, shrubs, and trees < 2 m tall suggested minimum avalanche frequencies of 1–2 years, while progressively taller and older trees indicated lower frequencies (Perla & Martinelli, 1976). Regional data are collated with local information to produce maps and models (Highland, 1997). Landslide susceptibility maps can sometimes indicate potential severity of landslides (Fig. 6.8; Larsen & Torres-Sánchez, 1998; Larsen, 2008). For example, in Spain, shallow (< 2 m deep) landslides were best predicted by daily rainfall totals whereas deeper (> 2 m) landslides were best predicted by annual net infiltration (annual rainfall minus evapotranspiration; Ferrer & Ayala, 1996). Two-dimensional terrain maps can be expanded in two more dimensions by reconstructing both the three-dimensional

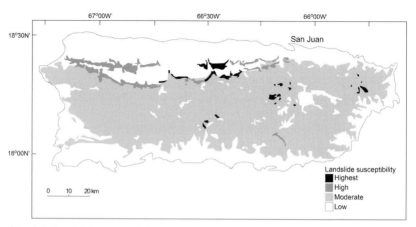

Fig. 6.8. Landslide susceptibility in Puerto Rico. From Larsen & Torres-Sánchez (1998) with permission from Elsevier.

structure of unstable slopes and the chronology of past landslides at a site (Brunsden, 2002; Petley, 2010). Such chronologies add a much needed temporal component to the usual spatial analyses. Hazard maps are potentially valuable planning tools for land managers, depending on the detail and quality of the data used to make them; they are also the only tool currently available for predicting deep-seated landslides (Sidle & Ochiai, 2006).

Risk models are less static than maps and more easily revised to reflect the dynamic conditions of slopes, provided there is adequate information about the geology, topography, hydrology, and climate (Larsen & Simon, 1993; Wang *et al.*, 2003). Earlier models can also be updated and revised as new tools become available (Chau & Lo, 2004). A model developed for a northern New Zealand watershed accounted for not only landslide susceptibility on 25 × 25 m grid cells, but also for the trajectories of sediment runoff and how soil redistribution up slope and down slope would affect future landslide frequency (Claessens *et al.*, 2007). Recent advances in landslide prediction include radar interferometry to detect early yet subtle landslide movements from satellites (Kondratyev *et al.*, 2002; Colesant & Wasowski, 2006), and increasingly sophisticated models of pore pressures in landslide zones (Iverson, 2005). Statistical tools to analyze landslide hazards include bivariate or multivariate approaches, multiple regression, logistic regression, discriminate analysis, neural networks, generalized additive models, random forests, boosted regression trees, and probabilistic analysis (Sidle & Ochiai, 2006; Ließ *et al.*, 2011;

Vorpahl *et al.*, 2012). Apart from purely statistical approaches, process-based models (also called physically based models) of slope stability incorporate a mechanistic understanding of landslide processes. One classical approach is the safety factor that calculates the ratio of stabilizing and destabilizing forces acting on a slope based on factors related to soil, vegetation, hydrology, and terrain (see Section 3.2; Sidle, 1992; Casadei *et al.*, 2003). Recent advancements integrate process-based and statistical models (Goetz *et al.*, 2011).

Biological features of landslides can help refine landslide hazard models (Sidle & Wu, 1999). For example, shrub growth rings have been used to determine re-sliding events in Germany (Gers *et al.*, 2001), thereby providing a history of past erosion patterns. In addition, vegetation composition sometimes correlates with landslide distribution (Fig. 6.9). In the northwestern U.S., landslides are more likely to occur in young forests (Turner *et al.*, 2010) and in areas of sparse vegetation and low root strength (Roering *et al.*, 2003). In the Himalayan Mountains, landslides are most likely to occur on slopes with < 40% cover of pine trees (*Pinus*), shrubs, or grasses, and least likely to occur where slopes are covered by multi-layered broadleaf forests (Tiwari *et al.*, 1986). In New Zealand, the distribution of kauri trees (*Agathis*) across the landscape resembled areas at risk for landslides (Claessens *et al.*, 2006). In Hong Kong, woodlands were less likely to slide than bare slopes or those dominated by grasses and shrubs (Zhou *et al.*, 2002). However, in northern India, road cuts below forests were more likely to slide than when forests were absent, perhaps because remaining forests survived on relatively inaccessible and unstable slopes (Haigh *et al.*, 1988). Landslide and tree fall disturbances were modeled in the Luquillo Mountains in Puerto Rico (Table 6.2; Pederson *et al.*, 1991). Using assumptions based on the few sources available for tropical landslides at the time, these authors were able to predict landslide frequencies (0.29% of forest affected year^{-1}) similar to one measured in the same forest by Guariguata (1990). Although Pederson *et al.* (1991) noted that slope and rainfall were important causes of landslides, they found that soil type was the most important factor for predicting landslides in this forest, which is a conclusion supported by more recent research (Larsen & Torres-Sánchez, 1996; Shiels *et al.*, 2008). Pederson *et al.* (1991) also suggested that improvements could be made to their model by accounting for recurring disturbances, plant succession, and unusual storm events. This modeling exercise demonstrates that when one or several landslide triggers dominate, even preliminary models can provide realistic estimates of landslide frequency. Because plants vary

Fig. 6.9. Vegetation patterns reflect former landslides (vertical white stripes and associated shrubby vegetation in center of photo) on cliffs at the North Rim of the Grand Canyon, U.S. Note the contrast with the less recently disturbed forested slopes (upper right of photo). Photograph by L.R. Walker.

Table 6.2. *Assumptions for a landslide simulation model for Puerto Rico's Luquillo Mountains (Pederson* et al., *1991). See text for details*

	Model assumptions
Triggers	Forest type, slope, soil type, and rainfall
Slope effect	Exponential increase in landslide probability with increase in slope, starting at 10% probability with slope of 0° and increasing exponentially to 65% probability with slope of 50°
Frequency	Mean: 3–6% of a forest erodes every 100 years[a]
Density	Maximum of 5×10^5 landslides in each 900 m^2 grid cell per month[1]
Size	Mean: 900 m^2
Disturbance interactions	Any tree fall within a grid increases landslide probability by 2.5%
Succession	No re-growth of vegetation after landslides

[a] *Source:* Garwood *et al.*, 1979.

in their ability to retain soil on slopes (Stokes *et al.*, 2009), deter erosion from raindrops (see Section 6.5.2), or modify precipitation patterns through changes in levels of evapotranspiration (Scatena & Larsen, 1991), comprehensive models should include biological parameters.

Predictions of how much damage a landslide will cause (severity) involve estimates of its volume, speed, and width and depth of the likely pathway, but also assessments of structures (or human lives) that might be affected. The physical attributes of landslides are determined by the geomorphological and climatological calculations noted above. The assessment of damage to infrastructures and human lives relies largely on past examples. In Iceland, after several snow avalanches killed 34 people in 1995, the government required that landslide and avalanche risk assessments be conducted in all vulnerable areas. Pooling geographically explicit hazard data on a regional scale with information about numbers of people in buildings (where they would be safer) or outside, Bell & Glade (2004) determined that loss of life in one region of Iceland would be 0.009 lives year^{-1} from landslides and avalanches. Because of their speed, frequency, and magnitude, debris flows were considered more of a threat than rock falls; they recommended that areas found to be high risk locations for debris flows be evacuated and buildings removed. Another method for determining landslide risk in urban areas is to include assessments of property values, landslide probability, and vulnerability of property. For example, if an urban area had a value of 100×10^9 ($100 billion), the probability of a landslide happening to that area in the next 10 years was one in 1000 (0.001 or 10^{-3}), and the vulnerability was one in 100 (0.01 or 10^{-2}). The product of $(100 \times 10^9) \times (10^{-3} \times 10^{-2})$ equals $1 million (Keller, 1996). Prevention costs that did not exceed $1 million might therefore be a wise investment given that the prevention reduced the landslide hazard to zero. Hazard ratings of rock falls along roads also address danger to humans, and they are based on such variables as the effectiveness of roadside ditches, road width, line of sight distance for oncoming vehicles (to allow evasive action), rock size, and rock fall history (Budetta, 2004).

Predictions of submarine landslides first involve detecting them. With devastating tsunamis that can reach shorelines in minutes, prediction of submarine landslides is important, but remains in its infancy (Bardet et al., 2003; Masson et al., 2006). In addition to using remote sonar and acoustic measurements, ocean cores, and terrestrial deposits, submarine landslides are most easily detected when they damage human structures, especially submarine cables and harbor facilities (Coulter & Migliaccio, 1966; see Section 2.2.1). Mitigation measures are usually taken only after major disasters prove the unreliability of the site. Following the 1964 Alaska earthquake, Anchorage and Seward both designated coastal strips off limits to development (see Fig. 2.4), while Valdez relocated the entire town to a more geologically stable site 5.5 km away (Hampton et al., 1996). Similar concerns occur around newly filled (or emptied) reservoirs where shifting hydrostatic pressures can cause slope instability (Günther et al., 2004).

6.5.2 Mitigation

In some cases, extensive intervention can prevent landslides, and prevention can be 10 to 2000 times less expensive than repairing damage following a landslide (Keller, 1996). However, such foresight (and the necessary political will and economic resource) is rarely available, so humans are usually relegated to mitigation of damage caused by past landslides and efforts to reduce damage from re-sliding (Cronin, 1992). Mitigation can involve increasing the resisting forces (Holtz & Schuster, 1996) by constructing physical structures to retain sediments and water or by redirecting runoff away from slopes. Retention in watersheds can be attempted through small check dams or large catchment basins; linings of the drainage surface called groundsills and bed girdles; and retaining

Fig. 6.10. Stabilization of roadside erosion with metal screens in Vermont, U.S. Photograph by L.R. Walker.

walls built from rock, soil, timbers, gabions, concrete, or steel (Ikeya, 1989; Rollins & Rollins, 1992; Takahashi, 2007; Larsen, 2008). Mesh from various materials, both organic and inorganic, as well as grout can be spread on slopes (Fig. 6.10), and clays can be heated to become less erosive. Dowels, nails, and anchors can be inserted into unstable soils and heavy bolts into unstable rocks to improve slope stability (Morton & Streitz, 1975; Sidle & Ochiai, 2006). Grading slopes can reduce land-slide risk, or benches can be cut into a slope when grading the entire slope is not feasible (Keller, 1996). However, with all retention efforts, both surface and subsurface drainage must be addressed, as increased soil pore pressure is the major cause of most landslides (Keller, 1996). For example, crops requiring flooded terraces can be replaced by ones that do not need flooding. Most check dams allow water and fine materials to pass through grates but retain large rocks (Schuster, 2000). Deep-rooted plants are often very effective in reducing pore pressure, provided they are allowed to grow and are not over-harvested for fodder and firewood, as has occurred extensively in Nepal (Amacher *et al.*, 1996; Bhatt & Sachan, 2004; see Section 6.4.2). Ultimately, any retention effort can be overwhelmed by major landslides, as occurred in Mie Prefecture, Japan in 2004, where many roads were destroyed by landslides during cyclones (Sidle & Ochiai, 2006).

Redirection of landslide-causing runoff results from installing drains at the surface or by burying drains and conduits (Krohn, 1992). Pore pressures can be reduced by drainage tunnels and bore holes to collect and redirect ground water (Oyagi *et al.*, 1996). Roads typically have culverts on the up hill side to reduce damage to the road bed, but culverts also can minimize erosion, particularly when the runoff is directed away from unstable surfaces and toward natural gullies. Blocked culverts can cause ponding and potential sliding (Piehl *et al.*, 1988). Similarly, walls or buildings can be oriented to direct flow along designated corridors (e.g., roads or valleys) and minimize exposure of buildings, or vulnerable natural areas (Larsen, 2008). Buffer zones that prohibit permanent buildings adjacent to drainages can reduce loss of lives and property. Large buildings can sometimes provide physical protection to residents during landslides (Larsen & Wieczorek, 2006). Diversion tunnels or spillways can reduce the likelihood of natural or man-made dams from failing and sending dangerous debris flows downstream (see Fig. 3.5; Schuster, 2000). Pumps and siphons can also reduce lake levels if dam failure seems imminent. Snow can be stabilized with structures that retain or redirect it to avoid avalanches. However, severe landslides often overwhelm constructed barriers or diversions, particularly if basins are not frequently cleaned out or if landslides come from unexpected directions. An additional problem is when physical structures lead to a false sense of security and additional development in landslide-prone terrain, the latter an illustration of Jevon's paradox (increased efficiency in resource use leads to increased use; Giampietro, 1999).

Activities to reduce erosion severity are generally disturbance-specific. Silvicultural practices that reduce soil erosion include partial cutting to leave some trees intact, particularly in gullies, along riverbanks, and on steep slopes (Sidle *et al.*, 1985; Dhakal & Sidle, 2003). Brush can be piled on slopes to reduce further re-sliding, but can be problematic when it traps sediments and overloads unstable soils (Sidle & Ochiai, 2006). Roads are likely contributors to landslides in logging operations (see Section 6.4.1), and minimizing their effects (using aerial cable removal, avoiding unstable slopes, planning storage operations on stable ground) reduces landslide damage (Sidle & Ochiai, 2006). Road location is critical, with fewer landslides resulting from roads that are built on stable substrates and in relatively flat terrain (e.g., ridges, valleys). Roads crossing old landslide scars are vulnerable because re-sliding can be aggravated by new

(a) Less stable

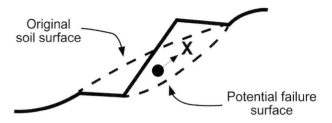

(b) More stable

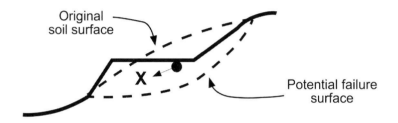

	Original center of gravity of the soil block
●	
X	Center of gravity of the soil block after the cut or fill has been completed

Fig. 6.11. Less and more stable ways to build a road on a slope. From Sidle & Ochiai (2006) with permission from The American Geophysical Union.

construction. Undercutting the base (toe) of a slope and overloading the top (crown) is destabilizing because it shifts the center of gravity upward; loading the toe and cutting back the crown is more stabilizing (Fig. 6.11; Sidle & Ochiai, 2006). However, down slope fill should be minimized or avoided completely (by carting away all loose material), because down slope fill is likely to slide in steep terrain. An exception is when the fill is stabilized by retaining walls. In general, reducing the overall length, width, and steepness of roads reduces potential for landslides. Pasture erosion can be reduced by keeping grazer densities low and fencing off steep sections and drainages that are vulnerable to sliding (Sidle & Sharma, 1996; see Section 6.4.2). High grazing intensities can cause more erosion and runoff due to reduced litter, vegetation, soil carbon, pore volume, and evapotranspiration (Krümmelbein *et al.*, 2009). Fire-triggered landslides can be mitigated by reducing fire frequency and intensity, conducting necessary clearings of steep slopes mechanically rather than with fire, and replanting slopes with fire-resistant or fire-resilient vegetation (Sidle & Ochiai, 2006; see Section 6.4.3). Choosing vegetation with characteristics that favor slope stability, while minimizing those that cause instability (see Table 3.2), is the recommended approach to mitigate landslides (Perla & Martinelli, 1976; Nott, 2006).

Effective mitigation measures result from widespread and persistent community support. Such measures include everything from a long-term commitment to the removal of sediments that build up in catchment basins, to ensuring public response to warnings, to pro-active education about hazards, to overall policy development that includes integration of multiple hierarchical and parallel interest groups and governmental agencies (Gori *et al.*, 2003). Mitigation of landslides in urban areas can occur through mapping of landslide risks, zoning, and incentives that are either positive (e.g., land swaps) or negative (e.g., costly landslide insurance) to avoid development in vulnerable areas. In high-density urban areas, building codes can be effective when they require geological inspections before construction can begin and limit the areas where urban development can occur. Deaths from landslides have declined since such codes were introduced in Los Angeles, California, Hong Kong, and Japan (Wong *et al.*, 1997; Smith, 2001). An informed citizenry is most likely to respond to warnings, support research into hazard management, and provide the basis for on-going political support (Larsen, 2008). Prevention measures need not be complex or costly, particularly if they are to find support among residents of mountainous regions in developing countries where most landslide fatalities occur (e.g., China, Colombia, Ecuador, Nepal, and Nicaragua). However, many fatalities also occur in more developed countries (e.g., Japan, Italy, and U.S.; Guzzetti, 2000; Mortality Statistics, 2011), so mitigation efforts can save lives wherever they are successful (Sidle, 2007). Typically, the major impediment to mitigation is a lack of political foresight (Schuster & Highland, 2007).

Warning signs that indicate when a slope is likely to fail can provide people with a chance to evacuate before an impending landslide, thereby leading to fewer deaths. Cracks in roads or dams, piles of accumulated debris in gullies, retrogressive slumps, leaning or split tree trunks, early successional vegetation, few large diameter shrubs or trees, and wetland vegetation are all possible signs of unstable slopes (Smith, 2001; Sidle & Ochiai, 2006). Rainfall sensors, rainfall threshold models, and effective communication links (e.g., trip wires, loud speakers, TV and radio alerts) to the affected public are all integral to successful warning systems (Giannecchini, 2005; Cavallo & Giannoni, 2006). Roads in California and Oregon have warning systems with voluntary compliance but in Japan, roads are closed to traffic when critical rainfall thresholds are reached and railroads are closed when there are earthquake alerts (Sidle & Ochiai, 2006). The U.S. National Weather Service and the U.S. Geological Survey developed a warning system for landslides in the San Francisco, California region that combined information on geologically susceptible areas with rainfall gauges and weather forecasts (Keefer *et al.*, 1987; Wilcox *et al.*, 2003). Hong Kong has 110 rain gauges that are linked to a landslide warning system (Petley, 2010). However, in addition to the difficulty of predicting a given landslide in a specific region, warning systems can be less effective when the region of forecasting is large, when rain gauges are rendered inoperable by erosion or excessive rain, where the landslide is too near at hand, or when populations fail to respond due to previous false alarms (Wilcock *et al.*, 2003; Larsen, 2008). Acoustic flow monitors on Mount Rainier, Washington give down slope urban residents 30 minutes' warning of potential debris flows; residents of Vargas, Venezuela (Table 6.1) would only have a maximum of 5 minutes because they live much closer to the unstable slopes (Larsen & Wieczorek, 2006). Finally, the initial landslide can be just the beginning of a series of landslides related to the initial slope failure. Re-sliding is often triggered by heavy rains following the first landslide (Petley, 2010). Thus, effective mitigation efforts need to take into account the risk of subsequent landslides.

6.5.3 Restoration

Restoration is a term that encompasses many processes (Table 6.3), but, in the broad sense that we use the term, it is the effort to re-establish some of the pre-landslide ecosystem structure and function. This goal can be approached initially through reclamation that stabilizes the landslide surface and ameliorates the harsh physical environment, but ultimately needs to include not only the biological components of an ecosystem (e.g., soil organisms, plants, dispersers, pollinators, herbivores, predators), but also

Table 6.3. *Definitions of types of restoration activities*

Term	Definition
Reclamation	Stabilization, amelioration, increase in utilitarian or economic value; rarely uses indigenous ecosystems as a model
Reallocation	Management that deflects succession to a land use with increased functionality
Rehabilitation	Actions that repair indigenous ecosystem function and structure
Bioremediation	The use of plants and microbes to reduce site toxicity (a kind of reclamation or rehabilitation)
Restoration *sensu lato*	Actions that reverse degradation and lead to partial recovery of pre-disturbance ecosystem structure and function (potentially including all of the above)
Restoration *sensu stricto*	Actions that lead to full recovery of pre-disturbance ecosystem structure and function

Modified from Aronson *et al.* (1993)

the more subtle ecosystem processes (e.g., nutrient cycling, primary productivity, successional dynamics; Table 6.4). Ideally for humans, landslide restoration also tries to re-establish any missing ecosystem services, such as water purification and slope stability.

Physical amelioration focuses on reducing the frequency of re-sliding (Cronin, 1992) and improving microsites to facilitate dispersal and establishment of organisms. As described in Section 6.5.2, there are many ways that landslides are stabilized, from adding retention walls or redirecting surface and subsurface runoff, to altering slopes through terraforming or construction of impermeable surfaces. Encasing a slope in an impermeable layer of plastic or concrete may be a successful short-term strategy; however, all artificial surfaces eventually degrade (Weisman, 2007) and lack the resiliency of vegetation and soil, which can repeatedly recover despite ongoing disruptions. Biological stabilization includes addition of cover plants to reduce surface splash, retention of soils through root growth, and facilitation of landslide colonization by other species (see Chapter 5). Together, physical amelioration and biological stabilization constitute reclamation, which focuses on increasing the utility or economic value of the site. Reclamation often introduces new species, new functions, and therefore new ecosystems to a landslide and it overlaps with the concept of reallocation (Table 6.3).

Table 6.4. *Restoration strategies for landslides.*

Restoration topic	Obstacles	Landslide applications	Selected references
Site amelioration	Re-sliding	Stabilize Add cover plants Divert runoff Terraform (re-shape slope) Make slope impermeable	Cronin, 1992; Chou et al., 2007; Morgan, 2007; Shiels et al., 2008; Shiels & Walker, in press
Carbon accumulation	Inorganic substrates	Mulch, add topsoil Add mature plants Limit grazing	Nakamura, 1984; Shiels et al., 2006
Nutrient availability	Infertility, decomposition	Fertilize, add topsoil Add nitrogen fixers and microbes Mulch for retention	Miles et al., 1984; Fetcher et al., 1996; Bellingham et al., 2001; Arunachalam & Upadhyaya, 2005; Shiels et al., 2006, 2008
Dispersal and colonization	Propagule establishment	Create favorable microsites (e.g., rip surface) Add bird perches Reduce seed predators Utilize legacies (e.g., seed banks) Promote sloughing and vegetative expansion from edges	Miles & Swanson, 1986; Myster, 1993; Senneset, 1996; Shiels & Walker, 2003; Velázquez & Gómez-Sal, 2007

(*cont.*)

Table 6.4. (cont.)

Restoration topic	Obstacles	Landslide applications	Selected references
Species diversity	Species dominance	Avoid monospecific thickets unless needed for stabilization and organic accumulation Plant local species and remove undesirable weeds	Maheswaran & Gunatilleke, 1988; Walker, 1994; Myster & Sarmiento, 1998; Negishi *et al.*, 2006; Velázquez & Gómez-Sal, 2009
Succession	Arrested or retrogressive trajectories	Promote stage transitions Do not over fertilize Mow or graze as needed Add functionally diverse species Promote connectivity with landscape Integrate with adjacent land uses Abandon restoration efforts if they are counterproductive	Lundgren, 1978; Negishi *et al.*, 2006; Velázquez & Gómez-Sal, 2008; Walker *et al.*, 2010a
Predictive models	Thresholds between stages, alternative stable states, landslide variability, stochastic events	Adaptive management (evaluate success of models) Model and promote many trajectories Model restoration of function, not composition	Davis *et al.*, 2004; del Moral *et al.*, 2007

Modified from Walker & del Moral (2008, 2009); Walker *et al.* (2009).

Rehabilitation attempts to re-establish ecosystem structures and functions that approximate conditions in the original ecosystem (restoration
sensu lato) but do not try to replicate them exactly (restoration *sensu stricto*;
Table 6.3). Rehabilitation of landslides focuses on accumulation of carbon
and nutrients, dispersal and establishment of organisms, enhancement
of species diversity, and promotion of desired community and ecosystem processes, including successional trajectories (Table 6.4). Carbon and
nutrient enhancement begin with physical mitigation of ongoing erosion
and the creation of surfaces that can retain leaf litter, mulch, or fertilizer.
The restoration of pre-landslide soil organisms is critical because without these organisms restoration efforts will be ineffective and nutrient
cycling will be limited. However, such restoration represents a difficult
task because most landslide organisms are lost through the initial disturbance. Pockets of soils that remain become very important nuclei from
which colonizing soil organisms can disperse (Francescato *et al.*, 2001).
Restoration activities can also promote sloughing of organic material
from surrounding soils (e.g., through direct addition to the landslide), an
example of one beneficial aspect of at least some on-going erosion. When
soil remnants are scarce, soil organisms must disperse onto landslides by
wind, water, or gravity (see Chapter 4). These early colonists often face
arid, unstable conditions on new landslides, yet for some, the open conditions provide competitor-free space to exploit. Mites and Collembola are
often among the first animal colonists, followed by predators including
ants and spiders (see Chapter 4). Many landslide-colonizing arthropods
depend on litter, so adding litter or creating microsites that entrap litter
(e.g., brush, swales, trenches) could potentially increase arthropod densities as well as nutrient cycling through the positive effects of litter on soil
microbes and decomposition. Earthworms and other burrowing animals
aerate soil and are positively correlated with the presence of soil bacteria
and leaf litter as well as soil carbon (Li *et al.*, 2005). These early colonists
are often crucial to the recovery of successional processes and ecosystem
functions. Soil organisms are central to plant nutrient uptake, largely
through symbioses such as nitrogen fixation and mycorrhizal fungi. Soil
bacteria and fungi help stabilize soils (Meadows *et al.*, 1994). Retention
or addition of soil organic matter improves conditions for soil organisms and subsequent plant nutrient uptake. Organic matter can be added
directly through additions of brush or other ground cover (Devkota *et al.*,
2006a, b) and through soil additions (Shiels *et al.*, 2006). Any substantive
restoration effort should address the soil fauna, although such efforts are
rarely attempted.

Fig. 6.12. Retention walls and plantings reduce erosion along the Beijing to Bangkok highway, southern China. Photograph by L.R. Walker.

Facilitated dispersal and establishment of plants and animals provide another critical focus of restoration efforts on landslides. Plants can be added to landslides as spores, seeds, seedlings, saplings, adults, or cuttings (Fig. 6.12). Success rates will be determined by initial site preparation, including stabilization and creation of adequate microsites (i.e., not too dry, hot, sunny, or infertile). Grass seeds are commonly sown because they germinate rapidly, root extensively, provide a thorough ground cover, and typically tolerate harsh environmental conditions. Vetiver grass (*Vetiveria zizanioides*) is planted on landslides in Nepal because it quickly grows roots that can reach depths of 4 m (Petley, 2010). However, grasses and other early colonists including scrambling ferns (Walker *et al.*, 2010a) can impede establishment of other plants. Re-vegetation is a critical component of landslide restoration that can contribute to both long-term slope stability and resiliency. Canopy structure and roots must be considered when choosing plants for restoration of landslides (Stokes *et al.*, 2009). Plant canopies and leaf litter intercept rainfall and reduce runoff while roots reinforce the stability of soil particles and can anchor unstable soils when they grow into more stable soils (Ghestem *et al.*, 2011). Large woody plants can reduce the effects of rock falls (Stokes *et al.*,

Fig. 6.13. Bamboo was planted to stabilize slopes along mountain roads in Puerto Rico. Photograph by L.R. Walker.

2007b). Perennial grasses, including bamboo (Fig. 6.13), can quickly stabilize erosive slopes (Cazzuffi *et al.*, 2007). Plant roots extract water from soil (which then evaporates) and create channels through which subsurface water can drain; both processes lower soil pore pressure and have a stabilizing effect on slopes. Plants also contribute to soil development;

well-developed soils, in turn, help to stabilize slopes because they dampen pore pressure and efficiently redistribute rainfall (Keim & Skaugset, 2003). Plants with nitrogen fixing symbionts not only increase soil fertility, but sometimes also act as important sources of leaf litter and microclimate amelioration. When they form thickets, nitrogen fixing plants can minimize soil erosion and arrest succession, allowing soils to develop (e.g., *Clitoria ternatea* in Nicaragua; Velázquez & Gómez-Sal, 2009). In the Kumuan Himalayas of northern India, seedlings of *Alnus nepalensis* planted on landslides contributed two to six times more nitrogen to the soil in 2 years than did other seedling species (Chaudhry *et al.*, 1996). Dense *A. nepalensis* growth also reduces erosion on slopes in the eastern Himalayas (Sharma & Ambasht, 1985).

Plants can also decrease slope stability; for example through transmission of wind forces from the air through the roots to the soil, or because they add mass to a slope (see Table 3.2; Sidle & Ochiai, 2006). Other potentially negative effects of plants on slope stability include increased evapotranspiration, which can lead to drier soils, increased cracks, and higher infiltration rates (Bell, 1998). Plants that are > 1 m tall can increase the erosive forces of raindrops coming through their canopies compared to plants that are closer to the ground (Fig. 6.14; Morgan, 2007). Transitions between types of vegetation cover (e.g., grass cover to forest or vice versa) that involve periods of bare soil are also conducive to erosion. Plants that are flammable can, upon burning, leave landslide soils exposed to erosion (see Section 6.4.3), particularly if fires are repeated (Goudelis *et al.*, 2007), or forests are logged following a fire on a slope (Spanos *et al.*, 2007). Efforts to reduce post-fire erosion can backfire, as found when grasses were introduced into sage brush habitat in California (U.S.) to reduce erosion but instead resulted in more erosion than the original vegetation (Rice *et al.*, 1969). Despite the potentially negative effects of plants on slope stability, re-vegetation is an essential restoration tool that must be used judiciously to avoid undesirable results (Nott, 2006; Stokes *et al.*, 2007a).

Plant–animal interactions have an important role in community development on landslides (see Chapter 4), and therefore can potentially be manipulated to improve landslide restoration; however, few studies have addressed this issue. The construction of artificial perches on Puerto Rican landslides attracted birds that deposited seeds and nitrogen-rich feces (Shiels & Walker, 2003). Ground-nesting ants can be important aerators of landslide soils and potentially affect plant colonization and restoration success through their selective consumption of seeds (Myster,

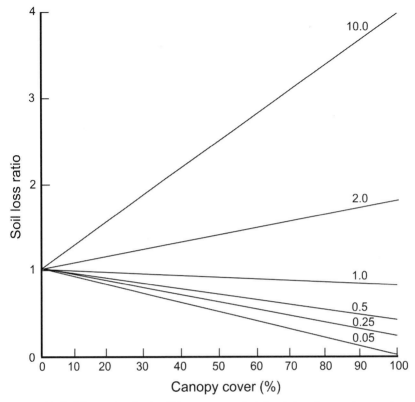

Fig. 6.14. Soil loss ratios for six different canopy heights (m) and cover (proportion of soil surface protected by vegetation cover). The ratio is the loss of surface soil particles when covered with vegetation divided by loss with no vegetation present. From Morgan (2007) with kind permission from Springer Science + Business Media B.V.

1997; Shiels, 2002). The role of pollinators has rarely been examined in succession. The successional status of the vegetation surrounding the landslide is presumably important because late successional stages do not always provide a ready source of pollinators for early successional landslide plants (Dale, 1986; Walker & del Moral, 2003). However, many primary seres are colonized by wind-dispersed, self-pollinating plants (Rydin & Borgegård, 1991; del Moral & Wood, 1993). When colonists are partially or fully self-incompatible, or when invertebrate or vertebrate pollinators are threatened (as on some tropical islands; Cox & Elmquist, 2000), pollination may become a critical factor for colonization (Carpenter, 1976; Compton *et al.*, 1994). The potential absence of suitable pollinators (Walker & Powell, 1999), as well as the lack of flower and seed production due to infertility in early primary succession (del Moral, 1993), should be considered for restoration, although we have no knowledge of such studies for landslides. Finally, mammals can be important to seed dispersal, soil mixing, herbivory, and re-establishment of food webs (see Chapter 4). Rodents are active on landslides and potentially important in transporting plant propagules between landslides and the surrounding landscape (Shiels, 2002; Samaniego-Herrera, 2003; Geertsema & Pojar, 2007). Burrowers such as rabbits, pikas, and rats increase vertical mixing of litter and soil profiles, thereby promoting decomposition and nutrient cycling as well as promoting spatial heterogeneity (Willig & McGinley, 1999). However, burrows can destabilize slopes and grazers such as rabbits can reduce ground cover, including plantings meant to stabilize a slope. Other large animals, including bears (Geertsema & Pojar, 2007), deer (James, 1973), and monkeys (Kaplan & Moermond, 2000) forage on landslides and increase connectivity between a landslide and its surrounding habitats. However, the precise role of animals in landslide restoration is poorly understood.

Enhancement of species diversity is a common restoration goal, in part to increase community resilience to repeated disturbances (Suding & Hobbs, 2009a). Increased diversity can also provide both functional redundancy and functional diversity. For example, on ten landslides in Puerto Rico, functional redundancy among several dozen woody pioneers meant that species composition varied greatly among landslides but all combinations had similar effects on succession (promotion of later successional woody plants; Walker et al., 2010a). Functional diversity was provided by other landslide colonists, particularly tree ferns and scrambling ferns, which inhibited plant succession. Restoration on these Puerto Rican landslides could optimize success by creating a mosaic of the three dominant life forms, each with its own benefits: the immediate erosion control of scrambling fern thickets, the fast growth of tree ferns, and the long-term successional advantages of woody pioneers. The use of mosaics of species has been suggested for the restoration of other degraded tropical habitats (Montagnini, 2001; Carnevale & Montagnini, 2002). Suppression of landslides can have potentially negative effects on species diversity when it reduces habitat diversity (Yamamoto et al., 1995) or ecosystem processes. In Central America, human expansion into mountains that are occasionally affected by multiple landslides may reduce overall landslide activity (e.g., by engineering slopes and converting them to artificial structures), thereby removing critical ecosystem processes such as gap formation and down slope transfer of organic matter and causing unknown consequences at landscape scales (Restrepo & Alvarez, 2006).

Another way that biodiversity has been increased is through road closures in areas where landslides are damaging wildlife habitat (e.g., sediment additions to salmon streams) or forest slopes (Forman *et al.*, 2003). Systematic closures of both private and public forest roads have begun in the U.S. and Canada (Havlick, 2002). Road closures have many ecological benefits, including limiting access by vehicles and humans, reducing road maintenance, and thereby not only reducing road-related landslides but improving conditions for sensitive and rare aquatic and terrestrial species (Liddle, 1997). Slopes with abandoned roads are gradually filled in by slumps into the road bed, and plant growth usually begins to stabilize the landslides formerly kept active through road maintenance and use. Techniques used in road closures that reduce landsliding include diagonal trenches across the road bed that divert road drainage to multiple points down slope to avoid gully formation, or complete decompaction of the road bed and reconstruction of the hill slope topography (Madej, 2001).

Long-term vegetation patterns are rarely considered in landslide restoration, but without some consideration of successional dynamics (including disturbance responses, species interactions, community assembly; see Chapter 5), restoration is unlikely to be successful (Walker & del Moral, 2008). One example demonstrates the value of a long temporal perspective. Claessens *et al.* (2006) found that a landslide hazard index modeled on the basis of physical parameters (e.g., hydrology, slope, aspect, and catchment area) was useful in predicting where kauri (*Agathis australis*) trees grew in New Zealand (see Section 6.5.1). Stands of kauri trees regenerate by colonizing recent disturbances such as landslides or fires in New Zealand, and then provide a long-term signal of that colonization event because of their longevity (often > 1000 years) and competitive exclusion of angiosperm tree species (Enright *et al.*, 1999). Restorers of erosive slopes in the region might consider the long-term stabilization provided by kauri trees (Claessens *et al.*, 2006).

Restoration is essentially the manipulation of succession, so it is important to realize that succession does not follow a predetermined trajectory but can vary, depending on many factors (Hobbs *et al.*, 2007). New landslide surfaces can, for example, be fertile or infertile, stable or unstable, with quite different successional trajectories and appropriate restoration strategies (Table 6.5; see Fig. 5.3; Walker *et al.*, 1996, 2009). While stabilization is of initial concern on most landslides, subsequent steps in landslide succession can also be critical. For example, landslides can be

Table 6.5. *Successional dynamics and restoration strategies for four different landslide substrate conditions*

Substrate condition	Successional dynamics	Restoration strategies
Unstable, infertile	Very slow; stochastic interruptions	Stabilize with plant cover; increase fertility
Stable, infertile	Slow; stress-tolerators dominate	Promote stress-tolerant ground cover; fertilize minimally
Unstable, fertile	Moderately fast; interrupted; variable rates of change	Stabilize
Stable, fertile	Fast; trajectory dependent on colonizers	Monitor; promote biodiversity

Modified from Walker *et al.*, 1996, 2009. The first condition typifies many slip faces and the last one many deposition zones.

vulnerable to erosion after the initial colonizing plants die back (Walker *et al.*, 2009). Restoration sometimes attempts to accelerate succession through the addition of later successional plants, but on landslides, such shortcuts of the normal successional sequence are unlikely to be successful without adequate soil development. How species interact can also alter assumptions about restoration. Introduction of a species that rapidly stabilizes landslide soils (e.g., a grass or a scrambling fern) may result in a delay of succession to later stages (Walker *et al.*, 2009; Walker *et al.*, 2010a), but may also allow seeds and organic matter to accumulate (Negishi *et al.*, 2006). Sometimes letting succession occur without any manipulation (unassisted succession) is the best approach to restoration, particularly in low-productivity ecosystems such as landslides (Fig. 6.15; Prach *et al.*, 2007).

Modeling landslide succession and results of specific restoration techniques can improve restoration success and indicate when certain efforts should be abandoned as counterproductive. Thresholds of effort needed to change a landslide ecosystem from one state to another can be modeled but are best determined through direct experience. Long-term observations of succession on landslides under different management strategies are important for validation and improvement of model predictions. Above all, restoration of landslides must follow a flexible approach, where lessons learned are applied through adaptive management to future efforts. Indeed, each landslide, despite similar treatment, can end

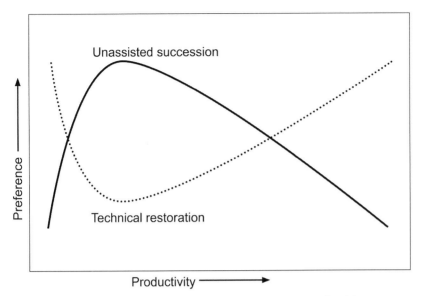

Fig. 6.15. Suggested mode of restoration based on ecosystem productivity. Technical restoration is likely to be more successful in very unproductive (e.g., infertile or toxic) or very productive (e.g., eutrophic) ecosystems. Unassisted succession can exceed in moderately productive ecosystems where dominance by a few competitive species is not expected. From Prach *et al.* (2007) with kind permission from Springer Science + Business Media B.V.

up following a distinct successional trajectory. Because of our incomplete knowledge of landslide succession, the stochastic nature of dispersal and repeated disturbances, and the multiple effects species have on one another, landslide restoration must aim for broad goals such as slope stabilization, sediment-free drainage, unassisted successional progression, and resilience in the face of repeat disturbances (Walker *et al.*, 2009). Most restoration activities also occur at limited spatial and temporal scales, whereas important ecological processes such as succession as well as geological triggers of landslides often occur at larger scales (see Fig. 2.1). To the extent that some ecosystem services are provided and landslide damage is mitigated, landslide restoration can be considered successful.

6.6 Conclusions

Humans have lived with landslides throughout their entire history, but early cultures were not densely populated enough to be significantly affected. Landslides actually offer humans a variety of benefits, including early successional plants used for food, fodder for animals, wood for fuel, and fertile soils for crops. However, humans are increasingly vulnerable to the dangers of landslides because, as our numbers increase, we have expanded our activities on slopes prone to landslides. Our activities have also increased landslide frequency and severity. Roads built across slopes are a common form of anthropogenic landslide generation. Expanding urban and suburban development are other widespread causes of landslides. Removal of original plant cover through forestry or agriculture generally leads to increased landslide frequency (Turner *et al.*, 2010) and often promotes invasion by non-native plants that may decrease biodiversity or be less able to stabilize slopes than the native flora. However, both fast-growing native and non-native plants that colonize landslides can potentially stabilize erosive slopes, while human activities can reduce overall landslide frequency when slopes are stabilized.

Technological efforts to predict future landslides now include a broad array of sophisticated monitoring and modeling tools. However, the stochastic nature of landslide timing, direction, and severity limits the effectiveness of such tools. Even the most likely landslide scenario often has unexpected parameters. Effective prevention of harm depends on a cooperative populace with a concern about future events. Nonetheless, there are numerous examples of successful mitigation of landslides, particularly when the causes and trajectories of previous local landslides are understood.

Biological factors are a part of any successful landslide mitigation or restoration effort. The biota is much more resilient than abiotic structures such as dams that ultimately fail. Something is known about how initially to stabilize slopes with vegetation and what types of root and shoot architectures are most useful. Much less is known about long-term efforts needed to maintain slope stability and recover ecosystem processes and services. Restoration that needs little or no maintenance is a worthy goal, but slopes are inherently unstable, particularly when modified by road cuts, grazing animals, or urban development. Therefore, local successes that stabilize local slopes and save lives are worthy achievements. Ultimately, human population densities in vulnerable regions will have to decline if landslide hazards are to be substantially reduced. Given the unrealistic nature of such a scenario, education about landslide hazards and full implementation of technological and biological tools need to be used.

7 · Large scales and future directions for landslide ecology

Key points

1. Landslide ecology is an emerging discipline that provides insights into both scientific and management issues. Scientifically, it explores nutrient cycling and soil development, plant physiological adaptations, dispersal and colonization dynamics, novel mixes of native and non-native species, and successional trajectories in an often inhospitable environment. Landslide ecology also integrates biological aspects of landslides into efforts to manage slope hydrology, soil erosion, and the stabilization of slopes.
2. Human–landslide interactions are becoming more common as human populations expand into mountainous terrain and climate change increases landslide frequency.
3. A landscape-level approach to landslide rehabilitation integrates topography, broad-scale climatic conditions, landslide density, patch dynamics, propagule dispersal, and coarse-scale predictive models.
4. We expect future contributions to landslide ecology will come from more effective technological tools to mitigate erosion and predict landslide hazards, an increased understanding of how plant–animal–soil interactions determine colonization patterns and successional trajectories, and practical contributions from efforts to use biological methods to stabilize landslides. Finally, we hope that the emergence of landslide ecology as a discipline will also improve our cultural perspectives of landslides, including the promotion of more sustainable uses of slopes and avoidance of erosion-prone areas.

7.1 Introduction

This book has demonstrated how landslides are not just geological processes but also ecological processes that structure landscapes and ecosystems in montane areas around the world. The physical aspects of landslides are complex but well studied; the biological and ecological aspects are equally complex but poorly studied. In addition to providing habitats for species that are gap specialists and initiating a series of species interactions over successional time, landslides also alter ecosystem parameters such as light regimes, nutrient cycling, and slope hydrology. Humans are key participants in the ecology of landslides because we use them, suffer from them, cause them, and sometimes try to manage them. Humans therefore have a multi-faceted and ambiguous relationship with landslides. We are vulnerable to the destruction that landslides cause, yet we also increase landslide frequency and severity by our inappropriate land use. We attempt to minimize potential damage by predicting the occurrence and location of landslides and by mitigating slope instability using dams, plantings, and other physical and biological tools. Once the damage has occurred, we try to restore slope stability, biodiversity, and ecosystem functions and services. Human–landslide interactions therefore occur across a wide range of spatial scales, from local, immediate concerns to the inclusion of populations and communities of landslides and their influence at larger spatial and temporal scales.

An understanding of landslide ecology is critical for several reasons: (1) landslides increase habitat heterogeneity and therefore have the potential to increase local and regional biodiversity; (2) landslides challenge our ability to understand a complex, rapidly changing ecosystem on often unstable and nutrient-poor substrates where retention of propagules, leaf litter, and soil is difficult (Larson *et al.*, 2000) and productivity is low; and (3) landslides re-shape landscapes by exposing rock-bound nutrients to weathering, thereby altering cycles of nutrients both locally and regionally through down slope influences on rivers and watersheds. Over geological time, landslides have influenced most landscapes and they continue to have widespread ecological and social effects (Sassa *et al.*, 2007). Further examination of these issues will help us pinpoint sources of altered water quality and hazardous terrain, understand physiological adaptations of landslide colonizers and their roles in succession, focus our efforts to conserve biodiversity, and evaluate the interplay of landscapes and disturbances. Ecological perspectives can advance both the understanding and manipulation of landslides. This chapter places the details of the previous chapters into the context of larger spatial and temporal scales and explores the future of ecological approaches to the study of landslides.

7.2 Human–landslide interactions

7.2.1 Land use changes

Human population growth has led to the expansion of human influences into most terrestrial and many submarine environments. Simultaneously, growing concentrations of humans in urban areas increase the local intensity of human influences on slopes. Because most human cultures exploit natural resources with little concern for long-term sustainability, higher densities of people lead to more resource extraction. Clearing vegetation and extracting soil, rock, and even water can destabilize slopes (see Chapters 3 and 6). Landslide frequencies have often increased as a demand for food, fuel, and shelter leads to expanded forestry and agriculture. Deforestation is driven by site-specific combinations of expansion of human activities for agriculture and infrastructure plus extraction of wood (Geist & Lambin, 2002). Expanding global markets provide economic incentives to clear forested slopes for crops such as coca leaves, corn, or tea (Sidle & Ochiai, 2006; López-Rodríguez & Blanco-Libreros, 2008). Fires, either accidental or intentional, and urbanization can also destabilize slopes (see Chapter 6; Goudie & Boardman, 2010). Fires are increasing in intensity and urbanization is expanding as human populations continue to grow. About half of all humans live in urban areas, and this ratio, which is steadily increasing, generally holds true for humans living in mountainous areas (Slaymaker, 2010). Mountain cities result in increased erosion because people build roads, homes, and other buildings on slopes; we also dam and channel the rivers for water and power. Mountain societies (e.g., many urban areas in the Andes) are increasingly likely to be composed more of low-income people who may lack adequate resources to adjust to disturbances caused by land use changes such as fires and landslides (Hewitt, 1997). Where human land use is so intense that terraforming has reduced landslide frequency and severity, the main loss is not of human lives but of ecosystem functions that landslides supply. These losses include reductions in nutrient redistribution and landscape heterogeneity (Restrepo & Alvarez, 2006).

7.2.2 Novel ecosystems

The rapid globalization of flora and fauna through human movements has led to the creation of novel mixtures of native and non-native species, often with poorly understood ecosystem consequences (Hobbs *et al.*, 2009). In most cases, we do not know whether such novel mixtures of species are more or less effective than native communities at stabilizing slopes. Our understanding of novel ecosystems is further complicated by novel, anthropogenic disturbances. For example, anthropogenic fires now denude slopes and promote erosion in areas not previously prone to erosion (Sidle *et al.*, 2004; Sidle & Ochiai, 2006). Insights into the relationships between novel ecosystems and landslide stability will influence future landslide mitigation and restoration efforts. Eventual dominance of landslide scars by a few successful, widespread, and usually introduced species is one scenario that would reduce biodiversity in landslide communities, but possibly increase predictability of landslide colonists across large geographical ranges. For example, non-native grasses invaded several Hawaiian landslides and reduced establishment and growth of native species (Restrepo *et al.*, 2003) but made it easier to predict the composition of further landslides. Novel ecosystems are likely to become more common in the future, not only from mixing of native and non-native species, but from realignments of species distributions due to climate change.

7.2.3 Climate change

Some studies have correlated landslide activity with changes in climate, particularly precipitation (Bovis & Jones, 1992; González-Diez *et al.*, 1996; Dale *et al.*, 2001), while other studies have found no such correlation (Innes, 1985). Linking climate change to landslides (Trauth *et al.*, 2003) is challenging because of the many variables that influence landslides in addition to climate (Sidle & Ochiai, 2006), including ones that are geological, hydrological, biological, and anthropogenic (Table 7.1; Fig. 7.1). Each of these factors may vary in time. For example, landslide triggers such as a particular rainstorm or earthquake are influenced by shifts in long-term trends in slope uplift, short-term temperature influences on evapotranspiration and pore pressure, and recent history of rainfall. At millennial time scales, landslides appear to be most frequent during cool, humid climates; at decadal scales the El Niño Southern Oscillation, the North Atlantic Oscillation, Asian monsoons, and the frequency and intensity of cyclones all appear linked to landslide occurrence (Borgatti & Soldati, 2010). Many prehistoric landslides were triggered by tectonic uplift from glacial retreats such as those that occurred at the end of the

Table 7.1. *Climate change implications and nine future directions for landslide ecology*

Climate change implication	Approach	Future directions
More variable weather and extreme events	Technology	Improve longevity of soil retention mechanisms; development of modular, replaceable units
	Ecology	Improve manipulation of succession for long-term slope stability
	Culture	Promote sustainable use of slopes and avoidance of erosion-prone areas
Spread of novel ecosystems	Technology	Improve mapping and modeling of native and novel ecosystems to forecast change and assist native ecosystem restoration
	Ecology	Determine optimal species mixes, optimal root architecture, and other biological tools to stabilize slopes
	Culture	Recognize and minimize the human role in spreading non-native species via land use patterns
More landslides; different slope failure thresholds	Technology	Improve predictive models and local applications
	Ecology	Develop robust, flexible restoration principles and applications that apply within and among ecosystems
	Culture	Develop flexible policies and infrastructures that recognize changing threats from landslides

Little Ice Age (Holm *et al.*, 2004). However, such variations in climatic factors are most applicable for predicting landslides at large spatial scales and are not as useful for understanding local slope dynamics (Schmidt & Dikau, 2004).

Current anthropogenic activities have altered climatic conditions and such changes will likely increase landslide activity (Bromhead & Ibsen, 1997; Lateltin *et al.*, 1997). Along with the expected 2–4 °C increase in global average temperature within the next 60–100 years (IPCC, 2007), we expect more variability in climatically controlled processes that trigger landslides. These include intensity and duration of rainfall, rate and extent of snow melt and glacial melt, frequencies of droughts and floods, stability of permafrost, river channel migration, and sediment loads in rivers (Dale *et al.*, 2001; Borgatti & Soldati, 2010). The exact nature and extent of

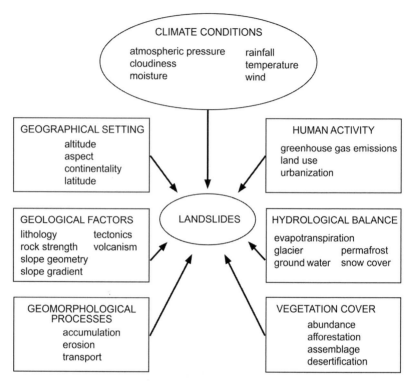

Fig. 7.1. A complex set of background factors influence slope instability and lead to specific triggers (capital letters) of landslides. Climatic influences are modified by geological, hydrological, biological, and anthropogenic variables. Modified from Borgatti & Soldati (2010) with permission from Cambridge University Press.

these climate changes on soil erosion will be measurable at local scales, but increased climatic variation, coupled with extensive, destabilizing land use changes, appears to be driving an increase in landslides. Factors that might offset a trend of increased erosion include stabilization of slopes by increased growth of plants in once arid regions, increased evapotranspiration that could lower pore pressure, and increased root growth due to higher carbon dioxide levels (Rogers *et al.*, 1994; Borgatti & Soldati, 2010).

One dramatic response to global warming is the unequivocal acceleration of glacial melting. In the short term (decades), this melting will probably lead to greater sediment transfer down slope and increased flooding (Slaymaker, 2010); both of these changes could cause an increased frequency of landslides in mountainous regions (Holm *et al.*, 2004; Hewitt,

2006). Newly exposed glacial sediments, not yet stabilized by plant growth or soil development, could be particularly vulnerable to erosion (Fischer *et al.*, 2006). These glacial sediments sometimes dam rivers during earthquake- or flood-triggered landslides, forming so-called glacial lakes. These lakes then can empty in catastrophic outburst floods (see Section 2.2.1). China, Nepal, and Tajikistan are examples of countries highly vulnerable to glacial lakes. In Tajikistan, earthquake-triggered landslides create lakes as large as the 17 km^3 Lake Sarez (Alford *et al.*, 2000). In 2008 in Szechwan, China, 30 lakes were formed by earthquake-triggered landslides. In Nepal, pro-active draining has been attempted to reduce the threat of glacial outburst floods (Slaymaker, 2010). In the long term (centuries), the frequency of landslides due to glacial melt water, high sediment loads in rivers, and channel instability may decline. However, that trend could be offset by an increased frequency of intense rainstorms, thereby maintaining high fluvial sediment loads and channel instability (Korup *et al.*, 2004). Similarly, changes in cyclone frequency, intensity, and direction can have widespread consequences for landslide erosion in such places as Taiwan (Dadson *et al.*, 2003).

Coupled with climate change, unprecedented manipulation and destabilization from anthropogenic land use will likely produce more landslides in the future. Local conditions will promote landslides if projections of more humidity and more irregularity in rainfall and temperature occur. Because landslide activity is likely to remain largely where it has always been (e.g., mountain slopes), efforts to mitigate future landslide damage have a clear, albeit broad geographical focus. Expansion of landslides to previously stable areas may occur, however (e.g., where permafrost melts or stabilizing vegetative cover is removed; Goudie, 2010). Predictive modeling can best contribute to specific recommendations for landslide hazard management at local scales, particularly where the critical details of land use effects on slope erosion can be incorporated (Sidle & Ochiai, 2006).

7.2.4 Landscape rehabilitation

A landscape perspective can aid rehabilitation efforts because it will incorporate spatial and temporal constraints common to all nearby landslides (Swanson *et al.*, 1988; Foster *et al.*, 1998). Landslides created by the same disturbance (populations of landslides; Restrepo & Alvarez, 2006) share a common date of origin and may therefore be linked through similar post-landslide disturbance regimes, common suites of colonizers, and similar successional trajectories. Alternatively, landslide successional trajectories can vary (Myster & Walker, 1997; Shiels *et al.*, 2006), even when the landslides are triggered by the same storm (Shiels *et al.*, 2008). Rehabilitation tactics should vary depending on such landscape-level attributes of landslides as patchiness, topographical location, climatic variables, and frequency (Swanson *et al.*, 1988). Landslide patchiness at a landscape scale influences succession in several ways. First, the variation in successional stage of all landslides in a given area influences the availability of airborne propagules for landslide colonization; and second, the degree of connectivity (e.g, corridors) among landslides influences the dispersal of colonists (see Chapter 4). The nature and distribution of landslide patches is highly influenced by human activities (Larsen & Santiago Román, 2001; Velázquez & Gómez-Sal, 2008). Topographical location influences rehabilitation success because landslides at ridge tops or on convex slopes are more likely to be rehabilitated than landslides found mid-slope or on concave slopes (Swanson *et al.*, 1988). One climatic variable influenced by landscapes is rainfall. Landslides facing the prevailing wind will receive more rainfall and can be harder to stabilize and revegetate than those in rain shadows. Conversely, drought can be an obstacle for landslides in the lee of the prevailing wind (rain shadow). Finally, frequency can affect rehabilitation, because landscapes with infrequent landslides (e.g., distant from tectonically active terrain) may be easier to re-vegetate than those with more frequent landslide disturbances. Large-scale landscape and even regional perspectives on rehabilitation benefit from models (e.g., of geochemical cycling and climate change) that are most effective at larger spatial and temporal scales than individual landslides (see Section 7.2.3; Restrepo *et al.*, 2003, 2009; Sidle & Ochiai, 2006).

7.3 Lessons learned

Investigation of the ecology of landslides provides insights for science and management. Scientifically, landslides help us understand disturbance ecology, soil formation and erosion, nutrient cycling in terrestrial and submarine habitats, species adaptations to disturbed environments, and ecological change or succession. Landslides provide insights into a broad array of other types of disturbances, including earthquakes, volcanoes, tsunamis, floods, and various anthropogenic activities (e.g., road construction, logging). Landslides are important to soil ecology because they expose rock-bound nutrients, trigger mixing of organic and inorganic layers, and result in net down slope movement of organic matter.

Landslides link terrestrial and aquatic ecosystems through sediment and nutrient transfers from river deltas, fjords, volcanic island shorelines, and continental shelves, with delayed effects on deeper submarine canyons and seafloors (Masson *et al.*, 2006). Terrestrial landslides transfer nutrients and carbon down slope but also promote colonization by new, often fast-growing plants (Sidle & Ochiai, 2006). Species adapted to landslides have met the challenges associated with dispersal, establishment on often unstable, dry, and infertile substrates, spatially heterogeneous microsites, steep environmental gradients, and competition with other colonists. Many kinds of species are successful colonists of landslides. These colonists may include cyanobacteria, fungi, ants, birds, rodents, ferns, grasses, various nitrogen fixing species, and wind-dispersed species of shrubs and trees. These species appear to be gap specialists rather than landslide specialists. Landslides, as examples of locations where succession occurs, inform us about how plants and other organisms colonize severe disturbances and then interact with each other and the physical environment over time. These lessons can augment knowledge obtained by studies of other types of primary succession where environmental conditions of severity (e.g., volcanic surfaces), instability (e.g., dunes, floodplains), and infertility (e.g., mine tailings) overlap with landslides (Walker & del Moral, 2003).

When other options are available, humans tend to avoid slopes prone to sliding. However, population pressures and the many resources found on sloped terrain (e.g., minerals, fertile soil, medicinal plants, firewood, and scenic vistas) mean that some humans decide to live with the danger of landslides. The unpredictability of a particular landslide event can lull people into thinking that where they live is stable (Larson *et al.*, 2000). It is harder to ignore more frequent landslides (e.g., on unconsolidated sands or clays) where erosion can occur with each severe rainstorm. Humans have also created new sources of slope instability from both additions of structures and fluids (e.g., reservoirs), to removal of rocks and soils for the construction of roads and buildings. Therefore, there is a positive feedback loop between expansion of humans onto unstable slopes and increased frequency and damage by landslides.

Human modifications of landslide-prone slopes provide opportunities to address experimentally the effects of various management scenarios. The study of erosion-prone slopes provides additional lessons about how to manage water and sediment flow and how to use plants and soil organisms to promote stabilization and restoration of ecosystem services. Hazard management can ameliorate local and sometimes even regional landslide problems. In a comparison of regional landslide hazards in the

Indian Himalayas and British Columbia (Canada), Singh & Pandey (1996) noted the positive role of management. Development of remote regions for logging, mining, agriculture, and tourism, and the road and railroad corridors used to access these regions, has led to increased landslides in both countries within the last few decades. Landslide damage has been more severe in India with limited management than in British Columbia with more widespread management. Lower population densities and public and financial support for mitigation efforts in British Columbia also helped minimize landslide frequency and severity. However, local human efforts at landslide mitigation and restoration are largely ineffective against stochastic natural disturbances (e.g., earthquakes) and global-scale anthropogenic disturbances (e.g., climate change and resulting changes in rainfall patterns).

7.4 Future directions

We suggest several areas where landslide ecology could develop in the next few decades. We organize them by technological, ecological, and cultural approaches following Walker (2012). We recognize that all of these approaches are essential to maximize flexibility in the face of the uncertainties of human land use and climate change (Table 7.1).

1. Technology is useful to mitigate local landslide disturbances and many slopes can now be engineered to reduce or avoid further erosion – at least during average rainstorm events. However, dams, walls, retention basins, and other erosion controls are all vulnerable to extreme rainstorms or earthquakes and also to eventual decay. Future technological advances could improve the longevity of such structures and develop modular units that can be more flexible in responding to a particular disturbance (e.g., allowing a dam to drain before it collapses) and can be replaced as needed.
2. Plants are potentially cheaper, longer-lasting, and more resilient to future disturbances than physical structures. Despite recent advances in understanding plant effects on soil stability (Ghestem et al., 2011), there is still much to be learned about root morphology and its consequences for preventing erosion, planting techniques, and individual species performances on different substrates. We expect continued improvement in such research and its applications.
3. Technological approaches are most effective when coupled with robust predictive models about slope stability. Models that incorporate the

latest knowledge in GIS, statistics, and remote sensing with ecological lessons about landslide and landscape dynamics have yet to be developed, but will represent a synergism of approaches and result in wider applicability of the models. Much benefit would be derived, for example, by successfully scaling robust climate model predictions about rainfall intensity down to local levels where, with appropriate accounting of local condition, direct action could be taken.

4. An important ecological topic to address is how plant and animal communities on landslides change over time. Succession on landslides involves plant–animal–soil interactions and is infrequently investigated, particularly as a vital, three-way dynamic. Examining these interactions on landslide communities across realistic time spans of years and decades will be an on-going challenge for landslide ecology. One unresolved question in this interaction is the role that nitrogen fixation and other symbioses have on soil development and successional trajectories of landslides. Another concern is the role that animals have on landslide stabilization and community development. How do pollinators, dispersers, burrowers, herbivores, and predators influence landslide succession? Also, is there any significant difference in stabilization rates or succession among landslides colonized by native plants and animals compared to those colonized by non-native species or landslides with novel mixtures of native and non-native species? To the extent that lessons learned from individual site studies can be extrapolated to other sites, the field of landslide restoration will benefit. Global generalizations across biomes are likely to be elusive, given the complexity and individuality of local conditions, but regional generalizations offer greater promise of success.

5. Another area of landslide ecology that could be improved is our understanding of the ecological responses to technological tools used in slope stabilization. Alterations of water flow on slopes can be technically sound but may not account for unexpected ecological responses such as weed invasions, root disruption of drains, or edge effects on surrounding vegetation. Research in the physiology of plants used to promote slope stability and individual plant effects on slope stability has outpaced its practical applications. How do plants with favorable root morphologies interact with each other? Under what environmental and substrate conditions are they most effective? How long do roots and plants on landslides live? Integrating the recent advances in physiological studies (Stokes *et al.*, 2007a, 2009) with practical slope management issues will be a fruitful avenue for further research.

6. Ecological restoration is the acid test of our understanding of ecosystem functions (Bradshaw, 1987) and of direct and urgent relevance to people affected by landslides. Successful, long-term, ecological restoration is less costly and more desirable than moving whole communities out of landslide zones, more resilient than physical structures to on-going disturbances, and a practical demonstration of a solid understanding of successional dynamics. Such restoration urgently needs exploration and will result in more resilient ecosystems when ecological lessons are incorporated (Hobbs *et al.*, 2007). Restoration will also benefit from a landscape perspective that incorporates plant and animal dispersal and topographical considerations.

7. Culturally, one approach to reduce future landslide damage is to discourage permanent settlements in landslide-affected areas, including both slopes and run-out zones below the slopes. Zoning or cultural taboos can help, particularly after a recent devastation when buildings are demolished (Hampton *et al.*, 1996). However, success will depend on broad community support of risk assessments, as recently conducted in Iceland (see Chapter 6; Bell & Glade, 2004). There is much need for future work on the cultural acceptance of risk assessment and its consequences for local community zoning choices. Developing an acceptable range of intensities of land use on unstable slopes (e.g., from minimal to limited to full access for grazing, recreation, construction) might facilitate the integration of societal and ecological requirements (Carreiro & Zipperer, 2011).

8. Another cultural approach is to promote more sustainable use of erosion-prone slopes. Intensive logging or urbanization on such slopes (and attendant roads and other construction) is untenable and is costly in the long term due to expense of future stabilization efforts and perhaps the loss of lives. Slopes where soils and vegetation are either kept intact or restored to maximize stability will have less cost and more benefits to communities (e.g., cleaner water and less danger of floods or landslides) than over-developed ones. Some of the potential benefits of not developing slopes include low-intensity recreational opportunities (hiking, skiing, berry-picking), wildlife refuges, and using slopes as educational tools (e.g., about geology, succession, or ecosystem services; Larson *et al.*, 2000). Future projects should integrate cultural attitudes with landslide management.

9. Changes in where we live and in how we use and value landslide-prone slopes will not be sufficient without policies to reinforce such approaches (Box 7.1). Education and warning systems help prepare a

Box 7.1 Will we ever learn?

When Europeans farmers colonized New Zealand in the mid 1800s, they found, to their delight, large swaths of native grasslands on which to graze their sheep. New Zealand quickly became a major wool exporter and the farmers introduced European grasses and removed native forests to improve grazing conditions. Efforts to maintain the grasslands included constant removal of secondary woody growth and the importation of rock phosphate from several Pacific Islands to fertilize the often nutrient-poor soils. By the 1970s, half of the country was in farmland, but the heavily grazed grasslands were not able to resist erosion and 10% of the land was considered severely eroded (Walker & Bellingham, 2011). Erosion was successfully reduced where trees such as Monterey pine (*Pinus radiata*) were grown, and in recent decades, many farmers switched to growing trees. However, when tree plantations are clear cut (typically every 25 years), the soils are again exposed and erode during rain storms (see Plate 15 and back cover image). In addition, many are again removing the trees to expand the lucrative dairy industry, with renewed soil exposure and extensive erosion. Kenneth Cumberland, a geographer from Auckland, wrote in the 1940s about the need to reforest New Zealand slopes (Cumberland, 1944). Recently, he lamented that, despite 60 years of knowledge about how to manage erosion and how costly each storm was, New Zealanders continue to overgraze their slopes. He ends a recent letter to a newspaper in Christchurch with the suggestion that the bill for tidying up the erosion from the next storm should perhaps go to those who have failed to address the problem (Cumberland & Cumberland, 2008). Would such a policy help improve the stewardship of the land?

population for the dangerous consequences of landslides, but green zones, nature reserves, or limits on roads and dwellings rarely succeed where they are strictly voluntary. Legislation at local levels can address specific concerns, while higher levels of government can tackle regional and larger issues such as the creation of national parks, limits to drilling, or locations of federal highways. Where destabilization is inevitable (e.g., along road cuts), enforceable guidelines can determine how stabilization is addressed and maintained while being realistic about local conditions and solutions to erosion.

Landslide ecology is a recent blend of the decades-old field of landslide science (Sassa *et al.*, 2007) and the century-old field of ecology (McIntosh, 1985). It is a natural extension of early work in primary succession that considered the ecological consequences of all severe disturbances on land (Clements, 1916). Landslide ecosystems resemble other severely disturbed habitats because they are colonized by pioneer species adapted to low nutrients, high light conditions, and on-going disruptions. Landslide ecosystems differ from many other severely disturbed habitats because of their chronic instability, the importance of gravity, and the central roles of rock, soil, and water movements. In other words, their geological aspects are more unusual than their biological characteristics. Nevertheless, for humans to stabilize effectively erosive slopes, the biological components of landslides cannot be ignored. We expect that as the field of landslide ecology develops it will serve to connect the field of landslide science, which has focused on physical aspects of landslides, with the field of ecology. We also foresee the applications of lessons from landslide ecology to a broad array of scientific and management topics including disturbance ecology, nutrient cycling, succession, biodiversity, and restoration. Progress in understanding landslide ecosystems will translate to more accurate predictions of future landslides and more resilient, long-term methods of ecosystem restoration on existing landslides. These improvements will be cost-effective, provide ecosystem services, and save lives.

Glossary

Abiotic Pertaining to non-living factors such as wind, temperature, erosion.

Actinorhizal Plants with a symbiosis with the nitrogen fixing actinobacteria *Frankia*.

Allelopathy Form of competitive inhibition based on the release of chemicals.

Anthropogenic Created or influenced by humans.

Avalanche Sudden flow of snow down a slope. A "dirty" avalanche includes soil and rock.

Biodiversity Number and proportional distribution of species in a specified location.

Bioerosion The erosion of hard ocean substrate including coral by living organisms such as worms, mollusks, and fish.

Biomass Mass of all organisms (living or dead) at a site.

Biotic Pertaining to living factors.

Bryophyte A non-vascular land plant that is a moss, hornwort, or liverwort.

Check dam A small dam built to reduce erosion and allow sediments to settle in drainage areas.

Chronosequence Space-for-time substitution that allows study of long-term succession.

Chute Often elongated region in the middle of the landslide through which material is transported from the slip face to the deposition zone. Also called zone of depletion or flow track.

Clay Very fine-grained sediment (< 0.002 mm diameter).

Collembola Springtails, an abundant and primitive group of wingless, insect-like arthropods.

Colluvium Gravity-transported sediments deposited at the base of a slope.

Competition Negative effect of two species on each other.

Creep Very slow form of mass wasting.

Crown Upper boundary of the slip face.

Debris Unconsolidated, mostly coarse (> 2 mm diameter), weathered rock and soil; regolith. Also can include branches, logs, and other loose vegetation remnants of any size.

Deposition zone Terminus of transported material. Also called the foot.

Disturbance Relatively abrupt event that causes a loss of biomass, ecosystem structure, or ecosystem function.

Driving forces Those forces that tend to make earth material slide.

Epiphyte Plant growing on another plant or surface without direct contact with the soil.

Evapotranspiration Transfer of water to the atmosphere by evaporation from humid surfaces plus transpiration by plants.

Facilitation Positive effect of one species on another, often in a successional context.

Fall Downward and outward movement of rocks or soil with exposed faces.

Fault A geological fracture with movement along either side.

Fjord Glacially eroded valley inundated by the ocean.

Floodplain The flat topography adjacent to a river produced by overbank flow and lateral migration of meanders.

Flow Movement of rock or soil influenced by gravity (see mass movement).

Fluvial Pertaining to rivers and streams.

Food web Set of connections among species based on which species are eaten by which other species.

Foot See deposition zone.

Forb Any broad-leaved, herbaceous seed plant that is not a grass or grass-like.

Frugivorous Fruit-eating.

Gabion Rock-filled wire cage used to stabilize slopes.

Gap specialist Species adapted to recently disturbed, high-light environments.

Gravel Unconsolidated, generally rounded fragments of rocks and minerals (> 2 mm diameter)

Hummocky terrain Land characterized by many small hills (< 15 m tall).

Hydrophytic A plant that grows partly or wholly in water.

Indeterminate growth Growth that continues throughout the lifespan of the organism.

Inhibition Competition, often in a successional context.

Jevon's paradox Increased efficiency of use of a resource increases rather than decreases the rate of consumption of that resource.

Landslide In the strictest sense, a sliding movement of a mass of rock, debris (loose rock or regolith), or earth (finer sediments with or without organic material) down a slope. In the broader sense used in this book, all types of slope failures or mass wasting that include slides, falls, flows, or combinations of these three types of movements and the habitats that are created.

Legacy Biological legacy is any life that survives a disturbance, e.g., buried seeds.

Liquefaction Fluid-like properties of clay-rich soils upon losing their shear strength.

Mass movement Movement of rock or soil influenced by gravity (see **Flow**); also called mass wasting.

Mass transport Movement of rock or soil by a transporting medium such as water, air, or ice.

Microsite Small-scale habitat; the immediate environmental conditions affecting an organism.

Macrosite Large-scale habitat; the broader environmental conditions affecting an organism.

Mycorrhizae Fungi that typically live in or on the surface of roots and aid plants in the absorption of water and nutrients in exchange for carbohydrates.

Nitrogen fixation Process of converting atmospheric nitrogen into forms usable by organisms.

Overland flow Flow of water on the surface of the earth not confined to channels. Results when precipitation rates exceed infiltration rates.

Permafrost Permanently frozen ground.

Pore pressure Pressure of ground water held in the pore spaces of soil or rock. Also called pore water pressure or pore fluid pressure.

Propagule Any reproductive unit adapted to dispersal, e.g., seed, spore, or vegetative part of a plant.

Rachis Central midrib of a fern leaf.

Regolith Loose rock and soil above bedrock.

Restoration Actions that reverse degradation and lead to partial (*sensu lato*) or full (*sensu stricto*) recovery of pre-disturbance structure and function. See Table 6.3 for associated terms.

Retrogressive landslide Landslide that continues to erode a slope, gradually moving further into and up the slope with each re-sliding.

Retrogressive succession Loss of complexity or function in latter stages of succession, often due to severe leaching of nutrients from surface soils.

Rhizome Horizontal or ascending stem growing at or below the soil surface.

Sand Grains of sediment 0.06–2 mm in diameter.

Saprolite Highly chemically weathered, "rotten" rock.

Scar New habitat created by a landslide as delineated by the surface of rupture (see Fig. 1.1).

Scarification Mechanical or chemical abrasion of a seed coat, which may promote germination.

Scarp See slip face.

Scrambling fern A fern with indeterminate growth that spreads across the soil or other vegetation.

Sediment Fine-grained material (mostly < 2 mm diameter) at the surface of the regolith.

Seed rain Aerially dispersed seeds.

Sere Sequence of successional stages.

Senescence Aging of organisms with reduction in function.

Shear strength Magnitude of stress that a soil can sustain without sliding.

Silt Fine sediments 0.002–0.06 mm in diameter.

Slide Landslide that moves by slumping or along a plane (translational slide).

Slip face Upper zone of landslide detachment, also called scarp or failure scar.

Slip plane Weakness plane in below-ground substrate where landslides occur when driving forces exceed resisting forces.

Slump Landslide that undergoes a rotation as it descends.

Soil Earth material so modified by biological, chemical, and physical processes that the material will support rooted plants.

Solifluction Soil movement down slope due to freeze – thaw cycles.

Spread Lateral expansion of a cohesive soil or rock mass.

Springtails *See* **Collembola**.

Stochastic Unpredictable.

Stolon Elongated, horizontal stem that forms new shoots at its end.

Submarine landslide A landslide that occurs in the ocean.

Succession Change in community structure and composition over time following a severe disturbance that removes most soil and organic matter (primary) or a less severe disturbance that leaves some soil and organic matter intact (secondary).

Swale pond Small body of water formed by in-filling of a depression or swale.

Talus Collection of rocks fallen from a slope.

Tectonic Referring to rock deformation.

Tension crack Crack formed by gravitational movement of a surface plane.

Terraform To reshape the geometry of a slope.

Toe Lower end of the deposition zone.

Trajectory Sequence of communities during succession.

Translational *See* **Slide**.

Tsunami Tidal wave.

Turbidity current Dense current of suspended sediments. Also called turbulent flow.

Watershed Land area that contributes water to a particular river system.

Weathering Breakdown of rocks due to biological, chemical, and physical processes.

References

Acevedo-Rodríguez, P. & Strong, M.T. (2005). Monocots and Gymnosperms of Puerto Rico and the Virgin Islands. *Contributions from the United States National Herbarium*, **52**, 1–415.

Achard, F., Stibig, H.-J., Eva, H.D., et al. (2010). Estimating tropical deforestation from Earth observation data. *Carbon Management*, **1**, 271–287.

Adams, J. (1980). Contemporary uplift and erosion of the Southern Alps, New Zealand. *Geological Society of America Bulletin Part II*, **91**, 1–114.

Adams, P.W. & Sidle, R.C. (1987). Soil conditions in three recent landslides in southeast Alaska. *Forest Ecology and Management*, **18**, 93–102.

Alcántara-Ayala, I. & Goudie, A. (2010). *Geomorphological Hazards and Disaster Prevention*. Cambridge: Cambridge University Press.

Alexander, D. (1993). *Natural Disasters*. New York: Chapman and Hall.

Alford, D., Cunha, S.F., & Ives, J.D. (2000). Mountain hazards and development assistance: Lake Sarez, Pamir Mountains, Tajikistan. *Mountain Research and Development*, **20**, 20–23.

Allen, R.B., Bellingham, P.J., & Wiser, S.K. (1999). Immediate damage by an earthquake to a temperate montane forest. *Ecology*, **80**, 708–714.

Allen, R.B., Bellingham, P.J., & Wiser, S.K. (2003). Forest biodiversity assessment for reporting conservation performance. *Science for Conservation*, **216**, 1–49. Wellington, New Zealand: New Zealand Department of Conservation.

Allison, S.D. & Vitousek, P.M. (2004). Rapid nutrient cycling in leaf litter from invasive plants in Hawaii. *Oecologia*, **141**, 612–619.

Alonso, E.E., Lloret, A., & Romero, E. (1996). Rainfall induced deformations of road embankments. In *Landslides*, eds. J. Chacón, C. Irigaray, & T. Fernández. pp. 97–108. Rotterdam: Balkema.

Alvarez, J. & Willig, M.R. (1993). Effects of treefall gaps on the density of land snails in the Luquillo Experimental Forest of Puerto Rico. *Biotropica*, **25**, 100–110.

Amacher, G.S., Hyde, W.F., & Kanel, K.R. (1996). Household fuelwood demand and supply in Nepal's Tarai and Mid-Hills: choice between cash and outlays and labor opportunities. *World Development*, **24**, 1725–1736.

Amatangelo, K.L. & Vitousek, P.M. (2009). Contrasting predictors of fern versus angiosperm decomposition in a common garden. *Biotropica*, **41**, 154–161.

Amezaga, J.M., Santamaría, L., & Green, A.J. (2002). Biotic wetland connectivity – supporting a new approach for wetland policy. *Acta Oecologica*, **23**, 213–222.

Aragon, E.L. (1975). Inhibitory effects of substances from residues and extracts of staghorn fern (*Dicranopteris linearis*). MS Thesis, University of Hawaii, Manoa, Hawaii, U.S.

Arno, S.F. & Hammerly, R.P. (1984). *Timberline Mountain and Arctic Forest Frontiers*. Seattle, Washington, U.S.: The Mountaineers.

Aronson, J., Floret, C., LeFloc'h, E., Ovalle, C., & Pontanier, R. (1993). Restoration and rehabilitation of degraded ecosystems in arid and semiarid regions. I. A view from the South. *Restoration Ecology*, **1**, 8–17.

Arunachalam, A. & Upadhyaya, K. (2005). Microbial biomass during revegetation of landslides in the humid tropics. *Journal of Tropical Forest Science*, **17**, 306–311.

Atkinson, I. (1989). Introduced animals and extinctions. In *Conservation for the Twenty-first Century*, eds. D. Western & M.C. Pearl. pp. 54–79. Oxford: Oxford University Press.

Augspurger, C.K. (1984). Seedling survival of tropical tree species: interactions of dispersal distance, light-gaps and pathogens. *Ecology*, **65**, 1705–1712.

Bansal, R.C. & Mathur, H.N. (1976). Landslides – the nightmare of hill roads. *Soil Conservation Digest*, **4**, 36–37.

Bardet, J.-P., Synolakis, C.E., Davies, H.L., Imamura, F., & Okal, E.A. (2003). Landslide tsunamis: recent findings and research directions. *Pure and Applied Geophysics*, **160**, 1793–1809.

Bardgett, R.D., Bowman, W.D., Kaufmann, R., & Schmidt, S.K. (2005). A temporal approach to linking aboveground and belowground ecology. *Trends in Ecology and Evolution*, **20**, 634–641.

Barry, J.P. & Whaling, P.J. (2003). Use of vesicomyrid clams as proxies for ageing submarine landslide events. *American Geophysical Union, Fall Meeting*, abstract #OS31A-07.

Batanouny, K.H., Stichler, W., & Ziegler, H. (1991). Photosynthetic pathways and ecological distribution of *Euphorbia* species in Egypt. *Oecologia*, **87**, 565–569.

Baur, B. & Baur, A. (1990). Experimental evidence for intra- and interspecific competition in two species of rock-dwelling land snails. *Journal of Animal Ecology*, **59**, 301–315.

Bea, R.G. (1971). How sea floor slides affect offshore structures. *Oil Gas Journal*, **69**, 88–91.

Bea, R.G., Wright, S.G., Sircar, P., & Niedoroda, A.W. (1983). Wave-induced slides in South Pass Block 70, Mississippi Delta. *Journal of Geotechnical Engineering, ASCE*, **109**, 619–644.

Bell, F.G. (1998). *Environmental Geology: Principles and Practice*. Oxford: Blackwell.

Bell, R. & Glade, T. (2004). Quantitative risk analysis for landslides – examples from Bíldudalur, NW-Iceland. *Natural Hazards and Earth System Sciences*, **4**, 117–131.

Bellingham, P.J. & Lee, W.G. (2006). Distinguishing natural processes from impacts of invasive mammalian herbivores. In *Biological Invasions in New Zealand*, eds. R.B. Allen & W.G. Lee. pp. 323–336. New York: Springer.

Bellingham, P.J., Walker, L.R., & Wardle, D.A. (2001). Differential facilitation by a nitrogen-fixing shrub during primary succession influences relative performance of canopy tree species. *Journal of Ecology*, **89**, 861–875.

Bellingham, P.J., Tanner, E.V.J., & Healey, J.R. (2005). Hurricane disturbance accelerates invasion by the alien tree species *Pittosporum ungulatum* in Jamaican montane rain forests. *Journal of Vegetation Science*, **16**, 675–684.

Benko, B. & Stead, D. (1998). The Frank Slide: a reexamination of the failure mechanism. *Canadian Geotechnical Journal*, **35**, 299–311.

Bergman, B., Johansson, C., & Soderback, E. (1992). The *Nostoc–Gunnera* symbiosis. *New Phytologist*, **122**, 379–400.

Bhatt, B.P. & Sachan, W.S. (2004). Firewood consumption along an altitudinal gradient in mountain villages in India. *Biomass & Bioenergy*, **27**, 69–75.

Bird, G., Brewer, P.A., Macklin, M.G., *et al.* (2008) River system recovery following the Novat-Rosu tailings dam failure, Maramures County, Romania. *Applied Geochemistry*, **23**, 3498–3518.

Boadu, F.K. & Owusu-Nimo, F. (2011). Exploring the linkages between geotechnical properties and electrical responses of sand-clay mixtures under varying effective stress levels. *Journal of Environmental and Engineering Geophysics*, **16**, 73–83.

Bonikowsky, L.N. (ed.) (2012). *The Canadian Encyclopedia*. http://www.thecanadianencyclopedia.com. Accessed 15 February 2012.

Bonuccelli, T., Luzia de Souza, M., & Zuquette, L.V. (1996). Landslides in urban areas: the triggering factors in the historical city, Ouro Preto, Brazil. In *Landslides*, eds. J. Chacón, C. Irigaray, & T. Fernández. pp. 117–124. Rotterdam: Balkema.

Borgatti, L. & Soldati, M. (2010). Landslides and climate change. In *Geomorphological Hazards and Disaster Prevention*, eds. I. Alcantara-Ayala & A. Goudie, pp. 87–95. Cambridge: Cambridge University Press.

Bovis, M.J. & Jones, P. (1992). Holocene history of earthflow mass movements in south-central British Columbia: the influence of hydroclimatic changes. *Canadian Journal of Earth Sciences*, **29**, 1746–1754.

Brabb, E.E. (1991). The world landslide problem. *Episodes*, **14**, 52–61.

Bradshaw, A.D. (1987). Restoration: an acid test for ecology. In *Restoration Ecology: A Synthetic Approach to Ecological Research*, eds. W.R. Jordan III, M.E. Gilpin, & J.D. Aber, pp. 23–29. Cambridge: Cambridge University Press.

Brenning, A. (2005). Spatial prediction models for landslide hazards: review, comparison and evaluation. *Natural Hazards and Earth System Sciences*, **5**, 853–862.

Brokaw, N.V.L. (1998). *Cecropia schreberiana* in the Luquillo Mountains of Puerto Rico. *The Botanical Review*, **64**, 91–120.

Bromhead, E.N. & Ibsen, M.L. (1997). Land-use and climate-change impacts on landslide hazards in SE Britain. In *Landslide Risk Assessment*, eds. D. Cruden & R. Fell. pp. 165–175. Rotterdam: Balkema.

Brown, V.K. & Gange, A.C. (1992). Secondary plant succession: how is it modified by insect herbivory? *Vegetatio*, **101**, 3–13.

Bründl, M., Bartelt, P., Schweizer, J., Keiler, M., & Glade, T. (2010). Review and future challenges in snow avalanche risk analysis. In *Geomorphological Hazards and Disaster Prevention*, eds. I. Alcantara-Ayala & A. Goudie, pp. 49–61. Cambridge: Cambridge University Press.

Brunsden, D. (1984). Mudslides. In *Slope Instability*, eds. D. Brunsden & D.B. Prior, pp. 363–418. New York: Wiley.

Brunsden, D. (2002). Geomorphological roulette for engineers and planners: some insights into an old game. *Quarterly Journal of Engineering Geology and Hydrogeology*, **35**, 101–142.

Brunsden, D. & Jones, D.K.C. (1980). Relative time-scales and formative events in coastal landslide systems. *Zeitschrift für Geomorphologie Supplement*, **34**, 1–19.

Bryant, J.P. & Chapin, F.S. III. (1986). Browsing-woody plant interactions during a boreal forest plant succession. In *Forest Ecosystems in the Alaska Taiga, a Synthesis of Structure and Function*, eds. K. Van Cleve, F.S. Chapin III, P.W. Flanagan, L.A. Viereck, & C.T. Dyrness, pp. 213–215. New York: Springer.

Bryne, M.M. & Levey, D.J. (1993). Removal of seeds from frugivore defecations by ants in a Costa Rican rain forest. *Vegetatio*, **107**/108, 363–374.

Budetta, P. (2004). Assessment of rockfall risk along roads. *Natural Hazards and Earth System Sciences*, **4**, 71–81.

Bull, W.B. (2010). Regional seismic shaking hazards in mountains. In *Geomorphological Hazards and Disaster Prevention*, eds I. Alcántara-Ayala & A.S. Goudie, pp. 5–12. Cambridge: Cambridge University Press.

Bull, W.B. & Brandon, M.T. (1998). Lichen dating of earthquake-generated regional rockfall events, Southern Alps, New Zealand. *Geological Society of America Bulletin*, **110**, 60–84.

Bulmer, M.H., Petley, D.N., Murphy, W., & Mantovani, F. (2006). Detecting slope deformation using two-pass differential interferometry: implications for landslide studies on Earth and other planetary bodies. *Journal of Geophysical Research*, **111**, E06S16 (10 pp.).

Bunce, M., Szulkin, M., Lerner, H.R.L., *et al.* (2005). Ancient DNA provides new insights into evolutionary history of New Zealand's extinct giant eagle. *PLOS Biology*, **3**, 1–3.

Bush, D.M., Neal, W.J., & Jackson, C.W. (2009). Summary of Puerto Rico's vulnerability to coastal hazards: risk, mitigation, and management with examples. *Geological Society of America Special Papers*, **460**, 149–165.

Butler, D.R. (2001). Geomorphic process-disturbance corridors: a variation on a principle of landscape ecology. *Progress in Physical Geography*, **25**, 237–248.

By, T., Forsberg, C.F., & Norem, H. (1990). Submarine slides: full scale experiment at Storglomvatn, Norway. *Norwegian Geotechnical Institute*, Report 522090–4. Cited in Locat & Lee (2002).

Caine, N. (1980). The rainfall intensity-duration control of shallow landslides and debris flows. *Geographical Annals Series A*, **62**, 23–27.

Callaway, R.M. (2007). *Positive Interactions and Interdependence of Plant Communities*. Springer: New York.

Callaway, R.M. & Walker, L.R. (1997). Competition and facilitation: a synthetic approach to interactions in plant communities. *Ecology*, **78**, 1958–1965.

Cammeraat, E., van Beek, R., & Kooijman, A. (2005). Vegetation succession and its consequences for slope stability in SE Spain. *Plant and Soil*, **278**, 135–147.

Camp, R.J. & Knight, R.L. (1998). Effects of rock climbing on cliff plant communities at Joshua Tree National Park, California. *Conservation Biology*, **12**, 1302–1306.

Campanello, P.I., Gatti, M.G., Ares, A., Montti, L., & Goldstein, G. (2007). Tree regeneration and microclimate in a liana and bamboo-dominated semideciduous Atlantic Forest. *Forest Ecology and Management*, **252**, 108–117.

Cannon, S.H. (2001). Debris-flow generation from recently burned watersheds. *Environmental and Engineering Geoscience*, **7**, 321–341.

Cannon, S.H., Kirkham, R.M., & Parise, M. (2001). Wildfire-related debris-flow initiation processes, Storm King Mountain, Colorado. *Geomorphology*, **29**, 171–188.

Cannone, N., Lewkowicz, A.G., & Guglielmin, M. (2010). Vegetation colonization of permafrost-related landslides, Ellesmere Island, Canadian High Arctic. *Journal of Geophysical Research – Biogeosciences*, **115**, article number G04020. doi:10.1029/2010JG001384

Carlton, G.C. & Bazzaz, F.A. (1998). Regeneration of three sympatric birch species on experimental hurricane blowdown microsites. *Ecological Monographs*, **68**, 99–120.

Carnevale, N.J. & Montagnini, F. (2002). Facilitating regeneration of secondary forests with the use of mixed and pure plantations of indigenous tree species. *Forest Ecology and Management*, **163**, 217–227.

Carpenter, F.L. (1976). Plant-pollinator interactions in Hawaii: pollination energetic of *Metrosideros collina* (Myrtaceae). *Ecology*, **57**, 1125–1144.

Carrara, A., Cardinali, M., Detti, R., *et al.* (1991). GIS techniques and statistical models in evaluating landslide hazard. *Earth Surface Processes and Landforms*, **16**, 427–445.

Carreiro, M.M. & Zipperer, W.C. (2011). Co-adapting society and ecological interactions following large disturbances in urban park woodlands. *Austral Ecology*, **36**, 904–915.

Casadei, M., Dietrich, W.E., & Miller, N.L. (2003). Testing a model for predicting the timing and location of shallow landslide initiation in soil-mantled landscapes. *Earth Surface Processes and Landforms*, **28**, 925–950.

Cavallo, A. & Giannoni, F. (2006). Natural risk warning: comparison of two methodologies. *Advances in Geosciences*, **2**, 335–338.

Cázares, E. & Trappe, J.M. (1994). Spore dispersal of ectomycorrhizal fungi on a glacier forefront by mammal mycophagy. *Mycologia*, **86**, 507–510.

Cazzuffi, D., Corneo, A., & Crippa, E. (2007). Slope stabilisation by perennial 'gramineae' in Southern Italy: plant growth and temporal performance. In *Eco- and Ground Bio-Engineering: The Use of Vegetation to Improve Slope Stability*, eds. A. Stokes, I. Spanos, & J.E. Norris, pp. 111–126. *Proceedings of the First International Conference on Eco-Engineering*, 13–17 September 2004. Dordrecht: Springer.

Chadwick, J., Dorsch, S., Glenn, N., Thackray, G., & Shilling, K. (2005). Application of multi-temporal high-resolution imagery and GPS in a study of the motion of a canyon rim landslide. *Journal of Photogrammetry & Remote Sensing*, **59**, 212–221.

Chapin, F.S. III, Matson, P.A., & Mooney, H.A. (2003) *Principles of Terrestrial Ecosystem Ecology*. New York: Springer.

Chau, K.T. & Lo, K.H. (2004). Hazard assessment of debris flows for Leung King Estate of Hong Kong by incorporating GIS with numerical simulations. *Natural Hazards and Earth System Sciences*, **4**, 103–116.

Chau, M.M., Walker, L.R., & Mehltreter, K. (In press). An invasive tree fern alters soil and plant nutrient dynamics in Hawaii. *Biological Invasions*, doi: 10.1007/s10530-012-0291-0.

Chaudhry, S., Singh, S.P., & Singh, J.S. (1996). Performance of seedlings of various life forms on landslide-damaged forest sites in Central Himalaya. *Journal of Applied Ecology*, **33**, 109–117.

Chaytor, J.D., ten Brink, U.S., Solow, A.R., & Andrews, B.D. (2009). Size distribution of submarine landslides along the US Atlantic margin. *Marine Geology*, **264**, 16–27.

Chazdon, R.L. & Fetcher, N. (1984). Photosynthetic light environments in a lowland tropical rain forest in Costa Rica. *Journal of Ecology*, **72**, 553–564.

Chen, H. (2006). Controlling factors of hazardous debris flow in Taiwan. *Quaternary International*, **147**, 3–15.

Chen, H., Chen, R.H., & Lin, M.L. (1999). Initiation of the Tungmen debris flow, eastern Taiwan. *Environmental & Engineering Geoscience*, **4**, 459–473.

Chester, D.K., Duncan, A.M., & James, P.A. (2010). Mount Etna, Sicily: landscape evolution and hazard responses in the pre-industrial era. In *Landscapes and Societies*, eds. I.P. Martini & W. Chesworth, pp. 235–253. New York: Springer.

Chien, H-C. (2007). Landslide alter orbatid mite communities in litter layers of a monsoon forest in southern Taiwan. MS Thesis, Institute of Life Sciences, National Cheng Kung University, Taiwan.

Chigira, M. & Oyama, T. (1999). Mechanism and effect of chemical weathering on sedimentary rock. *Engineering Geology*, **55**, 3–14.

Chigira, M. & Yokoyama, O. (2005). Weathering profile of non-welded ignimbrite and the water infiltration behavior within it in relation to the generation of shallow landslides. *Engineering Geology*, **78**, 187–207.

Chou, W.C., Lin, W.T., & Lin, C.Y. (2007). Application of fuzzy set theory and PROMETHEE technique to evaluate suitable ecotechnology method: a case study in Shihmen Reservoir Watershed, Taiwan. *Ecological Engineering*, **31**, 269–280.

Claessens, L., Verburg, P.H., Schoorl, J.M., & Veldkamp, A. (2006). Contribution of topographically based landslide hazard modeling to the analysis of the spatial distribution and ecology of kauri (*Agathis australis*). *Landscape Ecology*, **21**, 63–76.

Claessens, L., Schoorl, J.M., & Veldkamp, A. (2007). Modelling the location of shallow landslides and their effects on landscape dynamics in large watersheds: an application for Northern New Zealand. *Geomorphology*, **87**, 16–27.

Clarke, M.A. & Walsh, R.P.D. (2006). Long-term erosion and surface roughness change of rain-forest terrain following selective logging, Danum Valley, Sabbah, Malaysia. *Catena*, **68**, 109–123.

Clarkson, B.R. & Clarkson, B.D. (1995). Recent vegetation changes on Mount Tarawera, Rotorua, New Zealand. *New Zealand Journal of Botany*, **33**, 339–354.

Clements, F.E. (1916). *Plant Succession: An Analysis of the Development of Vegetation*. Publication 242, Washington, D.C.: Carnegie Institution of Washington.

Clements, F.E. (1928). *Plant Succession and Indicators*. New York: H.W. Wilson.

Close, U. & McCormick, E. (1922). Where the mountains walked. *National Geographic Magazine*, **41**, 445–464.

Coates, D.R. (1977). Landslide perspectives. In *Landslides*, ed. D.R. Coates, pp. 3–28. Washington, DC: Geological Society of America.

Coelho, C.O.A. (2006). Portugal. In *Soil Erosion in Europe*, eds. J. Boardman & J. Poesen. pp. 359–367. Chichester: Wiley.

Coleman, D.C., Crossley Jr., D.A., & Hendrix, P.F. (2004). *Fundamentals of Soil Ecology*, 2nd Edition. San Diego, California, CA, U.S.: Elsevier.

Colesant, C. & Wasowski, J. (2006). Investigating landslides with space-borne Synthetic Aperture Radar (SAR) interferometry. *Engineering Geology*, **88**, 173–199.

Compton, S.G., Ross, S.J., & Thornton, I.W. B. (1994). Pollinator limitation of fig tree reproduction on the island of Anak Krakatau (Indonesia). *Biotropica*, **26**, 180–186.

Conant, D.S. (1976). Ecogeographic and systematic studies in American Cyatheaceae. PhD Dissertation, Harvard University, Boston, Massachusetts, U.S.

Connell, J.H. & Slatyer, R.O. (1977). Mechanisms of succession in natural communities and their roles in community stability and organization. *The American Naturalist*, **111**, 1119–1144.

Cooper, M.R., Bromhead, E.N., Petley, D.J., & Grant, D.I. (1998). The Selborne cutting stability experiment. *Géotechnique*, **48**, 83–101.

Costa, J.E. & Schuster, R.L. (1991). Documented historical landslide dams from around the world. *U.S. Geological Survey Open-File Report*, 91–239.

Coulter, H.W. & Migliaccio, R.R. (1966). Effects of the earthquake of March 17, 1964, at Valdez, Alaska. *U.S. Geological Survey Professional Paper*, 542-C, 1–36.

Courchamp, F. & Caut, S. (2005). Use of biological invasions and their control to study the dynamics of interacting populations. In *Conceptual Ecology and Invasions Biology*, eds. M.W. Cadotte, S.M. McMahon, & T. Fukami, pp. 253–279. New York: Springer.

Courtney, R. & Mullen, G. (2009). Use of germination and seedling performance bioassays for assessing revegetation strategies on bauxite residue. *Water, Air and Soil Pollution*, **197**, 15–22.

Couture, R., Konrad, J.-M., & Locat, J. (1995). Analyse de la liquéfaction et du comportement non drainé des sables du delta de Kenamu (Project ADFEX). *Canadian Geotechnical Journal*, **32**, 137–155.

Cover, M.R., de la Fuente, J.A., & Resh, V.H. (2010). Catastrophic disturbances in headwater streams: the long-term ecological effects of debris flows and debris floods in the Klamath Mountains, northern California. *Canadian Journal of Fisheries and Aquatic Sciences*, **67**, 1596–1610.

Cowles, H.C. (1901). The physiographic ecology of Chicago and vicinity: A study of the origin, development, and classification of plant societies. *Botanical Gazette*, **31**, 73–108, 145–182.

Cox, P.A. & Elmquist, T. (2000). Pollinator extinction in the Pacific Islands. *Conservation Biology*, **14**, 1237–1239.

Crisafulli, C.M., Swanson, F.J., & Dale, V.H. (2005). Overview of ecological responses to the eruption of Mount St. Helens: 1980–2005. In *Ecological*

Responses to the 1980 Eruption of Mount St. Helens, eds. V.H. Dale, F.J. Swanson, & C.M. Crisafulli, pp. 287–299. New York: Springer.

Cronin, V.S. (1992). Compound landslides: nature and hazard potential of secondary landslides within host landslides. *Reviews in Engineering Geology*, **9**, 1–9.

Crozier, M.J. (1984). Field assessment of slope instability. In *Slope Instability*, eds. D. Brunsden & D.B. Prior, pp. 103–142. Chichester: John Wiley.

Crozier, M.J. (1986). *Landslides: Causes, Consequences and Environment*. London: Croom-Helm.

Crozier, M.J., Howorth, R., & Grant, I.J. (1981). Landslide activity during Cyclone Wally, Fiji: A case study of Wainitubatalu catchment. *Pacific Viewpoint*, **22**, 69–88.

Cruden, D.M. (1991). A simple definition of a landslide. *Bulletin of the International Association of Engineering Geology*, **43**, 27–29.

Cruden, D.M. & Fell, R. (1997). *Landslide Risk Assessment*. Rotterdam: Balkema.

Cruden, D.M. & Varnes, D.J. (1996). Landslide types and processes. In *Landslides: Investigation and Mitigation*, eds. A.K. Turner & R.L. Schuster, pp. 36–75. Special Report 247, Transportation Research Board, National Research Council. Washington, DC: National Academy Press.

Cruden, D.M., Keegan, T.R., & Thomson, S. (1993). The landslide dam on the Saddle River near Rycroft, Alberta. *Canadian Geotechnical Journal*, **30**, 1003–1015.

Crutchley, G.J., Gorman, A.R., & Fohrmann, M. (2007). Investigation of the role of gas hydrates in continental slope stability west of Fiordland, New Zealand. *New Zealand Journal of Geology and Geophysics*, **50**, 357–364.

Cumberland, K.B. (1944). *Soil Erosion in New Zealand: A Geographic Reconnaissance*. Wellington: Soil Conservation and Rivers Control Council.

Cumberland, K.B. & Cumberland, G. (2008). Poor land management. A letter to *The Press*, 24 September 2008, Christchurch, New Zealand.

Dadson, S.J., Hovius, N., Chen, H., *et al.* (2003). Links between erosion, runoff variability and seismicity in the Taiwan orogen. *Nature*, **426**, 648–651.

Dai, E.C. & Lee, C.F. (2002). Landslide characteristics and slope instability modeling using GIS, Lantau Island, Hong Kong. *Geomorphology*, **42**, 213–228.

Dai, E.C., Lee, C.F., & Nagi, Y.Y. (2002). Landslide risk assessment and management: an overview. *Engineering Geology*, **64**, 65–87.

Dale, V.H. (1986). Plant recovery on the debris avalanche at Mount St. Helens. In *Mount St. Helens: Five Years Later*, ed. S.A.C. Keller, pp. 208–214. Cheney, Washington, U.S.: Eastern Washington Press.

Dale, V.H., Joyce, L.A., McNultry, S., *et al.* (2001). Climate change and forest disturbance. *BioScience*, **51**, 723–734.

Dale, V.H., Swanson, F.J., & Crisafulli, C.M. (eds.) (2005). *Ecological Responses to the 1980 Eruption of Mount St. Helens*. New York: Springer.

Dalling, J.W. (1994). Vegetation colonization of landslides in the Blue Mountains, Jamaica. *Biotropica*, **26**, 392–399.

Dalling, J.W. & Iremonger, S. (1994). Preliminary estimate of landslide disturbance in the Blue Mountains, Jamaica. *Caribbean Journal of Science*, **30**, 290–292.

Dalling, J.W. & Tanner, E.V.J. (1995). An experimental study of regeneration on landslides in montane rain forest in Jamaica. *Journal of Ecology*, **83**, 55–64.

D'Antonio, C.M. & Vitousek, P.M. (1992). Biological invasions by exotic grasses, the grass/fire cycle, and global change. *Annual Review of Ecology and Systematics*, **23**, 63–87.

Davis, T.J., Klinkenberg, B., & Keller, C.P. (2004). Evaluating restoration success on Lyell Island, British Columbia using oblique videogrammetry. *Restoration Ecology*, **12**, 447–455.

Davis, W.M. (1909). The geographical cycle. In *Geographical Essays*, ed. D.W. Johnson, pp. 254–256. Oxford: Ginn & Co.

Dawson, B. (1995). *Crowsnest: An Illustrated History and Guide to the Crowsnest Pass*. Canmore, Alberta, Canada: Altitude Publishing.

DeBano, L.F. (2000). The role of fire and soil heating on water repellency in wildland environments: a review. *Journal of Hydrology*, **231**, 195–206.

DeBiase, R.A., Whipple, K.X., Heimsath, A.M., & Ouimet, W.B. (2010). Landscape form and millennial erosion rates in the San Gabriel Mountains, CA. *Earth and Planetary Science Letters*, **289**, 134–144.

de Boer, D.H. (1992). Hierarchies and spatial scale in process geomorphology: a review. *Geomorphology*, **4**, 303–318.

de la Cruz, M. & Dirzo, R. (1987). A survey of the standing levels of herbivory in seedlings from a Mexican rain forest. *Biotropica*, **19**, 98–106.

del Moral, R. (1993). Mechanisms of primary succession on volcanoes: a view from Mount St. Helens. In *Primary Succession on Land*, eds. J. Miles & D.H. Walton, pp. 79–100. Oxford: Blackwell.

del Moral, R. (2011). The importance of long-term studies of ecosystem reassembly after the eruption of the Kasatochi Island Volcano. *Arctic, Antarctic, and Alpine Research*, **42**, 335–341.

del Moral, R. & Walker, L.R. (2007). *Environmental Disasters, Natural Recovery and Human Responses*. Cambridge: Cambridge University Press.

del Moral, R. & Wood, D.M. (1993). Early primary succession on a barren volcanic plain at Mount St. Helens, Washington. *American Journal of Botany*, **80**, 981–992.

del Moral, R., Walker, L.R., & Bakker, J.P. (2007). Insights gained from succession for the restoration of landscape structure and function. In *Linking Restoration and Ecological Succession*, eds. L.R. Walker, J. Walker, & R.J. Hobbs, pp. 19–55. New York: Springer.

DeLong, H.B., Lieffers, V.J., & Blenis, P.V. (1997). Microsite effects on first-year establishment and overwinter survival of white spruce in aspen-dominated boreal mixedwoods. *Canadian Journal of Forest Research*, **27**, 1452–1457.

Dengler, N.G., Dengler, R.E., Donnelley, P.M., & Hattersley, P.W. (1994). Quantitative leaf anatomy of C_3 and C_4 grasses (Poaceae): Bundle sheath and mesophyll surface area relationships. *Annals of Botany*, **73**, 241–255.

Denslow, J.S. (1980). Gap partitioning among tropical rainforest trees. *Biotropica*, **12**, 47–55.

Denslow, J.S., Schultz, J.C., Vitousek, P.M., & Strain, B.R. (1990). Growth responses of tropical shrubs to treefall gap environments. *Ecology*, **71**, 165–179.

Denslow, J.S., Space, J.C., & Thomas, P.A. (2009). Invasive exotic plants in the tropical Pacific Islands: patterns of diversity. *Biotropica*, **41**, 162–170.

Derose, R.C., Gomez, B., Marden, M., & Trustrum, N.A. (1998). Gully erosion in Mangatu Forest, New Zealand, estimated from digital elevation models. *Earth Surface Processes and Landforms*, **23**, 1045–1053.

Devkota, B.D., Omura, H., Kubota, T., Paudel, P., & Acharya, K.P. (2006a). Vegetation restoration and root morphological features of colonized plants observed at a landslide scar, Matatirtha, Kathmandu, Nepal. *Banko Janakari*, **16**, 71–78.

Devkota, B.D., Paudel, P., Omura, H., Kubota, T., & Morita, K. (2006b). Uses of vegetative measures for erosion mitigation in mid hill areas of Nepal. *Kyushu Journal of Forest Research*, **59**, 265–268.

Devoe, N.N. (1989). Differential seeding and regeneration in openings and beneath closed canopy in sub-tropical wet forest. PhD Dissertation, School of Forestry and Environmental Studies, Yale University, New Haven, Connecticut, U.S.

Dhakal, A.S. & Sidle, R.C. (2003). Long-term modeling of landslides for different forest management practices. *Earth Surface Processes and Landforms*, **28**, 853–868.

Dhakal, A.S. & Sidle, R.C. (2004). Distributed simulations of landslides for different rainfall conditions. *Hydrological Processes*, **18**, 757–776.

Diaz, R.J., Cutter, G.R., & Rhoads, D.C. (1994). The importance of bioturbation to continental slope sediment structure and benthic processes off Cape Hatteras, North Carolina. *Deep-Sea Research II*, **41**, 719–734.

Diamond, J., Bishop, K.D., & Gilardi, J.D. (1999). Geophagy in New Guinea birds. *Ibis*, **141**, 181–193.

Dominik, T. (1956). Mycotrophy of poplars in their natural associations in Poland. *Roczniki Nauk Lesnych*, **14**, 247–266 (in English Translation, U.S. Dept. of Commerce Office of Technical Services Translation OTS 60–21382, 1961).

Douglas, I., Bidin, K., Balamurugan, G., *et al.* (1999). The role of extreme events in the impacts of selective tropical forestry on erosion during harvesting and recovery phases at Danum Valley, Sabbah. *Philosophical Transactions of the Royal Society London*, **354**, 1749–1761.

D'Souza, L.E., Reiter, M., Six, L.J., & Bilby, R.E. (2011). Response of vegetation, shade and stream temperature to debris torrents in two western Oregon watersheds. *Forest Ecology and Management*, **261**, 2157–2167.

Dung, B.X., Miyata, S., & Gomi, T. (2011). Effect of forest thinning on overland flow generation on hillslopes covered by Japanese cypress. *Ecohydrology and Hydrobiology*, **4**, 367–378.

Durand, L.Z. & Goldstein, G. (2001a). Growth, leaf characteristics, and spore production in native and invasive tree ferns in Hawaii. *American Fern Journal*, **91**, 25–35.

Durand, L.Z. & Goldstein, G. (2001b). Photosynthesis, photoinhibition, and nitrogen use efficiency in native and invasive tree ferns in Hawaii. *Oecologia*, **126**, 345–354.

Edwards, E.J. & Still, C.J. (2008). Climate, phylogeny and the ecological distribution of C_4 grasses. *Ecology Letters*, **11**, 266–276.

Egler, F.E. (1954). Vegetation science concepts I. Initial floristics composition, a factor in old-field vegetation development. *Vegetatio*, **4**, 412–417.

Ehley, P.L. (1986). The Portuguese Bend landslide: its mechanics and a plan for its stabilization. In *Landslides and Landslide Mitigation in Southern California*, ed. P.L. Ehley, pp. 181–190. Guidebook for field trip, Los Angeles, California: Cordilleran Section of the Geological Society of America.

Elias, R.B. & Dias, E. (2004). Primary succession on lava domes on Terceira (Azores). *Journal of Vegetation Science*, **15**, 331–338.

Elias, R.B. & Dias, E. (2009). Effects of landslides on the mountain vegetation of Flores Island, Azores. *Journal of Vegetation Science*, **20**, 706–717.

Elverhoi, A., Breien, H., De Blasio, F.V., Harbitz, C.B., & Pagliardi, M. (2010). Submarine landslides and the importance of the initial sediment composition for run-out length and final deposit. *Ocean Dynamics*, **60**, 1027–1046.

Enright, N.J., Ogden, J., & Rigg, L.S. (1999). Dynamics of forests with Araucariaceae in the western Pacific. *Journal of Vegetation Science*, **10**, 793–804.

Evans, S.G. & Bent, A.L. (2004). The Las Colinas landslide, Santa Tecla: a highly destructive flowside triggered by the January 13, 2001, El Salvador earthquake. *Geological Society of America Special Paper*, **375**, 25–38.

Evans, S.G., Couture, R., & Raymond, E.L. (2002). *Catastrophic landslides and related processes in the southeastern Cordillera: analysis of impact on lifelines and communities.* Geological Survey Canada, Natural Resources Canada.

Evans, S.G., Guthrie, R.H., Roberts, N.J., & Bishop, N.F. (2007). The disastrous 17 February 2006 rockslide-debris avalanche on Leyte Island, Philippines: a catastrophic landslide in tropical mountain terrain. *Natural Hazards and Earth System Sciences*, **7**, 89–101.

Fabbri, A.G., Chung, C.-J.F., Cendrero, A., & Remondo, J. (2003). Is prediction of future landslides possible with a GIS? *Natural Hazards*, **30**, 487–499.

Fagan, W.F. & Bishop, J.G. (2000). Trophic interactions during primary succession: herbivores slow a plant reinvasion at Mount St. Helens. *The American Naturalist*, **155**, 238–251.

Farris, M.A. (1998). The effects of rock climbing on the vegetation of three Minnesota cliff systems. *Canadian Journal of Botany*, **76**, 1982–1990.

Fastie, C.L. (1995). Causes and ecosystem consequences of multiple pathways on primary succession at Glacier Bay, Alaska. *Ecology*, **76**, 1899–1916.

Fenner, M. & Thompson, K. (2005). *The Ecology of Seeds.* Cambridge: Cambridge University Press.

Fernandes, N.F., Guimãraes, R.F., Gomes, R.A.T., et al. (2004). Topographic controls of landslides in Rio de Janeiro: field evidence and modeling. *Catena*, **55**, 163–181.

Fernández, D.S. & Fetcher, N. (1991). Changes in light availability following Hurricane Hugo in a subtropical montane forest in Puerto Rico. *Biotropica*, **23**, 393–399.

Fernández, D.S. & Myster, R.W. (1995). Temporal variation and frequency distribution of photosynthetic photon flux densities on landslides in Puerto Rico. *Tropical Ecology*, **36**, 73–87.

Ferreira, A.B., Zêzere, J.L., & Rodrigues, M.L. (1996). The Calhandriz landslide (Metropolitan area of Lisbon). In *Landslides*, eds. J. Chacón, C. Irigaray, & T. Fernández, pp. 31–38. Rotterdam: Balkema.

Ferrer, M. & Ayala, F. (1996). Landslides climatic susceptibility map of Spain. In *Landslides*, eds. J. Chacón, C. Irigaray, & T. Fernández, pp. 323–333. Rotterdam: Balkema.

Fetcher, N., Haines, B.L., Cordero, R.A., *et al.* (1996). Responses of tropical plants to nutrients and light on a landslide in Puerto Rico. *Journal of Ecology*, **84**, 331–341.

Fine, I.V., Rabinovich, A.B., Bornhold, B.D., Thomson, R.E., & Kulikov, E.A. (2005). The Grand Banks landslide-generated tsunami of November 18, 1929: preliminary analysis and numerical modeling. *Marine Geology*, **215**, 45–57.

Fischer, L., Kääb, A., Huggel, C., & Noetzli, J. (2006). Geology, glacier retreat and permafrost degradation as controlling factors of slope instabilities in a high-mountain rock wall: the Monte Rosa east face. *Natural Hazards and Earth System Sciences*, **6**, 761–772.

Flaccus, E. (1959). Revegetation of landslides in the White Mountains of New Hampshire. *Ecology*, **40**, 692–703.

Forman, R.T.T., Sperling, D., Bissonette, J.A., *et al.* (2003). *Road Ecology: Science and Solutions*. Washington, D.C.: Island Press.

Fort, M., Cossart, E., & Arnaud-Fassetta, G. (2010). Catastrophic landslides and sedimentary budgets. In *Geomorphological Hazards and Disaster Prevention*, eds. I. Alcantara-Ayala & A. Goudie, pp. 75–85. Cambridge: Cambridge University Press.

Fosberg, F.R. (1942). Uses of Hawaiian ferns. *American Fern Journal*, **32**, 15–23.

Foster, D.R., Knight, D.H., & Franklin, J.F. (1998). Landscape patterns and legacies resulting from large, infrequent forest disturbances. *Ecosystems*, **1**, 497–510.

Francescato, V. & Scotton, M. (1999). Analisi di vegetazioni colonizzatrici di frane su flysch e morena calcarea del bellunese. *L'Italia Forestale e Montana*, **6**, 324–349.

Francescato, V., Scotton, M., Zarin, D.J., Innes, J.C., & Bryant, D.M. (2001). Fifty years of natural revegetation on a landslide in Franconia Notch, New Hampshire, U.S. *Canadian Journal of Botany*, **79**, 1477–1485.

García-Fayos, P., García-Ventoso, B., & Cerdà, A. (2000). Limitations to plant establishment on eroded slopes in southeastern Spain. *Journal of Vegetation Science*, **11**, 77–86.

Garwood, N.C. (1985). Earthquake caused landslides in Panama: recovery of vegetation. *National Geographic Society Research Reports*, **21**, 181–183.

Garwood, N.C., Janos, D.J., & Brokaw, N. (1979). Earthquake-caused landslides: a major disturbance to tropical forests. *Science*, **205**, 997–999.

Gasiev, E. (1984). Study of the Usoy landslide in Pamir. *Proceedings of the Fourth International Symposium on Landslides*, **1**, 511–515.

Geertsema, M. (1998). Flowslides in waterlain muds of northwestern British Columbia, Canada. *Proceedings of the 8th Congress of the International Association of Engineering Geology and the Environment*, **3**, 1913–1921.

Geertsema, M. & Pojar, J.J. (2007). Influence of landslides on biophysical diversity–a perspective from British Columbia. *Geomorphology*, **89**, 55–69.

Geertsema, M. & Schwab, J.W. (1995). The Mink Creek earthflow, Terrace, British Columbia. *Proceedings of the 48th Canadian Geotechnical Conference*, Vancouver, B.C., **2**, 625–634.

Geist, H.J. & Lambin, E.F. (2002). Proximate causes and underlying driving forces of tropical deforestation. *BioScience*, **52**, 143–150.

Geist, V. (1971). *Mountain Sheep*. Chicago: Chicago University Press.

Gers, E., Florin, N., Gartner, H., *et al.* (2001). Application of shrubs for dendrogeo-morphological analysis to reconstruct spatial and temporal landslide movement patterns. A preliminary study. *Zeitschrift für Geomorphologie N.F.*, **125**, 163–175.

Ghahramani, A., Ishikawa, Y., Gomi, T., & Miyata, S. (2011). Downslope soil detachment-transport on steep slopes via rain splash. *Hydrological Processes*, **25**, 2471–2480.

Ghestem, M., Sidle, R.C., & Stokes, A. (2011). The influence of plant root systems on subsurface flow: implications for slope stability. *BioScience*, **61**, 869–879.

Giampietro, M. (1999). Economic growth, human disturbance to ecological systems, and sustainability. In *Ecosystems of Disturbed Ground, Ecosystems of the World 16*, ed. L.R. Walker, pp. 723–746. Amsterdam: Elsevier.

Giannecchini, R. (2005). Rainfall triggering soil slips in the southern Apuan Alps (Tuscany, Italy). *Advances in Geosciences*, **2**, 21–24.

Glade, T. (2003). Landslide occurrence as a response to land use change: a review of evidence from New Zealand. *Catena*, **51**, 297–314.

Glenn-Lewin, D.C., Peet, R.K., & Veblen, T.T., eds. (1992). *Plant Succession: Theory and Prediction*. London: Chapman and Hall.

Glynn, P.W. (1997). Bioerosion and coral reef growth: a dynamic balance. In *Life and Death of Coral Reefs*, ed. C. Birkeland, pp. 68–95. London: Chapman and Hall.

Goetz, J.N., Guthrie, R.H., & Brenning, A. (2011). Integrating physical and empirical landslide susceptibility models using generalized additive models. *Geomorphology*, **129**, 376–386.

Goh, C.J., Avadhani, P.N., Loh, C.S., Hanegraaf, C., & Arditti, J. (1977). Diurnal stomata and acidity rhythms in orchid leaves. *New Phytologist*, **78**, 365–372.

Gómez-Aparicio, L. (2009). The role of plant interactions in the restoration of degraded ecosystems: a meta-analysis across life-forms and ecosystems. *Journal of Ecology*, **97**, 1202–1214.

Gomi, T., Sidle, R.C., & Richardson, J.S. (2002). Understanding processes and downstream linkages of headwater systems. *BioScience*, **52**, 905–916.

González-Diez, A.G., Salas, L., de Teran, J.R.D., & Cendreno, A. (1996). Late Quaternary climate changes and mass movement frequency and magnitude in the Cantabrian region, Spain. *Geomorphology*, **15**, 291–309.

Gori, P.L., Jeer, S.P., & Highland, L.M. (2003). Enlisting the support of land-use planners to reduce debris-flow hazards in the United States. In *Debris-flow Hazards Mitigation: Mechanics, Prediction and Assessment*, eds. D. Rickenmann & C. Chen, pp. 1119–1127. Rotterdam: Millpress.

Goudelis, G., Ganatsas, P.P., Spanos, I., & Karpi, A. (2007). Effect of repeated fire on plant community recovery in Penteli, central Greece. In *Eco- and Ground Bio-Engineering: The Use of Vegetation to Improve Slope Stability*, eds. A. Stokes, I. Spanos, & J.E. Norris, pp. 337–344. *Proceedings of the First International Conference on Eco-Engineering*, 13–17 September 2004. Dordrecht: Springer.

Goudie, A.S. (2010). Geomorphological hazards and global climate change. In *Geomorphological Hazards and Disaster Prevention*, eds. I. Alcantara-Ayala & A. Goudie, pp. 245–255. Cambridge: Cambridge University Press.

Goudie, A.S. & Boardman, J. (2010). Soil erosion. In *Geomorphological Hazards and Disaster Prevention*, eds. I. Alcantara-Ayala & A. Goudie, pp. 177–188. Cambridge: Cambridge University Press.

Graettinger, A.H., Manville, V., & Briggs, R.M. (2010). Deposition record of historic lahars in the upper Whangaehu Valley, Mt. Ruapehu, New Zealand: implications for trigger mechanisms, flow dynamics and lahar hazards. *Bulletin of Volcanology*, **72**, 279–296.

Grant, F. (2012). http://www.nzherald.co.nz/tangiwai-rail-disaster/news/article.cfm?c_id=1500933&objectid=1592575. Accessed 25 February 2012.

Grau, H.R., Aide, T.M., Zimmerman, J.K., *et al.* (2003). The ecological consequences of socioeconomic land-use changes in postagriculture Puerto Rico. *BioScience*, **53**, 1159–1168.

Greene, H.G., Murai, L.Y., Watts, P., *et al.* (2006). Submarine landslides in the Santa Barbara Channel as potential tsunami sources. *Natural Hazards and Earth System Sciences*, **6**, 63–88.

Gryta, J.J. & Bartolomew, M.J. (1989). Factors influencing the distribution of debris avalanches associated with the 1969 Hurricane Camille in Nelson County, Virginia. *Geological Society of America Special Paper*, **236**, 15–27.

Guariguata, M.R. (1990). Landslide disturbance and forest regeneration in the Upper Luquillo Mountains of Puerto Rico. *Journal of Ecology*, **78**, 814–832.

Guariguata, M.R. & Larsen, M.C. (1990). Preliminary map showing location of landslides in El Yunque Quadrangle, Puerto Rico. *U.S. Geological Survey Open File Report* 89–257.

Günther, A., Carstensen, A., & Pohl, W. (2004). Automated sliding susceptibility mapping of rock slopes. *Natural Hazards and Earth System Sciences*, **4**, 95–102.

Gupta, R.P. & Joshi, B.C. (1990). Landslide hazard zoning using the GIS approach– a case study from the Ramganga Catchment, Himalayas. *Engineering Geology*, **28**, 119–131.

Guzmán-Grajales, S.M., & Walker, L.R. (1991). Differential seedling responses to litter after Hurricane Hugo in the Luquillo Experimental Forest, Puerto Rico. *Biotropica*, **23**, 407–413.

Guzzetti, F. (2000). Landslide fatalities and the evaluation of landslide risk in Italy. *Engineering Geology*, **58**, 89–107.

Guzzetti, F., Carrara, A., Cardinali, M., & Reichenbach, P. (1999). Landslide hazard evaluation: a review of current techniques and their application in a multi-scale study, Central Italy. *Geomorphology*, **31**, 181–216.

Habu, J. (2004). *Ancient Jomon of Japan*. Cambridge: Cambridge University Press.

Haeussler, S., Tappeiner, J.C., II, & Greber, B.J. (1995). Germination, survival, and early growth of red alder seedlings in the central Coast Range of Oregon. *Canadian Journal of Forest Research*, **25**, 1639–1651.

Haflidason, H., Sejrup, H.P., Nygård, A., *et al.* (2004). The Storegga Slide: architecture, geometry and slide development. *Marine Geology*, **213**, 201–234.

Hafner, D.J. (1993). North American Pika (*Ochotona princeps*) as a Late Quaternary biogeographic indicator species. *Quaternary Research*, **39**, 373–380.

Haigh, M.J., Rawat, J.S., & Baraya, S.K. (1988). Environmental correlations of landslide frequency along new highways in the Himalaya – preliminary results. *Catena*, **15**, 539–553.

Haigh, M.J., Rawat, J.S., Bartarya, S.K., & Rawat, M.S. (1993). Environmental influences on landslide activity: Almora Bypass, Kumaun Lesser Himalaya. *Natural Hazards*, **8**, 153–170.

Halvorson, J.J., Smith, J.L., & Kennedy, A.C. (2005). Lupine effects on soil development and function during early primary succession at Mount St. Helens. In *Ecological Responses to the 1980 Eruption of Mount St. Helens*, eds. V.H. Dale, F.J. Swanson, & C.M. Crisafulli, pp. 243–254. New York: Rotterdam.

Hamdouni, R.El, Irigaray, C., & Chacón, J. (1996). Landslides inventory and determining factors in the Albuñuelas river basin (Granada, Spain). In *Landslides*, eds. J. Chacón, C. Irigaray, & T. Fernández, pp. 21–30. Rotterdam: Balkema.

Hampton, M.A., Lee, H.J., & Locat, J. (1996). Submarine landslides. *Reviews of Geophysics*, **34**, 33–59.

Hancox, G.T., Perrin, N.D., & Dellow, G.D. (2002). Recent studies of historical earthquake-induced landsliding, ground damage and MM intensity in New Zealand. *Bulletin of New Zealand Society of Earthquake Engineering*, **35**, 59–94.

Hansen, A. (1984a). Landslide hazard analysis. In *Slope Instability*, eds. D. Brunsden & D.B. Prior, pp. 523–602. New York: Wiley.

Hansen, M.J. (1984b). Strategies for classification of landslides. In *Slope Instability*, eds. D. Brunsden & D.B. Prior, pp. 1–25. New York: Wiley.

Havlick, D.G. (2002). *No Place Distant*. Washington, D.C.: Island Press.

Heezen, B.C., Ewing, M., & Ericson, D.B. (1955a). Reconnaissance survey of the abyssal plain south of Newfoundland. *Deep-Sea Research*, **2**, 122–133.

Heezen, B.C., Ewing, M., & Menzies, R.J. (1955b). The influence of submarine turbidity currents on abyssal productivity. *Oikos*, **6**, 170–182.

Henkel, D.J. (1970). The role of waves in causing submarine landslides. *Geotechnique*, **20**, 75–80.

Herrington, R.E. (1988). Talus use by amphibians and reptiles in the Pacific Northwest. In *Management of Amphibians, Reptiles and Small Mammals in North America*, USDA Forest Service General Technical Report RM-166, eds. R.C. Szaro, K.E. Severson, & D.R. Patton, pp. 216–221. Flagstaff, Arizona: USDA Forest Service.

Heshmati, M., Arifin, A., Shamshuddin, J., Majid, N.M., & Ghaituri, M. (2011). Factors affecting landslides occurrence in agro-ecological zones in the Merek catchment, Iran. *Journal of Arid Environments*, **75**, 1072–1082.

Hewitt, K. (1997). *Regions of Risk: A Geographical Introduction to Disasters*. Harlow, U.K.: Addison-Wesley Longman.

Hewitt, K. (2006). Disturbance regime landscapes: mountain drainage systems interrupted by large rockslides. *Progress in Physical Geography*, **30**, 365–393.

Hewitt, K. (2009). Rock avalanches that travel onto glaciers and related developments, Karakoram Himalaya, Inner Asia. *Geomorphology*, **103**, 66–79.

Highland, L.M. (1997). Landslide hazard and risk: current and future directions for the United States Geological Survey's landslide program. In *Landslide Risk Assessment*, eds. D. Cruden & R. Fell, pp. 207–213. Rotterdam: Balkema.

Hilton, R.G., Galy, A., Hovius, N., Horng, M.-J., & Chen, H. (2011). Efficient transport of fossil organic carbon to the ocean by steep mountain rivers: an orogenic carbon sequestration mechanism. *Geology*, **39**, 71–74.

Hobbs, R.J., Jentsch, A., & Temperton, V.M. (2007a). Restoration as a process of assembly and succession mediated by disturbance. In *Linking Restoration and Ecological Succession*, eds. L.R. Walker, J.Walker, & R.J. Hobbs, pp. 150–167. New York: Springer.

Hobbs, R.J., Walker, L.R., & Walker, J. (2007b). Integrating restoration and succession. In *Linking Restoration and Ecological Succession*, eds. L.R. Walker, J. Walker, & R.J. Hobbs, pp. 168–179. New York: Springer.

Hobbs, R.J., Higgs, E., & Harris, J.A. (2009). Novel ecosystems: implications for conservation and restoration. *Trends in Ecology and Evolution*, **24**, 599–605.

Hodge, A., Robinson, D., & Fitter, A. (2000). Are microorganisms more effective than plants at competing for nitrogen? *Trends in Plant Science*, **5**, 304–308.

Hodkinson, I.D., Webb, N.R., & Coulson, S.J. (2002). Primary community assembly on land – the missing stages: why are the heterotrophic organisms always there first? *Journal of Ecology*, **90**, 569–577.

Holl, K.D. (1998). Do perching structures elevate seed rain and seedling establishment in abandoned tropical pasture? *Restoration Ecology*, **6**, 253–261.

Holm, H., Bovis, M., & Jakob, M. (2004). The landslide response of alpine basins to post-Little Ice Age glacial thinning and retreat in southwestern British Columbia. *Geomorphology*, **57**, 201–216.

Holtz, R.D. & Schuster, R.L. (1996). Stabilization of soil slopes. In *Landslides: Investigation and Mitigation*, eds. A.K. Turner & R.S. Schuster, pp. 439–473. Special Report 247, Transport Research Board, Washington, D.C.: National Academic Press.

Hong, Y., Adler, R.F., & Huffman, G.J. (2007). Satellite remote sensing for global landslide monitoring. *EOS, Transactions of the American Geophysical Union*, **88**, 357–358.

Hou, J.-J., Han, M.-K., Chai, B.-L., & Han, H.-Y. (1998). Geomorphological observations of active faults in the epicentral region of the Huaxian large earthquake in 1556 in Shaanxi Province, China. *Journal of Structural Geology*, **20**, 549–557.

Hou, P.-C.L, Zou, X., Huang, C.-Y., & Chien, H.-J. (2005). Plant litter decomposition influenced by soil animals and disturbance in a subtropical rainforest of Taiwan. *Pedobiology*, **49**, 539–547.

Huggett, R.J. (1998). Soil chronosequences, soil development, and soil evolution. *Catena*, **32**, 155–172.

Hughes, F., Vitousek, P.M., & Tunison, T. (1991). Alien grass invasion and fire in the seasonal submontane zone of Hawaii. *Ecology*, **72**, 743–746.

Hühnerbach, V. & Masson, D.G. (2004). Landslides in the North Atlantic and its adjacent seas: an analysis of their morphology, setting and behavior. *Marine Geology*, **213**, 343–362.

Hull, J.C. & Scott, R.C. (1982). Plant succession on debris avalanches of Nelson County, Virginia. *Castanea*, **47**, 158–176.

Hupp, C.R. (1983). Seedling establishment on a landslide site. *Castanea*, **48**, 89–98.

IAEG Commission on Landslides (1990). Suggested nomenclature for landslides. *Bulletin of the International Association of Engineering Geology*, **41**, 13–16.

Ibetsberger, H.J. (1996). The Tsergo Ri landslide: an uncommon area of high morphological activity in the Langthang valley, Nepal. *Tectonophysics*, **260**, 85–93.

Ikeya, H. (1989). Debris flow and its countermeasures in Japan. *Bulletin of The International Association of Engineering Geology*, **40**, 15–33.

Imaizumi, F., Sidle, R.C., & Kamei, R. (2008). Effects of forest harvesting on the occurrence of landslides and debris flows in steep terrain of central Japan. *Earth Surface Processes and Landforms*, **33**, 827–840.

Innes, J.L. (1985). Lichenometric dating of debris-flow deposits on alpine colluvial fans in southwest Norway. *Earth Surface Processes*, **19**, 519–524.

IPCC (2007). *Climate Change 2007: The Physical Science Basis. Contribution of Working Group I to the Fourth Assessment Report of the Intergovernmental Panel on Climate Change*, eds. Solomon, S., Qin, D., Manning, M., *et al*. Cambridge: Cambridge University Press.

Iverson, R.M. (2005). Regulation of landslide motion by dilatancy and pore pressure feedback. *Journal of Geophysics Research*, **110**, F02015, doi:10.1029/2004JF000268.

James, I.L. (1973). Mass movements in the upper Pohangina Catchment, Ruahine Range. *Journal of Hydrology (New Zealand)*, **12**, 92–102.

Jane, G.T. & Green, T.G.A. (1983). Morphology and incidence of landslides in the Kaimai Range, North Island, New Zealand. *New Zealand Journal of Geology and Geophysics*, **26**, 71–84.

Janos, D.P., Sahley, C.T., & Emmons, L.H. (1995). Rodent dispersal of vesicular-arbuscular mycorrhizal fungi in Amazonian Peru. *Ecology*, **76**, 1852–1858.

Janzen, D.H. (1973). Sweep samples of tropical foliar insects: effects of season, vegetation types, elevation, time of day and insularity. *Ecology*, **54**, 687–701.

Jenny, H. (1941). *Factors of Soil Formation*. New York: McGraw-Hill.

Jenny, H. (1980). *The Soil Resource: Origin and Behavior*. New York: Springer.

Jibson, R.W. (1989). Debris flows in southern Puerto Rico. *Geological Society of America Special Paper 236*, 29–55.

Jibson, R.W. & Keefer, D.K. (1989). Statistical analysis of factors affecting landslide distribution in the New Madrid seismic zone, Tennessee and Kentucky. *Engineering Geology*, **27**, 509–542.

Johnson, A.M. & Rodine, J.R. (1984). Debris flow. In *Slope Instability*, eds. D. Brunsden & D.B. Prior, pp. 257–361. Chichester: Wiley.

Johnson, E.A. & Miyanishi, K. (2008). Testing the assumptions of chronosequences in succession. *Ecology Letters*, **11**, 419–431.

Johnson, P.N. (1976). Changes in landslide vegetation at Lake Thomson, Fiordland, New Zealand. *New Zealand Journal of Botany*, **14**, 197–198.

Jones, F.O. (1973). Landslides of Rio de Janeiro and the Sierra das Araras Escarpment, Brazil. *U.S. Geological Survey Professional Paper 697*.

Kamai, T. Shuzui, H., Kasahara, R., & Kobayashi, Y. (2004). Earthquake risk assessments of large residential fill-slope in urban areas. *Journal of Japanese Landslide Society*, **40**, 389–399.

Kaplan, B.A. & Moermond, T.C. (2000). Foraging ecology of the mountain monkey (*Cercopithecus l'hoesti*): implications for its evolutionary history and use of disturbed forest. *American Journal of Primatology*, **50**, 227–246.

Kappelle, M., Avertin, G., Juárez, M.E., & Zamora, N. (2000). Useful plants within a campesino community in a Costa Rican montane cloud forest. *Mountain Research and Development*, **20**, 162–171.

Kay, E.A. (ed.) (1994). *A Natural History of the Hawaiian Islands*. Honolulu: University of Hawaii Press.

Kayen, R.E. & Lee, H.J. (1991). Pleistocene slope instability of gas hydrate-laden sediment on the Beaufort Sea margin. *Marine Geotechnology*, **10**, 125–142.

Keefer, D.K. (1984). Landslides caused by earthquakes. *Geological Society of America Bulletin*, **95**, 406–421.

Keefer, D.K. (1994). The importance of earthquake-induced landslides to long-term slope erosion and slope-failure hazards in seismically active regions. *Geomorphology*, **10**, 265–284.

Keefer, D.K. (2000). Statistical analysis of an earthquake-induced landslide distribution – the 1989 Loma Prieta, California event. *Engineering Geology*, **58**, 231–249.

Keefer, D.K. & Larsen, M.C. (2007). Assessing landslide hazards. *Science*, **316**, 1136–1139.

Keefer, D.K. & Wilson, R.C. (1989). Predicting earthquake-induced landslides, with emphasis on arid and semi-arid environments, In: *Landslides in Arid and Semi-arid Environments*, eds. P.M. Sadler & D.M. Morton, Vol. 2, Part 1, pp. 118–149. Riverside, California, U.S.: Inland Geological Society Southern California Publishing.

Keefer, D.K., Wilson, R.C., Mark, R.K., *et al.* (1987). Realtime landslide warning during heavy rainfall. *Science*, **238**, 921–925.

Keim, R.F. & Skaugset, A.E. (2003). Modelling effects of forest canopies on slope stability. *Hydrological Processes*, **17**, 1457–1467.

Keller, E.A. (1996). *Environmental Geology, 7th Edition*. Upper Saddle River, New Jersey: Prentice Hall.

Kelsey, H.M. (1978). Earthflows in Franciscan melange, Van Duzen River basin, California. *Geology*, **6**, 361–364.

Kerr, G.H. (2000). *Okinawa: The History of an Island People*. Tokyo: Tuttle Publishing.

Kessler, M. (1999). Plant species richness and endemism during natural landslide succession in a perhumid montane forest in the Bolivian Andes. *Ecotropica*, **4**, 123–136.

Kessler, M. (2010). Biogeography of ferns. In *Fern Ecology*, eds. K. Mehltreter, L.R. Walker, & J.M. Sharpe, pp. 22–60. Cambridge: Cambridge University Press.

Keys, D. (2000). *Catastrophe: An Investigation into the Origins of the Modern World*. New York: Ballantine Books.

Khan, B., Abdukadiri, A., Qureshi, R., & Mustaf, G. (2011). Medicinal uses of plants by the inhabitants of Khunjerab National Park, Gilgit, Pakistan. *Pakistan Journal of Botany*, **43**, 2301–2310.

Khazai, B. & Sitar, N. (2003). Evaluation of factors controlling earthquake-induced landslides caused by Chi-Chi earthquake and comparison with the Northridge and Loma Prieta events. *Engineering Geology*, **71**, 79–95.

Klink, C.A. & Joly, C.A. (1989). Identification and distribution of C_3 and C_4 grasses in open and shaded habitats in Sao Paulo State, Brazil. *Biotropica*, **21**, 30–34.

Kobayashi, S., Gomi, T., Sidle, R.C., & Takemon, Y. (2010). Disturbances structuring macroinvertebrate communities in steep headwater streams: relative importance of forest clearcutting and debris flow occurrence. *Canadian Journal of Fisheries and Aquatic Sciences*, **67**, 427–444.

Kojan, E. & Hutchinson, J.N. (1978). Mayunmarca rockslide and debris flow, Peru. In *Rockslides and Avalanches, 1, Natural Phenomena*, ed. B. Voight, pp. 316–361. Amsterdam: Elsevier.

Kondratyev, K.Y., Grigoryev, A.A., & Varotsos, C.A. (2002). *Environmental Disasters: Anthropogenic and Natural*. New York: Springer.

Koner, R. & Chakravarty, D. (2011). Earthquake response of external mine overburden dumps: a micromechanical approach. *Natural Hazards*, **56**, 941–959.

Korup, O., McSaveney, M.J., & Davies, T.R.H. (2004). Sediment generation and delivery from large historic landslides in the Southern Alps, New Zealand. *Geomorphology*, **61**, 189–207.

Krajick, K. (1999). Scientists and climbers discover cliff ecosystems. *Science*, **283**, 1623–1625.

Kristiansen, J. (1986). Blast-induced liquefaction of soils, a reference search. Norwegian Geotechnical Institute, Report 52209–1. Cited in Locat & Lee (2002).

Krohn, J.P. (1992). Landslide mitigation using horizontal drains, Pacific Palisades area, Los Angeles, California. *Reviews in Engineering Geology*, **9**, 63–68.

Kronfeld-Schor, N. & Dayan, T. (2003). Partitioning of time as an ecological resource. *Annual Review of Ecology, Evolution & Systematics*, **34**, 153–181.

Krümmelbein, J., Peth, S., Zhao, Y., & Horn, R. (2009). Grazing-induced alterations of soil hydraulic properties and functions in Inner Mongolia, PR China. *Journal of Plant Nutrition and Soil Science*, **172**, 769–776.

Kubešová, S. & Chytrý, M. (2005). Diversity of bryophytes on treeless cliffs and talus slopes in a forested central European landscape. *Journal of Bryology*, **27**, 35–46.

Kull, C.A. & Magilligan, F.J. (1994). Controls over landslide distribution in the White Mountains, New Hampshire. *Physical Geography*, **14**, 325–341.

Kurtaslan, B.O. & Demirel, Ö. (2011). Pollution caused by people's use for socioeconomic purposes (agricultural, recreation and tourism) in the Gölcük Plain Settlement at Bozdağ Plateau (Ödemis-Izmir/Turkey): a case study. *Environmental Monitoring and Assessment*, **175**, 419–430.

Lajczak, A. (2002). Slope remodelling in areas exploited by skiers: case study of the northern flysch slope of Pilsko Mountain, Polish Carpathian Mountains. In *Applied Geomorphology: Theory and Practice*, ed. R.J. Allison, pp. 92–100. Chichester: Wiley.

Lambers, H., Chapin, F.S., III, & Pons, T.L. (1998). *Plant Physiological Ecology*. New York: Springer.

Lambert, J.D.H. (1972). Plant succession on tundra mudflows: preliminary observations. *Arctic*, **25**, 99–106.

Langenheim, J.H. (1956). Plant succession on a sub-alpine earthflow in Colorado. *Ecology*, **37**, 301–317.

Large, M.F. & Braggins, J.E. (2004). *Tree Ferns*. Portland: Timber Press.

Larsen, M.C. (2008). Rainfall-triggered landslides, anthropogenic hazards, and mitigation strategies. *Advances in Geosciences*, **14**, 147–153.

Larsen, M.C. & Parks, J.E. (1997). How wide is a road? The association of roads and mass-wasting in a forested montane environment. *Earth Surface Processes and Landforms*, **22**, 835–848.

Larsen, M.C. & Santiago Román, A. (2001). Mass wasting and sediment storage in a small montane watershed: an extreme case of anthropogenic disturbance in the humid tropics. In *Geomorphic Processes and Riverine Habitat, Water Science and Application,* Volume 4, eds. J.M. Dorava, F. Fitzpatrick, B.B. Palcsak, & D.R. Montgomery, pp. 119–138. Washington, D.C.: American Geophysical Union Monograph.

Larsen, M.C. & Simon, A. (1993). A rainfall intensity-duration threshold for landslides in a humid-tropical environment, Puerto Rico. *Geografiska Annaler*, **75A**, 13–23.

Larsen, M.C. & Torres-Sánchez, A.J. (1990). Rainfall–soil moisture relations in landslide-prone areas of a tropical rain forest, Puerto Rico. *International Symposium on Tropical Hydrology*, 4th Caribbean Island Water Resources Congress, San Juan, Puerto Rico.

Larsen, M.C. & Torres-Sánchez, A.J. (1992). Landslides triggered by Hurricane Hugo in eastern Puerto Rico, September 1989. *Caribbean Journal of Science*, **28**, 113–125.

Larsen, M.C. & Torres-Sánchez, A.J. (1996). Geographic relations of landslide distributions and assessment of landslide hazards in the Blanco, Cibuco, and Coamo Basins, Puerto Rico. *U.S. Geological Survey Water Resources Investigations Report* 95–4029. San Juan, Puerto Rico.

Larsen, M.C. & Torres-Sánchez, A.J. (1998). The frequency and distribution of recent landslides in three montane tropical regions of Puerto Rico. *Geomorphology*, **24**, 309–331.

Larsen, M.C. & Wieczorek, G.F. (2006). Geomorphic effects of large debris flows and flash floods, northern Venezuela, 1999. *Zeitschrift für Geomorphologie*, **145**, 147–175.

Larsen, M.C., Torres-Sánchez, A.J., & Concepción, I.M. (1999). Slopewash, surface runoff, and fine-litter transport in forest and landslide scars in humid-tropical steeplands, Luquillo Experimental Forest, Puerto Rico. *Earth Surface Processes and Landforms*, **24**, 481–502.

Larson, D.W., Matthes, U., & Kelly, P.E. (2000). *Cliff Ecology: Pattern and Process in Cliff Ecosystems*. Cambridge: Cambridge University Press.

Lateltin, O., Beer, C., Raetzo, H., & Caron, C. (1997). Landslides in flysch terranes of Switzerland: causal factors and climate change. *Eclogae Geologicae Helvetiae*, **90**, 401–406.

Lavelle, P. & Spain, A.V. (2001). *Soil Ecology*. Dordrecht: Kluwer Academic Publishers.

Lawrey, J.D. (1980). Correlations between lichen secondary chemistry and grazing activity by *Pallifera varia*. *Bryologist*, **83**, 328–334.

Lecointre, J., Hodgson, K., Neall, V., & Cronin, S. (2004). Lahar-triggering mechanisms and hazard at Ruapehu Volcano, New Zealand. *Natural Hazards*, **31**, 85–109.

266 · References

Lee, H., Ryan, H., Kayen, R.E., et al. (2006). Varieties of submarine failure morphologies of seismically-induced landslides in Alaskan fjords. *Norwegian Journal of Geology*, **86**, 221–230.

Lerol, E., Rouzeal, O., Scanyic, J.-Y., Weber, C.C., & Vargas, C.G. (1992). Remote sensing and GIS technology in landslide hazard mapping in the Colombian Andes. *Episodes*, **15**, 32–35.

Levey, D. J. (1988). Tropical wet forest treefall gaps and distributions of understory birds and plants. *Ecology*, **69**, 1076–1089.

Lewis, N.K. (1998). Landslide-driven distribution of aspen and steppe on Kathul Mountain, Alaska. *Journal of Arid Environments*, **38**, 421–435.

Li, T. (1989). Landslides: extent and economic significance in China. In *Landslides: Extent and Economic Significance*, eds. E.E. Brabb & B.L. Harrod, pp. 271–287. Washington, DC: *Proceedings of the 28th International Geological Congress, Symposium on Landslides*.

Li, Y., Ruan, H., Zou, X., & Myster, R.W. (2005). Response of major soil decomposers to landslide disturbance in a Puerto Rican rainforest. *Soil Science*, **170**, 202–211.

Liddle, M. (1997). *Recreation Ecology: The Ecological Impact of Outdoor Recreation and Ecotourism*. New York: Chapman and Hall.

Ließ, M., Glaser, B., & Huwe, B. (2011). Functional soil-landscape modeling to estimate slope stability in a steep Andean mountain forest region. *Geomorphology*, **299**, 287–299.

Lin, W.-T., Lin, C.-Y., & Chou, W.-C. (2006). Assessment of vegetation recovery and soil erosion at landslides caused by a catastrophic earthquake: a case study in central Taiwan. *Ecological Engineering*, **28**, 79–89.

Lipman, P.W., Lockwood, J.P., Okamura, R.T., Swanson, D.A., & Yamashita, K.M. (1985). Ground deformation associated with the 1975 magnitude-7.2 earthquake and resulting changes in activity of Kilauea Volcano, Hawaii. *U.S. Geological Survey, Professional Paper 1276*.

Lipman, P.W., Normark, W.R., Moore, J.G., Wilson, J.B., & Gutmacher, C.E. (1988). The giant submarine Alika debris slide, Mauna Loa, Hawaii. *Journal of Geophysical Research*, **93**, 4279–4299.

Locat, J. & Lee, H.J. (2002). Submarine landslides: advances and challenges. *Canadian Geotechnical Journal*, **39**, 193–212.

Long, C.A. (2008). *The Wild Mammals of Wisconsin*. Sophia, Bulgaria: Pensoft Publishers.

Long, D., Smith, D.E., & Dawson, A.G. (1989). A Holocene tsunami deposit in eastern Scotland. *Journal of Quaternary Science*, **4**, 61–66.

López-Pamo, E., Barettino, D., Antón-Pacheco, G., et al. (1999). The extent of the Aznalcóllar pyritic sludge spill and its effects on soils. *Science of the Total Environment*, **242**, 57–88.

López-Rodríguez, S.R. & Blanco-Libreros, J.F. (2008). Illicit crops in tropical America: deforestation, landslides, and the terrestrial carbon stocks. *Ambio*, **37**, 1–3.

Lourens, S. & Nel, J.A.J. (1990). Winter activity of bat-eared foxes *Otocyon megalotis* in the Cape West Coast. *South African Journal of Zoology*, **25**, 124–132.

Lowe, S., Brown, M., Boudjelas, S., & De Poorter, M. (2000). *100 of the world's worst invasive alien species: a selection from the global invasive species database*. The Invasive

Species Specialist Group of the Species Survival Commission of the World Conservation Union. First published in *Aliens 12*, December 2000. Reprinted Nov. 2004. Auckland, New Zealand: Hollands Printing.

Lucchitta, B.K. (1978). A large landslide on Mars. *Geological Society of America Bulletin*, **89**, 1601–1609.

Lundgren, L. (1978). Studies of soil and vegetation development on fresh landslide scars in the Mgeta Valley, Western Ulugura Mountains, Tanzania. *Geografiska Annaler*, **60A**, 91–127.

Lundgren, L. (1980). Comparison of surface runoff and soil loss from runoff plots in forest and small-scale agriculture in the Usambara Mts., Tanzania. *Geografiska Annaler*, **62A**, 113–148.

Mackey, B.H., Roering, J.J., & Lamb, M.P. (2011). Landslide-dammed paleo-lake perturbs marine sedimentation and drives genetic change in anadromous fish. *Proceedings of the National Academy of Sciences (U.S.)*, **108**, 18905–18909.

Madej, M.A. (2001). Erosion and sediment delivery following removal of forest roads. *Earth Surface Processes and Landforms*, **26**, 175–190.

Magnússon, B., Magnússon, S.H., & Fridriksson, S. (2009). Developments in plant colonization and succession on Surtsey during 1999–2008. *Surtsey Research*, **12**, 57–76.

Maheswaran, J. & Gunatilleke, I.A.U.N. (1988). Litter decomposition in a lowland rain forest and a deforested area in Sri Lanka. *Biotropica*, **20**, 90–99.

Malanson, G.P. & Butler, D.R. (1984). Transverse pattern of vegetation on avalanche paths in the northern Rocky Mountains, Montana. *Great Basin Naturalist*, **44**, 453–458.

Malanson, G.P. & Cairnes, D.M. (1997). Effects of dispersal, population delays, and forest fragmentation on tree migration rates. *Plant Ecology*, **131**, 67–79.

Malouta, D.N., Gorsline, D.S., & Thornton, S.E. (1981). Processes and rates of recent (Holocene) basin filling in an active transform margin: Santa Monica Basin, California continental borderland. *Journal of Sedimentary Petrology*, **51**, 1077–1095.

Mangan, S.A. & Adler, G.H. (1999). Consumption of arbuscular mycorrhizal fungi by spiny rats (*Proechimys semispinosus*) in eight isolated populations. *Journal of Tropical Ecology*, **15**, 779–790.

Mark, A.F. & Dickinson, K.J.M. (2001). *Deschampsia cespitosa* subalpine tussockland on the Green Lake landslide, Hunter Mountains, Fiord Ecological Region, New Zealand. *New Zealand Journal of Botany*, **39**, 577–585.

Mark, A.F., Scott, G.A.M., Sanderson, F.R., & James, P.W. (1964). Forest succession on landslides above Lake Thomson, Fiordland. *New Zealand Journal of Botany*, **2**, 60–89.

Mark, A.F., Dickinson, K.J.M., & Fife, A.J. (1989). Forest succession on landslides in the Fiord Ecological Region, southwestern New Zealand. *New Zealand Journal of Botany*, **27**, 369–390.

Maser, C., Rodiek, J.E., & Thomas, J.W. (1979). Cliffs, talus, and caves. In *Wildlife Habitats in Managed Forests of the Blue Mountains of Oregon and Washington*, USDA Handbook 553, ed. J.W. Thomas, pp. 96–103. Washington, D.C: United States Department of Agriculture.

Masson, D.G., Harbitz, C.B., Wynn, R.B., Pedersen, G., & Løvholt, F. (2006). Submarine landslides: processes, triggers and hazard prediction. *Philosophical Transactions of the Royal Society A*, **364**, 2009–2039.

Matheson, J. (1995). Organization of forest bird and small mammal communities of the Niagara Escarpment, Canada. MS Thesis, University of Guelph, Canada.

Matsuoka, N. (2001). Solifluction rates, processes and landforms: a global review. *Earth-Science Reviews*, **55**, 107–134.

Matt, F., Almeida, K., Arguero, A., & Reudenbach, C. (2008). Seed dispersal by birds, bats and wind. In *Gradients in a Tropical Mountain Ecosystem of Ecuador: Ecological Studies*, eds. E. Beck, J. Bendix, I. Kottke, F. Makeschin, & R. Monsandl. Ecological Studies volume 198, pp. 157–165, The Netherlands: Springer Press.

Matthews, J.A. (1992). *The Ecology of Recently-Deglaciated Terrain: A Geoecological Approach to Glacier Forelands and Primary Succession*. Cambridge: Cambridge University Press.

May, C.L. & Gresswell, R.E. (2004). Spatial and temporal patterns of debris-flow deposition in the Oregon Coast Range, U.S. *Geomorphology*, **57**, 135–149.

McClanahan, T.R. & Wolfe, R.W. (1993). Accelerating forest succession in fragmented landscapes: the role of birds and perches. *Conservation Biology*, **7**, 279–288.

McDonnell, M.J. & Stiles, E.W. (1983). The structural complexity of old field vegetation and the recruitment of bird-dispersed plant species. *Oecologia*, **56**, 109–116.

McDowell, W.M. & Asbury, C.E. (1994). Export of carbon, nitrogen and major cations from three tropical montane watersheds. *Limnology and Oceanography*, **39**, 111–125.

McDowell, W.M., Sánchez, C.G., Asbury, C.E., & Ramos Pérez, C.R. (1990). Influence of sea salt aerosols and long range transport on precipitation chemistry at El Verde, Puerto Rico. *Atmospheric Environment*, **24A**, 2813–2821.

McIlveen, W.D. & Cole, Jr., H. (1976). Spore dispersal of Endogonaceae by worms, ants, wasps, and birds. *Canadian Journal of Botany*, **54**, 1486–1489.

McIntosh, R.P. (1985). *The Background of Ecology*. Cambridge: Cambridge University Press.

McKean, J. & Roering, J. (2004). Objective landslide detection and surface morphology mapping using high-resolution airborne laser altimetry. *Geomorphology*, **57**, 331–351.

McMillian, M.A. & Larson, D.W. (2002). Effects of rock climbing on the vegetation of the Niagara Escarpment in southern Ontario, Canada. *Conservation Biology*, **16**, 389–398.

Meadows, A., Meadows, P.S., Wood, D.M., & Murray, J.M.H. (1994). Microbiological effects on slope stability: an experimental analysis. *Sedimentology*, **41**, 423–435.

Medellin, R.A. (1994). Seed dispersal of *Cecropia obtusifolia* by two species of opposums in the Selva Lacandona, Chiapas, Mexico. *Biotropica*, **26**, 400–407.

Mehltreter, K. (2010). Fern conservation. In *Fern Ecology*, eds. K. Mehltreter, L.R. Walker, & J.M. Sharpe, pp. 323–359. Cambridge: Cambridge University Press.

Mehltreter, K., Walker, L.R., & Sharpe, J.M. (eds.) (2010). *Fern Ecology*. Cambridge: Cambridge University Press.

Meiners, S.J., Rye, T.A., & Klass, J.R. (2007). On a level field: the utility of studying native and non-native species in successional systems. *Applied Vegetation Science*, **12**, 45–53.

Melick, D.R. & Ashton, D.H. (1991). The effects of natural disturbances on warm temperate rainforests in south-eastern Australia. *Australian Journal of Botany*, **39**, 1–30.

Menéndez-Duarte, R., Marquínez, J., & Devolli, G. (2003). Slope instability in Nicaragua triggered by Hurricane Mitch: distribution of shallow mass movements. *Environmental Geology*, **44**, 290–300.

Metcalfe, D.J., Grubb, P.J., & Turner, I.M. (1998). The ecology of very small-seeded shade-tolerant trees and shrubs in lowland rain forest in Singapore. *Plant Ecology*, **134**, 131–149.

Metternich, G., Hurni, L., & Gogu, R. (2005). Remote sensing of landslides: an analysis of the potential contribution to geo-spatial systems for hazard assessment in mountainous environments. *Remote Sensing of Environment*, **98**, 284–303.

Meyer, D.F. & Martinson, H.A. (1989). Rates and processes of channel development and recovery following the 1980 eruption of Mount St. Helens, Washington. *Hydrological Sciences Journal*, **34**, 115–127.

Meyer, J.-Y. (1996). Status of *Miconia calvescens* (Melastomataceae), a dominant invasive tree in the Society Islands (French Polynesia). *Pacific Science*, **50**, 66–76.

Meyer, J.-Y. & Florence, J. (1996). Tahiti's native flora endangered by the invasion of *Miconia calvescens* DC. (Melastomataceae). *Journal of Biogeography*, **23**, 775–781.

Miles, D.W.R. & Swanson, F.J. (1986). Vegetation composition on recent landslides in the Cascade Mountains of western Oregon. *Canadian Journal of Forest Research*, **16**, 739–744.

Miles, D.W.R., Swanson, F.J., & Youngberg, C.T. (1984). Effect of landslide erosion on subsequent Douglas-fir growth and stocking levels in the Western Cascades, Oregon. *Soil Science Society of American Journal*, **48**, 667–671.

Millar, C.I. & Westfall, R.D. (2010). Distribution and climatic relationships of the American pika (*Ochotona princeps*) in the Sierra Nevada and western Great Basin; periglacial landforms as refugia in warming climates. *Arctic, Antarctic, and Alpine Research*, **42**, 76–88.

Millard, T. (2000). Channel disturbances and logging slash in S5 and S6 streams: an examination of streams in the Nitinat Lake area, southwest Vancouver Island. *Forest Research Technical Report TR-005*, Nanaimo, Canada: British Columbia Forest Service.

Mitton, J.B. & Grant, M.C. (1980). Observations on the ecology and evolution of quaking aspen, *Populus tremuloides*, in the Colorado Front Range. *American Journal of Botany*, **67**, 202–209.

Moles, A.T., Flores-Moreno, H., Bonser, S.P., *et al.* (2012). Invasions: the trail behind, the path ahead, and a test of a disturbing idea. *Journal of Ecology*, **100**, 116–127.

Monroe, W.H. (1964). Large retrogressive landslides in North-Central Puerto Rico. *U.S. Geological Survey Professional Paper 501-B*, pp. B123–125.

Montagnini, F. (2001). Strategies for the recovery of degraded ecosystems: experiences from Latin America. *Interciencia*, **26**, 498–503.

Montgomery, D.R. (1994). Road surface drainage, channel initiation, and slope stability. *Water Resources Research*, **30**, 1925–1932.

Moore, I.D., Norton, T.W., & Williams, J.E. (1993). Modeling environmental heterogeneity in forested landscapes. *Journal of Hydrology*, **150**, 717–747.

Moore, J.G. & Moore, G.W. (1984). Deposit from a giant wave on the Island of Lanai, Hawaii. *Science*, **226**, 1312–1315.

Moore, J.G., Clague, D.A., Holcomb, R.T., et al. (1989). Prodigious submarine landslides on the Hawaiian Ridge. *Journal of Geophysical Research*, **94**, 17645–17684.

Mora, S., Madrigal, C., Estrada, J., & Schuster, R.L. (1993). The 1992 Rio Toro landslide dam, Costa Rica. *Landslide News, Japan Landslide Society*, **7**, 19–22.

Moreiras, S.M. (2004). Landslide susceptibility zonation in the Rio Mendoza Valley, Argentina. *Geomorphology*, **66**, 345–357.

Morgan, R.P.C. (2007). Vegetative-based technologies for erosion control. In *Eco- and Ground Bio-Engineering: The Use of Vegetation to Improve Slope Stability*, eds. A. Stokes, I. Spanos, & J.E. Norris, pp. 265–272. Dordrecht: Springer.

Mortality Statistics (2011). http://www.nationmaster.com/graph/mor_vic_of_ava_lan_and_oth_ear_mov-avalanche-landslide-other-earth-movements. Accessed 17 January 2011.

Morton, D.M. & Streitz, R. (1975). Mass movement. In *Man and His Physical Environment*, eds. G.D. McKenzie & R.O. Utgard, pp. 61–70. Minneapolis, MN, U.S.: Burgess.

Moss, M.R. & Rosenfeld, C.L. (1978). Morphology, mass wasting and forest ecology of a post-glacial re-entrant valley in the Niagara Escarpment. *Geografiska Annaler*, **60A**, 161–174.

Murphy, H.T., Metcalfe, D.J., Bradford, M.G., et al. (2008). Recruitment dynamics of invasive species in rainforest habitats following Cyclone Larry. *Austral Ecology*, **33**, 495–502.

Myster, R.W. (1993). Spatial heterogeneity of seed rain, seed pool, and vegetative cover on two Monteverde landslides, Costa Rica. *Brenesia*, **39–40**, 137–145.

Myster, R.W. (1994). Landslide insects show small differences between an island (Puerto Rico) and the mainland (Costa Rica). *Acta Científica*, **8**, 105–113.

Myster, R.W. (1997). Seed predation, disease and germination on landslides in Neotropical lower montane wet forest. *Journal of Vegetation Science*, **8**, 55–64.

Myster, R.W. (2002). Foliar pathogen and insect herbivore effects on two landslide tree species in Puerto Rico. *Forest Ecology and Management*, **169**, 231–242.

Myster, R.W. & Fernández, D.S. (1995). Spatial gradients and patch structure on two Puerto Rican landslides. *Biotropica*, **27**, 149–159.

Myster, R.W. & Sarmiento, F.O. (1998). Seed inputs to microsite patch recovery on two tropandean landslides in Ecuador. *Restoration Ecology*, **6**, 35–43.

Myster, R.W. & Schaefer, D.A. (2003). Species and microsite effects on litter decomposition in a Puerto Rican landslide. *Community Ecology*, **4**, 157–162.

Myster, R.W. & Walker, L.R. (1997). Plant successional pathways on Puerto Rican landslides. *Journal of Tropical Ecology*, **13**, 165–173.

Myster, R.W., Thomlinson, J.R., & Larsen, M.C. (1997). Predicting landslide vegetation in patches on landscape gradients in Puerto Rico. *Landscape Ecology*, **12**, 299–307.

Naiman, R.J., Melillo, J.M., & Hobbie, J.H. (1986). Ecosystem alteration of boreal forest streams by beaver (*Castor canadensis*). *Ecology*, **67**, 1254–1269.

Nakamura, T. (1984). Vegetational recovery of landslide scars in the upper reaches of the Oi River, Central Japan. *Journal of the Japanese Forestry Society*, **66**, 328–332.

Nakashizuka, T., Iida, S., Suzuki, W., & Tanimoto, T. (1993). Seed dispersal and vegetation development on a debris avalanche on the Ontake volcano, Central Japan. *Journal of Vegetation Science*, **4**, 537–542.

Negishi, J.N., Sidle, R.C., Noguchi, S., Nik, A.R., & Stanforth, R. (2006). Ecological roles of roadside fern (*Dicranopteris curranii*) on logging road recovery in Peninsular Malaysia: Preliminary results. *Forest Ecology and Management*, **224**, 176–186.

Newton, A.C. & Healey, J.R. (1989). Establishment of *Clethra occidentalis* on stems of the tree-fern *Cyathea pubescens* in a Jamaican montane rain forest. *Journal of Tropical Ecology*, **5**, 441–445.

Nieto, A.S. & Schuster, R.L. (1991). Mass wasting and flooding induced by the 5 March 1987 Ecuador earthquakes. In *Landslides of the World*, ed. K. Sassa, pp. 220–223. Kyoto: Kyoto University Press.

Nieto, A.S., Schuster, R.L., & Plaza-Nieto, G. (1991). Mass wasting and flooding. *Natural Disaster Studies*, **5**, 51–82.

Nisbet, E.G. & Piper, D.J.W. (1998). Giant submarine landslides. *Nature*, **392**, 329–330.

Noguchi, S., Abdul Rahim, N., Baharuddin, K., *et al.* (1997). Soil physical properties and preferential flow pathways in a tropical rain forest, Bukit Tarek, Peninusular Malaysia. *Journal of Forest Research*, **2**, 115–120.

Norkko, A., Thrush, S.F., Hewitt, J.E., *et al.* (2002). Smothering of estuarine sandflats by terrigenous clay: the role of wind-wave disturbance and bioturbation in site-dependent macrofaunal recovery. *Marine Ecology Progress Series*, **234**, 23–41.

Nott, J. (2006). *Extreme Events: A Physical Reconstruction and Risk Assessment.* Cambridge: Cambridge University Press.

Oaks, S.D. & Dexter, L. (1987). Avalanche hazard zoning in Vail, Colorado: the use of scientific information in the implementation of hazard reduction strategies. *Mountain Research and Development*, **7**, 157–168.

Odum, E.P. (1959). *Fundamentals of Ecology,* 2nd Edition. Philadelphia, PA, U.S.: Saunders.

Oh, H.-J., Ahn, S.-C., Choi, J.-K., & Lee, S. (2011). Sensitivity analysis for the GIS-based mapping of the ground subsidence hazard near abandoned underground coal mines. *Environmental Earth Sciences*, **64**, 347–358.

Ohl, C. & Bussman, R. (2004). Recolonisation of natural landslides in tropical mountain forests of Southern Ecuador. *Feddes Repertorium*, **115**, 248–264.

Oliver, C.D., Adams, A.B., & Zasoki, R.J. (1985). Disturbance patterns and forest development in a recently deglaciated valley in the northwestern Cascade Range of Washington, U.S. *Canadian Journal of Forest Research*, **15**, 221–232.

Oliver-Smith, A. & Hoffman, S.M. (eds.) (1999). *The Angry Earth*. New York: Routledge.

O'Loughlin, C.L. & Pearce, A.J. (1976). Influence of Cenozoic geology on mass movement and sediment yield response to forest removal, North Westland, New Zealand. *Bulletin of the International Association of Engineering Geology*, **14**, 41–46.

O'Neill, R.V., DeAngelis, D.L., Waide, J.B., & Allen, T.F.H. (1986). *A Hierarchical Concept of Ecosystems*. Princeton, New Jersey: Princeton University Press.

Oyagi, N., Makino, H., & Mori, S. (1996). Landslide structure and control works at Nishitani landslide, Wakayama Prefecture, Japan. In *Landslides*, eds. J. Chacón, C. Irigaray, & T. Fernández, pp. 247–254. Rotterdam: Balkema.

Pabst, R.J. & Spies, T.A. (2001). Ten years of vegetation succession on a debris-flow deposit in Oregon. *Journal of the American Water Resources Association*, **37**, 1693–1708.

Pain, C.F. & Bowler, J.M. (1973). Denudation following the November 1970 earthquake at Madang, Papua New Guinea. *Zeitschrift für Geomorphologie*, Supplement Bd 18, 91–104. Cited in Pearce & Watson (1986) and Restrepo *et al.* (2009).

Pakeman, R.J., Attwood, J.P., & Engelen, J. (1998). Sources of plants colonizing experimentally disturbed patches in an acidic grassland, in eastern England. *Journal of Ecology*, **86**, 1032–1041.

Palkovic, L.A. (1978). A hybrid of *Gunnera* from Costa Rica. *Systematic Botany*, **3**, 226–235.

Pandey, A.N. & Singh, J.S. (1985). Mechanisms of ecosystem recovery: A case study from Kumaun Himalaya. *Recreation and Revegetation Research*, **3**, 271–292.

Parendes, L.A. & Jones, J.A. (2000). Role of light availability and dispersal in exotic plant invasion along roads and streams in the H.J. Andrews Experimental Forest, Oregon. *Conservation Biology*, **14**, 64–75.

Pareschi, M.T., Boschi, E., Mazzarini, F., & Favalli, M. (2006). Large submarine landslides offshore Mt. Etna. *Geophysical Research Letters*, **33**, L13302, doi:10.1029/2006GL026064.

Parise, M. & Jibson, R.W. (2000). A seismic landslide susceptibility rating of geologic units based on analysis of characteristics of landslides triggered by the 17 January, 1994 Northridge, California earthquake. *Engineering Geology*, **58**, 251–270.

Paull, C.K., Ussler, W., Greene, H.G., Barry, J., & Keaten, R. (2005). Bioerosion by chemosynthetic biological communities on Holocene submarine slide scars. *Geo-Marine Letters*, **25**, 11–19.

Pearce, A.J. & O'Loughlin, C.L. (1985). Landsliding during a M 7.7 earthquake: influence of geology and topography. *Geology*, **13**, 855–858.

Pearce, A.J. & Watson, A. (1983). Medium-term effects of two landsliding episodes on channel storage of sediment. *Earth Surface Processes and Landforms*, **8**, 29–39.

Pearce, A.J. & Watson, A. (1986). Effects of earthquake-induced landslides on sediment budget and transport over a 50-yr period. *Geology*, **14**, 52–55.

Pederson, N., Everham, E.M., III, & Sahm, J. (1991). Natural disturbance simulation in the Luquillo Experimental Forest, Puerto Rico. In *Toward Understanding Our Environment*, ed. J. McLeod, pp. 95–100. San Diego: The Society for Computer Simulation.

Peh, K.S.-H., Soh, M.C.K., Sodhi, N.S., *et al*. (2011). Up in the clouds: is sustainable use of tropical montane cloud forests possible in Malaysia? *BioScience*, **61**, 27–38.

Peltzer, D.A., Wardle, D.A., Allison, V.J., *et al*. (2010). Understanding ecosystem retrogression. *Ecological Monographs*, **80**, 509–529.

Perla, R.I. & Martinelli, M., Jr. (1976). *Avalanche Handbook*. U.S. Department of Agriculture, Forest Service, Agriculture Handbook 489, Washington, D.C.

Perotto-Baldiezo, H.L., Thurow, T.L., Smith, C.T., Fisher, R.F. & Wu, X.B. (2004). GIS-based spatial analysis and modeling for landslide hazard assessment in steeplands, southern Honduras. *Agriculture, Ecosystems and Environment*, **103**, 165–176.

Peruvian Times (2009). http://www.peruviantimes.com/31/yungay-1970-2009-remembering-the-tragedy-of-the-earthquake/3073/ Accessed 23 February 2012.

Peterson, D.M., Ellen, S.D., & Knifong, D.L. (1993). Distribution of past debris flows and other rapid slope movements from natural hillslopes in the Honolulu District of Oahu, Hawaii. *Open File Report 93–514*, pp. 1–34. U.S. Geological Survey, U.S. Department of the Interior, Honolulu, Hawaii.

Petley, D. (2010). Landslide hazards. In *Geomorphological Hazards and Disaster Prevention*, eds. I. Alcantara-Ayala & A. Goudie, pp. 63–73. Cambridge: Cambridge University Press.

Petley, D., Hearn, G.J., Hart, A., *et al*. (2007). Trends in landslide occurrence in Nepal. *Natural Hazards*, **43**, 23–44.

Pickett, S.T.A. (1989). Space-for-time substitutions as an alternative to long-term studies. In *Long Term Studies in Ecology*, ed. G.E. Likens, pp. 110–135. New York: Springer.

Pickett, S.T.A. & Cadenasso, M.L. (1995). Landscape ecology: spatial heterogeneity in ecological systems. *Science*, **269**, 331–334.

Pickett, S.T.A. & White, P.S. (eds.) (1985). *The Ecology of Natural Disturbance and Patch Dynamics*. New York: Academic Press.

Pickett, S.T.A., Collins, S.L., & Armesto, J.J. (1987). A hierarchical consideration of causes and mechanisms of succession. *Vegetatio*, **69**, 109–114.

Piehl, B.T., Beschta, R.L., & Pyles, M.R. (1988). Ditch-relief culverts and low-volume forest roads in the Oregon Coast Range. *Northwest Science*, **62**, 91–98.

Piper, D.J.W., Farre, J.A., & Shor, A.N. (1985). Late Quaternary slumps and debris flows on the Scotian Slope. *Geological Society of America Bulletin*, **96**, 1508–1517.

Pizano, C., Mangan, S.A., Herre, E.A., Eom, A.-H., & Dalling, J.W. (2011). Above- and belowground interactions drive segregation between two cryptic species of tropical trees. *Ecology*, **92**, 47–56.

Pla Sentís, I. (1997). A soil water balance model for monitoring soil erosion processes and effects on steep lands in the tropics. *Soil Technology*, **11**, 17–30.

Potts, D.F. & Anderson, B.K.M. (1990). Organic debris and the management of small channels. *Western Journal of Applied Forestry*, **5**, 25–28.

Prach, K. & Walker, L.R. (2011). Four opportunities for studies of ecological succession. *Trends in Ecology and Evolution*, **26**, 119–123.

Prach, K., Marrs, R., Pyšek, P., & van Diggelen, R. (2007). Manipulation of succession. In *Linking Restoration and Ecological Succession*, eds. L.R. Walker, J. Walker, & R.J.Hobbs, pp. 121–149. New York: Springer.

Prior, D.B. & Coleman, J.M. (1980). Sonograph mosaics of submarine slope instabilities, Mississippi River delta. *Marine Geology*, **36**, 227–239.

Prior, D.B. & Coleman, J.M. (1982). Submarine landslides – geometry and nomenclature. *Zeitschrift für Geomorphologie*, **4**, 21–33.

Prior, D.B. & Coleman, J.M. (1984). Submarine slope instability. In *Slope Instability*, eds. D. Brunsden & D.B. Prior, pp. 419–455. New York: Wiley.

Prior, D.B., Coleman, J.M., & Bornhold, B.D. (1982). Results of a known sea floor instability event. *Geo-Marine Letters*, **2**, 117–122.

Prior, D.B., Yang, Z.-S., Bornhold, B.D., *et al.* (1986). Active slope failure, sediment collapse, and silt flows of the modern subaqueous Huanghe (Yellow River) delta. *Geo-Marine Letters*, **6**, 85–95.

Punetha, N. (1991). Studies on atmospheric fern spores at Pithogarh (northwest Himalaya) with particular reference to distribution of ferns in the Himalayas. *Annual Review of Plant Science*, **13**, 146–161.

Putz, F.E. & Holbrook, N.M. (1988). Further observations on the dissolution of mutualism between *Cecropia* and its ants: the Malaysian case. *Oikos*, **53**, 121–125.

Rahman, A.-U., Nawaz Khan, A., Colllins, A.E., & Qazi, F. (2011). Causes and extent of environmental impacts of landslide hazard in the Himalayan region: a case study of Murree, Pakistan. *Natural Hazards*, **57**, 413–434.

Raven, P.H., Evert, R.F., & Eichhorn, S.E. (2005). *Biology of Plants,* 7th Edition. New York: W.H. Freeman.

Ravikiran, G., Raju, A.B., & Venugopal, Y. (2011). *Phytolacca americana*: A review. *International Journal of Research in Pharmaceutical and Biomedical Sciences*, **2**, 942–946.

Read, D.J. (1996). The structure and function of the ericoid mycorrhizal root. *Annals of Botany*, **77**, 365–374.

Reagan, D.P. & Waide, R.B. (eds.) (1996). *The Food Web of a Tropical Rain Forest.* Chicago: The University of Chicago Press.

Reddy, V.S. & Singh, J.S. (1993). Changes in vegetation and soil during succession following landslide disturbance in the central Himalaya. *Journal of Environmental Management*, **39**, 235–250.

Reice, S.R. (2001). *The Silver Lining: The Benefits of Natural Disasters.* Princeton, New Jersey: Princeton University Press.

Reid, L.M. & Dunne, T. (1984). Sediment production from forest road surfaces. *Water Resources Research*, **20**, 1753–1761.

Restrepo, C. & Alvarez, N. (2006). Landslides and their contribution to land-cover change in the mountains of Mexico and Central America. *Biotropica*, **38**, 446–457.

Restrepo, C. & Vitousek, P.M. (2001). Landslides, alien species, and the diversity of a Hawaiian montane mesic ecosystem. *Biotropica*, **33**, 409–420.

Restrepo, C., Vitousek, P., & Neville, P. (2003). Landslides significantly alter land cover and the distribution of biomass: an example from the Ninole ridges of Hawai'i. *Plant Ecology*, **166**, 131–143.

Restrepo, C., Walker, L.R., Shiels, A.B., *et al.* (2009). Landsliding and its multiscale influence on mountainscapes. *BioScience*, **59**, 685–698.

Rice, R.M., Corbett, E.S., & Bailey, R.G. (1969). Soil slips related to vegetation, topography, and soil in southern California. *Water Resources Research*, **5**, 647–659.

Rice, R.M., Ziemer, R.R., & Hankin, S.C. (1982). Slope stability effects of fuel management strategies: inferences from Monte Carlo simulations. *General Technical Report PSW-58*, pp. 365–371. Forest Service. Berkeley, CA: U.S. Department of Agriculture.

Richards, K. (2006). Sky view and weather controls on nocturnal surface moisture deposition on grass at urban sites. *Physical Geography*, **27**, 70–85.

Ricklefs, R., Kalin-Arroyo, M.T., Latham, R.E., *et al.* (1995). The distribution of global biodiversity. In *UNEP Global Biodiversity Assessment*, ed. V. Heywood, pp. 139–173. Cambridge: Cambridge University Press for the United Nations Environmental Program.

Riley, P.B. & Read, S.A.L. (1992). Lake Waikaremoana – present day stability of landslide barrier. In *Proceedings of the Sixth International Symposium on Landslides*, **2**, 1249–1255.

Robb, J.M. (1984). Spring sapping on the lower continental slope, offshore New Jersey. *Geology*, **12**, 278–282.

Roberts, B., Ward, B., & Rollerson, T. (2005). A comparison of landslide rates following helicopter and conventional cable-based clear-cut logging operations in the Southwest Coast Mountains of British Columbia. *Geomorphology*, **61**, 337–346.

Robinson, R.C., Sheffield, E., & Sharpe, J.M. (2010). Problem ferns: their impact and management. In *Fern Ecology*, eds. K. Mehltreter, L.R. Walker, & J.M. Sharpe, pp. 255–322. Cambridge: Cambridge University Press.

Roering, J.J., Schmidt, K.M., Stock, J.D., Dietrich, W.E., & Montgomery, D.R. (2003). Shallow landsliding, root reinforcement, and the spatial distribution of trees in the Oregon Coast Range. *Canadian Geotechnical Journal*, **40**, 237–253.

Rogers, H.H., Runion, G.B., & Krupa, S.V. (1994). Plant responses to atmospheric CO_2 enrichment with emphasis on roots and the rhizosphere. *Environmental Pollution*, **83**, 155–189.

Rollins, K.M. & Rollins, R.L. (1992). Case histories of landslide stabilization using drilled-shaft walls. *Transportation Research Record No. 1343, Rockfall Prediction and Control and Landslide Case Histories*, pp. 114–122. Washington, D.C.: National Academy Press.

Rose, A.B., Pekelharing, C.J., & Platt, K.H. (1992). Magnitude of canopy dieback and implications for conservation of southern rata-kamahi (*Metrosideros umbellata – Weinmannia racemosa*) forests, Central Westland, New Zealand. *New Zealand Journal of Ecology*, **16**, 23–32.

Rouse, W.C. (1984). Flowslides. In *Slope Instability*, eds. D. Brunsden & D.B. Prior, pp. 491–522. Chichester: Wiley.

Rozell, N. (1998). Avalanches, landslides, good for some. *Alaska Science Forum*, Fairbanks, Geophysical Institute, University of Alaska, 16 June, 1998.

Rudel, T.K., Perez-Lugo, M., & Zichal, H. (2000). When fields revert to forest: development and spontaneous reforestation in post-war Puerto Rico. *The Professional Geographer*, **52**, 386–397.

Russell, A.E., Raich, J.W., & Vitousek, P.M. (1998). The ecology of the climbing fern *Dicranopteris linearis* on windward Mauna Loa, Hawaii. *Journal of Ecology*, **86**, 765–779.

Russo, R.O. (2005). Nitrogen-fixing trees with actinorrhiza in forestry and agroforestry. In *Nitrogen Fixation in Agriculture, Forestry, Ecology, and the Environment*, eds. D. Werner & W.E. Newton, pp. 143–171. The Netherlands: Springer Press.

Růžička, V. & Zacharda, M. (1994). Arthropods of stony debris in the Krkonose Mountains, Czech Republic. *Arctic and Alpine Research*, **26**, 332–338.

Rydin, H. & Borgegård, S.-O. (1991). Plant characteristics over a century of primary succession on islands, Lake Hjälmaren. *Ecology*, **72**, 1089–1101.

Sage, R.F., Li, M., & Monson, R.K. (1999). The taxonomic distribution of C_4 photosynthesis. In *C_4 Plant Biology*, eds. R.F. Sage & R.K. Monson. San Diego, CA: Academic Press.

Sakai, A. & Ohsawa, M. (1993). Vegetation pattern and microtopography on a landslide scar of Mt Kiyosumi, central Japan. *Ecological Research*, **8**, 47–56.

Sakio, H. (1997). Effects of natural disturbance on the regeneration of riparian forests in Chibichu Mountains, central Japan. *Plant Ecology*, **132**, 181–185.

Samaniego-Herrera, A. (2003). Deslaves y sus effectos de borde sobre la communidad de roedores en un bosque mesófilo de montaña. MS Thesis, Instituto de Ecología, A.C., Jalapa, Veracruz, Mexico.

Sappington, J.M., Longshore, K.M., & Thompson, D.B. (2007). Quantifying landscape ruggedness for animal habitat analysis: A case study using bighorn sheep in the Mojave Desert. *The Journal of Wildlife Management*, **71**, 1419–1426.

Sassa, K., Fukuoka, H., Wang, F., & Wang, G. (eds.) (2007). *Progress in Landslide Science*. New York: Springer.

Scatena, F.N. & Larsen, M.C. (1991). Physical aspects of Hurricane Hugo in Puerto Rico. *Biotropica*, **23**, 317–323.

Schlesinger, W.H. (1991). *Biogeochemistry: An Analysis of Global Change*. New York: Academic Press.

Schmidt, J. & Dikau, R. (2004). Modelling historical climate variability and slope stability. *Geomorphology*, **60**, 433–447.

Schmidt, K.M., Roering, J.J., Stock, J.D., et al. (2001). The variability of root cohesion as an influence on shallow landslide susceptibility in the Oregon Coast Range. *Canadian Geotechnical Journal*, **38**, 995–1024.

Schowalter, T.D., Webb, J.W., & Crossley, Jr., D.A. (1981). Community structure and nutrient content of canopy arthropods in a clearcut and uncut forest ecosystem. *Ecology*, **62**, 1010–1019.

Schubert, K.R. (1986). Products of biological nitrogen fixation in higher plants: synthesis, transport, and metabolism. *Annual Review of Plant Physiology*, **37**, 539–574.

Schuster, R.L. (1995). Landslides and dams – a worldwide phenomenon. *Journal of the Japanese Landslide Society*, **31**, 38–49.

Schuster, R.L. (1996a). The 25 most catastrophic landslides of the 20th century. In *Landslides*, eds. J. Chacón, C. Irigaray, & T. Fernández, pp. 53–62. Rotterdam: Balkema.

Schuster, R.L. (1996b). Socioeconomic significance of landslides. In *Landslides: Investigation and Mitigation*, eds. A.K. Turner & R.L. Schuster, pp. 12–35. Special Report 247, Transportation Research Board, National Research Council. Washington, D.C.: National Academy Press.

Schuster, R.L. (2000). Outburst debris-flows from failure of natural dams. In *Debris-Flow Hazards Mitigation: Mechanics, Prediction, and Assessment*, eds. G.F. Wieczorek & N.D. Naeser, pp. 29–42. Rotterdam: Balkema.

Schuster, R.L. (2001). Landslides: effects on the natural environment. In: *Engineering Geology and the Environment*, eds. P.G. Marinos, G.C. Koukis, G.C. Tsiambaos, & G.C. Stournaras, pp. 3371–3387. Lisse: Swets & Zeitlinger.

Schuster, R.L. (2002). Usoi landslide dam, southeastern Tajikistan. *International Symposium on Landslide Risk Mitigation and Protection of Cultural and Natural Heritage*, pp. 489–505. Kyoto: Kyoto University Press.

Schuster, R.L. & Highland, L.M. (2007). Overview of the effects of mass wasting on the natural environment. *Environmental and Engineering Geoscience*, **13**, 25–44.

Schuster, R.L. & Kockelman, W.J. (1996). Principles of landslide hazard reduction. In *Landslides: Investigation and Mitigation*, eds. A.K. Turner & R.L. Schuster, pp. 91–105. Special Report 247, Transportation Research Board, National Research Council. Washington, D.C.: National Academy Press.

Schuster, R.L., Nieto, A.S., O'Rourke, E., *et al.* (1996). Mass wasting triggered by the 5 March 1987 Ecuador earthquakes. *Engineering Geology*, **42**, 1–23.

Schuster, R.L., Salcedo, D.A., & Valenzuela, L. (2002). Overview of catastrophic landslides of South America in the twentieth century. In *Catastrophic Landslides: Effects, Occurrence and Mechanisms*, eds. S.G. Evans & J.V. DeGraff, pp. 1–34. Boulder, CO, U.S.: Geological Society of American Reviews in Engineering Geology Volume **15**.

Schwab, J.W. (1983). Mass wasting: October-November 1978 Storm, Rennel Sound, Queen Charlotte Islands, British Columbia. *British Columbia Ministry of Forests Research Note*, **91**, 1–23.

Scott, G.A.J. & Street, J.M. (1976). The role of chemical weathering in the formation of Hawaiian amphitheatre-headed valleys. *Zeitschrift für Geomorphologie*, **20**, 171–189.

Sedell, J.R., Reeves, G.H., Hauer, F.R., Stanford, J.A., & Hawkins, C.P. (1990). Role of refugia in recovery from disturbances: modern fragmented and disconnected river systems. *Environmental Management*, **14**, 711–724.

Senneset, K., (ed.) (1996). Landslides. *Proceedings of the Seventh International Symposium on Landslides,* 17–21 June 1996, Trondheim, Norway, Volume 3, pp. 1489–1992. Rotterdam: Balkema.

Sharma, E. & Ambasht, R.S. (1985). Chemical soil properties under five age series of *Alnus nepalensis* plantations in the Eastern Himalayas. *Plant and Soil*, **84**, 105–113.

Sharpe, C.F.S. (1960). *Landslides and Related Phenomena: A Study of Mass-movements of Soil and Rock*. New Jersey: Pageant Books.

Shaw, C.G., III & Sidle, R.C. (1983). Evaluation of planting sites common to a southeast Alaska clearcut II. Available inoculum of the ectomycorrhizal fungus *Cannococcum geophilum*. *Canadian Journal of Forest Research*, **13**, 9–11.

Sheets, P.D. (1999). The effects of explosive volcanism on ancient egalitarian, ranked, and stratified societies in Middle America. In *The Angry Earth*, ed. A. Oliver-Smith & S.M. Hoffman, pp. 36–58. New York: Routledge.

Sheffield, L.M., Gall, A.E., Roby, D.D., Irons, D.B., & Dugger, K.M. (2006). Monitoring planktivorous seabird populations: validating surface counts of crevice-nesting auklets using mark-resight techniques. *Canadian Journal of Zoology*, **84**, 846–854.

Sheridan, R.P. (1991). Nitrogenase activity by *Hapalosiphon flexuosus* associated with *Sphagnum erythrocalyx* in cloud forest on the volcano La Soufrière, French West Indies. *Biotropica*, **23**, 134–140.

Shiels, A.B. (2002). Bird perches and soil amendments as revegetation techniques for landslides in Puerto Rico. MS Thesis, Department of Biological Sciences, University of Nevada, Las Vegas, Nevada, U.S.

Shiels, A.B. (2006) Leaf litter decomposition and substrate chemistry of early successional species on landslides in Puerto Rico. *Biotropica*, **38**, 348–353.

Shiels, A.B. (2011). Frugivory by introduced black rats (*Rattus rattus*) promotes dispersal of invasive plant seeds. *Biological Invasions*, **13**, 781–792.

Shiels, A.B. & Drake, D.R. (2011). Are introduced rats (*Rattus rattus*) both seed predators and dispersers in Hawaii? *Biological Invasions*, **13**, 883–894.

Shiels, A.B. & Walker, L.R. (2003). Bird perches increase forest seeds on Puerto Rican landslides. *Restoration Ecology*, **11**, 457–465.

Shiels, A.B. & Walker, L.R. (In press). Landslides cause spatial and temporal gradients at multiple scales in the Luquillo Mountains, Puerto Rico. In: *Ecological Gradient Analyses in Tropical Ecosystems, 54*, eds. G. González, M. Willig, & R. Waide. Ecological Bulletins.

Shiels, A.B., Walker, L.R., & Thompson, D.B. (2006). Organic matter inputs create variable resource patches on Puerto Rican landslides. *Plant Ecology*, **184**, 223–236.

Shiels, A.B., West, C.A., Weiss, L., Klawinski, P.D., & Walker, L.R. (2008). Soil factors predict initial plant colonization on Puerto Rican landslides. *Plant Ecology*, **195**, 165–178.

Shiels, A.B., Zimmerman J.K., García-Montiel, D.C., *et al.* (2010). Plant responses to simulated hurricane impacts in a subtropical wet forest, Puerto Rico. *Journal of Ecology*, **98**, 659–673.

Shimokawa, E. (1984). A natural process of recovery of vegetation on landslide scars and landslide periodicity in forested drainage basins. In *Symposium on Effects of Forest Land Use on Erosion and Slope Stability*, eds. C.L. O'Laughlin & A.J. Pierce, pp. 99–107. East–West Center Honolulu: University of Hawaii.

Shresta, D.P., Zinck, J.A., & Van Ranst, E. (2004). Modelling land degradation in the Nepalese Himalaya. *Catena*, **57**, 135–156.

Sidle, R.C. (1984). Relative importance of factors influencing landsliding in coastal Alaska. *Proceedings of the 21st Annual Engineering, Geology, and Soils Engineering Symposium*, pp. 311–325. Moscow, ID, U.S.: University of Idaho.

Sidle, R.C. (1992). A theoretical model of the effects of timber harvesting on slope stability. *Water Resources Research*, **28**, 1897–1910.

Sidle, R.C. (2007). Using weather and climate information for landslide prevention and mitigation. In *Climate and Land Degradation*, eds. M.V.K. Sivakumar & N. Ndiang'ui, pp. 285–307. Berlin: Springer.

Sidle, R.C. (2010). Hydrogeomorphic processes in temperate and tropical forests: effects of land use and scale. *Geography Compass*, **4**, 1115–1132.

Sidle, R.C. & Ochiai, H. (2006). *Landslides: Processes, Prediction, and Land Use.* Water Resources Monograph Series, volume 18. Washington, D.C.: American Geophysical Union.

Sidle, R.C. & Sharma, A. (1996). Stream channel changes associated with mining and grazing in the Great Basin. *Journal of Environmental Quality*, **25**, 1111–1121.

Sidle, R.C. & Swanston, D.N. (1982). Analysis of a small debris flow in coastal Alaska. *Canadian Geotechnical Journal*, **19**, 167–174.

Sidle, R.C. & Wu, W. (1999). Simulating effects of timber harvesting on the temporal and spatial distribution of shallow landslides. *Zeitschrift für Geomorphologie, N.F.*, **43**, 185–201.

Sidle, R.C., Pearce, A.J., & O'Loughlin, C.L. (1985). *Hillslope Stability and Land Use*, Water Resources Monograph, volume 11. Washington, D.C.: American Geophysical Union.

Sidle, R.C., Noguchi, S., Tsuboyama, Y., & Laursen, K. (2001). A conceptual model of preferential flow systems in forested hillslopes: evidence of self-organization. *Hydrological Processes*, **15**, 1675–1692.

Sidle, R.C., Taylor, D., Lu, X.X., *et al.* (2004). Interactions of natural hazards and humans: evidence in historical and recent records. *Quaternary International*, 118–119, 181–203.

Sidle, R.C., Ziegler, A.D., Negishi, J.N., *et al.* (2006). Erosion processes in steep terrain – truths, myths, and uncertainties related to forest management in Southeast Asia. *Forest Ecology and Management*, **224**, 199–225.

Sikes, D.S. & Slowik, J. (2010). Terrestrial arthropods of pre- and post-eruption Kasatochi Island, Alaska, 2008–2009: a shift from a plant-based to a necromass-based food web. *Arctic, Antarctic, and Alpine Research*, **42**, 297–305.

Silvera, K., Skillman, J.B., & Dalling, J.W. (2003). Seed germination, seedling growth and habitat partitioning in two morphotypes of the tropical pioneer tree *Trema micrantha* in a seasonal forest in Panama. *Journal of Tropical Ecology*, **19**, 27–34.

Sims, R.W. & Gerard, B.M. (1985). *Earthworms*. Bath: The Pitman Press.

Singh, J.S., Rawat, Y.S., & Chaturvedi, O.P. (1984). Replacement of oak forest with pine in the Himalaya affects the nitrogen cycle. *Nature*, **311**, 54–56.

Singh, R.B. & Pandey, B.W. (1996). Landslide hazard in Indian Himalaya and Canadian Rockies: a comparative analysis. In *Landslides*, eds. J. Chacón, C. Irigaray, & T. Fernández, pp. 63–69. Rotterdam: Balkema.

Singhroy, V. & Molch, K. (2004). Geological case studies related to RADARSAT-2. *Canadian Journal of Remote Sensing*, **30**, 893–902.

Slaymaker, O. (2010). Mountain hazards. In *Geomorphological Hazards and Disaster Prevention*, eds. I. Alcantara-Ayala & A.S. Goudie, pp. 33–47. Cambridge: Cambridge University Press.

Slocum, M.G., Aide, T.M., Zimmerman, J.K., & Navarro, L. (2004). Natural regeneration of subtropical montane forest after clearing fern thickets in the Dominican Republic. *Journal of Tropical Ecology*, **20**, 483–486.

Slocum, M.G., Aide, T.M., Zimmerman, J.K., & Navarro, L. (2006). A strategy for restoration of montane forest in anthropogenic fern thickets in the Dominican Republic. *Restoration Ecology*, 14: 526–536.

Smale, M.C., McLeod, M., & Smale, P.N. (1997). Vegetation and soil recovery on shallow landslide scars in Tertiary hill country, East Cape region, New Zealand. *New Zealand Journal of Ecology*, **21**, 31–41.

Smith, K. (2001). *Environmental Hazards: Assessing the Risk and Reducing Disaster,* 3rd Edition. London: Routledge.

Smith, R.B., Commandeur, P.R., & Ryan, M.W. (1986). Soils, vegetation, and forest growth on landslides and surrounding logged and old-growth areas on the Queen Charlotte Islands. British Columbia Ministry of Forests, Land Management Report 41.

Smith, S.D., Huxman, T.E., Zitzer, S.F., et al. (2000). Elevated CO_2 increases productivity and invasive species success in an arid ecosystem. *Nature*, **408**, 79–82.

Smyth, C.G. & Royle, S.A. (2000). Urban landslide hazards: incidence and causative factors in Niterói, Rio de Janeiro State, Brazil. *Applied Geography*, **20**, 95–117.

Soltis, D.E., Soltis, P.S., Morgan, D.R., et al. (1995). Chloroplast gene sequence data suggests a single origin of the predisposition for symbiotic nitrogen fixation in angiosperms. *Proceedings of the National Academy of Sciences, USA*, **92**, 2647–2651.

Spanos, I., Raftoyannis, Y., Goudelis, G., et al. (2007). Effecs of postfire logging on soil and vegetation recovery in a *Pinus halepensis* Mill. forest of Greece. In *Eco- and Ground Bio-Engineering: The Use of Vegetation to Improve Slope Stability*, eds. A. Stokes, I. Spanos, & J.E. Norris, pp. 345–352. Proceedings of the First International Conference on Eco-Engineering 13–17 September 2004. Dordrecht: Springer.

Spicer, R.A., Burnham, R.J., Grant, P., & Glicken, H. (1985). *Pityrogramma calomelanos,* the primary, post-eruption colonizer of Volcán Chichonal, Chiapas, Mexico. *American Fern Journal*, **75**, 1–5.

Stark, C.P. & Hovius, N. (2001). The characterization of landslide size distributions. *Geophysical Research Letters*, **28**, 1091–1094.

Staudacher, K. & Füreder, L. (2007). Habitat complexity and invertebrates in selected alpine springs (Schütt, Carinthia, Austria). *International Review of Hydrobiology*, **92**, 465–479.

Steiakakis, E., Kavouridis, K., & Monopolis, D. (2009). Large scale failure of the external waste dump at the "South Field" lignite mine, Northern Greece. *Engineering Geology*, **104**, 269–279.

Stern, M.J. (1995a). Vegetation recovery on earthquake-triggered landslides sites in the Ecuadorian Andes. In *Biodiversity and Conservation of Neotropical Montane Forests*, eds. S.P. Churchill, H. Balslev, E. Forero, & J.L. Luteyn, pp. 207–220. Bronx, New York, U.S.: The New York Botanical Garden.

Stern, M.J. (1995b). An inter-Andean forest relict: vegetation change on Pasochoa Volcano, Ecuador. *Mountain Research and Development*, **15**, 339–348.

Stewart, G. (2004). *The Tangiwai Disaster: A Christmas Eve Tragedy.* Wellington, New Zealand: Grantham House Publishing.

Stewart, G.H. (1986). Forest dynamics and disturbance in a beech/hardwood forest, Fiordland, New Zealand. *Vegetatio*, **68**, 115–126.

Stewart, M.M. & Woolbright, L.L. (1996). Amphibians. In *The Food Web of a Tropical Rain Forest*, eds. D.P. Reagan & R.B. Waide, pp. 274–320. Chicago: The University of Chicago Press.

Stokes, A., Spanos, I., & Norris, J.E. (eds.) (2007a). *Eco- and Ground Bio-Engineering: The Use of Vegetation to Improve Slope Stability*. Proceedings of the First International Conference on Eco-Engineering 13–17 September 2004. Dordrecht: Springer.

Stokes, A., Salin, F., Dzifa Kokutse, A., *et al.* (2007b). Mechanical resistance of different tree species to rockfall in the French Alps. In *Eco- and Ground Bio-Engineering: The Use of Vegetation to Improve Slope Stability*, eds. A. Stokes, I. Spanos, & J.E. Norris, pp. 155–164. Proceedings of the First International Conference on Eco-Engineering, 13–17 September 2004. Dordrecht: Springer.

Stokes, A., Atger, C., Bengough, A.G., Fourcaud, T., & Sidle, R.C. (2009). Desirable plant root traits for protecting natural and engineered slopes against landslides. *Plant and Soil*, **324**, 1–30.

Stringer, C. (2006). *Homo Britannicus: The Incredible Story of Human Life in Britain*. London: Penguin Group.

Suding, K.N. & Hobbs, R.J. (2009a). Threshold models in restoration and conservation: a developing framework. *Trends in Ecology and Evolution*, **24**, 271–279.

Suding, K.N. & Hobbs, R.J. (2009b). Models of ecosystem dynamics as frameworks for restoration ecology. In *New Models for Ecosystem Dynamics and Restoration*, eds. R.J. Hobbs & K.N. Suding, pp. 3–21. Washington, D.C.: Island Press.

Sultan, N., Cochonat, P., Foucher, J.-P., & Mienert, J. (2004). Effect of gas hydrate melting on seafloor slope instability. *Marine Geology*, **213**, 379–401.

Swanson, F.J. (1981). Fire and geomorphic processes. In *Proceedings of the Conference on Fire Regimes and Ecosystems*, ed. H.A. Mooney, pp 401–420. General Technical Report WO-26. Washington, D.C.: U.S. Department of Agriculture, Forest Service.

Swanson, F.J. & Dyrness, C.T. (1975). Impact of clear-cutting and road construction on soil erosion by landslides in the Western Cascade Range, Oregon. *Geology*, **7**, 393–396.

Swanson, F.J. & Franklin, J.F. (1992). New forestry principles from ecosystem analysis of Pacific Northwest forests. *Ecological Applications*, **2**, 262–274.

Swanson, F.J. & Major, J.J. (2005). Physical events, environments, and geological–ecological interactions at Mount St. Helens: March 1980–2004. In *Ecological Responses to the 1980 Eruption of Mount St. Helens*, eds. V.H. Dale, F.J. Swanson, & C.M. Crisafulli, pp. 27–44. New York: Springer.

Swanson, F.J., Kratz, T.K., Caine, N., & Woodmansee, R.G. (1988). Landform effects on ecosystem patterns and processes. *BioScience*, **38**, 92–98.

Swanston, D.N. (1991). Natural processes. In *Influences of Forest and Rangeland Management on Salmonid Fishes and their Habitats*, ed. W.R. Meehan. *American Fisheries Society Special Publication*, 19, 139–179.

Takahashi, T. (2007). *Debris Flow: Mechanics, Prediction, and Countermeasures*. London: Taylor and Francis.

Talbot, S.S., Talbot, S.L., & Walker, L.R. (2010). Post-eruption legacy effects and their implications for long-term recovery of the vegetation on Kasatochi Island, Alaska. *Arctic, Antarctic, and Alpine Research*, **42**, 285–296.

Tanner, E.U.J. (1983). Leaf demography and growth of the tree fern *Cyathea pubescens* Mett. Ex Kuhn in Jamaica. *Botanical Journal of the Linnean Society*, **87**, 213–227.

Tilman, D. (1985). The resource-ratio hypothesis of plant succession. *The American Naturalist*, **125**, 827–852.

Ting, I.P., Hann, J., Holbrook, N.M., *et al.* (1987). Photosynthesis in hemiepiphytic species of *Clusia* and *Ficus*. *Oecologia*, **74**, 339–346.

Tiwari, A.K., Mehta, J.S., Goel, O.P., & Singh, J.S. (1986). Geo-forestry of landslide-affected areas in a part of Central Himalaya. *Environmental Conservation*, **13**, 299–309.

Towhata, I. (2007). On failure of municipal waste landfill. In *Progress in Landslide Science*, eds. K. Sassa, H. Fukuoka, F. Wang, & G. Wang, pp. 147–149. New York: Springer.

Towns, D.R., Atkinson, I.A.E., & Daugherty, C.H. (2006). Have the harmful effects of rats on islands been exaggerated? *Biological Invasions*, **8**, 863–891.

Townsend, C.R., Begon, M., & Harper, J.L. (2008). *Essentials of Ecology, 3rd Edition*. Oxford, UK: Blackwell Publishing.

Trauth, M.H. & Strecker, M.R. (1999). Formation of landslide-dammed lakes during a wet period between 40,000 and 25,000 Yr B.P. in northwestern Argentina. *Palaeogrography, Palaeoclimatology, Palaeoecology*, **153**, 277–287.

Trauth, M.H., Bookhagen, B., Marwan, N., & Strecker, M.R. (2003). Multiple landslide clusters record Quaternary climate changes in the northwestern Argentine Andes. *Palaeogeography, Palaeoclimatology, Palaeoecology*, **194**, 109–121.

Tremper, B. (2008). *Staying Alive in Avalanche Terrain*. Seattle, WA: The Mountaineers Club.

Tryon, R.M. & A.F. Tryon. (1982). *Ferns and Allied Plants with Special Reference to Tropical America*. New York: Springer.

Tuba, Z., Slack, N., & Stark, L.R. (eds.) (2011). *Bryophyte Ecology and Climate Change*. Cambridge: Cambridge University Press.

Turner, T.R., Duke, S.D., Fransen, B.R., *et al.* (2010). Landslide densities associated with rainfall, stand age, and topography on forested landscaped, southwestern Washington, U.S. *Forest Ecology and Management*, **259**, 2233–2247.

Uniyal, S.K. Awasthi, A., & Rawat, G.S. (2000). Current status and distribution of commercially exploited medicinal and aromatic plants in upper Gori Valley, Kumaon Himalaya, Uttaranchal. *Current Science*, **82**, 1246–1252.

Usher, M.B. (1993). Primary succession on land: community development and wildlife conservation. In *Primary Succession on Land*, eds. J. Miles & D.W.H. Walton, pp. 283–293. Oxford: Blackwell.

Usher, M.B. & Jefferson, R.G. (1991). Creating new and successional habitats for arthropods. In *Conservation of Insects and their Habitats*, eds. N.M. Collins & J.A. Thomas, pp. 263–291. London: Academic Press.

Van der Burght, L., Stoffel, M., & Bigler, C. (2012). Analysis and modeling of tree succession on a recent rockslide deposit. *Plant Ecology*, **213**, 35–46.

Varnes, D.J. (1958). *Special Report 29: Landslides and Engineering Practice*. Washington, D.C.: National Academy of Sciences, Transportation Research Board.

Varnes, D.J. (1978). Slope movement types and processes. In *Landslides: Analysis and Control*, eds. R.L. Schuster & R.J. Krizek, pp. 11–33. Special Report 176. Washington, D.C.: National Academy of Sciences, Transportation Research Board.

Vázquez-Yanes, C. (1998). *Trema micrantha* (L.) Blume (Ulmaceae): a promising neotropical tree for site amelioration of deforested land. *Agroforestry Systems*, **40**, 97–104.

Vázquez-Yanes, C. & Smith, H. (1982). Phytochrome control of seed germination in the tropical rain forest pioneer trees *Cecropia obtusifolia* and *Piper auritum* and its ecological significance. *New Phytologist*, **92**, 477–485.

Veblen, T.T. & Ashton, D.H. (1978). Catastrophic influences on the vegetation of the Valdivian Andes, Chile. *Vegetatio*, **36**, 149–167.

Veblen, T.T. & Stewart, G.H. (1982). The effects of introduced wild animals on New Zealand forests. *Annals of the Association of American Geographers*, **72**, 372–397.

Veblen, T.T., Schlegel, F.M., & Escobar R.B. (1980). Structure and dynamics of old-growth *Nothofagus* forests in the Valdivian Andes, Chile. *Journal of Ecology*, **68**, 1–31.

Veblen, T.T., Kitzberger, T., & Lara, A. (1992). Disturbance and forest dynamics along a transect from Andean rain forest to Patagonian shrubland. *Journal of Vegetation Science*, **3**, 507–520.

Veblen, T.T., Hadley, K.S., Nel, E.M., *et al.* (1994). Disturbance regime and disturbance interactions in a Rocky Mountain subalpine forest. *Journal of Ecology*, **82**, 125–135.

Veblen, T.T., Kitzberger, T., Raffaele, E., & Lorenz, D.C. (2003). Fire history and vegetation changes in northern Patagonia, Argentina. In *Fire and Climatic Change in Temperate Ecosystems of the Western Americas*, eds. T.T. Veblen, W.L. Baker, G. Montenegro, & T.W. Swetnam, pp. 265–295. New York: Springer.

Velázquez, E. (2007). Sucesión ecológica temprana en un deslizamiento de ladera de grandes dimensiones en ambiente tropical seco, Volcán Casita, Nicaragua. PhD Dissertation, Universidad de Alcalá, Alcalá de Henares, Spain.

Velázquez, E. & Gómez-Sal, A. (2007). Environmental control of early succession in a landslide on a dry tropical ecosystem (Casita Volcano, Nicaragua). *Biotropica*, **35**, 601–609.

Velázquez, E. & Gómez-Sal, A. (2008). Landslide early succession in a neotropical dry forest. *Plant Ecology*, **199**, 295–308.

Velázquez, E. & Gómez-Sal, A. (2009a). Different growth strategies in the tropical pioneer tree *Trema micrantha* during succession on a large landslide on Casita Volcano, Nicaragua. *Journal of Tropical Ecology*, **25**, 249–260.

Velázquez, E. & Gómez-Sal, A. (2009b). Changes in the herbaceous communities on the landslide of the Casita Volcano, Nicaragua, during early succession. *Folia Geobotanica*, **44**, 1–18.

Versfeld, D.B. & van Wilgen, B.W. (1986). Impact of woody aliens on ecosystem properties. In *The Ecology and Management of Biological Invasions in Southern Africa*, eds. I.A.W. Macdonald, F.J. Kruger, & A.A. Ferrar, pp. 239–246. Oxford: Oxford University Press.

Vincent, K.R., Friedman, J.M., & Griffin, E.R. (2009). Erosional consequence of saltcedar control. *Environmental Management*, **44**, 218–227.

Vitousek, P.M. (1994). Potential nitrogen fixation during primary succession in Hawai'i Volcanoes National Park. *Biotropica*, **26**, 234–240.

Vitousek, P.M. & Walker, L.R. (1987). Colonization, succession and resource availability: ecosystem-level interactions. In *Colonization, Succession and Stability*, eds.

284 · References

A.J. Gray, M.J. Crawley, & P.J Edwards, pp. 207–224. Symposium of the British Ecological Society, vol. 26. Oxford: Blackwell.

Vitousek, P.M. & Walker, L.R. (1989). Biological invasion by *Myrica faya* in Hawai'i: plant demography, nitrogen fixation, ecosystem effects. *Ecological Monographs*, **59**, 247–265.

Vitousek, P.M., Asner, G.P., Chadwick, O.A., & Hotchkiss, S. (2009). Landscape-level variation in forest structure and biogeochemistry across a substrate age gradient in Hawaii. *Ecology*, 90: 3074–3086.

Vitousek, P.M., Gerrish, G., Turner, D.R., Walker, L.R., & Mueller-Dombois, D. (1995). Litterfall and nutrient cycling in four Hawaiian montane rainforests. *Journal of Tropical Ecology*, **11**, 189–203.

Vittoz, J.A. & Hacskaylo, E. (1974). Endo- and ectomycorrhizal associations in five *Populus* species. *Bulletin of the Torrey Botanical Club*, **101**, 182–186.

Vittoz, P., Stewart, G.H., & Duncan, R.P. (2001). Earthquake impacts in old-growth *Nothofagus* forest in New Zealand. *Journal of Vegetation Science*, **12**, 417–426.

Vorpahl, P., Elsenbeer, H., Märker, M., & Schröder, B. (2012). How can statistical models help to determine driving factors of landslides? *Ecological Modelling*, 293, 27–39.

Wagner, W.L., Herbst, D.R., & Sohmer, S.H. (1999). *Manual of the Flowering Plants of Hawaii*, Volumes 1 and 2, revised edition. Honolulu, Hawaii, U.S.: University of Hawaii Press.

Waide, R.B. (1996). Birds. In *The Food Web of a Tropical Rain Forest*, eds. D.P. Reagan & R.B. Waide, pp. 363–398. Chicago: The University of Chicago Press.

Wakatsuki, T., Tanaka, Y., & Matsukura, Y. (2005). Soil slips on weathering-limited slopes underlain by coarse-grained granite or fine-grained gneiss near Seoul, Republic of Korea. *Catena*, **60**, 181–203.

Walker, L.R. (1993). Nitrogen fixers and species replacements in primary succession. In *Primary Succession on Land*, eds. J. Miles & D.W.H. Walton, pp. 249–272. Oxford: Blackwell.

Walker, L.R. (1994). Effects of fern thickets on woodland development on landslides in Puerto Rico. *Journal of Vegetation Science*, **5**, 525–532.

Walker, L.R. (1999). Patterns and processes in primary succession. In *Ecosystems of Disturbed Ground, Ecosystems of the World 16*, ed. L.R. Walker, pp. 585–610. Amsterdam: Elsevier.

Walker, L.R. (2000). Seedling and sapling dynamics of treefall pits in Puerto Rico. *Biotropica*, **32**, 262–275.

Walker, L.R. (2011). Integration of the study of natural and anthropogenic disturbances using severity gradients. *Austral Ecology*, **36**, 916–922.

Walker, L.R. (2012). *Biology of Disturbed Habitats*. Oxford: Oxford University Press.

Walker, L.R. & Aplet, G.H. (1994). Growth and fertilization of Hawaiian tree ferns. *Biotropica*, **26**, 378–383.

Walker, L.R. & Bellingham, P.J. (2011). *Island Environments in a Changing World*. Cambridge: Cambridge University Press.

Walker, L.R. & Boneta, W. (1995). Plant and soil responses to fire on a fern-covered landslide in Puerto Rico. *Journal of Tropical Ecology*, **11**, 473–479.

Walker, L.R. & Chapin, F.S. III. (1987). Interactions among processes controlling successional change. *Oikos*, **50**, 131–135.

Walker, L.R. & del Moral, R. (2003). *Primary Succession and Ecosystem Rehabilitation*. Cambridge: Cambridge University Press.

Walker, L.R. & del Moral, R. (2008). Transition dynamics in succession: implications for rates, trajectories, and restoration. In *New Models for Ecosystem Dynamics and Restoration*, eds. R.J. Hobbs & K.N. Suding, pp. 33–49. Washington, D.C.: Island Press.

Walker, L.R. & del Moral, R. (2009). Lessons from primary succession for restoration of severely damaged habitats. *Applied Vegetation Science*, **12**, 55–67.

Walker, L.R. & Neris, L.E. (1993). Posthurricane seed rain dynamics in Puerto Rico. *Biotropica*, **25**, 408–418.

Walker, L.R. & Powell, E.A. (1999). Regeneration of the Mauna Kea silversword *Argyroxiphium sandwicense* (Asteraceae) in Hawaii. *Biological Conservation*, **89**, 61–70.

Walker, L.R. & Sharpe, J.M. (2010). Ferns, disturbance and succession. In *Fern Ecology*, eds. K. Mehltreter, L.R. Walker, & J.M. Sharpe, pp. 177–219. Cambridge: Cambridge University Press.

Walker, L.R. & Shiels, A.B. (2008). Post-disturbance erosion impacts carbon fluxes and plant succession on recent tropical landslides. *Plant and Soil*, **313**, 205–216.

Walker, L.R. & Smith, S.D. (1997). Impacts of invasive plants on community and ecosystem properties. In *Assessment and Management of Plant Invasions*, eds. J.O. Luken & J.W. Thieret, pp. 69–86. New York: Springer.

Walker, L.R. & Willig, M.R. (1999). An introduction to terrestrial disturbances. In *Ecosystems of Disturbed Ground, Ecosystems of the World 16*, ed. L.R. Walker, pp. 1–16. Amsterdam: Elsevier.

Walker, L.R., Zarin, D.J., Fetcher, N., Myster, R.W., & Johnson, A.H. (1996). Ecosystem development and plant succession on landslides in the Caribbean. *Biotropica*, **28**, 566–576.

Walker, L.R., Clarkson, B.D., Silvester, W., & Clarkson, B.R. (2003). Facilitation outweighs inhibition in post-volcanic primary succession in New Zealand. *Journal of Vegetation Science*, **14**, 277–290.

Walker, L.R., Velázquez, E., & Shiels, A.B. (2009). Applying lessons from ecological succession to the restoration of landslides. *Plant and Soil*, **324**, 157–168.

Walker, L.R., Landau, F.H., Velázquez, E., Shiels, A.B., & Sparrow, A. (2010a). Early successional woody plants facilitate and ferns inhibit forest development on Puerto Rican landslides. *Journal of Ecology*, **98**, 625–635.

Walker, L.R., Wardle, D.A., Bardgett, R.D., & Clarkson, B.D. (2010b). The use of chronosequences in studies of ecological succession and soil development. *Journal of Ecology*, **98**, 725–736.

Walker, T.W. & Syers, J.K. (1976). The fate of phosphorus during pedogensis. *Geoderma*, **15**, 1–19.

Walkinshaw, J. (1992). Landslide correction costs on U.S. state highway systems. *Transport Research Record*, **1343**, 36–41.

Wang, D., Cao, L., de Piao, C., Xue, Y.-D., & Wang, M. (2011). Study on high and steep slope stability of surface mine based on RFPA-SRM. *Journal of Coal Science and Engineering (China)*, **17**, 119–123.

Wang, W.-N., Chigira, M., & Furuya, T. (2003). Geological and geomorphological precursors of the Chiu-fen-erh-shan landslide triggered by the Chi-chi earthquake in central Taiwan. *Engineering Geology*, **69**, 1–13.

Wardle, D.A., Walker, L.R., & Bardgett, R.D. (2004). Ecosystem properties and forest decline in contrasting long-term chronosequences. *Science*, **305**, 509–513.

Waythomas, C.F., Scott, W.E., & Nye, C.J. (2010). The geomorphology of an Aleutian volcano following a major eruption: the 7–8 August 2008 eruption of Kasatochi Volcano, Alaska, and its aftermath. *Arctic, Antarctic, and Alpine Research*, **42**, 260–275.

Web of Science (2011). http://apps/webofknowledge.com/ Accessed 10 November 2011.

Webb, R.H., Ragland, H.C., Godwin, W.H., & Jenkins, O. (1978). Environmental effects of soil property changes with off-road vehicle use. *Environmental Management*, **2**, 219–233.

Weidinger, J.T., Schramm, J.-F., & Romero, E. (1996). On preparatory causal factors, initiating the pre-historic Tsergo Ri landslide (Langthang Himal, Nepal). *Tectonophysics*, **260**, 95–107.

Weisman, A. (2007). *The World Without Us*. New York: Picador.

Wells, A., Duncan, R.P., & Stewart, G.H. (2001). Forest dynamics in Westland, New Zealand: the importance of large, infrequent earthquake-induced disturbance. *Journal of Ecology*, **89**, 1006–1018.

Wemple, B.C., Jones, J.A., & Grant, G.E. (1996). Channel network extension by logging roads in two basins, western Cascades, Oregon. *Water Resources Bulletin*, **32**, 1195–1207.

Wemple, B.C., Swanson, F.J., & Jones, J.A. (2001). Forest roads and geomorphic process interactions, Cascade Range, Oregon. *Earth Surface Processes and Landforms*, **26**, 191–204.

Wentworth, C.K. (1943). Soil avalanches on Oahu, Hawaii. *Geologic Society of America Bulletin*, **54**, 53–64.

Westoby, M. (1984). The self-thinning rule. *Advances in Ecological Research*, **14**, 167–225.

Whelan, F. & Kelletat, D. (2002). Submarine slides on volcanic islands – a source for mega-tsunamis in the Quaternary. *Progress in Physical Geography*, **27**, 198–216.

Whitehead, D. (2011). Forests as carbon sinks – benefits and consequences. *Tree Physiology*, **31**, 893–902.

Whitehouse, I.E. (1982). Numerical assessment of erosion from old and recent photographs: a case study from a section of Highway 73, Canterbury, New Zealand. *Journal of the Royal Society of New Zealand*, **12**, 91–101.

Whitford, W.G., Depree, D.J., Hamilton, P., & Ettershank, G. (1981). Foraging ecology of seed harvesting ants, *Pheidole* spp, in a Chihuahuan Desert ecosystem. *American Midland Naturalist*, **105**, 159–167.

Wilcke, W., Valladarez, H., Stoyan, *et al.* (2003). Soil properties on a chronosequence of landslides in montane rain forest, Ecuador. *Catena*, **53**, 79–95.

Wilcock, P.R., Schmidt, J.C., Wolman, M.G., *et al.* (2003). When models meet managers: examples from geomorphology. *American Geophysical Union Monograph Series*, **135**, 27–40.

Wilke, S., McCafferty, G., & Watson, B. (2011). The archaeology of death on the shore of Lake Nicaragua. In: *Identity Crisis: Archaeological Perspectives on Social Identity*, eds. L. Amundsen-Meyer, N. Engel, & S. Pickering, pp. 178–188. Calgary, British Columbia: Chacmool Archaeological Association & University of Calgary.

Willig, M.R. & Gannon, M.R. (1996). Mammals. In *The Food Web of a Tropical Rain Forest*, eds. D.P. Reagan & R.B. Waide, pp. 399–431. Chicago: The University of Chicago Press.

Willig, M.R. & McGinley, M.A. (1999). The response of animals to disturbance and their roles in patch generation. In *Ecosystems of Disturbed Ground, Ecosystems of the World 16*, ed. L.R. Walker, pp. 633–658. Amsterdam: Elsevier.

Williams, J.C., Drummond, B.A., & Buxton, R.T. (2010). Initial effects of the August 2008 eruption on breeding birds and marine mammals, at Kasatochi Island, Alaska. *Arctic, Antarctic, and Alpine Research*, **42**, 306–314.

Willmott, W.F. (1984). Forest clearing and landslides on the basalt plateau of south east Queensland. *Queensland Agricultural Journal*, **110**, 15–20.

Wilson, D., Patten, R., & Megahan, W.P. (1982). Systematic watershed analysis procedure for Clearwater National Forest. *Transportation Research Record*, National Academy of Sciences, Washington, D.C., 892, 50–56. Cited in Schuster (2001).

Wolfe, L.M. (1987). Inflorescence size and pollinaria removal in *Asclepias curassavica* and *Epidendrum radicans*. *Biotropica*, **19**, 86–89.

Wood, J.R., Wilmshurst, J.M., & Rawlence, N.J. (2011). Radiocarbon-dated faunal remains correlate very large rock avalanche deposit with prehistoric Alpine fault rupture. *New Zealand Journal of Geology and Geophysics*, **54**, 431–434.

Wondzell, S.M. & King, J.B. (2003). Postfire erosional processes in the Pacific Northwest and Rocky Mountain Regions. *Forest Ecology and Management*, **178**, 75–87.

Wong, H.N., Ho, K.K.S., & Chan, Y.C. (1997). Assessment of consequence of landslides. In *Landslide Risk Assessment*, eds. D. Cruden & R. Fell, pp. 111–149. Rotterdam: Balkema.

Wu, W. & Sidle, R.C. (1995). A distributed slope stability model for steep forested hillslopes. *Water Resources Research*, **31**, 2097–2110.

Wunderle, J.M., Jr. (1995). Responses of bird populations in a Puerto Rican forest to Hurricane Hugo: the first 18 months. *Condor*, **97**, 879–896.

Wunderle, J.M., Jr. (1997). The role of animal seed dispersal in accelerating native forest regeneration on degraded tropical lands. *Forest Ecology and Management*, **99**, 223–235.

Wunderle, J.M., Jr., Díaz, A., Velásquez, I., & Scharron, R. (1987). Forest openings and the distribution of understory birds in a Puerto Rican rainforest. *Wilson Bulletin*, **99**, 22–37.

Wyllie, D.C. & Norrish, N.I. (1996). Stabilization of rock slopes. In *Landslides: Investigation and Mitigation*, eds. A.K. Turner & R.L. Schuster, pp. 474–504. Special Report 247, Transportation Research Board, National Research Council. Washington, D.C.: National Academy Press.

Xu, Q., Fan, X., Huang, R., *et al.* (2009). A catastrophic rockslide-debris flow in Wulong, Chongqing, China in 2009: background, characterization, and causes. *Landslides*, **7**, 75–87.

Yajima, T., Nakamura, F., Shimuzu, O., & Shibuya, M. (1998). Forest recovery after disturbance by the 1926 mudflow at Mount Tokachi, Hokkaido, Japan. *Research Bulletin of Experimental Forestry Hokkaido University*, **55**, 216–228.

Yamamoto, S.-I., Nishimura, N., & Matsui, K. (1995). Natural disturbance and tree species coexistence in an old-growth beech – dwarf bamboo forest, southwestern Japan. *Journal of Vegetation Science*, **6**, 875–886.

Yokota, S. & Iwamatsu, A. (1999). Weathering distribution in a steep slope of soft pyroclastic rocks as an indicator of slope instability. *Engineering Geology*, **55**, 57–68.

Yoo, K., Amundson, R., Heimsath, A.M., & Dietrich, W.E. (2006). Spatial patterns of soil organic carbon on hillslopes: integrating geomorphic processes and the biological C cycle. *Geoderma*, **130**, 47–65.

Yurkonis, K.A., Meiners, S.J., & Wachholder, B.E. (2005). Invasion impacts diversity through altered community dynamics. *Journal of Ecology*, **93**, 1053–1061.

Zarin, D.J. & Johnson, A.H. (1995a). Base saturation, nutrient cation, and organic matter increases during early pedogenesis on landslide scars in the Luquillo Experimental Forest, Puerto Rico. *Geoderma*, **65**, 317–330.

Zarin, D.J. & Johnson, A.H. (1995b). Nutrient accumulation during primary succession in a montane tropical forest, Puerto Rico. *Soil Science Society of America Journal*, **59**, 1444–1452.

Zasada, J.C., Sharik, T.L., & Nygren, M. (1992). The reproductive process in boreal forest trees. In *A System Analysis of the Global Boreal Forest*, eds. H.H. Shugart, R. Leemans, & G. Bonan. Cambridge: Cambridge University Press.

Zêzere, J.L., Reis, E., Garcia, R., et al. (2004). Integration of spatial and temporal data for the definition of different landslide hazard scenarios in the area north of Lisbon (Portugal). *Natural Hazards and Earth System Sciences*, **4**, 133–146.

Zhou, C.H., Lee, C.F., Li, J., & Wu, Z.W. (2002). On the spatial relationship between landslides and causative factors on Lantau Island, Hong Kong. *Geomorphology*, **43**, 197–207.

Ziegler, A.C. (2002). *Hawaiian Natural History, Ecology, and Evolution*. Honolulu, Hawaii: Hawaii University Press.

Ziegler, A.D., Giambellucca, T.W., Tran, L.T., et al. (2004). Hydrological consequences of landscape fragmentation in mountainous northern Vietnam: evidence of accelerated overland flow generation. *Journal of Hydrology*, **287**, 124–146.

Ziemer, R.R. (1981). The role of vegetation in the stability of forested slopes. *Proceedings of the 17th International Union of Forest Research Organization World Congress, Japan*: 297–308.

Zobel, D.B. & Antos, J.A. (1991). 1980 tephra from Mount St. Helens: spatial and temporal variation beneath forest canopies. *Biology and Fertility of Soils*, **123**, 60–66.

Zogning, A., Ngouaneta, C., & Tiafacka, O. (2007). The catastrophic geographical processes in humid tropical Africa: a case study of the recent landslide disasters in Cameroon. *Sedimentary Geology*, **199**, 15–29.

Index

298 · **Index**